# DESIGN FIRST
## Design-based planning for communities

David Walters

and

Linda Luise Brown

ELSEVIER

AMSTERDAM • BOSTON • HEIDELBERG • LONDON • NEW YORK •OXFORD
PARIS • SAN DIEGO • SAN FRANCISCO • SINGAPORE • SYDNEY • TOKYO

Architectural Press is an imprint of Elsevier

Architectural
Press

Architectural Press
An imprint of Elsevier
Linacre House, Jordan Hill, Oxford OX2 8DP
200 Wheeler Road, Burlington, MA 01803

First published 2004

**British Library Cataloging in Publication Data**
Walters, David
Design first: design-based planning for communities
1. City planning
I. Title II. Brown, Linda Luise
307.1'216

**Library of Congress Cataloging in Publication Data**
A catalog record for this book is available from the Library of Congress

ISBN 0 7506 5934 3

For Information on all Architectural Press publications
visit our website at www/architecturalpress/com

Typeset by Newgen Imaging Systems (P) Ltd., Chennai, India
Printed and bound in Great Britain

# Contents

# Acknowledgements

As with any enterprise of this nature, the authors wish to thank several people, especially colleagues at the Lawrence Group in Davidson, North Carolina – Craig Lewis, Brunsom Russum, Dave Malushizky and Catherine Thompson. These are fine professionals and friends as well as work partners.

Substantial thanks go out to colleagues on the faculty at the College of Architecture at the University of North Carolina at Charlotte. Bob Sandkam was incredibly patient in helping the authors improve their computer graphic skills in handling the images for the book. Our long-time friend and now Associate Dean at the College of Architecture, Dr Lee Gray, also deserves a big thank you for continually chiding the architect author to produce the book as an example for younger faculty. Even then, this book might not have happened without the good offices of another university colleague, Professor Chris Grech, an established author with the Architectural Press, who kindly introduced us to the publishers. At the Architectural Press we would especially like to thank Alison Yates and her colleagues for their consistent advice and support throughout the project.

In another context, we want to express our appreciation of Professor Robert Craycroft, a friend and ex-colleague from Mississippi State University, now retired after a long and distinguished career. Bob Craycroft introduced the architect author to the Neshoba County Fairgrounds featured in Chapter 4 in the mid-1980s and remains one of America's leading authorities on this little-known urban phenomenon. Professor Craycroft very kindly shared his expertise and photographs for this publication.

Nearer home, John Rogers, the administrator of the Charlotte Historic District Commission was also very helpful in providing local information about our home city, and for sterling service in reading several chapters of the manuscript. We have benefited from his thoughtful comments and advice. John's wife Amy also lent tremendous moral support, often expressed as delicious suppers provided on evenings when the authors were too exhausted to feed themselves.

Also in terms of moral support, the authors owe debts of gratitude to Johnice Stanislawski, the owner, and Courtney Devores, the manager of our local coffee shop, Queens Beans, next to our studio in Charlotte. We spent many hours reading over manuscripts while drinking copious amounts of their wonderful, shade grown, organic coffee!

And finally, we gratefully acknowledge that research for this book was supported in part by funds provided by the University of North Carolina at Charlotte.

Charlotte, NC

David Walters
and
Linda Luise Brown

# Credits

## CENTER OF THE REGION ENTERPRISE (Case Study 1)

### Project Team

*The Lawrence Group*
Craig Lewis
David Walters
Brunsom Russum
Dave Malushizky
Catherine Thompson
Ecem Ecevit
Paul Hubbman
Paul Kron
AnnHammond

*Karnes Research Company*
Michael Williams

*Kubilins Transportation Group*
Margaret Kubilins
Stephen Stansbury
Jonathon Guy

*Rose and Associates*
Kathleen Rose

### Triangle J Council of Governments Project Staff

John Hodges-Copple
Lanier Blum
September Barnes

### Community and Regional Partners

Town of Cary
City of Durham
Durham County
Town of Morrisville
City of Raleigh
Wake County
Research Triangle Foundation
Raleigh-Durham Airport Authority
Triangle J Council of Governments
Triangle Transit Authority
Capital Area Metropolitan Planning Organization
Durham-Chapel Hill-Carrboro Metropolitan
  Planning Organization

### Project Sponsors

Cisco
Duke Realty and Construction
Duke Power
Highwoods Properties
Roy E. Mashburn Jr.
John D. McConnell Jr.
Preston Realty
Progress Energy
Pulte Home Corporation
Research Triangle Regional Partnership
Southport Business Park
Teer Associates
Tillett Development Company
Toll Brothers
Tri Properties Inc.
Urban Retail Properties
White Ventures
York Properties
Additional support was provided by the U.S. Department of Transportation under a Transportation and Community Systems Preservation Program grant.

## CITY OF RALEIGH ARENA SMALL AREA PLAN (Case Study 2)

### Project Team

*The Lawrence Group*
Craig Lewis
David Walters
Brunsom Russum
Dave Malushizky
Nicole Taylor
Andrew Barclay

*ColeJenest & Stone*
Brian Jenest
Guy Pearlman

*Overstreet Studio*
Pat Newell

*Kubilins Transportation Group*
Stephen Stansbury
Jonathon Guy

*Karnes Research Company*
Michael Williams

## Local Government Partners

*City of Raleigh*
George Chapman
William Breazeale
James Brantley
Douglass Hill
Ed H. Johnson Jr.

*Triangle Transit Authority*
Juanita Shearer-Swink

## MOUNT MOURNE MASTERPLAN (Case Study 3)

*The Lawrence Group*
Craig Lewis
David Walters
Brunsom Russum
Dawn Blobaum

*Murray Whisnant Architects*
Murray Whisnant

*Town of Mooresville*
Erskine Smith

## GREENVILLE: HAYNIE-SIRRINE NEIGHBORHOOD MASTERPLAN (Case Study 4)

*The Lawrence Group*
Craig Lewis
David Walters
Brunson Russum
Dave Malushizky
Earl Swisher
Catherine Thompson
Ecem Ecevit
Nicole Taylor
Elizabeth Nash

*Overstreet Studio*
Pat Newell

*Kubilins Transportation Group*
Stephen Stansbery

*ColeJenest & Stone*
Brian Jenest
Fred Matrulli

*Upstate Forever*
Diane Eldridge

*Project Manager*
Julie Orr Franklin, Economic Development
Planner, City of Greenville

*Haynie-Sirrine Advisory Committee*
Felsie Harris
Andrea Young
Councilwoman Lillian Brock Fleming
John Fort
David Stone
Nancy Whitworth
Ginny Stroud

*Sirrine-Haynie Neighborhood Charrette Group*
Developer
    Rob Dickson
Property Owners
    John Fort and The Caine Company,
    David Stone
    C. Dan Joyner
The City of Greenville Department of Community
    and Economic Development
    Nancy Whitworth
    Julie Franklin
    Ginny Stroud
    Regina Wynder
IMIC Hotels
    David Walker,
    Sam Kelly, General Manager, Ramada Inn

## CORNELIUS TOWN CENTER (Case Study 5)

Master plan by Shook Kelly, Michael Dunning,
    project architect.
Transit-oriented Development by Duany
    Plater-Zyberk and Co.; amended by Cole Jenest
    and Stone.

# Introduction

## *History, theory and contemporary practice*

Toward the end of 2002, the authors were guests at a dinner party in Fayetteville, Arkansas, a pleasant American college town of 60 000 people in the Ozark Mountains. Sharing the table were the town's mayor, planning officers from town hall, local architects, developers, and spouses. The Fayetteville area is one of the few urbanized parts of Arkansas, an otherwise rural state in the American South just west of the Mississippi River. Combinations of generic commercial strip developments and poorly laid out residential suburbs, typical examples of 'suburban sprawl,' are endangering the special features and qualities of that town's local landscape. The degradation of the environment that makes the community a desirable place to live and work is a story repeated in America from coast to coast.

The subject of the evening's discussion was how to improve the way the town could grow, how to move away from conventional sprawl and toward a more attractive, and more environmentally and economically sustainable pattern of development. This kind of development, labeled 'Smart Growth,' has generated much discussion in America since the mid-1990s, but despite an abundance of professional, media, and political interest, its principles are far from universally accepted at the time of writing in 2003. Advocates of progressive development face an uphill struggle against the power, money, and conservatism of the American real estate, transportation and construction lobbies that exert influence over American politicians and control the development patterns of many towns and cities across the land.

That evening around the Fayetteville dinner table confirmed something significant to us. Here in microcosm was the most important audience for our book. Our convivial dinner party comprised intelligent men and women, concerned about the future of their community but unsure how to achieve the desired improvement.

Their priority was action, not academic analysis. Time was short as conventional sprawl development eroded the quality of life in their town a little bit more each day. They wanted to know what ideas to use and how to use them. They wanted assurance that new ideas came with some provenance, and that other communities had used them successfully. The purpose of our visit to Fayetteville was to discuss those precise issues, to give civic leaders and professionals an abbreviated synopsis of the material in this book and direct them toward smarter planning and better urban design.

Our message to the folks in Fayetteville was the same as the one contained herein: think in three dimensions as urban designers and not in two dimensions like land planners. We call this approach *planning by design*, applying principles of three-dimensional urban design to the problems and processes of urban and community planning. Most of these problems revolve around basic issues such as development versus conservation, or the public good of the community versus private rights of individual property owners. We believe that designing the physical form, infrastructure, and appearance of urban and suburban areas in detail is more effective in mediating these conflicts than conventional two-dimensional land-use planning. In this book we explain why that is, and how the process works.

Because one of the authors is English, Americans often ask us how British towns are able to conserve their historic fabric and surrounding green landscape, picturesque qualities much admired by transatlantic visitors. When we explain the process of government regulation of private land, our questioners, previously eager to find some lessons to follow, often become perplexed – even angry – at the thought of cooperative planning ideas for the 'public good' being applied to private property. In the USA, few people are quick to accept the values underpinning the British system or the extent of government intervention in the planning and development process, even for benign purposes of conservation and community enhancement.

In Britain the growth versus development discussion is slanted towards conservation of national and local heritage. The 1999 report *Towards an Urban Renaissance* produced by the government-appointed Urban Task Force, led by the architect peer Lord (Richard) Rogers of Riverside, gave rise to the subsequent White Paper, *Our Towns and Cities: the Future: Delivering an Urban Renaissance*, introduced by the Labour government in 2000. The White Paper identifies key points of urban policy at a national level, focusing on redevelopment of existing 'brownfield' sites and improved public transportation rather than 'greenfield' urban expansion and the extended use of the private automobile. Though British critics have voiced their displeasure at their government's perceived delay and weakness in acting on the urban principles established in its policy documents, at least there *is* a policy. In America, there is little evidence of any national agenda for sustainable urban or environmental policies. Quite the contrary. Initiatives to improve the cities and the environment enacted by President Clinton between 1992 and 2000 are being rolled back in the Republican administration of George W. Bush.

The United States of America is 40 times the size of the UK, but has only five times its population. Given this large size and low density, there is relatively uncritical enthusiasm for urban growth, despite environmental problems and disturbing social factors such as an increasing polarization between the (mainly white) wealthy and highly mobile residents of the suburbs and the (mainly black and Hispanic) poorer populations isolated in dilapidated sections of the inner city. Calls for change can be heard as the negative aspects of suburban sprawl – environmental pollution, loss of open space, heavy traffic, and long commutes – impinge on the public's consciousness, but the vast majority of communities continue to grow more or less unchecked. In some fast-growing towns that have undergone disturbing amounts of change, citizen-based outcries have risen to halt development altogether, but rarely in the American political system is stopping growth a realistic option. For the 'no-growth' lobby to succeed, so many constraints would need to be placed on private property that many legal experts believe these limits could not easily withstand challenges in the courts relative to rights guaranteed under the Fifth Article of Amendment to the United States Constitution, which states that no 'private property shall be taken for public use without due compensation.' While the purchase of land by the state for public projects such as road building is generally well accepted, controlling the development potential of private land for less

immediately tangible community benefits is harder to uphold.

Many citizens regard government action to limit what they can do with their land as a 'taking' under the provisions of the Constitution. For example, reducing residential density, or clustering homes to protect the quality of water in local streams (by minimizing the impermeable site area caused by buildings and driveways) is good public policy, but it may take away some sale value of the land compared to what the property owner could expect under a conventional sprawl scenario. While the American Supreme Court would not agree that this partial devaluation constitutes a 'taking,' (viz. the Court's 1978 decision in *Penn Central Transportation Company v. City of New York*) property rights advocates and developers hold the threat of aggressive legal action over many timid municipalities.

Helping to resolve issues like alternative development scenarios for land is one of the advantages of our method of designing in full view of the public, using intensive design 'charrettes' or participatory workshops. In these venues, concepts like the housing clusters that can potentially benefit the community through less polluted run-off into streams can be illustrated clearly. A perspective drawing of dwellings carefully integrated into a protected landscape is worth a dozen abstract planning diagrams of the same concept. Citizens understand the issues more easily and are likely to support the proposed design solutions, and opponents may even be persuaded that the ideas have merit.

This hypothetical example illustrates the theme of the book – how communities can radically improve both their process of town planning and their finished product of town building by using three-dimensional urban design techniques. When we work in communities large or small, we usually focus on the public spaces – streets, squares, parks, and so forth – and design them in considerable detail, because these spaces are the core of any community, the real armature of public life. This process often includes designing the architectural elements of the buildings that define and enclose these public spaces – the façades, entrances, and massing that contribute to the general appearance seen from eye level. We integrate the specifics of a building's use into this design process, but use is not always a determining factor because it often changes, sometimes several times within a building's lifespan. It is more important to get the relationships between building-to-building and building-to-public space correct. These are – or should be – long-term issues.

During community workshops, we also work with transportation planners to design traffic circulation and parking arrangements, and to integrate transportation into public spaces. It's these public spaces, defined by buildings and landscape, that form the framework of the master plan for the community, and the development economist on our team ensures our solutions are economically viable. We then encode our three-dimensional design solutions in simplified and graphically rich regulations for implementation and development control so that over time the community will build itself in accordance with the master plan. Our case study examples illustrate variations of this method used on sites as small as an urban block and as large as a region of 60 square miles, and in the very last chapter we draw these threads together in a way that links the smallest scale of the block to the largest frame of the region.

Our case studies focus on American communities seeking to implement Smart Growth strategies by means of environmentally sensitive suburban expansion and infill, and the redevelopment of older urban areas. This emphasis goes hand-in-hand with the resurgence of traditional concepts of city design in America under the rubric of New Urbanism. We are sympathetic to the ideals and ambitions of New Urbanism (one of the authors is a signatory of the founding Charter), and we discuss this movement in some detail in Chapter 3. We are especially keen to dispel some of the myths and misconceptions surrounding New Urbanist concepts, and to demonstrate their connections to many similar ideas from the past 200 years on both sides of the Atlantic.

Although our work is developed from a New Urbanist agenda, this book is not a review of the greatest hits of New Urbanism, something achieved well by Katz (1994) and Dutton (2000). Our case studies are analysed from *inside* the urban planning process. They are projects in which the authors have played lead roles, usually in association with the North Carolina office of The Lawrence Group, a firm of architect-planners based in St. Louis, Missouri. We have specifically organized our case studies to illustrate the full variety of urban scales, from the region, to the city, the town, the neighbourhood, and down to the scale of an individual urban block, and in so doing we exemplify a key theme of the Charter of the New Urbanism: the town planning and urban design principles inherent in New Urbanism are relevant and applicable at all scales and in all situations. It is a comprehensive way of looking at patterns of human settlement.

Our examples are works in progress, for city building is a continuous activity; it is never finished. Some case studies have achieved very successful results; others have hit snags during implementation. But all of them provide valuable lessons in their content and their narrative.

We stated earlier that our audience for the book wanted plans for action, not academic analysis. But no proposals for the planning and design of communities should be used out of their historical and theoretical context. As academics as well as practitioners, we love the histories and theories of design and planning, partly for their own sake as fascinating knowledge, but also because they help us design and plan well. Without a grounding in history and theory, all design becomes contingent on fleeting circumstances – be they financial, personal, political, or locational. As practitioners, we know just how powerful these contingent forces can be, sometimes positively, often negatively. We therefore use theory and history as the firm structure and platform for our work, and we have traced the interconnections between urban ideas with some care. We explain how contemporary planners and architects like ourselves have arrived at our present set of beliefs, and why we adhere so strongly to them.

But this isn't an exhaustive history of the Anglo-American city. That's not our purpose. Rather, we discuss key historical and theoretical concepts of contemporary planning and urban design, often highlighted by the authors' personal experiences and anecdotes, to illustrate a practical approach that is consciously *informed* by history. This historical sense, and its awareness of intellectual and physical precedent, shapes and enriches the ideas we bring to bear on contemporary urban planning problems. But while context and precedent are crucially important, designers need not be slaves to perceived history. Simply wrapping contemporary buildings in historical wallpaper diminishes architectural and urban design to the level of pastiche, always a dangerous tendency in postmodern design. It is important to distinguish between using precedent creatively in community design (good) and retreating into nostalgic formulas (bad). Accordingly we try to clarify this difference throughout the text as we discuss concepts and methods.

Serious scholars of urban history will find little new material here that hasn't been covered in many other histories and polemics (Blake, 1974; Booker, 1980; Hughes, 1980; Ravetz, 1980; Coleman, 1985; Hall, 1988; Campbell, 1993; Kunstler, 1993; Lubbock, 1995; Gold, 1997). But we review this story with a reader in mind for whom this may be unfamiliar territory. And we approach the discussion with a particular question in mind: why do we teach our students the opposite of what we were taught by our professors thirty-five years ago? We were taught the doctrine of modernism only to spend our professional lives fighting against its urban legacy in our towns and cities.

We now embrace the same principles of city design rejected by modernist pioneers. Instead of trying to obliterate traditional public space (the so-called 'death of the street' so eagerly sought by Le Corbusier and others), we conceive the city once again as a defined, if discontinuous, network of urban spaces – a public realm of streets and squares. In an expanding world of virtual realities and electronic spaces, we believe the creation of real places for public life is more important than ever. But is our advocacy of traditional urban forms merely the swing of the historical pendulum? Is it a transient phenomenon, a collection of concepts that flourishes, then withers as we move back to a revived, neo-modernist position in a few decades? Or have we rediscovered something fundamental about cities and the human need for public life in public space? The cliché about not understanding where you're going if you don't know where you've been has never been more relevant.

Our perspective on problems and opportunities facing American towns and cities is sharpened by comparisons to British practice regarding urban expansion and revitalization of older areas. As we noted earlier,

several American dilemmas are similar to British problems, while others are substantially different – bred of disparate geographies and cultural priorities. We hope these themes of comparison and contrast between American and British urban experiences render the book valuable for audiences in both countries. British readers can relate American lessons to their own situations, and American professionals can understand ways in which British practice might inform their own daily battles for better design in cities and suburbs.

We appreciate the privilege of working in communities, designing with citizens in public forums to forge visions, templates and policies that will guide the future growth of the places where the participants live and work. We also enjoy working within a complex intellectual lineage traceable to previous centuries. We take pleasure in knowing that our small efforts are part of a much larger narrative of town building.

We said at the beginning that this book is aimed at architects, planners, developers, planning commissioners, elected officials, and civic-minded citizens. Students of architecture and planning constitute another very important audience. These are the young men and women whose charge it is to continue the fight to make better, more humane, ecological and beautiful cities. Whichever group you belong to, and whether you are reading this book in America, Britain, or elsewhere, we hope you find within its pages some inspiration to serve a community, large or small, and help it to grow more smartly. By this, all of us benefit.

# PART

# I

# History

# Paradigms lost and found dilemmas of the Anglo-American city

## SYNOPSIS

In this first chapter, we examine four aspects of British and American city design, and in so doing we introduce several concepts that will be elaborated in subsequent chapters. First, we try to answer the questions that are often posed by practicing architects and planners about the value of history. 'Why bother with history?' they ask. 'How are the events and ideas of a hundred years ago relevant to my work today?'

To help evaluate these questions, we discuss in the second section some of the ideologies and attitudes that have shaped our cities today – the founding assumptions of modernist architecture and planning as they were theorized and practiced in the middle decades of the twentieth century. The buildings created from these ideas spawned a legacy of unforeseen urban problems, and by the late 1960s and 1970s, the lack of success of modernist design generated anti-modernist reactions. These coalesced around reawakened interest in traditional forms of urbanism, such as the street and the square, which had been explicitly rejected by modernist theory and practice.

The third section examines aspects of these reactionary movements. We discuss some of the reasons for this reversal in attitudes, a theme that will be consistent throughout the book, and we look at some of the work that resulted from this more consciously historical perspective. In the final section of this opening chapter we confront one of the ironies of our period. At the very time of the revival and renewed ascendancy of traditional urbanism, revolutions in information technology and media have created a whole series of virtual worlds, communities and electronic places that threaten to render the public spaces of our towns and cities obsolete. Where does

this leave the urban designer today? Is an urbanism based around a revived representation of traditional public space still relevant?

## THE ROLE OF HISTORY

The community design professions have several choices today regarding the role of history. From one perspective, the architect or planner may choose to ignore history altogether in pursuit of a vision of an unfettered future. Or, thinking that the search for solutions to today's complex urban design problems leaves no time or place for the 'esoteric' study of times past, a working professional may choose to pigeonhole history in the realm of academia.

Conversely, the professional who views his or her efforts as being part of a larger narrative, one that acknowledges the past as being relevant to the problems of contemporary practice, will likely address the role of history more positively. We hold this latter view regarding the importance of history to urban design and planning. Some of the urban concepts and values we use in our work stretch back (at the very least) to the beginning of the industrial revolution in the late eighteenth century. We will argue in several places throughout the book that some urban concepts are 'timeless,' and can be found in western cultures in many periods of history, but for our purposes here, the late 1700s usefully define the beginning of what we might call the modern era in city design. It was then, just to the south of London, that the first modern suburbs started to develop.

As a pair of seasoned teachers and practitioners, we strongly believe we are more effective when we understand the sources and the histories of the urban design and planning concepts that we use. They did not arrive fully formed at our pencil tips and computer keyboards! Some continue recent trends, or reclaim discarded or outdated concepts; others are deliberate reactions against perceived mistakes of the past. Our ideas come with a history, and we are guided in our practice by the knowledge of how they were derived and how they have been used (and misused) by professionals in previous times and places.

But first we must be careful to define what constitutes our 'history'. Historians and critics are often tempted to seek some overarching 'grand narrative' as a framework for their arguments (we are no different in this regard except that we are wary of the process and its results!) and for much of the twentieth century the history, theory and practice of modern architecture was presented as a unified, coherent story by writers such as Hitchcock and Johnson (1932), Pevsner (1936), Richards (1940), and Giedion (1941). In this tale of the 'International Style,' the heroes were Le Corbusier, Walter Gropius, Ludwig Mies van der Rohe, Ludwig Hilbersheimer, the artists and architects at the Bauhaus, and other pioneers of the modern movement. Under the intellectual leadership of this new avant-garde, a primary task of modern architects was to rid society of the environmental and social evils of the polluted industrial city, where workers lived miserable lives, crowded into unsanitary slums. In place of the old, corrupt Victorian city, modern architects envisioned a bright, new healthy environment, full of sun, fresh air, open space, greenery and bold new buildings free of the trappings of archaic historical styles. It was a terrific vision and a fulfilling professional mission.

The replacement of cities perceived as outdated and corrupt brought a bright new optimistic face to urban design. In war-ravaged Britain during the 1950s, new blocks of flats rose heroically from the rubble. Some were sited, like those at Roehampton, in west London, in park-like settings deliberately reminiscent of Le Corbusier's evocative drawings (see Figure 1.1).

All was not sweetness and light, of course. Implementation of the vision varied, and a tangible gap was revealed between the promise of the utopian vision and 'real-life' achievements on the ground. Within a couple of decades, the planning and design philosophies of the modernist agenda were being questioned by the public. Planners and architects first took a defensive position. They suggested that the bleak urban environments people were complaining about were simply the result of the great visions of

**Figure 1.1** Alton West Estate, Roehampton, London, London County Council Architects' Department, 1959. Bold versions of Le Corbusier's Unité d'Habitation are set in the soft landscape of south London, creating an image of the modernist dream. Compare this image with Figure 1.4.

the masters being interpreted by less talented pupils, but increasing popular discontent, particularly against programs of urban reconstruction in Britain and urban renewal in America, gradually made the modernist position untenable.

Within these unpopular urban settings, the architecture itself was disliked; the new buildings were decried as dull and boring boxes. While architects loved to use concrete, either poured-in-place or as precast panels, citing its 'honesty' or 'integrity,' the public perceived this material as unfriendly and hostile. The uniformity and abstraction of the International Style puzzled and dismayed a public used to a richer and more conventional architectural language of historical detail and imagery, even in the most modest of buildings. Over time, redeveloped urban areas bred a form of distaste and antagonism among residents who lived and worked there. In particular, the large tracts of semi-public space that were the norm in much urban redevelopment from the 1950s through the early 1970s, gave rise to unforeseen and uncomfortable ambiguities about social behavior. This 'free' space for sunlight and greenery prescribed by modernist doctrine was achieved only through the destruction of old patterns of streets and urban blocks.

This open space was neither truly public nor private, and its consequent lack of spatial definition blurred boundaries and territories, raising issues of control and management, and ultimately of crime and personal security. Few people living in the large, modern housing redevelopments of slabs and towers favored by modernist theory felt safe or comfortable, or felt sufficient ownership of the open spaces around the new buildings to help take care of them. The list of failings in urban renewal and redevelopment schemes grew to such length and seriousness that ultimately it was impossible to treat these problems as teething troubles or poor applications of visionary ideas by less-talented designers. As urban historian John Gold has pointed out, a movement predicated on functionalism as a core belief could not withstand criticism about its dysfunctional consequences (Gold, 1997: pp. 4–5).

The conclusion was unavoidable: the ideas themselves were seriously flawed. Critic Charles Jencks famously ascribed the 'death of modernism' to the precise moment of 3.32 p.m. on July 15, 1972, when high-rise slab blocks in the notorious Pruitt-Igoe housing project in St. Louis, Missouri were professionally imploded by the city (Jencks, 1977: p. 9). Completed as recently as 1955, the buildings had been abandoned and vandalized by their erstwhile inhabitants to a degree that made them uninhabitable. Earlier, in 1968, a gas explosion and the consequent partial collapse of another high-rise block at Ronan Point in east London severely eroded the British public's confidence in the safety of modernist high-rise residential construction.

The tensions of urban life burst into the open during the British urban riots of the 1980s. Like their American precedents in the 1960s, the riots were the product of a clash between mainstream white culture and a black subculture built on deprivation and disadvantage, and were mainly focused on older urban areas of concentrated poverty, such as Toxteth in Liverpool, Moss Side in Manchester, Handsworth in Birmingham and Brixton in south London. The unrest and violence reached spectacular levels with the Broadwater Farm conflagration in Tottenham, north London, in 1985, and this was significantly different from the other urban areas of racial tension. Broadwater Farm was a 'prizewinning urban renewal project of 1970, (which) had proved a case study of indefensible space; its medium-rise blocks, rising from a pedestrian deck above ground-level parking, provided a laboratory culture for vandalism and crime' (Hall, 2002: p. 464).

There were several influential efforts to link this urban unrest directly to the failures of modern architecture and planning (e.g. Coleman, 1985). Although the social, racial and economic situation in 1980s Britain that bred the riots was far more complex than the cause-and-effect argument about the physical environment, the simplistic connection was a compelling one in the public mind. It was easier to blame the architecture than to deal with the deep-seated problems of social inequity and racial tension. With the hacking to death of a British policeman at Broadwater Farm and hundreds of riot police assailed by fire bombs, the tragic modernist blocks came to stand, like Pruitt-Igoe before them, for everything bad with modernist city planning and architecture.

Thus, what were truths for one generation quickly became doubts and finally anathema to the next. Faced with this ideological void, the younger generation of architects and planners sought to construct a new set of beliefs, and several premises of modernist urbanism were radically overhauled, and in many cases overturned. Many aspects of the search for new concepts focused around the recovery of more human-scaled spaces and an architectural vocabulary that connected with public taste. As we discuss more fully in Chapter 3, early postmodern architecture in the USA during the 1970s and 1980s incorporated ornamental classical details and elements of pop culture in an effort to bridge the communication gap between architects and the public. In the UK, this trend to glitzy ornamentation was also present, but a more substantive move was a return to an appreciation of vernacular building types and traditional urban settings. Just as the inclusion of ornament and kitsch into postmodern architecture was a conscious violation of modernist principles – a definitive rejection of the reductive, abstract aesthetics that had ruled professional taste for several decades – postmodern urbanism resurrected the traditional street, identified in modernist thinking as the villain and cause of urban squalor.

This renewed appreciation of traditional urban forms was presaged by Jane Jacobs in her landmark book *The Death and Life of American Cities* (Jacobs, 1962). Her description of the vitality and life on the streets of her New York neighborhood contrasted poignantly with the crime and grime of the urban wastelands produced by urban renewal, and while her criticism of modernist planning and architecture was largely dismissed by professionals during the 1960s, by the 1980s her book had become a standard text within this developing counter-narrative. Le Corbusier soon became the arch-villain of the new history, with his revolutionary and draconian proposals for 'The City of Tomorrow' identified as the source of everything bad about modernist urbanism (see Figure 1.2). Like countless other urban design professionals caught in the midst of this great revision of architectural and planning ideology over the last 30 years, we (the authors) have often promoted our ideas of traditional urban form and space by

**Figure 1.2** Le Corbusier's vision of The Contemporary City for Three Million Inhabitants, 1922. Tower blocks isolated in space and mid-rise slabs disassociated from the streets and set apart in landscape became the standard typologies for city building after World War II. (*Drawing courtesy of the Le Corbusier Foundation*)

contrasting them with a 'conveniently adverse picture of modernism' and its failings (Gold, p. 8).

In developing the new, improved grand narrative of postmodern city design during the 1970s and 1980s, professionals turned to smaller scale opportunities instead of striving for new social and physical utopias. Architects started taking note of what was already in place and sought to enhance the urban fabric rather than erase it. The study of history and context became important again, and designers focused on 'human-scaled' development, with a particular emphasis on the creation of defined public spaces, often taking the form of streets and squares, as settings for a reinvigorated public life.

Our wholesale abandonment of modernist principles and their replacement by a radical return to premodern ideas poses something of a dilemma. Based on the belief that modernist architects and planners made serious errors about many aspects of city planning and design, we tell ourselves we won't repeat the same mistakes, and consider our ideas much more appropriate to the task of city design. Here in America, our working concepts are based on traditional values of walkable urban places instead of the car-dominated asphalt deserts produced in the search for a drive-in utopia. We promote mixing uses once again, where for five decades functions were rigidly segregated, and we seek to involve the public directly in the making of plans instead of drawing them in the splendid isolation of city halls or corporate offices. We feel certain that these ideas are the right ones for the task of repairing the city and advancing the cause of a sustainable urban future.

But how can we be sure? After all, the modernist architects and planners we now criticize so harshly felt a similar degree of certainty in their mission and ideology. Have we merely replaced one professional paradigm with another that is also destined to fail, despite our good intentions? In the face of this conundrum, architects and planners must affirm their principles and their commitment to action; our cities and suburbs have a myriad of problems that demand urgent solutions. But, being neither fundamentalist nor unilateral, we must simultaneously reserve room for doubt, and be open to question. We have to allow the possibility that we are wrong, just as our predecessors were wrong before us! However, unlike our modernist forebears, we embrace the study of history and precedent in our work, and we heed George Santayana's words: 'Those who cannot remember the past are condemned to repeat it' (Santayana, 1905: p. 284).

Accordingly, we pay particular attention to how modernist architecture and planning operated *on the ground*, the place where people were affected by it most directly. By observing the transformations of the nineteenth-century industrial city wrought by modernist pioneers and their disciples in Britain and America, we gain insight into the values and ideas that shape our post-industrial city today.

## MODERNISM IN OPERATION

The story of city design is not straightforward. Even in our abbreviated history, themes weave and in and out of each other to form a complex tapestry. From our postmodern perspective we often mistake modernism for a monolithic construct, but this is far from the case. In architecture the early modernisms of Michel de Klerk, or Hans Scharoun and Hugo Haring, were far different from the unified vision that sprang into three-dimensional reality in 1927 at Stuttgart's influential Weissenhoff Siedlung. This model housing settlement, master-planned by Ludwig Mies van der Rohe and heavily influenced by Le Corbusier, included housing prototypes from most of the important European modern architects. This orchestrated concentration of crisp white stucco

**Figure 1.3** Kiefhoek Housing Estate, Rotterdam, J.J.P. Oud, 1925–29. Until Le Corbusier's doctrines were embodied in the all-encompassing Athens Charter of 1933, other modernists pioneers such as Oud were reluctant to abandon the street.

**Figure 1.4** Tower block in Benwell, Newcastle-upon-Tyne, UK, 1970. All too often the modernist vision of 'towers in the park' was reduced to towers in the urban wasteland by bad design and cheap building. Housing was seen merely as a political issue of numbers of units constructed rather than an integral element of city building.

boxes established the architectural language that was to become the International Style, but even within this homogeneity, subtle differences remained (see Figure 1.3).

Architect-inspired modernism also affected much theory and practice in planning during the years following World War II. The legacy of urban renewal still dominates thinking about postwar planning to such an extent that it is easy to believe that everything devolves from Le Corbusier's erasure of the traditional city and its replacement with the City of Towers in the Park. There was much more to it than that.

British planner Sir Peter Hall cites the different strands of twentieth-century planning thought at some length, but for our purposes they can be summarized under six headings, beginning with the urban replacement approach advocated by Le Corbusier and Ludwig Hilbersheimer. The second strand comprises the Garden City and its legacy; the third involves attempts to create the Regional City; and the fourth features Beaux Arts monumental master planning. Strand number five encompasses transportation and its impact on urban form; and the sixth incorporates democratic populism in civic design, providing opportunities for citizens to take charge of planning their own neighborhoods (Hall, 2002).

Hall also makes note of one of history's bitter jests of the twentieth century: many of the radical ideas of urban visionaries like Ebenezer Howard, Le Corbusier and Frank Lloyd Wright lay fallow for

years, only to reappear in later periods transformed into parodies of their former selves. Ironically, America's endless sprawl finds some of its origins in F. L. Wright's Broadacre City, for example, while many soulless suburban developments in British green fields are touted as direct descendants of Howard's Garden Cities. In cities across both nations, Le Corbusier's vision of gleaming skyscrapers in a lush and verdant landscape was constructed as cheap and shoddy towers rising amidst urban rubble (see Figure 1.4).

Today's urban designer is heir to all six strands of modernism, and we will deal with all of them during our discourse throughout the book. Each is important, but it is the legacy of urban renewal or 'comprehensive development' that colors community memories most vividly. The relative success of Garden Cities in postwar Britain pales in comparison with the memories of bulldozed neighborhoods and collapsed tower blocks. American families still recall with bitterness being forced from their homes in the 1960s to make way for grandiose civic plazas and monumental buildings.

The evidence of urban renewal's physical and social destruction in the name of community progress is undeniable. Many slums that needed to be torn down were justly demolished, but what replaced them was often a concrete dystopia that bred only desperation, despair and a new generation of social malaise. And along with the slums, other communities were demolished that deserved to remain and be refurbished rather than wrecked. Jane Jacob's passionate indictment of modernist architecture and planning in *The Death and Life of Great American Cities* describes how professionals were blind to the character and potential of older, shabby but still functional urban neighborhoods (Jacobs, 1962). This criticism resonates across 40 years. In the UK, the remark attributed to Prince Charles that planners destroyed more buildings in British cities in the years after World War II, than Hitler's *Luftwaffe* managed in all the years of bombing captures the sense of outrage at some of the acts of our predecessors.

Yet, these were not the deeds of urban vandals, bent on the destruction of communities. This may have been the unintended result, but the plans and designs were produced and implemented by well-meaning professionals intent on serving the public good. These architects and planners were concerned with the problems of the vast industrial city, where millions of people lived in great hardship with low rates of life expectancy and high rates of infant mortality. When we look at photographs of endless acres of grim, soot-grimed British terrace housing without a single tree in sight and blanketed by an ever-present pall of pollution, we must remind ourselves just how bad those conditions were. A new city of bright, modern buildings sited amidst an infinite park-like landscape with plenty of sun and clean, fresh air presented a compelling vision of urban improvement. No wonder architects and planners wanted to obliterate those miserable conditions and the past that created them!

A generation of gifted, younger designers educated in Britain during the 1950s and 1960s were imbued with a passionate desire to serve society, and saw their role in remaking the physical environment of cities as a public service akin to the National Health Service. Already by 1950 more than 50 percent of architects were employed in public service (Gold: p. 191). Early in the process of rebuilding war-torn Britain under the auspices of the 1947 Town and Country Planning Act, there were less than 1700 planners to staff 1400 planning authorities! It was young, recently graduated architects who eagerly filled many of the vacancies, bringing a strong three-dimensional design perspective to the new planning regimes (Gold: p. 190). Whatever else we say about them, we must give our modernist predecessors full credit for genuine humanitarian and social concern.

The urban renewal process that dominated Anglo-American cities in the 1950s and 1960s was, broadly speaking, a marriage of Le Corbusier's *tabula rasa* approach with single-function zoning. For several decades following World War II, professional thinking about urban redevelopment was dominated by models of widely spaced towers rising in open space and tidy planning diagrams of colored zones that separated the different parts of city life into distinct spatial areas. Modernist theory was not primarily structured around the everyday lives of people and the spaces they inhabited; instead it sought to change these informal patterns to others that were more orderly and rational in physical and technical circumstances. The planning orthodoxy derived from the urban visions of Le Corbusier and Hilbersheimer was compelling in its abstract technical clarity, and that very strength – the abstract spatial syntax and belief in technical systems – contained the core of its demise.

This theory had to be experienced to understand fully the power and implications of its doctrine. During the 1960s and even later, architectural students in Britain were routinely taught to find little value in old patterns of urbanism. Le Corbusier's famous disparagement of the street as an 'oppressive trench' and a 'donkey path' was an oft-quoted dictum in design studio (Le Corbusier, 1925, 1929). To the modernist pioneers in the early decades of the twentieth century the industrial city represented the values of old, corrupt Europe, and was seen as largely responsible for the poor living conditions of the working classes. Its elimination was considered a high priority. Little value was attached to older buildings or to existing urban configurations; they were perceived as part of the problem, not the solution. By the 1960s, the worst physical conditions in British cities had been substantially eradicated, but countless acres of old terraced housing stood as silent witness to the industrial past that was fast disappearing. To architects and planners alike, these neighborhoods stood in the way of progress, and their continued demolition was a way to cleanse society of the residual evils of the industrial city. It didn't really matter if the buildings and streets weren't technically slums. It was sufficient that they were old and decaying. The possibility that they could be refurbished and the neighborhood brought back to life was not one that students were encouraged to pursue.

The overwhelming sense that these old buildings had no value extended into a general perception that the past itself held little merit for design professionals. Historical thinking and the use of precedent were intentionally divorced from the design process; in their place newness and originality of form were prized above all other attributes. One of the authors vividly remembers receiving high marks for a student project at architecture school in the mid-1960s proposing the complete physical destruction of an English mining community of streets, houses and shops and its replacement by a series of tall hexagonal towers in open landscape.

Two examples that illustrate the process of remaking the modernist city are found in Birmingham, England, and Charlotte, North Carolina, in the USA. As early as the mid-1950s British urban renewal, or 'comprehensive redevelopment' programs in the center of cities like Birmingham demolished much of the historic core along with whole sections of the inner city. Though large new buildings gave the effect of high density, these redevelopment schemes dramatically reduced the population by about half, from about 120 people per acre to 60 (300 persons per hectare down to 150). Birmingham urban designer Joe Holyoak witnessed this process firsthand in the 1960s as a young architect:

> The dense complexes of working class houses, factories and workshops, corner shops and pubs, unrelieved by green spaces, built on loose grids of streets, pierced by canals and railways, were being comprehensively swept away. They were being replaced by a pattern which had elements both of Le Corbusier's geometric, high-rise *Ville Radieuse* and Parker and Unwin's curvilinear, low-rise Garden Suburb. (Holyoak, 1993: p. 59)

Despite the abundance of Corbusian rhetoric enthusiastically imported by city architects, this development pattern replaced only about half of the number of dwellings. In Birmingham alone there was an exodus of nearly 50 000 working-class residents to new suburbs and to expanded and new towns nearby (inelegantly referred to as 'overspill'). With regard to the new inner city housing, Holyoak reports that there was:

> ... plenty of evidence that the rehoused residents ... were at first very pleased with their new conditions. They had modern homes with kitchens, bathrooms and central heating, modern schools for their children to attend, and grass and trees about them. But the losses were also being documented in books such as *Family and Kinship in East London* (Young and Willmott, 1992) and *The Forgotten People* by the Vicar of Ladywood (Power, 1965), who described the changes taking place around his (Birmingham) church. Of course, there was simply the sudden, traumatic disappearance of

a familiar landscape. But there was also the break-up of complex kinship structures; the emergence of single-class areas; the inconvenience caused by the zoning of land uses, which eliminated such things as corner shops; and above all, the fragmentation of the community's collective sense of its own identity. (Holyoak: p. 60)

Holyoak reminds us that 'distance lends enchantment,' and the nostalgia we feel when looking at old photographs of vanished neighborhoods must be balanced by the memory of the physical poverty that these images also represented. Yet what speaks to us most directly in old photographs of children playing in the street and housewives gossiping on the doorstep is the 'quality of immediacy evident in the physical environment'. Holyoak defines this as:

> ... the close juxtaposition of the private and public realms, with the private shaping the public, the concentration of people together to produce a social intimacy, and the close relationship of those various places which form aspects of the same life – house, shops, pub, school, church and work. (Holyoak: p. 60)

Immediacy carried to excess can lead to overcrowding, as in the case in the industrial slums, but this feeling of shared togetherness in public space carried an important component of neighborhood cohesion. The absence of this type of shared space where fresh bonds of community could be nurtured in the new housing areas fostered feelings of alienation among families only a few years after they moved into their new homes.

While Birmingham and other British cities were tearing down their old neighborhoods in the name of progress, American cities were pursuing their own brand of civic improvement by means of the wrecking ball. Issues of racial and societal segregation in both nations are too intricate to mention with any depth in the context of this book, but the struggle by American blacks for equality and civil rights during the 1960s added an unavoidable racial dimension to the intentions and process of urban demolition and slum clearance in American cities. Charlotte, North Carolina, in the American South was typical in this regard.

Over the 25 years between 1949 and 1974, the American Federal Urban Renewal Administration provided large sums of money to cities for ambitious urban redevelopment. The federal program's original intention was to improve housing conditions for the urban poor by clearing slums and building new homes. Cities used federal government money to clear away decrepit neighborhoods and then sold the land to developers at bargain prices so the private sector could build affordable new dwellings. At least, that was the theory.

American mayors and their councils loved the program because it didn't require them to spend much local money. Developers also liked it, as they were able to buy prime development land very cheaply. It wasn't long before lobbying by municipalities and the development industry persuaded Congress to expand (or loosen) the objectives of rehousing the poor to include other urban uses. During the 1950s, increasing amounts of land cleared of human shelter could be developed for non-residential (i.e. more profitable) purposes.

North Carolina-based historian Tom Hanchett chronicled Charlotte's actions during the urban renewal era in his book *Sorting Out the New South City*, in which he explains how and why Charlotte '... used more than $40 million in federal money to flatten inner city neighborhoods and replace them with glistening new developments' (Hanchett: p. 249). One area in particular was the focus of these efforts, Brooklyn, a densely built black neighborhood in Charlotte's Second Ward, immediately to the east of the central business district (see Figure 1.5). Taking advantage of still looser federal guidelines that allowed housing to be demolished for almost any use deemed 'better' by the city, Charlotte's business and political leadership (they were essentially the same thing) sent a fleet of bulldozers into the black neighborhood. Between 1960 and 1967, the city razed almost every structure to the ground.

Local media heartily endorsed this demolition. The head of the Charlotte Redevelopment Authority, an urban administrator who had been hired away from the city of Norfolk, in Virginia, was profiled in a Charlotte newspaper with an enthusiastic headline: 'Heart of Norfolk Blitzed in Urban Renewal.' The article stated approvingly, that '... this 250 year old seaport has never been bombed by an intercontinental ballistic missile, although it sometimes seems a little that way' (Hanchett: p. 249). In Charlotte, a similar orgy of demolition '... made no pretense at creating better quarters for the residents. Not a single new housing unit went up to replace the 1480 structures that fell to the bulldozer. Urban renewal displaced 1007 Brooklyn families' (Hanchett: p. 250). It wasn't only homes that were destroyed, it was black businesses, too. 'The old district's density and central

**Figure 1.5** The Brooklyn neighborhood, Charlotte, NC, USA, early 1950s. Every building in this African-American community but one or two on the urban blocks in the fore and middle ground of this aerial view were demolished in the federally funded urban renewal programs of the 1960s. The area is now dominated by extensive complexes of government buildings, parking lots, and a large church with a white congregation. A new plan has recently been completed that will, over time, restore part of the block structure and promote mixed income housing. (*Photo courtesy of the Charlotte Historic District Commission*)

location had provided a warm environment for small shops ... Urban renewal displaced 216 Brooklyn businesses. Many never reopened' (Hanchett: p. 250). Along with homes and businesses, the social fabric of the community was comprehensively dismantled. Churches, social clubs, the one black high school in Charlotte, the city's only black public library were all pounded into rubble. An entirely self-sustaining community was effectively wiped out (Rogers, 1996).

Having cleared the land, the city constructed a palatial government district with a high-rise city hall, new law courts and jails, and a showpiece park. Other development included sundry offices and a large church for an all-white congregation. The city widened streets throughout the area, providing easier access between the city center and the wealthy white suburbs to the east. The scale of the destruction differed dramatically between black areas and others where the population was white. In white areas not far from the Brooklyn neighborhood the city used much more restraint, demolishing only a few blocks here and there.

These blatant racial politics were not uncommon in American cities at that time, and certainly added extra complexities to the tasks of the architectural and planning professionals that rarely existed in the work of their British counterparts. But even without the race factor, it took a long while for these professionals to appreciate the disparity between initially good intentions and terrible results. One reaction to these urban injustices was a groundswell of radical community activism by younger designers. In America, 'advocacy planning' opened a new revolutionary paradigm of democratic populism for architects and planners, with young professionals directly serving small community-based organizations from store-front offices. Using their expertise and idealism, they helped communities oppose government bureaucracy, often by direct political confrontation rather than by alternative design work. In Britain a very similar phenomenon developed under the rubric 'community architecture'.

In graduate school in the late 1960s in England, one of the authors became immersed in community architecture, and attempted to complete his urban design studies by means of community activism in an underprivileged city neighborhood. His professors informed him that this kind of work did not constitute urban design; if he wanted to graduate, he should get down to some 'real design.' Retiring his activism to evenings and weekends, the author duly produced a half-hearted urban megastructure that obligingly obliterated the community to the liking of his professors. No questions were posed to him concerning the social consequences of the design.

This pedagogical slant was by no means unusual in British architectural schools of the period. In this context, books that criticized modernist doctrine, such as Jane Jacobs' *The Death and Life of American Cities* (1962) on a social and planning level, and Gordon Cullen's *Townscape* (1961), from an urban design perspective, were routinely dismissed as flawed. Jacobs' book was belittled as being merely the writings of someone who was not a designer and therefore simply didn't understand architecture and planning. Her gender was also invoked as another reason to diminish her arguments. Even Lewis Mumford, a hero of progressive planning in the USA, belittled her ideas as 'Mother Jacobs' Home Remedies' in a scathing review of the book in the New Yorker magazine (Mumford, 1962).

Cullen's work, based upon subjective visual experience, was criticized on the grounds that it was too 'romantic' and lacked scientific rigor. A similar charge had been lodged by Le Corbusier in 1929 against Camillo Sitte and his important book *City Building According to Artistic Principles* published in 1889. Sitte's book was a closely researched effort to establish an empirical basis for the aesthetics of public space in older European cities. Sitte focused on the sensory experience of being in a place, and documented the plans of hundreds of urban squares in an effort to distill some defining principles for a spatial order of pragmatic irregularity rather than the ubiquitous rectangular geometries of nineteenth-century speculative urban development.

However, for Le Corbusier irregularity was merely romantic and shallow picturesqueness, something he considered a false ambition in urbanism. Writing in *The City of Tomorrow*, the young Swiss architect extolled the virtues of orthogonal planning in dogmatic opposition to Sitte's carefully studied variety. In his opinion, picturesqueness was 'a pleasure which quickly becomes boring if too frequently gratified,' and that, by contrast, 'the right angle is lawful, it is part of our determinism, it is obligatory' (Le Corbusier, 1929: pp. 210, 21). Le Corbusier admitted being initially 'subverted' by Sitte's ideas as a younger man before returning to the true path of reason. In the Foreword to *The City of Tomorrow* Le Corbusier wrote:

> I read Camillo Sitte, the Viennese writer, and was affected by his insidious pleas in the direction of picturesque town planning. Sitte's demonstrations were clever, his theories seemed adequate; they were based on the past, and in fact WERE the past, but a sentimental past on a small and pretty scale, like the little wayside flowers. His past was not that of the great periods, it was essentially one of compromise. Sitte's eloquence (turned) architecture away, in the most absurd fashion, from its proper path ... When in 1922 ... I made my panorama of a City of Three Million Inhabitants, I relied only on the paths of pure reason .... (Le Corbusier; 1929: p. xxv)

Despite decades of intellectual antipathy towards experiential urbanism, always dubbed picturesque and romantic by its opponents, as if these were somehow irredeemably negative traits, the more humanistic ideas and the vocabulary of human-scaled spaces contained in that approach gradually began to win converts among the design and planning professions during the early 1970s. In Britain, Garden City style planning had continued through the New Town program after World War II, and the environments in these new 'garden cities' were much more popular with the public than the architectural heroics of urban redevelopment. The 'picturesque' revival reconnected with this venerable tradition to the benefit of both camps. Architects and planners had finally built a bridge to span the chasm between professional theory and popular taste. This alliance formed a focus for the anti-modernist reaction that had been building during the 1960s and 1970s.

## ANTI-MODERNIST REACTIONS

The radical tactics of street demonstrations and vocal opposition to government plans employed by British community architects and American advocacy planners noted above was part of the anti-establishment ideological change in Europe and America during the late 1960s and early 1970s. The young professionals were reacting against the recent mistakes and omissions of urban policy and design in political ways, but there were other, more intellectual critiques of modernism emerging at the same time, ones that had their roots in the 1950s. This lineage begins most clearly with the work of a post-World War II generation of young architects, most particularly those associated with the group known as Team 10.

This group was entrusted with the preparations for the tenth meeting of CIAM (the Congrès Internationaux d'Architecture Moderne) that took place at Dubrovnik in 1956. At the core of this group, which took its name from the number of the CIAM conference, was a smaller circle of professionals who had come together in Doorn, Holland in 1954 and set out a critique of CIAM doctrine from earlier conferences in the 'Doorn Manifesto' (Gold: p. 230). This group, comprising architects Aldo van Eyck, Peter Smithson, John Voelcker, Jacob Bakema and Daniel van Ginkel, together with a social economist Hans Hovens-Greve, argued specifically that CIAM's overly technical view of city functions failed to deal with 'human associations,' or the social fabric that sustained the city and its people.

CIAM's doctrine about cities had been spelled out clearly in 1933, during the movement's fourth conference, and in the celebrated Athens Charter, written largely under the auspices of Le Corbusier. The Congress was only five-years old in 1933, having been founded in 1928 at La Sarraz in Switzerland as a means of propagating the agenda of modern architecture. Specifically, it sought to unite a series of disparate architectural experiments into an international movement with common intentions and cohesion around the building style that had emerged strongly the previous year at the Weissenhoff exhibition.

As a relief from the political tensions in Europe, CIAM's famous fourth conference was held aboard the steamer S.S. *Patris II* as it sailed across the Mediterranean from Athens to Marseilles. On board, elements of the most notable, one might say notorious manifesto of modern city design were formulated. The crusading document we know today as the Athens Charter is in fact a substantial and subsequent rewriting of CIAM IV's original maritime proceedings. The mild-mannered technical language of the original notes, *Les Annales Techniques*, was transformed by a series of working groups, influenced heavily by Le Corbusier, into a hard-hitting, dogmatic manifesto that eventually appeared in 1942 under Le Corbusier's sole authorship (Gold, 1997).

The Charter narrowly defined the modern city under four main categories – Dwelling, Work, Recreation and Transportation – each with its distinct location and urban form. A fifth heading briefly discussed historic buildings and suggested it was appropriate to conserve buildings if they were true remnants of the past. However, the tone of the document implied that no avant-garde architect or planner associated with the modern movement could or should allow these irrelevant past cultures to interfere with the grand work of making the new city. Absent from the text of the Charter was any meaningful discussion of the social, economic or architectural character of existing residential or mixed-use neighborhoods.

However, the Charter's rhetoric was powerful, and its vision compelling in its distilled abstraction of human functions. The urban ideas enshrined in the text became guiding principles and doctrine for many architects and planners involved in rebuilding British and European cities after World War II. But while many professionals in the new postwar generation were persuaded by the promise of a crisp, clean technical future, others began to question the doctrine. Radicals like those involved in the Doorn Manifesto quickly discerned an intellectual vacuum in postwar thinking about urban architectural and social issues. For example, all that could be said at CIAM VIII in 1951, structured around the theme of 'The Urban Core,' was that the center city itself should be designated as a functional zone, and include 'open space' to which citizens would be spontaneously attracted in some mysterious and unspecified fashion. It was becoming all too clear that CIAM's model of the Functional City had been formulated in ignorance of how cities actually worked.

In opposition to these large-scale, technical and abstract generalizations, Team 10, which grew out of the Doorn group, proposed an urbanism that valued 'the personal, the particular and the precise' (Banham, 1963). In the words of Aldo van Eyck, one of Team 10's founders, 'Whatever time and space mean, place and occasion mean more' (van Eyck, 1962: p. 27). The tenth conference in Dubrovnik in 1956 signaled the end of CIAM as an organization and an intellectual force. But the power of the modernist view of the city, with its single-use zones divided by major highways, and new large buildings constructed as singular, unrelated objects in the open space laid bare by the demolition of old neighborhoods, lasted for another twenty years. It created the city we now fight to reform.

In contrast to the abstraction of city plans inspired by Le Corbusier, the work of younger architects who came to prominence in the 1950s through their association with Team 10 demonstrated a concern to enrich modernism with a sense of social realism that it lacked. The urban designs of one such architect, Ralph Erskine, revealed his special sensitivity to human behavior and community dynamics.

Erskine's work in the northern British city of Newcastle-upon-Tyne is particularly relevant to our story, as it provided a dramatic counterpoint to the general set of values, assumptions and procedures that pertained to most British urban renewal programs, and to a large degree in America also. The bulk of city redevelopment in Britain during the 1960s continued to follow an impersonal process of slum clearance with old neighborhoods replaced by large-scale residential projects. In this bureaucratic process, homes were 'housing units,' and residents were regarded as passive consumers and quantified merely as numbers to be rehoused. There was little or no sense of partnership between city planners and the public, and the bureaucratic process often bred bitter conflict. Residents resented being forcibly rehoused, while paternalistic city architects and planners couldn't understand why people weren't grateful for their efforts to provide them with newer, better accommodation. It wasn't only young idealistic professionals who waged a campaign to change the urban renewal process. Ralph Erskine, already a well-established architect, came to prominence in Britain for doing just that.

Although born in Britain, Erskine had developed as a major architectural figure in his adopted homeland of Sweden, gaining a reputation for well-designed housing schemes that were sensitively adapted to site,

climate and community. When Erskine was appointed architect for the massive Byker redevelopment project in 1968, the Newcastle city authorities intentionally embarked on a more progressive policy of urban redevelopment, but it is doubtful whether they had any real inkling of where this appointment would lead.

What the Newcastle city fathers got for their good intentions was a mini-revolution in urban redevelopment. Erskine stood the standard process on its head, involving the residents as partners and forging a strong bond between the community and the designers. Erskine's partner, Vernon Gracie, lived on-site for many years during the rebuilding process in a flat above the drawing office set up in an old corner store, previously a funeral parlor, which became as much a community resource space as a professional drawing office. In this program of urban redevelopment that lasted for 14 years, Erskine and his team showed what could be done when urban designers took community values seriously. Suddenly there was a real alternative to the standard urban renewal procedures that had devastated so many communities.

Erskine's design team evolved a new process, and derived an architecture that was contemporary in its details but which grew from an understanding of the traditional pedestrian scale of urban space (see Figure 1.6). The architect author of this book was privileged to be associated with Erskine's office in the early 1970s, an experience that healed his damaged faith in the profession of architecture, and invigorated his lifelong pursuit of democratic urban design.

**Figure 1.6** Housing at Byker, Newcastle-upon-Tyne, Ralph Erskine, 1968–82. Despite the fame of the Byker Wall (seen in the background) most of the housing at Byker is two and three storeys organized around intimate urban spaces.

The significance of Byker was manifold but the facts of its achievements have been eclipsed by its mythology. The project was such a progressive and optimistic counterpoint to 'normal' urban redevelopment at the time that the successes of Erskine's project team were touted as panaceas for almost all urban problems. Apart from the successful design, the two main accomplishments publicized by most commentators were citizen involvement in the rehousing process and in the retention of population in the community. That the facts themselves demonstrate something different takes little away from the efforts and achievements of the architects.

Apart from one preliminary exercise, residents were not involved in detailed design decisions. Instead, their participation evolved to a more general level of forming strong bonds of trust between architects and residents – to an extent unusual in any such relationship. Erskine wanted to elevate the residents to the status of primary clients, but his contractual relationship with the city, and the city's complex bureaucracy made the task unfeasible. This led to some ambiguity regarding Erskine's ability to fulfill all his promises to the local people.

But there was no such doubt regarding the role the architects' office played in the community. The old corner shop became an informal community resource center. It was a focal place in the life of the neighborhood, where residents could obtain information and see the designers of their community at work. This level of mutual respect allowed the architects a relatively high level of freedom to interpret the community's needs into three-dimensional forms and spaces. As shown in Figure 1.6, they developed an original architectural language for the new buildings, having more to do with Erskine's personal aesthetic than local precedent, and created an intimate 'jumble' of urban spaces instead of the long bleak streets.

Demolition of Byker's housing stock began in 1966, two years before Erskine's appointment, and by 1969 the population had dropped from nearly 18 000 to 12 000. Normally, areas like Byker, covering 81 hectares (202 acres) were demolished in one fell swoop. Residents were rehoused permanently in other parts of the city, and the web of community connections and relationships was destroyed, along with all physical traces of old buildings. Instead of this soulless process, Erskine persuaded the Newcastle city authorities to clear away the old rows of 'Tyneside flats' on a much smaller scale, only a few streets at a time. This more selective schedule was intended to mesh with the phasing of rebuilding, so that residents could be quickly rehoused in new dwellings. Erskine planned to accommodate 9000 of the resident population in new homes at a density of 247 persons per hectare (100 per acre) – in American terms, about 38 dwellings per acre. This was considerably lower than the original housing densities, but allowed also for 1.25 car parking spaces per dwelling. The city authorities expected the remaining few thousand residents to relocate elsewhere by their own choice.

Despite these good intentions, substantial construction delays dislocated this intermeshing program of demolition and rebuilding, and toward the end of the project the number of original residents rehoused within their community numbered nearer 5000 (Malpass, 1979). Even though the architects did not achieve all their intended social goals, they did save and refurbish several important community buildings, including schools, pubs and clubs. One of these, the Shipley Street baths, was incorporated into the now-famous Byker Wall that bounds the northern edge of the community for a distance of one-and-a-half miles, dramatically following the topography (see Figure 1.7).

Erskine's Byker redevelopment provided a viable alternative to standard planning procedures and the architectural vocabularies of British urban redevelopment. But other changes were in the works in Britain in the early 1970s. A book with the poignantly polemic title *Architecture versus Housing* comprehensively cataloged the failings of modernist housing initiatives, and provided a biting critique of bureaucratic policies and insensitive designs (Pawley, 1971). Two years later, in 1973, the RIBA Journal published a short article by Richard MacCormac entitled 'Housing form and land use: new research,' which demonstrated that the desired densities of 250 persons per hectare (approximately 38 dwellings per acre in American terms) could be achieved by interlocking courts of terraced houses. All the homes had private gardens, and the density targets were achieved without recourse to the publicly despised high-rise flats. Built projects using MacCormac's approach, such as Pollards Hill, in Merton, South London (1977), by the Borough of Merton Architects' Department, bear a strong resemblance to the influential American plan of Radburn New Town in New Jersey of 50 years earlier by Clarence Stein and Henry Wright. In both cases, cul-de-sac vehicle courts bring cars to one side of the houses which open up to parkland and pedestrian greenways on the other, all organized within a large 'superblock' of major roads.

The extensive influence the design of Radburn had upon subsequent developments is discussed further

**Figure 1.7** The Byker Wall, Newcastle-upon-Tyne, Ralph Erskine. Designed originally to shield the low-rise housing from the noise of an urban motorway that was never built, the Byker Wall has become the dominant symbol and landmark of the Byker redevelopment. It is mainly lived in by elderly residents who enjoy magnificent views across the valley of the River Tyne.

in Chapter 2, but for our narrative here it is important to observe its effect in other British public housing schemes of the early to mid-1970s. Typical of this design ethos, for example, are large residential areas in the new town of Runcorn, outside Liverpool in northwest England. Here we can see clear Radburnesque principles in the layouts of vehicle cul-de-sacs and pedestrian paths along greenways leading to local schools, bus stops, a day care nursery, an elderly persons' home, community centers, and shopping areas. In contrast to the crisp white modern terraces of Pollards Hill, the neighborhoods of Palace Fields and The Brow at Runcorn are built in a low-key brick and pitched roof aesthetic, a stripped-down vocabulary derived from traditional housing forms.

Vernacular imagery also provided the impetus behind many other designs in the public and private sectors in the UK during the early 1970s. Housing schemes were designed once more using traditional streets and closes and an architecture that specifically recalled the regional vernacular. Typical of this kind of development was Oaklands Park in Dawlish, a seaside town in the southwest of England, designed by the now defunct firm of Mervyn Seal and Associates, where the architect author worked for part of that decade. Oaklands Park drew inspiration from the townscape examples of Gordon Cullen, combined with an appreciation of the local vernacular architecture found in the fishing villages of southwest England. Although many architects regarded this use of vernacular imagery as a betrayal of modernist ideals, 'neo-vernacular' housing performed well in the marketplace, and before long earned professional recognition – in the case of Oaklands Park, by winning a national design award from the British Department of the Environment (see Figures 4.13–4.15).

These pioneering projects of the early 1970s often met official opposition from planners, but it was not long before these very design principles and imagery became ensconced as the prevailing wisdom in local authority design guides. The most famous of these was the pioneering *Design Guide for Residential Areas*, published by the County Council of Essex in 1973 and discussed further in Chapter 3. A very clever variant of this townscape-based approach – one that has largely faded from professional memory – was illustrated by Ivor de Wolfe in the pages of the *Architectural Review* in 1971, and published later that year as *Civila: the End of Sub Urban Man*.

This project created a vision for a new town on industrial wasteland in the English midlands, and it stands out for a couple of reasons. First, it was designed entirely in three-dimensional perspective vignettes, comprising artfully composed photographic collages of existing buildings. Second, *Civila* included many 'heroic' modernist structures, but instead of standing isolated in space, here they were juxtaposed closely with their neighbors. As Figure 1.8 illustrates, this created a dense urban fabric of almost medieval complexity, but rendered without recourse to romantic or nostalgic urban imagery. But this powerful polemic attempt to marry the spatial complexity of the townscape approach to urbanism with contemporary architectural aesthetics – a poem to an invigorated modernism – failed to affect British urban development proposals. At the very time of its

**Figure 1.8** The 'Town Wall' in Civilia, an imaginary city on reclaimed land in the English midlands, 1971. Traditional townscape is constructed from modernist buildings. (*Photo-collage courtesy of The Architectural Press*)

**Figure 1.9** Suburban house designs in the inner city; Birmingham, UK, 1980s.

publication, cities were becoming shaped less by public projects and more by privately financed designs. Private developers had little interest in polemical positions, and chose instead to build housing of the most conservative and traditional kind, dwellings that were guaranteed to sell in the marketplace.

This return to smaller scale, and more traditional development led to an unexpected consequence in British inner cities – the suburbanization of the center during the 1980s. It was less a matter of density, which had already been substantially reduced by the towers and slabs of urban renewal, and more a matter of image. The immediate origins of this change can be found in the 1970s with substantial reductions in public home-building programs and the energy crisis of 1974, 'which made inner urban areas more attractive to the middle class' (Holyoak: p. 60).

Private developers were quick to sense this opportunity, and bought up land cheaply in the central areas, either abandoned industrial sites or unloved areas of the 1960s era housing, already severely dilapidated. Developers, and the architects who worked for them, did not share the high-style modernist aspirations of their public sector colleagues at City Hall. Instead, they had a range of house designs that sold well in the suburbs and were economical to build. It was therefore easy for private builders to construct large numbers of these commercially popular but uninspired and low-density (by English standards) houses that made the suburbanization of inner city areas complete. Combined with Britain's growing political conservatism during the 1980s, and

> ... the emphasis by the Thatcher government on placing private and family interests above the collective, led to inner urban areas coming to look more like slightly compressed versions of the suburbs; rows of neovernacular two storey houses, each with a small front garden with a car parking space, but with little in the way of communal resources – house production rather than city building' (Holyoak: p. 62). (See Figure 1.9.)

The 1980s found British cities without a coherent strategy for revitalization, with neither the private nor the public sectors being able to grapple effectively with the problem on their own. One government response during the Thatcher years was to diminish, or in the case of the Greater London Council, destroy the power local authorities had over development in their areas. New fast-track 'Enterprise Zones' were set up in decayed central city areas, such as the London Docklands, to lure private investment with the guarantee of minimal interference from local government. The successes and failures of these initiatives during the 1980s are discussed in more detail in Chapter 5, but one major reaction to their perceived American-style imbalance of private power over public interest has been the development of much more proactive local planning and design initiatives in British cities during the 1990s. During the last decade of the twentieth century, this reversion of policy has connected with consciously traditional types of urban forms and patterns in cities, involving mixtures of uses, pedestrian scale and spatial enclosure (see Figure 1.10).

Similar renewed interest in traditional urban values, patterns and imagery was evident in America during the 1980s. Beginning in that decade, the

urban form of the traditional European city enjoyed a renaissance in American architecture and urbanism, especially in American academia, through the influential writings of people like Christopher Alexander at Berkeley (Alexander, 1977, 1987), and Michael Dennis and Colin Rowe at Cornell (Rowe and Koetter, 1978; Dennis, 1981). From that time onward, the work of Aldo Rossi and the Italian Neo-Rationalists became better known to students, and European theorists like Leon Krier began to influence a new generation of younger architects. Among these were Andres Duany and Elizabeth Plater-Zyberk, the two people most often credited with initiating the movement that became known in America as New Urbanism.

The volumes of existing material about Seaside, the Duany and Plater-Zyberk landmark project in the Florida panhandle, make it unnecessary to add to that body of literature which has charted the 1982 design's progress from an affordable alternative community to a fantasy playground for the consciously cute upper-middle class (Krieger and Lennertz, 1991; Mohney and Easterling, 1991; Brooke, 1995; Sexton, 1995). It is a strange and wonderful place, but Seaside has been over-hyped to the point that it has become the victim of its own success. The alternative urbanism that Seaside offered has spawned dozens of second- and third-rate imitations as developers and architects copied superficial details without understanding the deeper philosophy. Its idiosyncratically romantic appearance has been parodied in a myriad of developments to the extent that New Urbanism itself is often misconstrued in the public's mind as comprising merely picket fences and front porches (see Figure 1.11).

Seaside is such a particular place that it is now of little use as a precedent for everyday design in more typical American communities, but there is no doubt that this small development on Florida's Gulf coast struck the important first blow in America's battle against conventional suburbia. However, a more important contribution to reordering the suburbs was Duany and Plater-Zyberk's innovative example of using graphic codes as the primary means of development control. In the context of ever more cumbersome American zoning books of dense and dull verbiage, the crisp and elegant depiction of the rules regarding building arrangement, street design and appropriate uses was a revelation. We discuss this important issue further in Chapter 5.

Seaside started a whole reappraisal of what was possible to build in America's suburbs, and began the movement

**Figure 1.10** Modern versions of traditional urban forms; Gloucester Green market square, Oxford, UK, 1987–90.

**Figure 1.11** Seaside, Florida, Duany and Plater-Zyberk, 1982. This modest development became the poster child of traditional urbanism, but soon became the victim of its own success with escalating house prices, fostering the (unfair) image of New Urbanism as the exclusive province of an elite middle class.

initially known as Neo-Traditional Development or Traditional Neighbourhood Development (TND). As we discuss in detail in Chapter 3, the co-mingling of Duany and Plater-Zyberk's TND on the east coast with Peter Calthorpe's experiments with 'pedestrian pockets,' or Transit-Oriented Development (TOD) on the west coast in the late 1980s gave rise to the movement now known as New Urbanism in 1993. In the subsequent 10 years, these once radical ideas about city and suburban design have gained considerable acceptance in the development community. However, many battles remain to be fought; it is still much easier in America to produce standard suburban sprawl than to create sustainable mixed-use urban communities.

In academia, it was New Urbanism's historicist leanings that engendered a negative reaction in many American schools of architecture. The return to traditional types of urbanism came under challenge from academic architects who saw this reversion to traditionalism as a retreat from the high intellectual ground of modernity, or the convoluted games of postmodernity, into the reactionary romance of nostalgia. Moreover, professors at prestigious architectural institutions found it uncomfortable, even demeaning, to be associated with ideas that were gaining currency in the 'soiled' world of the marketplace. But more important than this American squabble, the relevance of traditional urbanism was challenged by revolutionary developments in another sphere – in information technology. The creation of 'virtual'

space on the Internet as a competitor to 'real' space in communities poses new challenges and dilemmas for our society, and for the professions of architecture and planning. It is to that conflict of paradigms that we must now direct our attention.

## REAL PLACES AND VIRTUAL COMMUNITIES

This technological challenge to traditional urban space is not the first one in the history of the modern city. For an earlier example we have to return briefly to the 1960s, when the dispersed scale of the new automobile landscape in America threatened to make the traditional city obsolete. Even in Britain during the 1960s, proponents of picturesque urban design, the kind so neatly captured in Gordon Cullen's book *Townscape*, were still in the minority. This approach to the design of pedestrian-friendly urban spaces remained alive in Britain in only a very watered down manner in the layout of several postwar New Towns. In America, similar design principles that had been characteristic of that country's Romantic Garden Suburbs of the 1890s through the 1920s all but disappeared in the decades after World War II.

Designers like Cullen stayed focused on these kinds of urban spaces because they believed they could foster a sense of community and belonging that was demonstrably absent in the voids between the towers and slabs of high-rise housing and in the dull repetition of developer-produced suburbia. The placelessness of modernist cities and suburbs was critiqued more savagely by commentators like Ian Nairn, who, starting in the 1950s, routinely castigated examples of miserable civic design in a regular column in the *Architectural Review* entitled 'Outrage,' and extended this argument into the books *Outrage* and *Counter-attack against Subtopia* (Nairn, 1955, 1957). More often than not these bad examples were in suburban situations that Nairn and others felt lacked any sense of cohesion or traditional urbanity. Cullen's beautifully illustrated book dealt with the same subject matter, but its message pushed architects more gently towards a re-appreciation of traditional spaces and city textures and this concern blended easily with Jane Jacobs' American praise for the traditional streets of her New York urban neighborhood.

But at the very time in the early to mid-1960s, that some architects and urbanists were retracing their steps toward the traditional city, progressive planners began to challenge these concepts as outmoded and unrealistic in the new culture based on expanded personal mobility and the automobile. Not surprisingly this challenge came from America, where, in 1963 and 1964, the academic planner Melvin Webber from Berkeley, California, wrote two influential articles entitled *Order in Diversity: Community without Propinquity* and *The Urban Place and the Nonplace Urban Realm*, in which he rejected models of the city based on traditional spatial patterns. Webber and others argued that it was a mistake to critique the expanding city as shapeless sprawl, and to long for traditional streets and squares, because this missed the point that the car had changed the relationship between space and time in cities. People now conceptualized distance not in miles, but in minutes, based on the time it took to drive to their destinations. Propinquity, being near everything one needed, was no longer a necessity for mobile families. Instead of defined physical places in the traditional townscape sense of spatial enclosure and walking distances, the new city was based on a pattern of dispersal, where individuals and families constructed their sense of the city from a series of physically discontinuous locations, connected only by driving. The city was no longer experienced as an integrated hierarchy of places and neighborhoods. Instead it became a non-hierarchical network where locations were equalized by their accessibility by car.

Webber's argument that the automobile would release people from the ties that bound them to particular places, and open up new possibilities of mobility

and connections with a wide variety of locations, coincided with the explosive growth of American suburban development in the 1950s and 1960s. New housing subdivisions, shopping centers and office parks were built on open land with few spatial constraints, and connected by the ubiquitous system of what were then high-speed commuter freeways. The real point of Webber's thesis, however, was not simply that it was possible to move around easily to lots of different places, or that a new architecture could evolve from the technologies of movement, but that at a deep, fundamental level, *place didn't matter anymore*. Instead of community being grounded in a particular location, a new pattern of social relationships could be created from weaving together the disparate strands of daily life from a variety of generic locations. In this context, argued Webber and other academic planners, traditional urban forms were simply irrelevant.

In Britain, the Archigram movement of the 1960s and 1970s extended this thesis with inspiring images of 'walking cities' that carried everything needed to sustain life and culture in their famously massive tortoise-like forms. A few years later, the same group proposed a contradictory 'soft' architecture that placed more emphasis on fast-changing technical systems that could 'plug in' to any existing building situation and provide environmental and cultural services that could enrich all locations. The place didn't matter, and the character of the buildings in any location was immaterial. Drawing on a unique blend of science fiction and science fact, Archigram elaborated the theme that technology can render geographic location unimportant by supplying all necessary support systems without primary recourse to the natural or urban worlds.

This shifting equation between propinquity and accessibility has remained a central issue for architects, planners, geographers and cultural critics (Sennett, 1971, 1974; Castells, 1989, 1997; Harvey, 1989; Soja, 1989; Jameson, 1991; Howell, 1993; Watson and Gibson, 1995; Mitchell, 1995, 1999). Many have expounded at length on this dilemma, offering various interpretations regarding the urban politics of power and place. For Webber and his colleagues forty years ago, the issue was originally one of new equations between physical distance and ease of personal travel, but the information technology revolution of the 1990s has radically changed the parameters of the discussion.

Webber, Archigram, and many other designers, planners, and critics reordered physical space relative to new technologies, but real space was still the medium of human discourse. Proponents of our new digital society have argued that our computer-rich culture, redolent with electronic spaces, has superseded all such discussions (Mitchell, 1995; Kelly, 1998; Gilder 2000 and others). The virtual spaces of the Internet, available to everyone with a computer, have brought Marshall McLuhan's 'global village' to fruition. Some even suggest that traditional community life is obsolete, and that virtual space will replace physical space as the primary medium of personal, commercial and cultural dialogue. The 'electronic cottage' in the wilderness is now a reality, and information technology, these same critics argue, has rendered traditional urban places obsolete at an even more fundamental level than Webber predicted. Once more the street is under attack. Michael Dear goes so far as to say that 'the phone and the modem have rendered the street irrelevant' (Dear, 1995: p. 31).

As designers of physical, inhabited space, many architects are naturally loath to accept this conjecture, preferring to investigate the writings of authors who offer an alternative conclusion: in a society that enables us to live and work anywhere we like, the places we choose to inhabit become *all the more precious* and important.

The first argument against the dispersal and 'death of place' scenario is that commerce still clusters. While routine office work in the service sector has been farmed out to towns all across America, and to cities in developing countries, companies in key innovative business sectors such as information technology, design, financial services, law and health care operate differently. They tend to concentrate their operations in certain key places – Manhattan, Chicago, the San Francisco Bay Area, Austin Texas, Boston or Seattle, to name just a few. This phenomenon has given rise to what is referred to as the 'human capital theory' of economic and urban growth.

Simply stated, the theory of human capital argues that traditional reasons for city growth – location near natural resources or convenient transportation routes – no longer apply. Now, the crucial factor for future economic development is the human resource of highly educated and productive people, not the conventional wisdom of reducing the costs of doing business by making and transporting things as cheaply as possible. A leading proponent of the human capital theory, Joel Kotkin, suggests that through this new lens, wealth will accumulate wherever 'intelligence clusters' evolve, whether this is a big city or a small town (Kotkin, 2001, in Florida, 2002: p. 221). Other notable economists such as Robert Lucas and Edward Glaeser show in their research that

human capital – groupings of creative, productive, original innovators and problem solvers – is the main impetus of urban development and wealth creation (Florida: p. 222).

Author Richard Florida takes this well-established premise one stage further in his book *The Rise of the Creative Class*, where he notes that many experts on urban and regional growth have emphasized the importance of places as incubators of creativity and new industries (Florida: p. 219). Contrary to expectations, the New Economy that was supposed to destroy place and render cities obsolete, increasingly makes place more relevant by clustering activities around real concentrations of people in real places. The question posed by Florida is not whether companies cluster, but why do they cluster in some locations and not others? What role does physical place play in this process?

Florida's research strongly suggests that companies locate in close proximity to one another to recruit from concentrations of talented people who spur innovation and create economic growth (Florida: p. 220). Unlike their parents and grandparents, creative people today don't simply settle where the jobs are. They gather in places they like to live and which are centers of creativity in themselves. Creative people look for places where they can make friends easily, find acceptance of diverse lifestyles, enjoy a wide variety of recreation and entertainment and live productive and stimulating lives.

Florida's 'creative class' comprised 30 percent of America's workforce in 2002. They are scientists, computer professionals and programmers, architects, engineers and graphic and product designers, entrepreneurs, educators, artists, musicians and entertainers. Around this core clusters a broader group of other creative professionals in business and finance, law and health care. It is this 30 percent of America's workforce, Florida concludes, that will provide the energy and talent to power the next generation of economic growth and wealth creation.

In essence, the informal, flexible, and intensive work habits of people like the authors – professors/ architect/artist/writers – have moved from what used to be the fringes of the marketplace into the economic mainstream. These workplace characteristics contrast with those of the tightly organized corporate professionals of yesterday, and Florida's thesis is supported by the latest research into workplace trends. English architect-author Frank Duffy, a world authority on office design, predicts that the days of the large-scale corporate headquarters are numbered.

In their stead are new innovative types of office environment based on more flexible work patterns that suit creative professionals (Duffy, 1997).

The members of this new creative class are drawn to places that offer a range of economic opportunities, a stimulating environment, and amenities for people with diverse lifestyles. In America, such places as Cambridge and Boston, Massachusetts; Seattle; San Francisco; Austin; Boulder, Colorado; Gainesville, Florida and Santa Fe, New Mexico provide the stimulation, diversity and richness of experience desired by these creative people (Florida: p. 11). Generic suburbia, bland at best, alienating at worst, cannot meet these requirements. Creative professionals prefer communities that have a distinctive character, diversity, are accepting of difference, and that offer lifestyle options. Such attributes are nurtured by the quality and attractiveness of physical places – a lively street scene, an arts district, a thriving music scene and older neighborhoods with interesting and unique buildings.

The relationship of this theory of the 'creative class' to urban form is amplified by the research of Ray Oldenburg, whose book *A Great Good Place* documents the role of 'third places' in modern society. Home and work are the first two places, and the third comprises venues like bookstores, cafés and coffee shops which support a community's social vitality, and where a 'stranger feels at home' (Oldenburg: p. xxviii). These informal gathering spots amplify and extend the communal space of the street, and provide relief from patterns of focused work or a single lifestyle and provide a setting for group gatherings.

Such places work best as part of a walkable neighborhood, and this book was written in one such setting, in a space cleared from canvasses in the front room of a two-room painting studio on the second floor of an old brick building. Beneath us are a picture framing shop and a beauty salon. Next door is a digital animation studio over an art gallery, and a coffee shop. A few yards up the street is a one-person car repair business. Across the street are the studios of an artists' cooperative, the offices of Charlotte's weekly African-American newspaper, the premises of a replacement window company, a second-hand business furniture showroom, and a funky restaurant. Beyond the new light rail tracks outside our window stands a block of recently constructed apartments and small offices for architects, financial advisors, and interior decorators opposite some older buildings containing an antique store.

More apartments are under construction on the next block, adjacent to the neighborhood fried chicken take-away restaurant, and at the south end of the street a cluster of converted warehouses are home to several design firms, including UNC-Charlotte's Community Design Studio. One block to the east and north are more restaurants, bars and offices, two large apartment complexes, two more thriving car repair businesses and a barbed wire compound with secondhand cars for sale. Our street is slowly evolving into the 'Main Street' of a new urban village with a diverse population, and we frequently take breaks and drop into the coffee shop just to chat, see our neighbors, meet our students, chat to strangers or to read over what we've just written. At the end of the day, we can stride half-a-mile up the sidewalk by the rail line to the gym to work out, or walk a leisurely seven blocks to home. This predilection for neighborhood and community doesn't mean that we abhor virtual space. On the contrary, we are connected to the Internet as we write, and we communicate the daily trivia of our lives on our mobile phones. The point is, we *could* do this anywhere, but we *choose* to do it in an attractive urban place (see Figure 1.12).

This vignette is increasingly typical of developing neighborhoods, and we feel lucky to be part of one such special place. Contrary to Melvin Webber's thesis of the 1960s that place doesn't matter any more, and the predictions of techno-futurists that 'geography is dead,' research increasingly demonstrates the opposite: place itself is fast becoming the main organizing feature of economic activity. Even while arguing that electronic space is more important than physical

**Figure 1.12** Camden Road, Charlotte, NC. At the heart of an evolving urban neighborhood, the street outside the authors' studio is occasionally taken over by an arts and crafts market.

place, Kevin Kelly, a leading prophet of the 'geography is dead' theme, qualifies this assertion by admitting that distinctive places retain their value, and that this value will increase despite the non-spatial dimension of information technology (Kelly: pp. 94–5, in Florida: p. 219).

Given their flexible and unpredictable work schedules, creative professionals require access to recreational and entertainment opportunities at a moment's notice (see Figure 1.13). They increasingly act 'like tourists in their own city' (Lloyd and Clark, 2001, in Florida: p. 225) and require amenities close at hand, within walking distance if possible. There is only one kind of urbanism that can meet this need: the traditional public spaces of street and square, park and boulevard.

At an urban design conference in Melbourne, Australia, in 2001, author Joel Garreau, best known

**Figure 1.13** Working in a beautiful urban place. An anonymous worker telecommutes with mobile phone and laptop from the quayside in Dartmouth, Devon. When we can work anywhere, we're likely to choose a beautiful place.

for his seminal book *Edge City*, noted that cities are changing faster today than at any time for 150 years, and that computers are reshaping our urban world to favor places that provide and nourish face-to-face contact. Garreau expressed his belief that the urban future could 'look like the eighteenth century, only cooler.' Edge cities and downtowns 'that are sterile and charmless will die.' In common with the observations of Richard Florida, Garreau believes the primary purpose of future cities will be to provide optimum conditions for face-to-face contact, an ancient but still primary human need (Garreau, 2001). In this context, good urban design and traditional public space are crucial in providing the appropriate environment for these human activities. We would go so far as to say that New Urbanism in America, derided by opponents in academia as a reactionary, nostalgic movement, in fact provides the best opportunity to create the urbanity necessary for the creative class – and ultimately the rest of us – to function fruitfully. Other critics mock this search for a more walkable urban future as the 'café society' and often dub such efforts at community building as 'latté towns.' These commentators, pontificating from the sidelines, see such urban villages only as the commodification of urban experience, reducing the richness of public life to mere spectacle and entertainment courtesy of Starbucks, The Gap, Victoria's Secret and Williams-Sonoma. We're well aware of these dangers in newly minted developments of the type we'll discuss later in more detail, but even so, we beg to differ. In contrast to our critics, we believe the (re)creation of traditional urban places offers the best hope of a sustainable urban future for America's cities and suburbs.

As witness to this belief, a symposium entitled 'Thinking Creatively For Our Economic Future' featuring Richard Florida at the University of North Carolina at Charlotte in April 2003, brought together nearly two hundred people from the Charlotte region to brainstorm ideas that would increase the economic competitiveness for the city and surrounding counties in the global marketplace. There were only a handful of design professionals in the audience, but of all the dozens of innovative ideas discussed, the top recommendation of the day by a large margin was the creation of new urban spaces and public places where people could connect with each other and thus spur the creation of ideas. This strategy is called 'designing for collisions,' and we think of this by a simple analogy of molecules bumping into each other and creating reactions. The more molecules that bump around in a space the more creative collisions occur, resulting in yet more innovative encounters. This creative energy is precisely the opposite of the passive consumer culture portrayed by several critics of traditional urbanism (Kaliski, 1999; McDougall, 1999). The greater the density of occupation, and the more eclectic the mixture of uses in the neighborhoods around the public space, the higher will be the energy quotient and the greater the potential for economic development.

We dispute the often-made assertion that somehow, the urban life in these places isn't authentic, and that the only valid, creative urban activities take place in marginalized neighborhoods amidst nondescript surroundings (Chase et al., 1999). While every city needs unloved and unlovely places that can be appropriated cheaply, or at no cost, for unprogrammed uses by individuals and groups outside the mainstream, there is a major inconsistency in academic efforts to glorify these acts as somehow more profound or better than actions taken in public space by the middle classes. Appropriating urban space for culturally specific activities by individuals and groups of all complexions is a valid endeavor, and needs to be facilitated wherever possible – even at the expense of social discomfort, as in protest rallies and demonstrations. A culturally diverse city needs different places for different activities, but for critics to disparage the business meetings, local commerce, spontaneous conversations, and kids' homework activities in places like our local coffee shop as mere 'simulation' of urbanism is nonsense. Authentic cultural production can take place in attractive surroundings as well as in abandoned parking lots.

We expand on this theme in Chapters 3, 4 and 6, and on the relevance of 'urban village' type development in Britain and America. We believe strongly that such mixed-use, walkable neighborhoods really can become the inclusive crucibles of creativity, sustainability and economic development in an increasingly uncertain global environment. In our attempt to 'think globally,' we design towns and cities locally, street by street and block by block.

# Cities, suburbs and sprawl

## SYNOPSIS

In America, the main battles for a sustainable urban future will be fought in the suburbs, as they pose the most difficult political terrain for design and environmental improvement. Accordingly, a large part of this chapter is devoted to untangling the interwoven strands of suburban history and their influence on present-day practice. The nineteenth century witnessed a lot of cross-reference between suburban development in Britain and America, and we review this history in some detail to counter a prevailing American misconception of the suburb as a particularly American (and twentieth-century) phenomenon.

Suburbs developed first in eighteenth-century England and the story of their origin and development there and in America – first as a companion and later as a rival to the city – is a complex one. It includes many diverse sources of aesthetic inspiration and many influences from the socio-economic conditions and cultural values of various periods of Anglo-American history since the beginnings of the Industrial Revolution. Within this elaborate tale are important reminders and examples that can help us understand our present condition. Moreover, illuminated by our renewed appreciation of the relevance of traditional forms of urbanism to contemporary cities and suburbs, this history contains vital precedents for our most advanced urban thinking today.

Since World War II, suburbs in America have developed in a somewhat different pattern from those in Great Britain, due in part to different cultural attitudes about the development of private property and restrictions on suburban growth. Whereas Britain practiced (more or less) a policy of containment and green belt preservation around towns and cities,

America countenanced no such restrictions, and what began in the 1950s as an optimistic search for a convenient, affordable, drive-in utopia, turned during the 1990s into a conflicted landscape of polarized opinion about the burdens of growth – sprawl, congestion, pollution and loss of open space. The second part of the chapter examines this devolution of the American environment from the positive connotations of 'suburb' to the negative image of 'sprawl.' The problems associated with spread-out, low-density development have led in America to the rise of the 'Smart Growth' movement, an important factor that we shall examine in Chapter 3.

## THE EVOLUTION OF THE ANGLO-AMERICAN SUBURB

We ended the previous chapter by referring, rather grandly, to New Urbanism, and traditional urbanism in general, as the best hope for a sustainable future. Our conviction that New Urbanism does offer an opportunity to achieve Smart Growth from both environmental and economic perspectives, is deeply colored by the American experience of uncontrolled suburban sprawl and the abandonment of traditional urbanism during the decades from 1950 through the 1980s. Areas of many British cities suffered similar fates at the hands of well-intentioned architects and planners during the period of urban renewal in the 1950s to early 1970s, but the urban form of British cities didn't disintegrate the way it did in post-World War II America. While traditional urban forms were threatened in the UK, they were never completely rejected. In America they all but died on the vine.

The application of modernist doctrine through the process of urban demolition and rebuilding certainly contributed to the decline of urban form in America, but even more destructive was the emergence of a completely car-dominated culture. The automobile, a powerful instrument of convenience, demanded easy access to such an extent that developers, planners, and architects allowed its needs to override almost every other consideration of urban space and building design. Designing for the car contributed to the decline of urban form in city centers as countless buildings were demolished for parking lots, a practice facilitated by American property tax laws.

Land is generally taxed in America according to its 'highest and best use'. If a building sits on a parcel of land, the property owner pays taxes based on the productive use of that structure, whether occupied or not. If the owner demolishes the building, his or her tax bill drops quite dramatically: now the best use for the land is only a car park, and it's taxed at a lower rate. Add to this saving a steady income from parking fees, and the property owner has a substantial incentive for demolition. The loss of older buildings in this manner has reduced many American city centers to the ubiquitous but arid formula of a cluster of office towers surrounded by oceans of asphalt parking lots (see Figure 2.1).

In suburban America the process was, and remains, just as stark. Since the 1950s the placement of commercial buildings has been dictated by a simple

**Figure 2.1** Office towers and adjacent surface parking lots, Charlotte, NC, 2003. In a new plan for this part of the city, this area is being reclaimed to become a two-block park over four levels of underground parking. The park will be framed with mid-rise housing, offices and shops. A new light rail line is being constructed immediately adjacent to this area.

formula: buildings were set way back from the street to make room for large, asphalt car parks in front, and without buildings close to the street to advertise themselves, large signs were positioned at the curb to catch the eye of the passing customer. The building at the back of the site became nothing but a blank box for commerce (it didn't need windows to lure pedestrian shoppers) and simply draped itself with another large sign or gaudy fake façade to guide the shoppers to the entrance. It was a singular recipe for convenience that gave little or no thought to larger issues of community aesthetics or pedestrian space.

Architects largely ignored this commercial strip as a populist environment that offered no scope for their design talents, and which, moreover, was beneath their professional dignity. It wasn't until 1972 that Robert Venturi, Denise Scott Brown and Steven Izenour startled the profession into reconsidering the suburban environment with their book *Learning from Las Vegas*, (as we shall discuss further in Chapter 3), and even then there was little positive response from architects for another decade.

Planners were similarly ineffectual. They created generic zoning plans and regulations that dealt with land purely as a commodity rather than an eco-system, and regulated site layouts purely for the convenience of automobile traffic. It was as if Ian McHarg's treatise *Design with Nature* had never been written, and America's fine tradition of urbanism had never existed. Having painted broad brush categories of land use across the map, planners then spent most of their time administering petty details of entrance drives and landscape buffers. Neither profession was looking at the patterns and character of suburban development from an urban design or environmental perspective.

In defense of architects and planners, the pace and extent of this suburban growth in America in the decades after the end of World War II was overwhelming. It was difficult for anybody to get a grasp of the extent of the production of new suburbs. Growth was so dramatic and intense that a clear understanding of its causes and precedents was hard to come by in the midst of all the activity. Very few people thought that history had much relevance, but they were wrong.

The urge to live in the suburbs has a long history. Two thousand years ago, when the *villa suburbana* was the residence of choice for the Roman elite who lived on large country estates outside the city, suburban living already carried a distinguished pedigree. The Latin word, *suburbanus*, meaning 'near the city,' provides the etymological definition, but we can trace the history of suburban retreats for wealthy citizenry even farther back, to sixth century BC Babylon. However, it was during the Middle Ages in Europe that extensive suburban settlements accrued around most cities, often in poor areas outside city walls where inhabitants were unable to avail themselves of city services and protection. At this time the sense of 'suburban' changed; a definition in the Shorter Oxford English Dictionary shows that as late as 1817, 'suburban' meant 'having inferior manners, the narrowness of view attributed to residents in suburbs'. Another dictionary definition deflates the suburb as 'a place of inferior, debased, and especially licentious habits of life'. In contrast, 'urbane' retains its meaning of being sophisticated, refined and elegant.

The more immediate origins of modern suburbia lie in the late eighteenth century at the beginning of the Industrial Revolution, in the countryside to the south of London. This new development marked a return to the original, positive connotations of living outside the city. Elite merchants in the British capital, echoing the Roman tradition, conceived the notion of a rural preserve where families could escape the increased congestion and pollution resulting from the early stages of London's transformation to an industrial metropolis. From these beginnings, the physical and social form of the suburbs evolved under the impetus of transportation technologies, and during the latter half of the nineteenth century trams and urban railways extended the suburbs into a literal and metaphoric 'middle landscape' between city and country for the wider middle class.

We shall examine the development of the modern suburb in Britain and America around three themes. The first traces the development of the suburb as an element of the changing form and patterns of the city, due in large part to rapid developments in transportation technology and other technical advances of the Industrial Revolution. This technical capacity for urban expansion combined with the opportunities for developers to make large profits on the conversion of cheap rural land to urban uses, thus accelerating the trend. The second theme focuses on the upsurge of a new 'romantic' aesthetic that gripped the public's imagination; and the third concerns changes in the values and structure of family life during the late eighteenth and nineteenth centuries. Together, these forces engineered a revolution in the whole metropolitan structure, and in the relationships between city and countryside.

In divergence to the unflattering definitions of an earlier time, during the late eighteenth and nineteenth centuries the term suburbia came to mean a high-quality, low-density environment characterized by a preponderance of single-family middle-class homes in a park-like setting. It excluded industry, most commerce, and all lower classes except for servants. In contrast to this exclusivity, the core of the eighteenth-century city comprised a dense mixture of uses and classes. A basic principle of a city like London, and the early American settlements in the British colonies along the eastern seaboard, was that work and home were naturally combined within each house, and the house was located in a place that was good for business. For most urban occupations, this meant being in the bustling center of town.

The concept of single-use districts, so basic to our design of the twentieth-century city, was unknown in the premodern city. Most middle-class commercial enterprises were extensions of the family, and so the businessman lived above his office or shop, stored his goods in the cellar, and often housed apprentices and trusted employees in the attic (Fishman, 1987: p. 7). Moreover, the dwellings of the wealthy were often cheek-by-jowl with the tenements of the poor. Wealthy families occupied large town houses that fronted the principal streets, and the poor crowded into the alleyways and courtyards to the rear (Fishman: p. 8). The inhabitants of these inferior dwellings were usually the servants of the upper classes or the workers in the multitude of small workshops that clustered around the houses of the merchants who dealt in their products.

To understand this sharing of public space by people of widely disparate character, it is important to remember that English society of this time, just before the onset of the Industrial Revolution in the mid-to-late eighteenth century, was still very much a caste system. The 'social distance' between upper and lower classes was so clearly understood by all concerned that the privileged elite felt little need to separate themselves from the poor by physical distance. The poor occupied the same public spaces as the rich, but were simply 'invisible' to their wealthy betters until they were needed to perform menial or commercial tasks.

This situation seems strange to our contemporary social mores, where urban spaces, particularly in America, tend to be separated by use, race and economic class. It illustrates how much our modern suburb is the product of nothing less than a complete transformation of urban values. At a fundamental level, established meanings of the city center as the fashionable focus of wealth and the urban edge as the place of poverty have been inverted. Only recently during the 1990s have some city centers begun to enjoy a renaissance of urban life and activity.

'Family values,' one of the most clichéd phrases of modern society, have also been redefined. In the late 1700s, all members of a middle-class family played an important role in business affairs, living, working and sharing the same spaces. This integrated model progressively fragmented to a condition where business in the city became the exclusive province of men, and child rearing became the responsibility of women in the suburbs. This paradigm shift was spurred by two sets of forces – one economic, the other, religious.

Before the Industrial Revolution, the structure of the middle-class family was often an economic one, based on these shared business responsibilities between fathers, wives, sons, daughters and other extended family members. However, the developing capitalist economy increasingly redefined work less as a collaborative effort and more as a set of specialized tasks, and this separation of roles combined with emerging Evangelical religious ideas that defined individual holiness as a function of a morally virtuous family life. Over the course of several decades straddling the turn of the eighteenth century into the nineteenth, these changes gradually led to the replacement of extended family ties based on economic cooperation by ones based more on emotional attachment around the nucleus of husband, wife and children (Fishman: p. 33–5). As noted above, the husband and wife performed newly defined roles; the man became the sole breadwinner and the woman assumed total responsibilities for bringing up the children to the extent that it took her out of the urban workforce. This model of middle-class family life became so ubiquitous during the nineteenth and twentieth centuries that it assumed the status of a fundamental principle of Anglo-American culture. Only during the 1980s and 1990s did this spatial gender gap began to close, with the reintegration of women back into the urban (and suburban) workplace as part of a more general demographic shift away from the nuclear family stereotype, and (in America) as a matter of economic necessity due to the increasing cost of maintaining a suburban lifestyle.

As these new nuclear families evolved in the early 1800s, their members focused less on extended economic familial connections, and more on their own emotional relationships within the small group.

To this end, families sought to separate themselves from the workplace – and from the intrusions of that working environment into the home. The idea of the family dwelling came to be conceived as a wholly domestic environment, insulated from other pressures, and to meet these new demands the traditional city house – what we would now refer to as a 'live-work unit' – was no longer suitable. There was little or no space for the middle-class family to nurture the growing bonds of intimacy in a dwelling that was open to customers and the commercial activities of city business, storing goods, and even housing employees. These merchants and bankers however, had in their grasp the financial resources and ambition to reorder the physical patterns of the city to meet their new needs.

And so they did, building new houses near the villages that surrounded London. Wealthy bankers and merchants created a new type of living in these villages that reflected their changing values. To the educated minds of the eighteenth century, a renewed appreciation of nature and the man-made landscape became a hallmark of sophisticated taste, and instead of a place of rural poverty, the countryside was seen as a charmingly picturesque setting, ripe for new homes within easy commuting distance by private carriage.

But the city bourgeoisie could not emulate the landed gentry living in their country estates far from urban centers; middle-class merchants and bankers were tied to the city's web of commercial operations where they earned their living. The first suburban homes were thus regarded as weekend places for the family to escape the pressures of intrusive city life, much like the Roman *villa suburbana*. These classical antecedents went hand-in-hand with the other major element of the new aesthetic taste: the affection for landscape, and in particular, the picturesque landscaped garden. This sensibility had its roots in the large-scale reconfiguration of country estates during the eighteenth and early nineteenth centuries by designers and tastemakers such as Capability Brown, Humphrey Repton, Payne Knight, and Uvedale Price.

In contrast to the French tradition of landscape gardening based on clear formal geometries (e.g. Versailles) English taste in the late eighteenth century evolved to the ideal of seeking visual pleasure in the landscape by subtle man-made improvements that looked 'natural.' The idea was empiricist – to stimulate emotions in the viewer by appealing to his or her senses – and to this end a certain irregularity or 'picturesque roughness' in the composition was to be preferred over 'symmetrical beauty.' Because this new fashion in landscape design had little precedent, designers often turned to the paintings of Claude Lorrain(1600–82) and Nicolas Poussin (1594–1665) for inspiration. Evocative landscapes with scaled-down crags, pastoral scenes ready-made for sheep and shepherds, and romantic 'follies' of ruined classical temples and gothic fragments became the environments of choice for the British aristocracy.

Following this elite aesthetic, a group of villas was constructed during the decade 1790–1800 at Clapham, south of London, around a common open space that became a picturesque park in miniature, thus creating the first true proto-suburb (Fishman: p. 52). Public space blended seamlessly with private gardens to create surrogate Gardens of Eden as settings for new modes of family life.

It wasn't long before these weekend retreats became full-fledged homes, where wives and children stayed while husbands commuted each day into the city by private horse-drawn carriage. This cultural shift was aided and abetted by a strong economic incentive. Suburban residential expansion beyond the normal boundaries of the city transformed cheap agricultural land into profitable building plots. Suburbia was a good investment as well as a good setting for family life (Fishman: p. 10).

The image of the middle-class suburb as a romantic garden where the virtues of the city merged with those of the countryside became the dominant model on both sides of the Atlantic for development beyond established city boundaries. English precedents such as John Nash's Regents Park, with its surrounding terraces and adjacent Park Village, in London (1811–41) and Decimus Burton's Calverly Park in Tunbridge Wells, (1827–28), are important in this regard.

American designers traveled to England during the first half of the nineteenth century to see these and other examples that predated any similar developments in the USA (Archer, 1983: pp. 140–1). It is important to note that these changes in taste and values, and the transatlantic exchanges of information, both predated the technologies of mechanized public transportation. The cultural template for suburbia had been created by 1830; the role of the railway was to bring this new style of life within reach of the whole spectrum of the middle class, and ultimately sections of the working classes too. Typical early examples, well known to American experts, were Victoria Park in Manchester and Rock Park Estate in Cheshire, across the River Mersey from Liverpool (Archer: p. 143). Dating from 1837, both these designs featured detached

and semi-detached (duplex) houses, landscaped parks, and curving roadways.

The new suburban lifestyle of the first half of the nineteenth century soon established a coherent physical expression of building form and land use. To create an attractive and profitable enterprise, new developments generally applied four planning principles that are still relevant today, and could describe most suburban residential developments built in the USA since 1950. These were: a uniformly low density of development enhanced by open landscaped areas; a homogeneous single class population for economic and social stability; the availability of convenient but carefully screened and segregated commercial areas; and lastly, the creation of a plan in a coordinated manner by a single developer (Archer: pp. 141–2).

The scope and location of this type of development were vastly extended by the growth of mass transportation that was part of the progressive industrialization of society during the nineteenth century in Britain and America. In the USA in particular, this growth gave rise to what became the dominant model of suburbia until the 1920s – the middle-class commuter suburb organized around a train station or streetcar stop. The railway station was normally located centrally in the plan for obvious reasons of convenience, and commuters walked back and forth between home and the station every day, thus giving rise to a compact urban plan.

This is the precise concept that drives the design of new Transit-Oriented Developments (TODs) in America today. In both historic and contemporary examples, a network of clearly organized and connected streets leads to the train station, and development is clustered within the radii of five- and ten-minute walking distances. In the USA, this arrangement has become a near-binding typology in its own right (see Figure 3.5). This spatial principle of a short walk to transit was also evident in the design of the American railroad suburbs' junior sibling, the streetcar suburb of the late nineteenth and early twentieth centuries. This smaller scale technology provided more frequent stops and allowed more flexible layouts varying between a clustered center and a looser and less dense plan form as illustrated in Figure 2.2.

As we have noted, the concept that the suburb combined the positive values of the country and the city was one of its founding assumptions from the late eighteenth century onward, and this sensibility expanded quickly during the nineteenth century. In 1847, the New York architect William Ranlett published the first American design for a suburban village

**Figure 2.2** Coolidge Corner, Boston, Massachusetts. This mature suburban centre in Boston thrives around a stop on the city's elderly Green Line light rail system. (Photo by Adrian Walters)

**Figure 2.3** Riverside, Chicago, Frederick Law Olmsted, 1869. A curving street sweeps alongside a park towards the local 'town center' designed around the commuter railroad station with service to central Chicago.

layout that incorporated detached villas in a picturesque landscaped setting after the English fashion (Archer: p. 150). Three years later, in 1850, the American architect A. J. Downing described in his influential essay 'Country Villages,' a design for an ideal suburb with a central landscaped park and wide, curving, tree-lined streets. Downing's concepts, gleaned from travels to many English examples, pre-figure several important American suburbs during the next 20 years, including most notably Llewellyn Park, New Jersey (developed from 1853 onwards by Llewellyn Haskell, a New York businessman, and designers Alexander Jackson Davis and Howard Daniels); and Riverside, just south of Chicago (1869) by Frederick Law Olmsted (see Figure 2.3).

By the time Olmsted was commissioned to design Riverside, the blending of picturesque aesthetics with the new conceptual synthesis of city and countryside was firmly established as a key planning principle for suburban residential development on both sides of the Atlantic. Riverside, designed with direct rail access to Chicago, promised to provide a better life than the middle class found in the city, with homes set amidst attractive landscape. This proved a winning combination, and Olmsted's creation became a model development and a precedent for innumerable subsequent suburbs, influencing design not only in the USA but also exporting this influence back to Britain, the original source of many of its attributes.

This suburban impetus throughout the nineteenth century can thus be thought of as a combination of the 'pull factor' of the countryside and the 'push factor' of the overcrowded industrial cities. The raw energy of the Industrial Revolution generated large population increases in the major industrial cities in Britain and America, but the concentration of commercial operations within the urban cores made the land values too high and the environment too polluted for superior residential development. The poorer classes, with no resources to relocate or to pay for suburban transportation, were trapped in an inner ring of unsanitary and overcrowded slums within walking distance of the mills and factories at the urban core. By contrast, the more affluent bourgeoisie moved as far from the center as their means and transportation options would allow, settling in new suburban communities. Here they could enjoy countryside amenities yet still travel to work in the city with relative ease. One of the very first American examples of this new commuter suburb was New Brighton, laid out on Staten Island in New York Harbor in 1836, and bearing a marked resemblance to the resort suburb of the same name near Liverpool, England, built four years earlier in 1832 (Archer: p. 153).

While due attention is paid to the importance of English origins and prototypes for the garden suburb, it is important not to underestimate the indigenous American influences of the New England villages, and the Jeffersonian ideals of the individual gentleman farmer and democratic land development. The American president's distaste for the city as the prime venue for American society was well documented, as was his deep philosophical preference for the virtues of country living. Thus the garden suburb, with its rural aesthetic and low density, seemed to embody key attributes of American life. The city could be kept at a distance, and the suburb embodied sound real estate principles – making money by converting cheap agricultural land to desirable residences. For millions of Americans in search of the good life it was, until recently, a near-perfect solution.

This evolution of the garden suburb had one other important attribute: it presaged the creation of the Garden City ideal at the end of the nineteenth century that in turn catalyzed much urban and suburban design theory and practice throughout the twentieth century. However, as we have outlined, the romantic suburb was a middle-class phenomenon, and there was another important component of the nineteenth-century vision of a Garden City arcadia: the development of model industrial villages for the working classes.

Early industrial villages such as New Lanark, Scotland (1793) Lowell, Massachusetts (1822), and Saltaire in England (1851), illustrated a strain of philanthropic concern by industrialists and their architects, and a growing sense of the need for socially responsible planning and urban reform. Other industrial villages such as Pullman (1880) outside Chicago, and the English examples of Port Sunlight (1888), Bournville (1895) and New Earswick, (1903) all contributed to this ideology.

The social ideals of nineteenth-century reformers John Ruskin and William Morris were influential in this regard. Enlightened British industrialists Sir Titus Salt, W.H. Lever, and the chocolate magnates – Rowntrees and Cadburys – adopted these ideals in their attempts to improve the desperate conditions of industrial workers. These philanthropists constructed company towns in the clean air and natural beauty of the English countryside beyond the 'corruption' of the city. Salt built Saltaire outside Bradford; Lever constructed Port Sunlight outside Liverpool. George Cadbury developed Bournville southwest of Birmingham; and perhaps most importantly, the Rowntrees created New Earswick north of York using designs by Barry Parker and Raymond Unwin (see Figures 2.4 and 2.5).

The planned communities of Port Sunlight and New Earswick in particular demonstrate a picturesque architectural character in their buildings and an artful layout of streets and public spaces. These features, together with the reliance upon nearby cities, confirmed their places in the lineage of romantic suburban settlements. American examples like Lowell or Pullman, while

**Figure 2.4** Port Sunlight, near Liverpool, UK, begun 1888. Soap magnate William Lever employed over thirty architects in the design of this industrial model village. It is characterized by picturesque groupings of traditional buildings in counterpoint to the long, neo-classical that forms the axis of the plan leading to the Lady Lever Art Gallery, completed in 1922.

**Figure 2.5** New Earswick, near York, UK, Parker and Unwin, 1903. The housing in this model village was commissioned by Joseph Rowntree, a York industrialist famous for his chocolate products, to provide affordable housing for low-income workers. Residency was open to all applicants in need, and was not limited to employees of Rowntree's nearby chocolate factory. The housing layout illustrates the early development of Parker and Unwin's picturesque composition and spatial arrangement.

sharing many of the philanthropic intentions, or at least, the enlightened self-interest of their British counterparts, were composed of well planned but rather severe urban dwellings, owing nothing to the growing popular taste for romantic imagery. It wasn't until

Frederick Law Olmsted's design in 1890 for the planned industrial village of Vandergrift, Pennsylvania, that American industrial towns began to follow their English counterparts by incorporating picturesque suburban aesthetics (Stern: p. 9). The twin trends of social reform and romantic aesthetics reached their pinnacle of physical exposition in Barry Parker and Raymond Unwin's designs for the new town of Letchworth (1904) 30 miles north of London. This self-financed new settlement was the first built example of what would become one of the most important planning ideas of the twentieth century – Ebenezer Howard's Garden City.

Howard had published his radical proposal for Garden Cities a few years earlier in 1898, under the title *Tomorrow: A Peaceful Path to Real Reform*. Born in Britain in 1850 and having lived in America, notably Chicago, for several years during the 1870s, Howard understood the implications of the new garden suburbs in Britain and America very well. He appreciated that the railway had made rural areas directly accessible to existing towns and cities, and this accessibility was fundamentally changing the long-standing rationales of urban location and urban form: large populations could be shifted to and from remote rural areas if efficient mass transportation could be provided. As noted earlier, one of the most powerful reasons for moving outside cities was the availability of cheap land in the countryside, and in Howard's time this land was especially undervalued. In addition to the national urban problems of industrial overcrowding and squalor in British cities, poverty in the rural areas was also endemic. Britain's agricultural industry in the decades before the turn of the century was plagued by a recession, and Howard's intention was not only to relieve urban congestion but also to alleviate rural poverty by the transformation of depressed rural areas into prosperous new towns.

Howard's practical scheme would utilize the revenue created by the conversion of cheap farmland to urban use to finance the development of new cities by reinvesting the profits from the sale of residential and industrial sites in the public infrastructure of the community. Despite Howard's unwillingness to commit to any specific town plan, his famous planning diagrams clearly illustrated the importance he placed on this public infrastructure. He located the public institutions at the heart of the community and surrounded them by a park. In its turn, this open space was bordered by a linear, glass-roofed structure enclosing all the retail functions of the city, very

much the precursor of today's shopping mall. Radiating from this center, residential areas incorporated sites of all sizes for a mixture of social classes, and beyond these lay the industrial and manufacturing zone. This was served by a railway ring and bordered by farmland which functioned as a greenbelt to define the edges of the community and to limit growth in accordance with the proposed population figure of thirty-two thousand people (see Figure 2.6).

While Howard gave a diagrammatic order to the plan of the Garden City, it was Parker and Unwin who derived its architectural form in their plan of Letchworth. The two designers were the conscious inheritors of the same Victorian reformist social responsibility that inspired the industrial magnates Lever, Rowntree and Cadbury, and they combined this mission with the picturesque aesthetic principles from the English eighteenth- and nineteenth-century traditions. There is no evidence that Parker and Unwin were aware of the American garden suburbs when they were designing Letchworth: their precedent was the recent revival of interest in English vernacular architecture and its incorporation into what is commonly called the 'Queen Anne Style' (Barnett: p. 71). This aesthetic had been successfully applied to recent housing, particularly in highly picturesque schemes such as Bedford Park in London by Norman Shaw and others dating from the 1870s.

Parker and Unwin first developed their town planning technique and vernacular village composition in the model settlement of New Earswick outside York, for the Rowntree Chocolate Trust noted previously, where they had been influenced by the work of C.F.A. Voysey (see Figure 2.5). The architectural duo retained this picturesque approach in their design for Letchworth and added some more formal geometries to create a partial synthesis of axial and informal planning ideas. With groups of houses, they created carefully contrived architectural compositions, relating them to topography and other natural and climatic determinants. For example, the location of industry on the east side of town meant that the pollution was blown away from residential areas (Barnett: p. 72).

Rather than being on the periphery as in Howard's diagram, the railway at Letchworth bisects the town. Nothing in evidence resembles the fully glazed shopping mall; instead there is a traditional shopping area with a main street. Howard, Parker, and Unwin were no dogmatic visionaries. They were sympathetic with local conditions, and they adapted their ideals to the realities of the place. The success of Letchworth lies

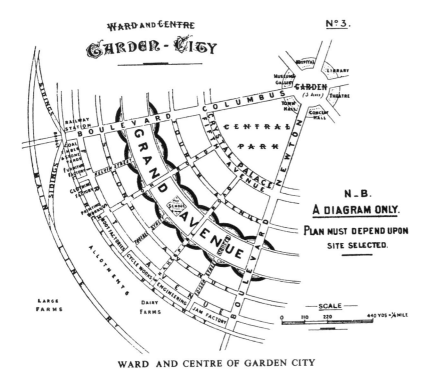

WARD AND CENTRE OF GARDEN CITY

**Figure 2.6** Ebenezer Howard's Garden City diagram (detail). (Diagram courtesy of M.I.T Press)

in its ability to represent Howard's radical ideas in a totally non-threatening way, evoking the pleasant environment of traditional English villages (Barnett: p. 73) (see Figure 2.7).

In this sense Letchworth is the direct precursor of much New Urbanist work in America from the 1990s, when radical town planning ideas in America were given form by conservative, traditional architectural aesthetics. The use of traditional neoclassical and vernacular aesthetics in the work of firms such as Duany Plater-Zyberk and Urban Design Associates soothed public fears and facilitated commercial acceptance of New Urbanist planning practice (while at the same time infuriating modernists and academics). It's very likely that if a more adventurous, contemporary architectural language had been used in American New Urbanist developments, the movement's planning concepts would have been subjected to a much more difficult process of public acceptance.

This mixing of radical planning with conservative architecture is another example of the close interweaving of history with present circumstances, and the advantages and shortcomings of this marriage are discussed in more detail in Chapter 3. Now that New Urbanism is moving into the mainstream, it

**Figure 2.7** Housing at Letchworth Garden City, Parker and Unwin, 1904. Parker and Unwin progressively refined their techniques of housing design and layout. Note the attention to three-dimensional composition with a gable form terminating the visual axis while the street curves away to the right.

remains to be seen whether this gives its practitioners confidence to attempt more contemporary aesthetics. This theme also resurfaces in the Case Studies where our desire to create progressive, forward-looking architecture is always in tension with the conservatism of public taste and the realities of community politics.

As important as Letchworth was in giving urban form to ideas of a new social and cultural order, Parker and Unwin's subsequent commission, Hampstead Garden Suburb, designed in association with Sir Edwin Lutyens in 1905, has proved more influential in the practice of urban and suburban design (Barnett: p. 73). By the early years of the twentieth century, the area north of Hampstead in north London remained a pocket of rural landscape threatened with suburban encroachment on all sides. With the extension of the London Underground railway to nearby Golders Green, the site was ripe for development. The client, Henrietta Barnett, a prominent social reformer, conceived a community comprised of people of different incomes, while the architects saw the opportunity to develop further Howard's ideas of a managed synthesis of town and country. The combination of concepts created a coalition of urban and arcadian environments designed to assist in the breaking down of rigid class barriers. Once again, these social ideals prefigure New Urbanist ambitions to bring order to the suburbs, and to create diverse communities, open to different sectors of society, in direct opposition to the segregation by income so prevalent in conventional American suburbia.

By the time they began their work on Hampstead Garden Suburb in 1905, Parker and Unwin had become aware of the theories of Camillo Sitte, and Unwin's own 1909 book, *Town Planning in Practice: an Introduction to the art of designing Cities and Suburbs*, contained significant sections on the design of public spaces and streets that incorporated many of Sitte's ideas. Unwin was probably familiar with the first French edition of Sitte's writings published in 1902 under the title of *L'Art de Batir les Villes*, because there was no full translation in English until 1965 (although passages were approvingly quoted by Hegemann and Peets in their influential *The American Vitruvius: An Architect's Handbook of Civic Art*, published in America in 1922). Indeed Unwin refers almost exclusively to Sitte's medieval precedents, to the exclusion of classical, Renaissance, and Baroque examples. This purely medieval bias was not one contained in Sitte's original publication, but one which dominated the 1902 and 1918 French editions, and which stemmed from bizarre editorial decisions by his translator, Camille Martin. A medievalist by training and preference, Martin substituted French

and Belgian examples for the German and Austrian precedents used by Sitte, and eliminated all reference to Baroque urbanism. The Frenchman's motivations have been discussed by George and Christianne Collins in their extensive introduction to the 1986 critical edition of Sitte's original text.

As we discussed briefly in Chapter 1, Sitte's approach to urban design was not based on the logic of abstract geometries, but rather on what a pedestrian would see and experience when walking through the spaces of a city. This approach was validated by Unwin in his work, and later in the 1960s by Gordon Cullen, whose concept of 'Serial Vision' was formulated from similar principles. This emphasis on the pedestrian has caught the attention of contemporary urban designers, who stress, particularly in America, the reactivation of public space and the creation of 'Walkable Communities' as an alternative to car-dominated sprawl.

The idea of the city comprehended as a series of pedestrian views was close to the idea of the English landscape picturesque garden, where follies would be located to terminate vistas and for other visual effects, and at Hampstead, Parker and Unwin used this sensibility to create a plan of greater conceptual clarity than had been evident in their previous work. Despite a disappointingly weak design by Sir Edwin Lutyens for the central area, which isolated monumental buildings in space in a manner at odds with Unwin and Sitte's precepts of urban enclosure, Parker and Unwin developed a residential layout that was architecturally stronger and urbanistically tighter than Letchworth. It included a pair of very fine Germanic entrance buildings on the main Finchley Road, incorporating shops and housing in a dynamic interplay of symmetry and asymmetry (see Figure 2.8).

The influence of Letchworth and Hampstead Garden Suburb crossed to America almost immediately with the design of Forest Hills Gardens, a model streetcar suburb of New York City, started in 1909 using designs by Frederick Law Olmsted Jr and Grosvenor Atterbury (Barnett: p. 76). Around the railway station, Atterbury created an attractive enclosed urban space as the entrance to the community and the beginning of a sequence of spaces that were organized as, in the opinion of one critic, 'a metaphoric journey from town to country' (Stern: p. 34).

The next most vivid manifestation of garden city concepts also took place in America as a direct result of the nation's entry into World War I in 1917. This created an immediate demand for housing for

**Figure 2.8** Hampstead Garden Suburb, Parker and Unwin, 1907. Mixed-use buildings on Finchley Road. Unwin's admiration for German medieval architecture is evident in the design of these buildings at the main entrance into the suburb.

the dramatically increased population of industrial workers around manufacturing locations. Federal agencies supported design and construction programs for 25 000 homes, and Charles Whittaker, editor of *The Journal of the American Institute of Architects* lobbied to ensure that these new homes were not designed as barracks – but as permanent communities. Whittaker strenuously publicized the work of Raymond Unwin, who was in charge of the British war-housing program, and who had argued forcefully for the British construction effort to be considered a permanent investment in housing provision (Barnett: p. 78). Frederick Law Olmsted Jr was given control of the American planning effort, and in the endeavor to create permanent communities of good quality, he appointed talented designers to lay out the new communities. Among them was John Nolen, a great admirer of Parker and Unwin, and

whose reputation as a rising star in American planning was enhanced by his design of a fine new town at Kingsport, Tennessee.

During the nineteenth century it had been the railway that exerted most influence on urban and suburban form, but around the time of World War I the private automobile began to make its impact felt. As the next major technological development in transportation, even relatively primitive cars brought about a dramatic increase in personal mobility. The suburbs no longer had to be located at railway stations or along streetcar lines. The notion of designing urban space as a function of walking distance to and from town centers or transit stops began to fall into disuse, to be replaced by new planning concepts scaled to the dimensions and speed of the car.

A pair of early twentieth-century suburbs, Beverly Hills, Los Angeles (commenced 1906) and the Country Club District in Kansas City, Missouri (commenced 1907 with its famed commercial core, Country Club Plaza dating from 1922), indicated the impending spatial revolution heralded by the automobile. These layouts included facilities such as upmarket shopping centers accessible by road rather than rail, broad boulevards and longer blocks. Larger block sizes reduced the cost of constructing intersections and cross-streets, but they also eliminated the very features that provided a more intimate scale and choice of route to the pedestrian. As one of the few planners of the period to recognize some of the impacts the car would have upon the layout of towns, John Nolen made a significant contribution to this evolving form of urbanism. In his 1918 design of Mariemont, outside Cincinnati, Ohio, he dispensed with any railway connections to the larger city, attempting instead to integrate the car into a garden suburb layout.

Despite these precursors, a new form of suburban development specific to the automobile age did not arise until 1928, with plans for an American new town at Radburn, New Jersey. Conceived as an American counterpart to Letchworth and Welwyn Garden City (Britain's second Garden City, begun in 1921), only a fraction of Radburn was completed (one neighborhood) due largely to the onset of the Great Depression in 1929. Nonetheless, the plans of its designers, Clarence Stein and Henry Wright, proved immensely influential. At a stroke, Radburn turned suburban design on its head, using multiple dead-end streets within a long, curving arterial loop road in place of a connected network of streets and smaller blocks.

While Parker and Unwin had invented cul-de-sacs and used them to good effect at Hampstead Garden

Suburb, they were relatively few in number, being exceptions for specific circumstances rather than the general rule. At Radburn, the opposite was true: cul-de-sacs dominated the street layout. Instead of normal sized urban blocks with a connected street network, Stein and Wright's basic unit of planning was the 'superblock,' a large area defined by a system of arterial roads, which were designed for the automobile rather than pedestrians. The extensive circumference of these arterial loops contained a multitude of cul-de-sacs, and this system of vehicle circulation was kept quite separate from pedestrian paths. No longer did cars and pedestrians share the same public space. Homes accepted the service of the car to one side of the dwelling, but opened on another face to green footpaths that led to large and attractively landscaped open spaces. These communal green areas were segregated from vehicles and crossed by pedestrian paths leading to community facilities and other neighborhoods via underpasses. In the completed scheme, pedestrians would have rarely needed to cross a busy street (see Figure 2.9).

As an interesting side note to the continued transatlantic trading of ideas and precedents, it is worth recording that Barry Parker visited America in the 1920s, where he met with Stein and Wright. He was so impressed with Radburn that he incorporated several of its features into his 1930 designs for Wythenshawe, a huge satellite community in Manchester, England, that has some legitimate claim to be called England's third Garden City (Hall: p. 111).

In the burgeoning world of private car ownership, safety was an increasing concern, and Stein and Wright were intent on creating a secure environment for pedestrians and cyclists. This logic of separating vehicles from pedestrians, so radical in the 1930s, became a planning principle in many types of development during the 1950s and 1960s when efficient movement of cars became preeminent in the minds of planners and engineers. Multi-leveled circulation systems had been a staple of many futuristic urban visions from Leonardo da Vinci onwards, including in the twentieth century, Antonio Sant'Elia's *La Citta Nuova* (1912), Le Corbusier's *Plan Voisin* (1925), Hugh Ferris' *Metropolis of Tomorrow* (1929), and the New York City Regional Plan, also from 1929.

In Britain, an over-simplistic reading of Sir Colin Buchanan's 1963 report for the government entitled *Traffic in Towns* raised this concept of vertical segregation of people and cars to an almost universal precept for city design, evident in massive projects like London's Barbican (see Figure 2.10). Stein and

**Figure 2.9** Radburn, New Jersey, Clarence Stein and Henry Wright, 1928. This innovative separation of cars and pedestrians in the interests of safety was hailed by many as the new model of suburban design. However, it started a trend that has led to the banal sterility of suburban layouts as the quality of the pedestrian environment progressively diminished in America.

Wright's limited instances of vertical separation however, have a more modest precedent, that of Olmsted and Vaux's plan for Central Park in New York where pedestrian paths dip below roads that cross the park on rustic bridges.

At the suburban scale, vertical separation did not mature into a defining principle, but the use of lots of cul-de-sacs branching from a few collector and arterial streets did. The collective assumption by highway engineers and developers was that travel demand would not increase beyond the expected population growth, and that this new hierarchical system, that saved developers money when compared with gridded layouts, would be able to meet the future demand. This belief held sway for several decades, to the extent that it became the governing suburban layout type since the 1950s in America, and to a lesser extent in Britain. What the engineers, planners and developers didn't foresee was the demographic shift of the

**Figure 2.10** The Barbican, London, Chamberlain, Powell and Bon, 1954–75. This 40 acre (16 hectare) development in the heart of London extended the theme of separation of vehicles and pedestrians into the vertical plane. While this was a seductive urban theory, in practice the results were often inhuman. Streets were turned into dark service tunnels or canyons, while the pedestrian upper levels became little more than wind blown concrete wastelands. There is a pleasant urban space in the middle of the development around the Barbican Concert Hall, but this is small recompense for the brutal mutilation of the city fabric.

population into more, smaller households as it increased (a factor with many implications that we will examine in more detail later). By the 1980s and even more so during the 1990s, the traffic demands imposed by these unforeseen numbers of households far outpaced the ability of hierarchical road systems to cope with the increased load.

Despite all the evidence of traffic congestion on the few connector streets, and the access problems of subdivisions with only one way in and out, the return to the traditional network of connected streets has been slow and difficult. Cul-de-sac layouts have been enshrined in American highway engineers' design manuals for several decades and only in 1994 did traditional models of gridded and connected layouts receive provisional official backing by the Institute of Transportation Engineers' report on *Traffic Engineering for Neo-Traditional Neighborhood Design*.

No analysis of suburban precedents is complete without mentioning Frank Lloyd Wright's Broadacre City (1935). In a (successful) attempt to reingratiate himself with an American society that had marginalized him during the 1920s as a talented genius too difficult to work with, Wright prepared designs for a city based on his perception of truly American principles. In this polemic contrast to the European ideas

of Le Corbusier, Walter Gropius and Ludwig Hilbersheimer, Wright also explicitly rejected the American tradition of the romantic garden suburb with its curving streets and history of public transit. Instead, Wright established a regular square grid on a flat prairie landscape divided by high-speed roads. Railroads and streetcars were abolished; in Wright's vision, every American adult was entitled to one automobile.

Within this grid, most inhabitants lived in single-family houses on an acre of land. If Wright's low-density design layout was prophetic of post-World War II suburbia in America, so was his Usonian housing prototype, a private family space focused away from the public realm of the street. This rejection of the shared world of the pedestrian street was prophetic of American suburbia several decades later, where the private automobile that Wright construed as a liberating technology for American families now controls the American domestic environment. Today, houses lurk behind garage doors that dominate the streetscape to the exclusion of pedestrians.

Some individual pieces of Wright's vision have become generic features of the American landscape, including clusters of service stations, grade separated highways, towers rising amidst open space, and ubiquitous low-density housing. But the suggestion that Broadacre City was the precursor to contemporary suburbia is overstated. Taken as a whole, Broadacre City differs from suburbia in several fundamental aspects (Alofsin, 1989). Wright's plan integrated many different uses: farms, manufacturing and industry, a variety of housing types and open space, together with communal markets, schools and places of worship were all dovetailed into an inclusive framework. In this regard, it established almost the opposite of the segregation of uses and classes common in American suburbia today.

The modernist designs of the city and the suburbs mentioned here and in the previous chapter share one thing in common: the extensive use of large highways to structure movement and shape the city. Until the late 1990s, highway engineers exerted the most determining effect on the form of American cities (and most British cities, too). In America, the public realm of streets and sidewalks began to vanish as car-based spatial formulas drove decisions in urban design plans, from the scale of regional road networks to individual site plans. Criteria for roadway design had everything to do with the efficiency of vehicle movement and almost nothing to do with the needs of pedestrians. If pedestrians were considered at all,

**41**

they were regarded as impediments to brisk traffic movement, and figured as such in the transportation engineers' calculations.

Pedestrians became a rare sight in most suburban areas in America. Odd as it seems to British eyes, developers ceased to build sidewalks along residential streets even in the most affluent American suburbs, with the consequence that any pedestrian who did venture out was forced either to walk in the street, sharing the road dangerously with passing cars or to stride across other people's front lawns. In an increasingly car-based world, walking became equated with suspicious behavior, practised only by the poor or the deviant. Not until the late 1990s did walkability become once again a sought-after attribute of daily suburban life, and for millions of Americans living in the suburbs that sprouted around cities all across the country between 1960 and 1990, pedestrian convenience remains an impossible dream.

American popular mythology tends to credit the private sector with the phenomenal growth of the suburbs after World War II. The design concepts that underpin the suburban environment are often mistakenly believed to be a simple reflection of consumer preference – the free market in operation. That's not quite true. While private development and construction companies did indeed produce the vast majority of home designs for private buyers, the suburban boom in America was largely promoted by actions by the federal government. As early as the 1930s the Federal Housing Administration (FHA) began to develop a national planning code, resulting in the FHA Minimum Planning Standards. With input from the social planner Clarence Perry (whose work on neighborhood design we shall discuss in Chapter 3) the code was based largely on the ideas of architect-planners Clarence Stein and Henry Wright, best known for their work at Radburn. Given the planning concepts of Radburn, it's not surprising that Stein and Wright's influence led to the belief, institutionalized by the new government code provisions, that the traditional grid-iron form of the American town could not accommodate the automobile (Solomon, 1989: p. 24). Instead, the 1930s code imposed a pattern of separated curvilinear enclaves that held some minimum evocation of the nineteenth-century Romantic Garden Suburb together with a pared-down diagram of Radburn's cul-de-sac planning.

As we have noted earlier, car-orientated planning became the dominant philosophy that guided private development from the 1930s onward, characterized by large enclaves of housing separated from each other and linked only by arterial roads catering solely to the movement of vehicular traffic. Radburn's compensating network of connecting green space was quickly deleted; it used up too much profitable land. The mass-market suburbs of the early 1950s like Levitttown, simply featured large blocks of curving streets with the number of connecting cross-streets reduced to save cost. This framework of reduced connectivity set the pattern for the present day whereby layouts since the 1980s have been dominated by a myriad of dead-end streets branching off a series of artlessly meandering 'collector streets' that connected the housing subdivision to the larger arterial roadways. Needless to say, these few streets that did connect became over-burdened by traffic from all the cul-de-sacs, leading to increased congestion, driver frustration and longer journey times (Southworth and Ben-Joseph, 1997: p. 107).

The impact of these federal Minimum Planning Standards was felt across America after World War II, when the great suburban expansion of the 1950s and 1960s was fuelled by a surge of home ownership by returning servicemen and others financed under the provisions of the Federal GI Bill. Federal Mortgage Insurance – a means of changing the lending practices of financial institutions to bring home-ownership within the reach of millions of less affluent Americans – was available only on homes and subdivisions that complied with the government's Minimum Planning Standards. This linkage soon led to a standardization of housing layout from coast to coast.

The production of individual houses had already become much more uniform. Starting in the 1930s, in an effort to reduce costs so as to compete better in the reduced housing market after the Depression, the housing industry streamlined itself in terms of mass-produced designs and developer financing. This process accelerated in the late 1940s and 1950s as the housing industry, capitalizing on the experience gained from mass-production techniques during wartime, rushed to meet the new demand for inexpensive housing. Developers and builders were able to borrow large sums from savings and loan institutions (akin to building societies in England) to finance large subdivisions of nearly identical houses. They achieved considerable economies of scale by this process, enhancing their own profit margins, and enabling them to build yet more subdivisions to the same standardized formula. The American author spent her early years in a house in one such development in the 1950s, and while it's

**Figure 2.11** Post-war American suburbia, early 1950s. One of the authors plays with her mother in the front yard of their new suburban home in Illinois. Although small, and located in what began as bleak environments, these new suburban bungalows represented a major improvement in living standards for many working and middle-class American families. (Photo courtesy of the estate of Dee A. Brown)

easy to criticize the design of these houses from a contemporary perspective, there's no doubt they once represented a substantial increase in the quality of the domestic environment available to first-time home-buying families (see Figure 2.11).

This suburban boom, seen as an unreservedly good thing by earlier American generations, now, in the early years of the twenty-first century appears laden with problems, especially in its land-consuming patterns of low-density uses and related environmental and social consequences. Our current epithet of 'sprawl' signifies our society's growing distaste for this suburban phenomenon, and we must now turn our attention to examining this transformation.

## FROM SUBURB TO SPRAWL: THE DEVOLUTION OF THE AMERICAN ENVIRONMENT

The federally supported suburban house building boom in America during the 1950s and 1960s was so enormous that the mass migration of those able to afford a new home in the suburbs sent the central areas of cities into a decline. This explosion of suburban development, and the parallel decline of American city centers during that period and subsequent decades is a very well researched and documented phenomenon (Jackson, 1985; Fishman,

1987; Rowe, 1991; Kunstler, 1993; Langdon, 1994; Kay, 1997; Duany et al., 2000). An underlying trend of this phenomenon was the shift in racial demographics often referred to as 'white flight,' indicating the increasing polarization of mainly white, wealthy suburbs and the poorer, predominantly black inner cities.

This movement of the more affluent sections of society to the periphery, leaving the poor in the center was not new in the history of the Anglo-American city. We noted in the first section of this chapter how, from the late eighteenth century onward, in England and America, it was first the upper classes and later the middle classes who moved to the suburbs, leaving the poor trapped in the inner city. The urban exodus after World War II simply continued this pattern, but with one important difference: the city center jobs that the poorer classes relied on, together with the downtown stores and other activities, gradually moved out to the suburbs, too, leaving the centrally located, low-paid workers with reduced access to employment, shopping and recreation.

Demographically the new suburbanites of the 1950s and 1960s were almost all middle-income families, the vast majority of them white, and these predominantly young families who 'joyously moved into the new homes' were pursuing their own dreams, and, understandably, not worrying much about the problems they left behind (Jackson: p. 244). The financial deals and easy payment terms available on new houses in the suburbs made moving out to new subdivisions so much more attractive than staying in the center and renovating older properties, where financing was much harder to obtain. Accessibility and distance were not problems in the new periphery because of the big increase in personal car ownership, and petrol was very cheap. Increasingly, commercial enterprises of all sorts constructed new buildings next to the new suburban highways for better access, and offices and shopping centers relocated in the suburbs to be near their white-collar workforce and consumers.

The evacuated housing areas around the inner city were thus starved of investment, and quickly declined in property values. This low cost housing was thus occupied by poorer individuals and families, often renting from absentee landlords who picked up swathes of formerly decent housing very cheaply. These older housing areas and their lowly paid or unemployed residents thus began their combined spiral of physical, social and economic decline, and the central business districts of many American cities found themselves surrounded by newly decaying residential areas, a bleak situation that only increased the rate of business relocation to the suburbs. This self-reinforcing cycle of decay and depression remained largely unbroken until the 1980s, when many of these centrally located housing areas began to be reclaimed by the pioneering members of the middle class who had grown increasingly dissatisfied with their suburban lifestyle.

During the decades of this suburban building boom, the attention of most architects was not focused on the decaying inner cities, or on the single-family houses and the commercial strips of the suburbs. Most of the everyday fabric of America's suburbs was constructed with very little thought to design except in the most superficial ways. The profession generally concerned itself with the more upscale suburban building types of enclosed shopping malls and office parks. Here buildings stood alone as objects in (sometimes) landscaped space, each trying to outdo its competitors in terms of external appearance and visual gimmicks. As in the residential subdivision, the public realm of shared pedestrian space disappeared by neglect and omission (see Figure 2.12).

The exception to this decline of the pedestrian environment was the much-examined transformation of the American Main Street into the pedestrian space of the suburban shopping mall. Leading this transformation was the Austrian-American architect

**Figure 2.12** Medical insurance office building, Chapel Hill, NC, 1970s. Many architects became seduced in the 1960s and 1970s with abstract formalism and minimalism. So much attention was focused on the form of the object that little consideration was given to the qualities of public space around and between structures.

Victor Gruen, the person generally credited with inventing this new building type in the late 1950s and early 1960s. Gruen's initial vision was a recreation of Main Street without the cars, but with the inclusion of civic facilities such as post offices and community rooms. He was eager to carry forward a wider spectrum of social activities than simply shopping into the new suburban environment, but by the early 1970s, Gruen admitted that the market forces that drove the allocation of money-making space in malls made the incorporation of non-retail, civic functions all but impossible (Gruen: p. 39: Kaliski: p. 92). Shopping was, by this time, an activity increasingly divorced from the other functions of daily life. Only in the late 1990s has this begun to change with the design and development of a new generation of mixed-use 'town centres' (Bohl, 2002).

American society was slow to recognize the transformation of the good life in the suburbs to the perils and problems of sprawl. Jerry Adler's article 'Bye-Bye, Suburban Dream: 15 ways to fix the suburbs', in *Newsweek* (May 1995) was followed by James Howard Kunstler's cover story 'Home from Nowhere' in the *Atlantic Monthly* magazine in September 1996. These populist polemics against the prevailing suburban lifestyle and its spatial pattern reached a wide audience and opened up a national debate, but several social scientists, geographers, environmentalists and architects had been pulling together various critiques of urban and suburban conditions in America dating initially from the 1950s and reemerging again in the 1980s (Riesman, 1950; Whyte, 1956; Gans, 1967; Clawson, 1971; Krier, 1984; Spirn, 1984; Baldassare, 1986; Cervero, 1986; 1989; Whyte, 1988; Kelbaugh, 1989; Putnam, 2000).

These and other analyses illustrated the major changes on urban form since 1950 as a result of ideological, technological, and economic forces. As we have seen, from the 1950s onward, rising car ownership, combined with population increases, extended America's urbanized areas further, faster and at lower densities than previous decades. Riesman, Whyte and other researchers categorized suburbia as being boringly homogenous and a place lacking in individuality and rich human experience, while Gans, in his study of the superficially homogenous community of Levittown, strongly refuted these assertions. The debate continues to rage on to this day, informing such 1990s Hollywood movies as *The Truman Show* and *American Beauty*.

This dissolution of the American urban fabric begun in the 1950s increased during the 1980s and

1990s as the electronic information revolution challenged many conventional assumptions about urban space and urban life, and Americans have come to regard this expansive phenomenon as a recent problem. But such physical expansion of cities was nothing new, nor particular to America. In the years between World Wars I and II, the land area of London doubled while the population increased by only 30 percent, from six-and-a-half million to eight-and-a-half million people (Clawson and Hall: p. 33). Much of this phenomenal upsurge took the form of suburbs sprawling along the main arterial roads leading out of the city, and enlarged communities developing around new underground train stations. This rapid urban growth gave rise to cries about protecting the countryside from shoddy development that are almost identical to those heard today.

However, recent experiences in many American cities have elevated this pattern to even higher levels. The extent of this dramatic push towards lower densities and larger land acquisitions for urban purposes is illustrated most vividly by the case of Cleveland, Ohio. Here the population *decreased* by 11 percent between the years of 1970 and 1990, but the land area of the metropolitan area actually *increased* by 33 percent! (Benfield et al., 1999). Detroit, Michigan provides similar figures for the same 20-year period. Its population declined by 7 percent yet its land area grew by 28 percent. Pittsburgh, Buffalo and Dayton all followed this same paradoxical trend. Most other major cities in the USA increased their population during the same period and continue to do so. Of the 100 largest urbanized areas in the country, 71 cities grew in both population and land area, some very dramatically, while 11 experienced no population growth (or decreased in numbers) yet increased in area (www.sprawlcity.com). This growth occurred almost exclusively at the suburban edge: between 1950 and 1970, American suburbs grew in population more than eight times faster than central cities, by 85 million people compared to 10 million.

The growth followed new market opportunities with little thought for the consequences, but by the late 1980s the effects of this suburban migration of people and wealth was more clearly seen: the centers of most American cities, once proud hubs of commerce and culture, became hollow shells. Dallas, Texas, during the 1980s provides a perfect illustration of the conditions in the city center at that time. White, middle-class office workers drove in from the suburbs, parked their cars in parking decks, walked through air-conditioned pedestrian bridges or skywalks into their office towers, went for lunch and shopped in the internal pedestrian malls linked together in the lower floors of the office buildings, walked back through the skywalks to their cars at the end of the day and drove home. Not once did the typical office worker set foot on the streets, or engage in any pedestrian activity that was part of external public space. On some days, before they skywalked back to their cars after work, they might even catch a Maverick's basketball game via subterranean passages. The streets – hot and unpleasant in the summer months – were predominantly the territory of the black and Hispanic lower class workers and the unemployed.

This dystopian downtown scene contrasted with affluence in the suburbs, where development gobbled up green fields for new residential subdivisions and shopping centers at an astonishing rate. In the same period from 1950–1970, the consumption of land for residential purposes in greater Chicago grew at an amazing 11 times faster than the region's population. This suburban expansion has continued almost unchecked despite the radical improvement of many American city centers during the 1990s.

America lost 4 million acres of *prime* farmland to urban use during the decade from 1982 to 1992. That equates to 1.6 million hectares, or an area nearly as big as Wales. That may not sound much in the context of the huge American continent, but it doesn't count other, less productive rural areas that are also converted to housing subdivisions, shopping malls and office parks. The speed at which this overall transformation takes place is hard to contemplate. The city of Charlotte, North Carolina, for example, converts open space to suburbs at the rate of 41 acres per day, or 1.7 acres per hour! (Brookings Institution, 2002). Nationally, this process of urbanization is equivalent to gobbling up land a rate of 45.7 acres per hour, every day (Benfield et al., 1999).

It wasn't residential use alone that expanded the suburbs. During those same two decades from 1950 to 1970 the suburbs provided 75 percent of all new jobs in the retail and commercial sectors. To use a dramatic example, between 1970 and 1990 the consumption of land for industrial and commercial uses in greater Chicago increased by 74 percent, 18 times the rate of that metropolitan area's population growth.

Meanwhile, the decline of central cities continued, often in dramatic ways, with increasing instances of stark poverty, rising crime, homelessness and other major problems, often associated with drug abuse. By 1990, the flight of the residential middle class from the city center was all but complete, and many suburbanites, too busy congratulating themselves on their realization of the American Dream, had excised the problems of the deserted downtowns from their minds. A single-family, detached house on the family's own property, even if the land measured less than half an acre, was an acceptable substitute for the American pioneer's dream of a 'little house on the prairie.'

The report *Measuring Sprawl and its Impact: the Character and Consequences of Metropolitan Expansion* identified sprawl as the

> ... process in which the spread of development across the landscape far outpaces population growth. The landscape sprawl creates has four dimensions: a population that is widely dispersed in low-density development; rigidly separated homes, shops, and workplaces; a network of roads marked by huge blocks and poor access; and a lack of well-defined, thriving activity centers, such as downtowns and town centers. Most of the other features usually associated with sprawl – the lack of transportation choices, relative uniformity of housing options or the difficulty of walking – are a result of these conditions. (Ewing et al., 2002: p. 3).

Fiscal impacts of unrestrained suburban expansion can be added to this list of factors; these land use decisions generate direct costs for the public purse. They require new infrastructure of roads, water mains and sewer connections to serve undeveloped land on the edges of urban areas. The new populations need fire and police protection – more personnel, new buildings, extra equipment. Suburban families setting up home in new areas need new schools for their children to attend. The money for these new expenses has to come from somewhere, and the American system of public finance demands that most costs for community services be borne locally through property taxes and sales taxes. Where the costs to support growth exceed the tax income municipalities receive from new households, part of the price to accommodate newcomers falls on existing residents through general tax increases, often creating friction between existing residents and newcomers. A study in Salt Lake City, Utah, demonstrated that low-density sprawl would cost as much as $15 billion in infrastructure and public services – approximately $30 000 per household (Calthorpe and Fulton, 2001: p. 2). Despite the protestations of the real estate industry, growth rarely pays for itself.

This inequity has given rise to several efforts to pass these costs of growth onto the newcomers who have generated the need for extra services in the form of impact fees, that is, extra fees per new dwelling charged by the municipality to developers. These fees are then put toward the cost of providing new community services, thus reducing the tax burden on existing residents. These impact fees can vary from a few hundred dollars to several thousand, and developers (who dislike this system intensely) pass these fees directly onto homebuyers in the form of increased house prices. Critics of impact fees point to the fact that this system makes new housing more expensive, thus making it less affordable to people of low or moderate incomes.

At a larger scale, several studies have shown that these new costs for providing community services to expanding suburban areas can be minimized through compact development. A well-known examination of comparative development patterns in New Jersey estimated that the state of New Jersey could save several billion dollars in infrastructure costs if its urbanized areas developed in compact patterns instead of extended sprawl (Burchell and Listokin, 1995). In addition to reducing the costs of public services, other studies show that compact development can also reduce actual housing costs by between 6 and 8 percent (Burchell, 1997).

Another quirk in the structure of American public sector finance that differentiates it from British practice also causes great difficulty in creating and funding policies of sustainable growth in metropolitan areas. Because public funding is largely locally based as opposed to centrally administered, there is greater competition among municipalities for certain types of development that generate more tax revenue than expenditure. For example, a large new out-of-town shopping center will generate new property taxes and sales tax revenue from all the goods sold, with relatively little cost to the local authority – possibly new water and sewer connections and police and fire protection. This type of commercial development does not generate any need for new schools, libraries or other expensive community facilities, and thus the local authority makes a net profit from this kind of development, receiving more tax money from the project than it expends on services. This contrasts with typical residential development, which usually costs the municipality more money to service with all necessary facilities than it receives in taxes.

Towns and cities therefore compete fiercely with each other to attract large retail and office developments to their community, usually in suburban locations, and financial considerations often override all others. Issues of environmental impacts, loss of open space and even traffic congestion find it hard to match the need for local authorities to raise their own money for community services. In this competitive context, it's very difficult (some would say impossible) to undertake collaborative regional planning that coordinates the design of sustainable transportation and land-use patterns across several different local authorities. Currently each municipality takes decisions that within their own limited boundaries might be rational, but which in the larger regional context can be exactly the opposite.

Most American cities, while homogeneous on the ground, are divided into different political jurisdictions that compete with one another for new development to improve their tax base. Atlanta, Georgia, for example, is an agglomeration of 73 different local authorities, comprising the original city of Atlanta and a multitude of surrounding suburban towns and counties. As Atlanta's urban area grew, its municipal boundaries didn't expand with it. Instead, the new built-up areas were claimed by the formerly rural counties around the original city, leaving the city of Atlanta landlocked within its suburbs, all of which have grown into towns in their own right. The complete extent of the extended Atlanta metropolitan area, with its population of 4 112 198 (in 2003), comprises the city of Atlanta, 20 counties and 143 independent towns!

For the British reader, a theoretical analogy might be if the city of Birmingham were composed of many different towns, each having its own town council, planning staff, police force, fire brigade – and budget. Most taxation would be local, and different councils, say, Edgbaston and Ladywood, for example, would have different rates of property tax on homes and businesses, and of sales tax (VAT) on the goods bought in the stores. 'Towns' nearer the center might have larger percentages of poorer inhabitants, and would therefore have trouble raising enough revenue to maintain good levels of public services, while the wealthier municipalities in the suburbs would always have the upper hand in attracting new jobs, shopping centers and affluent residents. What in the UK is a unified administrative area capable of coordinated planning and allocation of resources would thus become a fractured metropolis of increasing disparity between rich and poor communities. The nearest Britain has come to experiencing this state of affairs was in London during the 1980s, when Prime Minister Margaret Thatcher abolished the Greater London Council and left the capital city to be run by

a series of squabbling and unequal borough councils. It wasn't until the late 1990s that the process of restoring unified local government for London was commenced under Tony Blair's administration with the election of a new Mayor for the whole metropolitan area.

Profligate patterns of suburban expansion also bring with them problems of air and water pollution that cross America's myriad municipal boundaries. Polluted surface water run-off from a large suburban shopping center in one town may flow into the river that supplies drinking water for the adjacent community. But if the upstream town desperately needs the taxes from the shopping center to pay for new schools it may very well pay no heed to the pleas of its downstream neighbor. Problems of pollution are well-documented in American technical literature (Benfield et al., 1999) and we don't wish to duplicate facts and figures here to an unnecessary degree, but a few instances will help drive home the need for dramatic changes to current attitudes and policies.

The expanding nature of America's suburbs requires that most people drive everywhere for everything they need in their normal daily lives. In a country dominated by large distances and large vehicles with low gas mileage, it is quite possible to spend a gallon of gas to buy a gallon of milk. Using the 20-year period between 1970 and 1990 again as a reliable benchmark, vehicle miles travelled (VMT) increased at four times the increase in the driving-age population (Benfield et al., 1999). For many people today, it's virtually impossible to live without a car. There is no alternative, for the widely spaced suburbs cannot be served conveniently or economically by public transportation. Some wealthier families 'need' three or four vehicles to support their suburban lifestyle.

Twenty-first century Americans drive so much because the goods and services they require each day are separated into single-use zones, and the roads between them have been designed for vehicle use only. Walking in this environment often requires walking in the roadway, endangered by traffic, or on some muddy, scruffy unpaved verge. America is increasingly becoming a land of private affluence and public squalor, as the public realm decays through lack of use, or use by only those members of society whose mobility is limited.

All this driving translates directly into unhealthy air quality caused by carbon monoxide exhaust, nitrous oxides, and other carcinogenic and toxic air pollutants. Many American cities regularly have 'bad air' days, or smog-alert days when health authorities advise citizens not to go outside if they have respiratory problems.

European cities are by no means immune from this problem, but there is one crucial difference: alternative, less polluting types of transportation are often available. In most American cities, the car is the only realistic means of moving around. Every American suburban area has places where office workers eat lunch at restaurants within a quarter-mile from where they work, but where it is physically impossible or unsafe to walk. In twenty-first century America, even going for lunch with a group of colleagues involves a multitude of car trips.

The haphazard, spread-out development patterns of sprawl dramatically affect air quality; equally dramatic is their impact on the quality of water in America's creeks, streams and rivers. It's now fairly well understood that natural landscapes are generally permeable, allowing rainwater and snowmelt to percolate slowly into the ground and filtering out most pollutants naturally. In cities and suburbs, by contrast, large areas of ground are paved or built over with impervious materials, thus forcing stormwater to run-off quickly into waterways without benefit of any natural filtration, and picking up man-made pollutants such as car oil and other everyday chemicals as it flows. Even when tallying densities as low as one house per acre, the math adds up to approximately 10 percent of the site being covered with buildings and concrete driveways, paths and patios. Shopping centers typically cover between 75 and 95 percent of their site's area with this impervious construction. As a result, run-off pollution is now America's main threat to ecologically sound water quality. Forty percent of the nation's rivers are significantly polluted, leading to diminution of fish stocks, public health problems and loss of recreational venues (Benfield et al., 1999).

Added to these serious environmental problems are the visible attributes of suburban sprawl. Much of it, especially the commercial areas, is incredibly *ugly* (see Figure 2.13). The caustic critic James Howard Kunstler sums up this American dilemma:

We drive up and down the gruesome, tragic suburban boulevards of commerce, and we're overwhelmed at the fantastic, awesome, stupefying ugliness of absolutely everything in sight – the fry pits, the big-box stores, the office units, the lube joints, the carpet warehouses, the parking lagoons, the jive plastic townhouse clusters, the uproar of signs, the highway itself clogged with cars – as though the whole thing had been designed by some diabolical force bent on making human beings miserable. (Kunstler, 1996a: p. 43).

**Figure 2.13** Generic commercial sprawl in the American city. South Boulevard, Charlotte, NC, 2003. Every piece of this visual and functional mess is the result of developers following planning regulations that focused on the minutiae of individual projects with no regard for the larger urban whole.

It is interesting to compare Kunstler's 1996 critique of the suburban environment to that of British architectural critic and cartoonist Osbert Lancaster, writing in 1959:

If an architect of enormous energy, painstaking ingenuity and great structural knowledge, had devoted years of his life to the study of how best to achieve the maximum of inconvenience … and had the assistance of a corps of research workers ransacking architectural history for the least attractive materials and building devices known to the past, it is just possible, though highly unlikely, that he might have evolved a style as crazy as that with which the speculative builder, with no expenditure of mental energy at all, has enriched the landscape on either side of our great arterial roads … Notice the skill with which the (buildings) are disposed, that ensures that the largest possible area of countryside is ruined with the minimum of expense. (Lancaster: p. 152)

Medical and psychological evidence reveals that ugly surroundings are not good for us. University research in Texas and Delaware indicates that our reactions to visual clutter 'may include elevated blood pressure, increased muscle tension, and impacts on mood and work performance' (Benfield et al., 1997). Recent studies have also linked health problems such as obesity and diabetes to a badly-designed, unwalkable environment (Killingsworth et al., 2003; US Dept of Health and Human Services, 2001; Srikameswaram, 2003).

The litany of problems that accompanies suburban sprawl, especially its ugliness, the loss of open space, health issues, environmental pollution and the pressure continually to increase tax rates to fund new community services comprise the most evident symptoms of America's urban tribulations. But many in the development community who construct conventional strip centers and residential subdivisions dismiss these objections, claiming the continued market success of low-density spread-out development indicates that it's what people want. They reject the criticisms of ugliness as the subjective aesthetics of a snooty middle-class elite; they cast environmental objections as the rantings of 'tree-hugging' extremists. Nothing, in their view, outweighs a successful financial return within the limited 10-year time frame of their development cycle. From this perspective, success in the marketplace equates to success in society at large.

For many years the developers' financial equations of suburban development went unchallenged, but more recently they have been subjected to closer scrutiny. The fiscal impacts of sprawl are now much better understood in terms of their real costs to society and the taxpayer, issues that the development community has gladly overlooked in its analyses. This sharper economic sense is one of the factors that has led to the upsurge of interest in development that is more sustainable in terms of its longer term environmental and fiscal impacts. Generally labelled Smart Growth, this search for a wiser use of land

and resources has prompted a slew of publications, each promoting a similar agenda of environmental conservation and more compact, space-efficient development (Benfield et al., 1999; Benfield et al., 2001; Booth et al., 2002; O'Neill, 2002). An increasing number of professionals and the public realize our generation is simply passing on to our children and grandchildren the costs to clean up the civic and environmental mess our society produces today.

But like many cities in Britain, American urban areas are plagued by many other dilemmas apart from suburban sprawl, the solutions to which must be part of any Smart Growth policy. Both countries suffer from increasing separation by race and income in urban areas (and the consequent problems of social inequity and ghettoization) and on top of this, American cities still struggle with issues of disinvestment in central cities, the deterioration of suburbs that date from the 1950s and 1960s, and the erosion of the culture's built heritage by thoughtless

**Figure 2.14** First Ward Place, Charlotte, NC, 1997–2001. Under the auspices of the US governments HOPE VI program, and following New Urbanist design principles, several cities have transformed blighted urban areas into attractive mixed-income neighborhoods like this Charlotte example.

**Figure 2.15** Lindberg Center, Atlanta, Cooper Carry architects, 1998–2003. The Bell South telecommunications company has consolidated its regional offices as the centerpiece of this large mixed-use development built on top of and around a MARTA train station in Atlanta, Georgia.

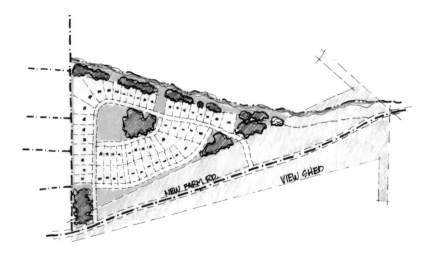

**Figure 2.16** Conservation subdivision design. On greenfield sites, new development can minimize its negative aspects and engender a sense of place by clustering in more compact layouts to preserve existing landscape amenities and ecologies. (Drawing courtesy of The Lawrence Group)

demolition or careless stewardship. For each of these quandaries, private or public organizations are trying to reverse the downward trend, sometimes with impressive local success. In America, several cities can now point to major downtown improvements during the 1990s, with thousands of new city center dwellers bringing with them renewed retail development to supplement the traditional concentrations of office space. The intransigent problem of building afford-able housing and integrating it into the community is at least being tackled with some serious intent (see Figure 2.14).

New transportation infrastructures, usually light rail or streetcars, are beginning to spur a series of urban redevelopments in more central locations that provide a partial antidote to continued peripheral

expansion (see Figure 2.15). Some new developments on greenfield sites are taking a more compact, envi-ronmentally friendly form with an urbanized core and walkable neighborhoods (see Plate 5). Other subdivision designs around the edges of cities empha-sise the conservation of existing landscapes as an environmental resource and a generator of economic value (see Figure 2.16). All these types of develop-ment have their place in the lexicon of Smart Growth, and formed the foundations of New Urbanist theory and practice some years before Smart Growth became the rallying cry it is today in America. Accordingly, in the next chapter we turn our attention specifically to the principles of New Urbanism, the evolution of the movement, and its intersection with Smart Growth.

Theory

# Traditional urbanism: New Urbanism and Smart Growth

## SYNOPSIS

In the first part of this chapter we analyze New Urbanism and trace its evolution over the last two decades of the twentieth century, relating it to similar urban concepts – both historical American precedent and parallel strands of European urban design. We begin this brief history of traditional urbanism in an unlikely place – Las Vegas, home of the 'strip', and the antithesis of the traditional city. The analysis of the American roadside environment and the commercial strip by Venturi et al. (1972) in their book *Learning from Las Vegas* was an important event in the demolition of modernist urban theory; it created room for the development of new ways of thinking about urbanism in America.

We explore the parallel developments of Traditional Neighborhood Development and Transit-oriented Development and their fusion to create New Urbanism. In particular, we look at the environmental agenda of Transit-oriented Development and connect this urban-based vision with the third main element of New Urbanist theory and practice, the conservation of rural landscapes and ecologies, staying 'rural by design.' This union of urban and rural perspectives creates the strongest link between New Urbanism and the Smart Growth movement in America, to the point where the two terms are almost synonymous.

In the second section we discuss the concepts embodied in the term Smart Growth, and note the extensive overlap of this environmentally based vision of America with New Urbanism. Lastly, we examine some of the myths and misconceptions that exist concerning the agendas of Smart Growth advocates, many of them deliberately fostered by opponents of Smart Growth and New Urbanism. We revisit, and

counter, some other strands of opposition to the use of traditional urban forms that exist within academia and the architectural profession.

## THE ORIGINS, CONCEPTS AND EVOLUTION OF NEW URBANISM

We've never liked the name 'The New Urbanism.' In our work with communities, we stuck to 'traditional town planning' or 'neo-traditional development' as long as we could, but the momentum of general usage, and the branding of traditional urban forms as New Urbanism was eventually irreversible.

We didn't like the term because it got in the way of our work in community design. Most American suburban communities grappling with suburban growth pressures don't want to be 'new.' Newness, in the form of new development, is seen by many as the source of the problems growth brings. And many communities we work with, except those that comprise neighborhoods within cities, don't want to be urban. Citizens moved out of the cities to the suburbs precisely to avoid urbanity, or at least what they perceived as urban. So the name erected two unnecessary barriers from the outset.

In our practice, we now tend to use the terms 'New Urbanism' and 'Smart Growth' as synonyms. Indeed, because of our discomfort with the title 'New Urbanism' we have come to use Smart Growth almost universally, liberally sprinkled with references to traditional neighborhood design and 'urban villages.' The English heritage and experience of one of the authors means he has been designing with the concepts now classified as New Urbanism since the 1970s, long before the term was coined, and some time before its precursor, Neo-Traditional Development was invented in America in the early 1980s. However, the lineage of the design and planning movement in America that became New Urbanism is important to review, as several misconceptions still attach themselves to the public's (and the design professions') understanding of the term.

The name 'The New Urbanism' was consciously chosen in the early to mid-1990s to mark the merging of Traditional Neighborhood Development, developed on the east coast of America by Duany and Plater-Zyberk (2002), with Transit-oriented Development which evolved synchronously on the west coast largely through the work of Peter Calthorpe, Doug Kelbaugh, and Daniel Solomon. The conjoined movement developed a manifesto for urbanism in the postmodern city specifically as a counterpoint to the Charter of Athens, the 1942 document that codified the modernist view of urbanity. The new charter, the Charter of The New Urbanism, was signed into being at the Fourth Congress of The New Urbanism in 1996 at Charleston, South Carolina. This urbanism, based on the return to traditional urban forms and typologies, was defined as 'new' in contrast to the old and discredited urban language of modernism. And it was to be 'urban' by creating a coherent urban structure to counteract the faults of a sprawling suburban model of city development.

However, this rebirth of traditional urbanism in the 1980s did not happen in a vacuum: it was necessarily preceded by the final demise of modernist urban theory that came to pass during the 1970s. During those years American architects had been faced with two stark facts about their contributions to the nation's cities – the failure of modernist design theories in the inner city programs of urban renewal – and the profession's lack of any success in shaping suburbia into an attractive and efficient form. The year 1972 in particular administered two unsettling shocks to architects: the publication of *Learning from Las Vegas* by Robert Venturi, Denise Scott Brown and Steven Izenour marked the end of modernism in architecture and planning as effectively as the demolition of the Pruitt-Igoe housing blocks in that same year. Venturi, Scott Brown and Izenour made implicit common cause with Melvin Webber's 'Nonplace Urban Realm' of the early 1960s to the extent they considered traditional urban forms no longer relevant, but, most shockingly, they declared that modernist concepts of architectural style and form were similarly obsolete. Instead of modernist doctrine that placed emphasis on the sculptural form and constructional integrity of buildings,

Venturi and his colleagues proposed an architecture that was based much more on signs and symbolic communication. They threw down the gauntlet to a profession still mesmerized by European modernism by placing the products of American popular culture on a par with Corbusian aesthetics.

Developed from a 1968 essay, *A Significance for A&P Parking Lots*, the message of *Learning from Las Vegas* was an exhortation to architects not to reject the popular culture of their time, but to elevate it to a subject worthy of serious study, just as pop artists had challenged the aesthetic values of high modernism a decade earlier. The subtext of the argument was that the space of the commercial strip, or of highway travel in general, was a more valid architectural and cultural experience for Americans than the traditional, enclosed space of European plazas. For Venturi and his co-authors, the most relevant works of architecture along the highway were the commercial signs rather than buildings. If architecture was about communication of meaning to the general public, then the symbolism of the large signs was more effective than modernist abstract aesthetics.

To further this message, Venturi and Scott Brown organized an exhibition in Washington DC, in 1976, entitled 'Signs of Life: symbols in the American City,' which examined popular symbolism in the family house, the American Main Street (almost defunct by that time), and the commercial suburban strip. Architects and planners didn't have to like Venturi and Scott Brown's thesis, but one fact was undeniable: for the first time in over thirty years, architectural theory was re-embracing the suburbs. *Learning from Las Vegas* validated the process of learning from existing and commonplace landscapes; indeed the authors considered this intellectual reversion a praiseworthy and revolutionary act (Venturi et al., 1972).

For thirty years or so, the study of the symbolic iconography of the American strip has continued to provide fodder for esoteric academic studies at schools and colleges of architecture, but has done little to improve the physical environment. Reclassifying something that was ugly and inefficient as visually rich and significant didn't alter the fact that suburbia was developing in a manner that was detrimental to the city, its citizens, and its environment. However, Venturi's subversive text breached the intellectual dam of modernism in a crucial way, and other possibilities for design began to open up. If it was valid to study the existing landscape, then was it possible that older American landscapes, those of the traditional town, might also hold some lessons?

There was one other positive urban result from American architects' fascination with the brash road-side vernacular of the Strip and its signs and symbolic meanings. This emphasis on semiotics captured the imagination of a profession keen to reconnect with public sentiment, and initially led to several years of superficial façadism in postmodern architecture. Architects slathered classical or populist images on the façades of their buildings – to little lasting effect – but these designs did at least lay the groundwork for a crucial lesson. The renewed emphasis on the design of building façades independent from the building's plan meant that it was possible once again to regard the external walls of buildings as *urban* elements, responsive to conditions in the exterior public realm.

To understand the revolutionary implications of this seemingly modest change, we have to remember that modernist buildings didn't have façades. This was a word banned from design studio in the 1950s and 1960s for its decadent, historicist overtones. Instead, the building's external walls were designed as elevations, raising the plan in three dimensions with the expectation that the disposition of windows, doors and other elements of the wall would reflect the needs of the ground plan with functional precision. As reasonable as this may have been on one level, this focus on a building's appearance as predominantly the expression of its internal func-tions meant that external factors such as adjacent buildings and the urban context had little or no role to play in the building's aesthetics. As an extension of this attitude, as we noted in Chapter 1, architects in the 1950s and 1960s had dismissed the study of con-text itself as having much value, and existing build-ings were often viewed as inconsequential and in the way, as Figure 3.1 indicates.

Architects slowly relearned the lesson of history that external walls need not merely enclose and express the building's internal functions, but could independently shape and modulate external space. This shift allowed architects to go further, and study the traditional role of buildings as definers of public space instead of sim-ply objects in space. From here it was only a short step to designing new buildings that specifically responded to their context – a setting that included adjacent buildings, the public spaces of the city, and the pat-terns of human activity within those spaces.

Within ten years of architectural modernism's intel-lectual decline, this fledgling interest in contextualism connected in the USA with a growing interest in the traditional vernacular architecture and urbanism of American towns and cities. This nexus received its earliest expression by the vacation community of Seaside in the Florida panhandle, designed by Andres Duany and his wife, Elizabeth Plater-Zyberk in 1981–82 (see Figure 1.11). Seaside featured modern

**Figure 3.1** Office buildings, Newcastle-upon-Tyne, Ryder and Yates, architects, 1970. Many buildings from the 1970s were quite sophisticated structures, The office building on the left, for example, is designed as a giant beam from which the floors are suspended by cables enclosed in stainless steel cruciform mouldings, creating large open-plan floor areas. Despite such cleverness, buildings often demonstrated a crushing insensitivity to their context and the urban scale of the city. Other buildings of the late modernist period were far less clever. The example in the photograph on the right is just terrible. The new slab has no redeeming features whatsoever. It is a testament to the aesthetic power of the adjacent Victorian building that it even holds its own against this monstrous intrusion into the city fabric. Such design outrages are particularly poignant in Newcastle, which has a marvellous early Victorian urban structure and architectural legacy.

interpretations of traditional domestic building types and a pattern of streets and public spaces actively reminiscent of traditional American towns and suburbs from the nineteenth and early twentieth centuries. Beneath its quirky aesthetics, the design provided a radical critique of contemporary suburban planning, with its emphasis on well-defined public spaces and a vision based primarily on the visual character of buildings and spaces rather than their uses. The plan of Seaside featured a range of traditional urban forms, designed as a series of grids overlaid with diagonal axes focusing on the town center, and providing key locations for monumental buildings. The streets were designed as narrow pedestrian 'rooms' along which cars could move at slow speed, and which often terminated at a public building or public space. Garages were accessed from the rear, by means of narrow alleyways.

The effect of Seaside was dramatic; for the first time in several decades, a suburban development was constructed with some sense by being a unified place, like a traditional neighborhood or town in miniature. But the modest development by these two architects was so far beyond conventional thinking in the early 1980s, that it took another decade, until the mid-1990s before American planners tentatively embraced 'neo-traditional development.' Almost another decade followed before the development community, through their 'think-tank' the Urban Land Institute (ULI), embraced these same architectural and planning principles. By this time, neo-traditional development had morphed into New Urbanism and the ULI began to hold workshops and conferences on the topic in the late 1990s. By the time of writing in 2003, the Institute had produced several publications explaining how their members could create traditional towns in line with New Urbanist principles (ULI, 1998; Eppli and Tu, 1999; O'Neill, 1999; Booth et al., 2002; Bohl, 2002).

This conscious process of morphing Traditional Neighborhood Development with Transit-oriented Development to create New Urbanism in the mid-1990s brought together the two most radical strands of avant-garde urbanism in America. Traditional Neighborhood Development had its roots in historical examples of American urbanism such as the 'pre-automobile' neighborhoods of streetcar suburbs and commuter rail suburbs that were built around many cities in the late 1800s and the early decades of the twentieth century. At a reduced scale, American small towns of the same period provided similar useful precedent. Duany and Plater-Zyberk realized that the planning concepts and physical attributes of such places, with their human scale and lively mix of uses,

were as appropriate to postmodern America as when they were originally developed, sixty to one hundred years ago. The authors' neighborhood of Dilworth, in Charlotte, for example, with its network of pedestrian-friendly streets, restaurants, offices and stores is as lively, attractive and relevant now as it was when it was first laid out one hundred years ago as Charlotte's first streetcar suburb. In 1903, the level of car ownership was miniscule. Now in our neighborhood automobiles number at least two, often three per family. For a system of streets, spaces and buildings to continue to function very well given this major technological change speaks highly of its robust and flexible design principles. History presents us with a model that suggests neighborhoods like ours will be as valid in the future as they were in the past. Thus, the radicalism of Traditional Neighborhood Development was predominantly a conservative ethos; this contrasts with the compatible but more environmentally progressive spirit of Transit-oriented Development.

Part of this radical conservatism derives from the considerable influence of the European urbanist, Leon Krier. Duany and Plater-Zyberk acknowledge the impact of Krier, and his neo-rationalist ideas derived from the European city, on the planning of Seaside. Krier was a consultant during the design process of that landmark community, and has remained an important contributor to New Urbanist theory. Duany described hearing a lecture on traditional urbanism by Krier while he and Plater-Zyberk were still working in Arquitectonica, the Miami architectural firm best known for its flashy high-rises. As a result, the husband and wife team underwent a profound change of direction in their work. (http://applied.math.utsa.edu/krier/).

In Europe during the 1970s, Krier was a leading advocate of the Movement for the Reconstruction of the European City, whose major themes included: the preservation of historic centers; the use of historic urban types and urban patterns such as the street, the square and the neighborhood (or *quartier* in Krier's lexicon) as the basis for new city development; and the reconstruction of single-use residential 'bedroom suburbs' into articulate mixed-use neighborhoods. While the specific European urban pattern s and types were transformed by their travel across the Atlantic during the following decade, these underlying theoretical principles became founding concepts for Traditional Neighborhood Development in the 1980s and made their way into New Urbanist theory in the 1990s.

Krier's focus on the European urban quarter was matched by Dauny and Platter-Zyberk's revived interest in the American neighborhood concept of social planner Clarence Perry, first promulgated in the early 1920s and more fully developed as part of the 1929 First Regional Plan of New York. Perry was active in the American Regional Planning Association with Lewis Mumford and Clarence Stein and Henry Wright, the architect-planners of Radburn. Perry's training as a sociologist had taught him the importance of cohesive neighborhoods as political, social, and even moral units of a city. Moreover, Perry lived in the New York railroad suburb of Forest Hills Gardens (noted in Chapter 1), and this experience stimulated his concept of the neighborhood unit as the fundamental unit of city planning. In his 1929 monograph for the Regional Plan of New York, Perry wrote from first-hand experience about the value of high quality urban design in fostering the good spirit and character of a neighborhood, and created a plan diagram of a typical neighborhood layout (Perry, 1929: pp. 90–3; in Hall, 2002: p. 132). This diagram illustrated a hypothetical area bounded by major roads with community facilities, including a school and a park, at the center (see Figure 3.2).

Central to Perry's concept was the ability of all residents to walk to those facilities they needed on a daily basis, such as shops, schools and playgrounds. The size of the neighborhood was determined by a five-minute walking distance from center to edge, approximately 1/4-mile, creating a population of about 5000 people, large enough to support local shops but small

enough to generate a sense of community (Broadbent p. 126). The street pattern was a mixture of radial avenues interspersed with irregular straight and curving grids with small parks and playgrounds liberally scattered throughout. Shopping was located along the edge at the intersections of the main roads within the five-minute walking distance for most residents.

Duany and Plater-Zyberk developed this same concept and updated it for American urban conditions of the late twentieth century. In their *Lexicon of New Urbanism* (DPZ, 2002) they illustrated a similar sized urban area, bounded by highways, and scaled to the five-minute, 1/4-mile walk. In this contemporary version, more extensive commercial development is located along the edges of the bounding highways, and a street of mixed-use buildings leads from one corner into the central public park, where community institutions and some local shops are located. The school has moved to the edge, due to much larger space requirements for playing fields and parking, and this educational facility is now shared between neighborhoods. Duany and Plater-Zyberk's street grid is tighter and more organized than Perry's but is similar in concept to the original (see Figure 3.3).

Duany and Plater-Zyberk's understanding how powerful diagrams can be in regulating development and promoting good urban design is one of the most important contributions to urban design and town planning in contemporary America. This claim is based on the duo's revolutionary innovation of graphic

NEIGHBORHOOD UNIT 1927

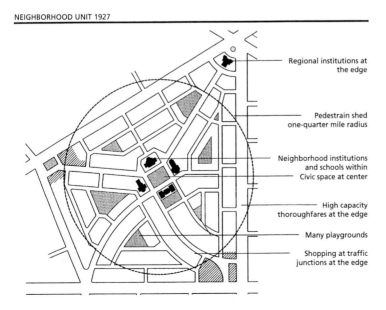

Regional institutions at the edge

Pedestrain shed one-quarter mile radius

Neighborhood institutions and schools within Civic space at center

High capacity thoroughfares at the edge

Many playgrounds

Shopping at traffic junctions at the edge

**Figure 3.2** Clarence Perry's Neighborhood Unit, 1927. The circle illustrates a five-minute (approximately 1/4 mile) walk from the center. (*Diagram (2002 version) courtesy of Duany Plater-Zyberk and Company*)

TRADITIONAL NEIGHBORHOOD DEVELOPMENT 1997

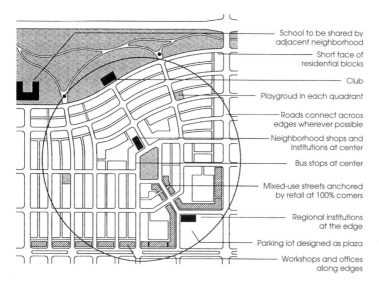

School to be shared by
adjacent neighborhood

Short face of
residential blocks

Club

Playgroud in each quadrant

Roads connect across
edges wherever possible

Neighborhood shops and
institutions at center

Bus stops at center

Mixed-use streets anchored
by retail at 100% corners

Regional institutions
at the edge

Parking lot designed as plaza

Workshops and offices
along edges

**Figure 3.3** Traditional Neighborhood, 1997, as designed by Duany Plater-Zyberk and Company. As with Figure 3.2, the circle represents a five-minute walk from the center. (*Diagram courtesy of Duany Plater-Zyberk and Company*)

development codes as the means of making sure developments are controlled by concepts of good urban design in three dimensions, rather than by the conventional means of two-dimensional diagrams of land use and dense tomes of legal language. The role of design-based codes is central to this book: they are exemplified in several of our case studies, and discussed in detail in Chapters 5 and 10, so here we will simply highlight their importance. In Seaside and subsequent projects, Duany and Plater-Zyberk established the practice of encoding all the salient features of building forms, types of urban space (streets, squares, parks and so on) into a simple-to-read sheet of diagrams that created the physical vocabulary for building the community. Into these three-dimensional templates were then inserted conditions pertaining to building use. This is exactly the opposite of conventional planning practice, where use of buildings or land is paramount and issues of physical design are usually relegated to detailed legal language that tries, inadequately, to describe details for the arrangements of buildings and spaces. Learning from Duany and Plater-Zyberk's breakthrough in the early 1980s, the authors developed their first graphic, design-based code for the town of Davidson, NC, in 1995 (Keane and Walters, 1995) (see Figure 3.4). This example was indicative of work by several architect-planners in communities across North America during the mid-1990s, searching to find ways of translating Duany and Plater-Zyberk's code for a privately controlled development like Seaside into a document that

operated for all circumstances in the fully public realm of city zoning (City of Toronto, 1995; Hammond and Walters, 1996).

This issue of coding remains a crucial one because most aspects of this traditionally based urbanism are still illegal under many conventional American zoning ordinances that control development in American towns and cities (Langdon, 2003a). These outdated ordinances, developed in the decades after World War II, provide the framework of detailed regulations that have implemented the modernist and suburbanized view of the city, categorized by low-density single-use developments separated out across the landscape. As we discuss in detail in Chapter 5, the solution adopted by New Urbanist designers has been to rewrite development codes based on models of traditional urbanism, and to persuade municipalities to implement these as parallel or substitute zoning regulations.

If a renewed appreciation of traditional American urbanism and a breakthrough in development coding were the main highlights of Traditional Neighborhood Development, the equivalent emphasis of Transit-oriented Development was made clear in its title: it renewed the severed connection between urban form and public transportation. Transit-oriented Development embodied many similar and complimentary ideas as its Traditional Neighborhood Development companion concerning traditional urban patterns, but it evolved specifically from the concept of the 'Pedestrian Pocket.' This was essentially

**58**

a small town, or 'urban village' organized primarily with the needs of the pedestrian in mind, like the pre-automobile suburbs that formed the basis for Traditional Neighborhood Developments, but developed around new public transit – usually light rail – that enabled residents of one 'pocket' to travel conveniently to others and to a major metropolis (Kelbaugh, 1989). Once again the concept of the five-minute walk defined the scale of the development, five minutes being established as the maximum distance an average American will walk to catch transit (see Figure 3.5). Walking distance apart, there are remarkable similarities between the TOD vision and Ebenezer Howard's concept of Garden Cities, where a series of independent communities would be located around a major metropolis and connected together by railways.

This full transit vision has not yet been implemented anywhere in the USA, although Portland, Oregon, perhaps comes closest, but the marked upsurge of interest in light rail transit in cities across the USA is a testament to the power of the original Pedestrian Pocket/Transit-oriented Development concept. The City of San Diego was one of the first to adopt Calthorpe's Transit-oriented Development principles in an official city ordinance in 1992 (Calthorpe Associates, 1992). Many other cities have followed suit with similar codes prepared by the other consultants who have mastered the techniques of Transit-oriented Development. Transit-Oriented Development has thus managed to extend the same planning and urban design ideas found in Traditional Neighborhood Development into a regional context by connecting existing places and new communities along fixed transit corridors, primarily utilizing light rail or commuter rail technology. Each transit stop can catalyze a neighborhood planned for a mixture of higher-density uses within a five- or ten-minute walking radius (1/4–1/2-mile) organized around pedestrian-friendly streets, squares and parks.

Traditional Neighborhood Developments and Transit-oriented Developments were relatively few in number during the 1980s. Seaside in Florida (1982), and Kentlands, near Washington DC (1988), by DPZ provided the leading built examples. Peter Calthorpe's Laguna West, near Sacramento, California followed in 1990. Both types of development became far more common during the 1990s, due largely to avid proselytizing of the ideas around the nation by Duany, Plater-Zyberk, Calthorpe and others (Duany and Plater-Zyberk, 1991; Calthorpe, 1993), but also to changing national demographics of smaller, more diverse households for whom more compact, walkable, and mixed-use neighborhoods

were attractive places to live. These two movements coalesced in the formation of the Congress for the New Urbanism (CNU) in 1993, which has held annual congresses every year since that date. The basic tenets of the movement were defined in the Charter of the New Urbanism, which was ratified in 1996, and which established guiding principles and paradigms for postmodern urbanism.

The Charter (reproduced in Appendix I) is organized into four sections: (i) an untitled preface of general statements; (ii) the Region – Metropolis, City and Town; (iii) the Neighborhood, District, and Corridor; and (iv) the Block, the Street and the Building (Congress for the New Urbanism, 1998, 2000). The document first emphasizes coherent urban design and planning at a regional scale, promoting the renewed urbanity of existing areas, and the increased urbanity of new development. This focused urbanism is balanced by a concern for the environmentally sustainable relationship between any metropolis and its agrarian hinterland and natural landscapes. The subsequent sections spell out the movement's concerns for the reconstruction of American cities at a variety of scales, utilizing many of the concepts articulated previously by Leon Krier and his fellow neo-rationalists in their manifestoes for the reconstruction of the European city, and adapting them to American practice.

The Charter is a manifesto for physical and social change in American towns and cities. New Urbanism aims to alter the ways people understand and build the places where they live and work, superceding modernist concepts of separated single-use zoning areas, buildings isolated in open space and an environment dominated by the automobile. Instead, the main organizing principles involve: the creation of compact, defined urban neighborhoods, comprising a compatible mixture of uses and housing types; a network of connected streets with sidewalks and street trees to facilitate convenient and safe movement throughout neighborhoods for all modes of transportation; the primacy of the pedestrian over the automobile; the integration of parks and public spaces into each neighborhood; and the placement of important civic buildings on key sites to create a strong visual structure of memorability. In short, it was an endorsement of the forms and types of traditional urbanism that had been presaged in some avant-garde sectors of American academia a decade and a half earlier, as noted in Chapter 1.

One of the most important applications of these New Urbanist ideas is in the design and planning of new projects on infill 'grayfield' sites, usually the

## Lot Type/Apartment Building

### Building Placement/Parking/Vehicular Access

### Encroachment/Pedestrian Access

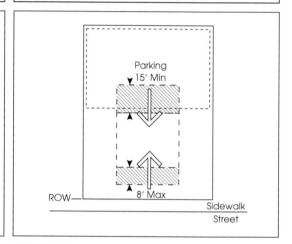

1. Buildings shall be placed on the lot within the zone represented within the hatched area.

2. In most cases, the build to line will be 15' behind street ROW. Special site conditions such as topography, pattern of lot widths, or setbacks of existing buildings permit a larger setback. In urban conditions, apartments may be set up to the property line at the sidewalk, including corner conditions.

3. Building facades shall be generally parallel to front property lines. All buildings shall front onto a public street. All ground floor residential units with exterior access shall front a public street, unless specifically exempted by one of the provisions of Section 8.1.

4. Parking shall be located to the rear of the building.

5. Points of permitted access to the parking indicated by arrows.

6. Hedges, garden walls, or fences may be built on property lines or as the continuation of building walls. A garden wall, fence, or hedge (min. 3' in height) shall be installed along any street frontage adjacent to parking areas.

7. Trash containers shall be located in the rear parking area (see Parking Regulations).

8. Mechanical equipment at ground level shall be placed on the parking lot side of building and away from buildings on adjacent sites.

1. For buildings set back from sidewalk, balconies, stoops, stairs, open porches, bay windows, and awnings are permitted to encroach into setback area up to 8'.

2. Attached decks are permitted to encroach into the rear setback up to 15 feet.

3. For buildings set up to the sidewalk, upper level balconies, bay windows and their supports at ground level may encroach a maximum of 5'0" over the sidewalk.

4. Main pedestrian access to the building and to individual units is from the street (indicated by larger arrow), unless specifically exempted by one of the provisions of Section 8.1. Secondary access may be from parking areas (indicated by smaller arrow).

Description:
    The apartment building is a residential building accommodating several households. In traditional towns, this building type coexists with a variety of other building types. A successful contemporary design permits its integration with other residential types through the coordination of site and building design (see Architectural Regulations). Apartment complexes should be one or more separated buildings similar in their scale on the public street to large detached housing.

Special Conditions:
    1. The intention of buildings in all locations must be to relate the principal facade to the sidewalk and publicspace of the street.

    2. Corners: Setback at street corners will generally replicate frontage conditions. However, side setbacks on a minor street may be less than the front dimension.

    3. Within the limits described, front and side setbacks will vary depending upon site conditions. Setbacks should be used in a manner which encourages pedestrian activity. Squares or spatially defined plazas within building setback areas can act as focal points for pedestrians.

| Building Type/Apartment Building | |
|---|---|
| Permitted height and uses | Architectural standards |

### Permitted height and uses

Varies

36' Max.*

Residential
Use

8' Max.

1. Building height shall be measured as the vertical distance from the highest finished grade relative to the street frontage, up to the eaves or the highest level of a flat roof.

2. The height of parapet walls may vary depending on the need to screen mechanical equipment.

3. Building height to ridge may vary depending on the roof pitch.

4. Permitted uses are indicated above.

### Architectural standards

Principles

A. To perpetuate the unique building character of the town and its environs, and to re-establish its local identity, development shall generally employ building types that are sympathetic to the historic architectural vocabulary of the area in their massing and external materials.

B. The front elevations facing the street, and the overall massing shall communicate an emphasis on the human scale and the pedestrian environment.

C. Each building should be designed to form part of a larger composition of the area in which it is situated. Adjacent buildings should thus be of similar scale, height, and configuration.

D. Building silhouettes should be generally consistent. The scale and pitch of roof lines should thus be similar across groups of buildings.

E. Porches should form a predominant motif of house designs, and be located on the front or to the side of the dwelling. When attached to the front, they should extend over at least 15% of the front facade. All porches should be constructed of materials in keeping with those of the main building.

F. Front loaded garages, if provided, shall meet the standards of Section 8.16.

G. At a minimum, the Americans with Disabilities Act standards for accessibility shall be met.

Configurations

A. Main roofs on residential buildings shall be symmetrical gables or hips with a pitch of between 4:12 and 12:12. Monopitch (shed) roofs are allowed only if they are attached to the wall of the main building. No monopitch shall be less than 4:12. All accessory buildings shall have roof pitches that conform to those of the main building.

B. Balconies should generally be simply supported by posts and beams. The support of cantilevered balconies should be assisted by visible brackets.

C. Two wall materials may be combined horizontally on one facade. The "heavier" material should be below.

D. Exterior chimneys should be finished in brick or stucco.

Techniques

A. Overhanging eaves may expose rafters.

B. Flush eaves should be finished by profiled molding or gutters.

**Figure 3.4** Excerpts from the Regulating Code for Davidson, NC, Walters and Keane, 1995. These two code pages establish the three-dimensional controls for apartment buildings in terms of urban form and building scale and massing. The emphasis here and in all other aspects of the code is making sure that buildings contribute effectively to making properly defined public spaces – the streets, squares and parks of the community. (*Diagrams courtesy of the Town of Davidson, NC*)

T. O. D. PATTERN

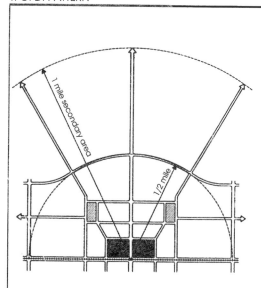

**Figure 3.5** Transit-oriented Development diagram. Developed originally as the 'Pedestrian Pocket' by Peter Calthorpe in the late 1980s, the concept of TOD has become widespread across the USA. This diagram, along with Figures 3.2 and 3.3 are taken from *The Lexicon of The New Urbanism* by Duany Plater-Zyberk and Company. *(Diagram courtesy of Duany Plater-Zyberk and Company)*

location of failed shopping malls or other outdated commercial development (CNU, 2002). Calthorpe's successful reconstruction of an 18-acre derelict mall in Mountain View, California (1996–2001) into a mixed-use neighborhood where all residents live within a five-minute walk to a train station exemplifies this trend. This more integrated vision of an energy efficient, and less car-dependent lifestyle embodied in Transit-oriented Development derives from the longstanding interest among Calthorpe and his west coast collaborators in environmental and ecological issues, dating from their work on architecture and renewable energy in the 1970s. This agenda for a more sustainable urban environment has become a central one for many architects and planners who consider themselves New Urbanists, and during the 1990s it married with a rural counterpart developed by the planner Randall Arendt, and exemplified in his influential book, *Rural by Design: Maintaining Small Town Character* (Arendt, 1994).

Arendt's main contribution to New Urbanism and Smart Growth has been to approach the design of small town environments from the position of preserving the rural character of the surrounding countryside threatened by suburban expansion. His design approach first establishes the important rural features and landscape components of the property to be developed, safeguards these areas from building activity, and only then inserts new development carefully into the natural setting. By clustering development, more land can be set aside as permanently protected open space, and in many instances this ethos of landscape preservation has added considerable value to new housing. Americans have shown they will spend more money to live near protected green space (see Figure 2.16).

With careful planning at the community scale, these areas of open space can be connected together to create a long-lasting green infrastructure for the environmental benefit of the community (Arendt, 1994, 1996). One downside of this otherwise admirable approach is that the extra economic value conferred on properties developed in this manner raises the cost of housing above the level many people can afford. To overcome this objection, the town of Davidson, North Carolina, has enacted a zoning ordinance that both requires the preservation of 50 percent open space in new greenfield developments, and the provision of 12.5 percent of the new housing to be at price ranges refined as affordable, that is, accessible to people earning 80 percent of the national median income (Davidson, 2000). Taken together, these visions of urban and rural sustainability provide the strongest argument for New Urbanism in its alliance with the Smart Growth movement, and indeed, for New Urbanism to be synonymous with Smart Growth.

While Leon Krier was a major influence on the development of this New Urbanist agenda, his was by no means the only European influence. The work of several architects and urbanists who played crucial roles in the historical development of the Anglo-American city also contributed to New Urbanist theory and practice. A reprise of the range of influences brings back into focus several personalities we have already met earlier in the text. We have noted that Ebenezer Howard's Garden City reform movement, with its emphasis on well-planned, self-contained new towns served by transit and defined by large tracts of productive countryside, was also an important precedent for the TOD strand of New Urbanist theory. The work of Raymond Unwin, and his brother-in-law Barry Parker has also been crucial. We explained in Chapter 2 how Unwin and Parker gave tangible form to Howard's Garden City ideals in the English new town of Letchworth (1904) and Hampstead Garden Suburb in north London (1907). Unwin's book, *Town Planning in Practice* (1909) spread his planning and urban design ideas through Europe and America early last century, and the volume's recent republication in America (1994) has revived the relevance of the work to postmodern urban designers.

We have also clarified how Unwin himself was increasingly influenced by the work of the Austrian teacher and designer Camillo Sitte, whose book *City Planning according to Artistic Principles* (1889) set out principles regarding the artful composition of public space. Werner Hegemann and Elbert Peets (1922) summarized Sitte's findings for American professionals in the 1920s with the publication of their *The American Vitruvius*, and the book's republication in 1990 brought Sitte's work before a whole new generation of American urban designers. Hegemann and Peets also provided examples of European Garden Cities as well as codifying Beaux Arts concepts for American use. In addition, they illustrated America's own traditions of the City Beautiful movement, and their revived handbook became a seminal text for New Urbanist design in the 1990s.

In Europe there were other parallel movements in urban design that predated New Urbanism by several decades in some instances, but without notable influence at the time of the American movement's inception. This can largely be explained by the fact that despite their common emphasis on the street and the pedestrian, these parallel movements were picturesque and empiricist in inspiration as opposed to the rationalist approach to urbanism espoused by Krier. We explore this duality further in Chapter 4, but briefly we mean that the picturesque approach is based on understanding the city through human sensory experience (primarily visual), and this reliance on personal experience is a hallmark of empiricist philosophy. By contrast, Krier's approach uses typologies, or pre-existing patterns of urban form and space as the basic *a priori* building blocks of urbanism. This *a priori* deductive reasoning, which in design puts a higher priority on essential and unchanging consistencies of urbanism rather than the vagaries of visual experience, is deeply embedded in the rationalist strand of western philosophical thought.

In Britain, the previously mentioned work of Gordon Cullen provided a paramount example of the picturesque approach, and we have described how his book *Townscape* (1961) became a seminal work about pedestrian-scaled urban environments based on traditional elements of streets and squares. From the 1970s onward, this approach to urbanism gave rise to neotraditional developments in Britain under the rubric 'neo-vernacular design,' or 'pseudo-vernacular' to its critics. This trend was formalized with the publication of the official County of Essex *Design Guide for Residential Areas* (1973), a visual code book that established the principles of good (i.e. traditional) urban design which new developments were expected to follow. The Introduction complains that few people in the County of Essex were happy with the 'dreary suburban uniformity' of postwar housing. New buildings lacked any defining characteristics that made them specific to the region, and the regulations were intended to spur a 'more varied and imaginative approach' to design (County Council of Essex, 5). Using regulations to promote innovation might seem a counter-intuitive process, but the point of the Essex publication and others like it was to promote tighter, more pedestrian-friendly layouts of a type that were not achievable by means of developers' standard suburban designs. The new layout principles demanded design thinking of a higher standard, but at the same time, their basis of traditional forms made them easily understandable to professionals and lay people alike (see Figure 3.6).

In Spain, this neotraditional direction was presaged in 1929 by the idiosyncratic picturesque development of the *Pueblo Español*, or 'Spanish Village' as part of that year's international exhibition in Barcelona. Only a few hundred yards from Mies van der Rohe's modernist icon, the Barcelona Pavilion, the architectural team of Reventós, Folguera, Nogues and Utrillo created a brilliant encapsulation of traditional Spanish townscape. Organized as a warren of small streets linking three plazas, the urban composition faithfully recreated examples of Spanish vernacular buildings, and disposed them in ways that created a myriad of beautiful urban vignettes. A popular tourist destination ever since its creation, it was markedly out of step with the avant-garde architectural and urban doctrines of the times, and this masterwork has remained largely unknown and unappreciated by architects and planners for decades (see Figure 3.7).

Similar picturesque approaches to urban composition were also evident in France, exemplified by the 'Provincial Urbanism' of Jacques Riboud at La Verrière-Maurepas in St. Quentin-en-Yvelines outside Paris (1966). Seven years later, in southern

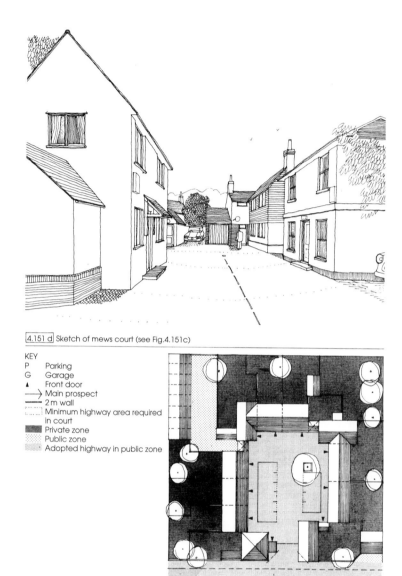

4.151 d Sketch of mews court (see Fig.4.151c)

KEY
P    Parking
G    Garage
▲    Front door
——▶  Main prospect
———  2 m wall
······  Minimum highway area required
       in court
▨    Private zone
     Public zone
     Adopted highway in public zone

**Figure 3.6** A page from the original 1973 version of the Essex 'Design Guide for Residential Areas.' These drawings illustrate the precept of using modest buildings to create coherent, spatially enclosed public space. (*Illustration courtesy of Essex County Council*)

France, Françoise Spoerry expanded on this use of traditional and picturesque urban forms in his resort development at Port Grimaud (1973) and later hilltown developments at nearby Gassin.

Most recently, during the late 1980s and 1990s, in tandem to New Urbanism, a new interest in 'urban villages' has developed. In Britain, under the impetus of HRH Prince Charles, and his planning advisor, the ever-present Leon Krier, this work focuses on the creation of sustainable mixed-use urban developments as the incremental building blocks of urban expansion

and redevelopment. The intent is to facilitate high quality but affordable urban living while preserving the economic and environmental resources of the countryside. One tangible result of this initiative has been the new village of Poundbury, outside Dorchester designed by Leon Krier in 1988, and the first phase of which was completed in 1997 (see Figure 3.8). In its idiosyncrasies and royal patronage, Poundbury has limited use as a precedent for everyday urbanism just as Seaside's unexpected success as a playground for the very affluent has curtailed its

**Figure 3.7** Pueblo Espanol, Barcelona, Reventós, Folguera, Nogues and Utrillo, 1927. Faithful reproductions of traditional Spanish architecture are used to re-create an intimate urban scale and sense of place. Created for the international exhibition of 1927, it remains a popular tourist destination today.

**Figure 3.9** Kirchsteigfeld, Potsdam, Germany, Rob Krier, 1992–2003. Rob Krier, brother of Leon, has used similar traditional urban typologies of street and square, but this new German suburb has been built with refreshingly crisp and clean contemporary aesthetics. Similar successful urban design in the USA is all too often rendered in clumsy, pastiche neo-classicism.

**Figure 3.8** Poundbury, Dorset, Leon Krier, 1988–97. Although cleverly designed by Leon Krier, Poundbury's overt traditional and neo-classical architecture has led several critics to dismiss this variant of New Urbanism as merely an exercise in nostalgia.

applicability to other sites in America. However, Poundbury is notable for Krier's use of picturesque composition, marking a move away from his previously strong rationalist roots. More important in the development of urban villages has been the general acceptance in the UK of this type of development at higher densities as the best approach to inner city regeneration, witnessed by new projects in Manchester, Birmingham, Liverpool and Bristol (Baker, 2003).

In mainland Europe since the mid-1970s, Leon Krier's brother Rob Krier has been steadily amassing a series of collaborative projects and built works that in their spatial language are indistinguishable from New Urbanism, and which are based largely on re-establishing continuity with the traditional form of the European city. This work is exemplified by the master plan by Krier–Kohl Architects for the new city district of Kirchsteigfeld, in Potsdam, Germany, a typological essay in streets, squares and perimeter blocks designed between 1992 and 1997 and partially complete in 2003 (Krier, R., 2003: pp. 84–99). What sets this and other European developments apart from spatially similar developments in America is the complete lack of historicist architecture in the build-out of the plan, accomplished by over thirty separate architectural firms. Instead of cornice mouldings and classical columns, the buildings at Kirchsteigfeld match crisp, contemporary aesthetics with traditional urban forms (see Figure 3.9).

This European neorationalist approach to city design displayed in the work of the Krier brothers, Aldo Rossi and others, and the neotraditional picturesque townscape popular in Britain, both emphasize the art of contextual relationships between buildings, and the importance of well-defined public space. This view of the human-scaled city found its American counterpart in the work of Paul Goodman,

Kevin Lynch, and Jane Jacobs during the early 1960s. Lynch's seminal work *Image of the City* (1960) introduced the powerful idea of making the city 'legible' to the user through the coding and manipulation of simplified urban elements such as districts, paths, edges, nodes and landmarks. Jacobs, in her powerful indictment of modernist city planning, *The Death and Life of American Cities* (1962), specifically reminded architects of the importance of the street in city life, though the message fell on deaf ears for at least another decade. The same points were repeated in Britain in 1973 by Nicholas Taylor in his book *The Village in the City*, where he argued for the return to traditional patterns of public and private space, front and back gardens, porches and streets as the necessary armature of community life (Taylor, 1973).

## NEW URBANISM AND SMART GROWTH

The three strands of New Urbanism that we have described earlier, Traditional Neighborhood Development, Transit-oriented Development and design for rural conservation, weave an agenda for more sustainable patterns of development that is virtually synonymous with Smart Growth. Planners, local government officials, citizens and an increasing number of developers have shown great interest in New Urbanist design, particularly in areas that are experiencing growth-related conflicts. Many see New Urbanism as an approach that enables a community's growth to be channeled into a physical form that is more compatible with the scale of existing neighborhoods, discourages excessive auto use, is less costly to service, and uses less land and natural resources. These attributes provide a pretty good description of Smart Growth, and although many definitions of Smart Growth exist in America from organizations like the Smart Growth Network, the National Resources Defense Council, the Sierra Club and the Urban Land Institute, to name only a few, there is common agreement around a basic set of principles.

Smart Growth means developing in ways that are environmentally responsible, economically viable, and well designed. A reasonable expectation, you might agree. But as we've seen, most suburban development in America over the last few decades fails these basic tests. Disused strip centers degrade the environment, suburban subdivisions cost more tax dollars to service that are recouped in property taxes, and an awful lot of suburbia is poorly laid out and shoddily built.

We have to do better, and to the three central criteria noted earlier we would add an important fourth: the ways that new developments are generated and regulated should involve citizens and stakeholders in an open democratic forum. Not only should urban public spaces be democratically open in their use; the ways they are produced should also be democratically transparent. But this public debate does not necessarily mean 'consensus.' Too often a search for consensus means agreeing around the lowest common denominator, the most minimal set of concepts that offend the least number of people. Time and again we have seen this process strip away all the best features of a proposal, until the scheme that's finally agreed upon is an empty shell, even a travesty of its original content and format. It is not consensus that's important; the crucial factor is a concentrated, open debate, to provide a fair and equal opportunity for concerned citizens to state their points of view. In this way officials who have to take the tough decisions are fully informed, and they know that different opinions have been aired during the design process.

This open process can be difficult, but the temptation to avoid this forum and to design developments behind closed doors away from the inconvenience and messiness of public scrutiny leads to equally severe problems. The attitude that 'the professionals know best' was invalidated by the errors architects and planners made during the modernist period of city building. To these mistakes we would add the very poor quality of private sector developments where architects and planners were minimally involved. Clearly, designers, planners and developers can all benefit from citizen involvement in creating their visions, however complicated and messy this process might be. In the case studies we discuss these issues in more detail, and examine how concentrated urban design charrettes can provide the best opportunities for mediating conflicts and educating a community about its future options.

Many citizens' groups are vocal in their opinions, and they have every right to demand the opportunity to speak about their ideas. But just because they're vocal doesn't mean they're right; many Smart Growth initiatives have been squashed by wrongheaded local opposition. Sometimes Smart Growth policies are enacted by government over the objections of local pressure groups, a process that requires considerable courage by elected representatives. It also means they, and their constituents, need to distinguish between myths and facts about Smart Growth. Indeed, much opposition to Smart Growth arises from misconceptions and misunderstandings about the relevant issues, and it is worth reviewing the basic principles and some of the most common errors before we go any further.

Not quite an error, but an important clarification concerns the similarities and differences between Smart Growth and 'sustainable development'. These terms are often used interchangeably, and we, the authors, are guilty of that on occasion. There is much overlap between the two concepts, and all physical design concepts that constitute Smart Growth support sustainable development. However, the adjective 'sustainable' adds a deeper dimension (Porter, 2000: p. 2). It implies a profound respect for long-term conservation of natural resources, energy conscious (green) building design and the enhancement of a community's human capital, raising important issues of social justice and equity. Appendix II sets out our set of Smart Growth principles dealing primarily with the physical design of communities, and adds a note or two *(in italics)* where sustainable development extends and deepens these concepts. Here we summarize some of the most important points under the headings of General Policies, Planning Strategies, and Urban Design Concepts.

## General policies

1. Plan collaboratively amongst municipalities within a region.
2. Target public investment to support development in key areas and to discourage development in others. Extend suburban areas only in locations where they can be supported by existing public facilities and services, or by simple and economic extensions of these services.
3. Reinforce the centers of cities, towns and neighborhoods. Locate regional attractions in city centers wherever possible, not in suburban locations.
4. Make development decisions predictable, fair, and cost effective. Involve community stakeholders and citizens in the decision-making process. Require zoning decisions to follow the adopted plan.
5. Provide incentives and remove some legislative barriers to persuade and enable developers to do the right thing. Make it easy to build smart developments and harder to build sprawl.

*Planning strategies*

6. Integrate land use and transportation planning to minimize the number of trips by car and the distances driven. Provide a range of transportation choices to mitigate congestion.
7. Create a range of affordable housing opportunities and choices.
8. Preserve open space around and within the community, as working farmland, areas of natural beauty or areas with fragile environments.
9. Maximize the capacity of existing infrastructure by reusing derelict urban sites and filling in gaps in the urban fabric. Preserve historic buildings and neighborhoods and convert older buildings to new uses wherever possible.
10. Foster a distinctive sense of place as a building block of community development.

*Urban design concepts*

11. Create compact, walkable neighborhoods with connected streets, sidewalks and street trees to make walking to work, to school, to the bus stop or train station, or just walking for pleasure and exercise, safe, convenient and attractive. Integrate offices and shops, along with community facilities such as schools, churches, libraries, parks, and playgrounds into neighborhoods to create places to walk to and reduce vehicle trips. Design for densities that can support active neighborhood life. (The Denver Regional Air Quality Council estimated that urban designs that follow these guidelines can reduce the Vehicle Miles Travelled (VMT) by as much as 10 percent (Allen, p. 16)).
12. Make public spaces the focus of building orientation and neighborhood activity. Move large car parks away from streets and screen them with buildings.

To all of which we would add:

13. Think three-dimensionally! Envision your community in urban design detail.

The concepts embodied in this list will be elaborated and exemplified in the Case Study section later in this book, but as noted earlier, it is important to separate myths about Smart Growth from the facts. Sometimes these myths are the result of honest misunderstandings; othertimes they are created by deliberate exaggeration and distortion of the facts by opponents of Smart Growth (of which, more later).

## MYTHS AND CRITICISMS OF SMART GROWTH AND NEW URBANISM

There are half-a-dozen myths in particular that circulate freely in American debates about Smart Growth, and it is important to put the record straight. These are:

1. Smart Growth is code for 'no growth.'
2. Smart Growth is all about high density.
3. Smart Growth is all about cities and wants to get rid of suburbs.
4. Smart Growth is anti-car.
5. Smart Growth doesn't work in the marketplace.
6. Smart Growth means more regulations that slow development and increase costs.

Let's take the first two points together; they are clearly in opposition to each other, which should tell us something straight away about the muddled thinking that still exists about this topic. Many developers are very suspicious about Smart Growth, fearing it will at the very least make life harder (see Myth no. 6) and at worst drive them out of business as citizens' groups urge more and more restrictions on development in order to stop growth in their community. Neighborhood groups on the other hand, often imagine that Smart Growth is either a plot by architects and planners forcing a high-density lifestyle upon them for some socialistic purpose, or it's a conspiracy by developers to get rich by building as many homes as possible on any given piece of land.

Before correcting these two myths, it is important to clarify the issue of density, for what is perceived as high density in an American residential neighborhood would be considered average or even low in Britain. In many public meetings we've held on this topic, Americans used to living in places that have only one or two houses per acre complain strongly about 'high' densities of 10 dwellings per acre. For comparative purposes, 10 units per acre (25 dwellings per hectare) is the average density currently built in British suburbs in 2000. However, the national government's Planning Policy Guidance Note (PPG3, 2000) regards this as too low, and recommends a minimum of 30 dwellings per hectare net, and a preferred range of between 30 and 50 dwellings per hectare net (12–20 units per acre). (These British figures are calculated on the net site area that excludes major roads and landscape buffers, so the actual gross densities to equate with American figures would be slightly lower.)

To extend this comparison, Parker and Unwin's model village at New Earswick, begun in 1902, is about 11 dwellings per acre, a figure consistent with that of the New Town of Runcorn, designed at a 'low' density in the 1970s to 'reduce overcrowding.' These differences in suburban community norms between America and Britain are less evident in the redevelopment of central urban areas. In a city like Charlotte, densities for downtown living range from older neighborhoods with four houses per acre to new mid-rise apartments at 100 dwellings per acre (26–650 persons per hectare). Foregoing the lowest densities in this spectrum, the range of medium to high numbers (20 units per acre and up) are broadly in line with British practice.

While attitudes to density in Britain and America vary, the fact that towns and cities will continue to grow is consistent in both countries. A 'no growth' strategy is impossible to uphold. The British government announced in February 2003 a major new development initiative for south-east England to cope with the anticipated need for as many as 800 000 new homes by 2030 in that part of the country (http://news.bbc.co.uk/2/hi/uk_news/england/2727399.stm). In America, the US Bureau of the Census expects the country's population to grow by 58 million people by 2020, or more than 21 percent.

While growth is inevitable, the way it is handled is not, and as shown by the 12-point list of principles earlier, Smart Growth advocates support many different strategies to improve the quality of development. Denser development is only one of many tactics. Density alone means nothing; in the wrong place it can be harmful, but as part of a more comprehensive strategy of mixed-use neighborhoods and alternative transportation choices – buses, trains, bicycles, walking – it is definitely part of the solution. The positive attributes of this strategy include a more walkable, less polluted environment, less reliance on the car, and easy access to shopping and employment.

Development should occur across a range of scales and densities depending on the situation and site conditions. Around transit stations that form the centers of new neighborhoods, in areas that have a mixture of uses, and along bus routes, densities should be medium to high, between 20 and 80 dwellings per acre (130–520 persons per hectare). This puts a large number of people in locations where they can reduce the use of their cars by riding trains and buses, and where they can walk conveniently to other uses in the neighborhood. Importantly, large apartment complexes should *not* be built in places that are distant from other facilities and only accessible by car. This just causes extra traffic and pollution as large numbers of new residents drive everywhere for everything. One of the conventional American land-use planning tools, zoning land near large roads as high density 'multi-family' apartments as a buffer between the highway and single-family neighborhoods, is therefore one of the least smart things to do.

In locations that are purely residential, densities should be lower, from 2 to 20 dwellings per acre (13–130 persons per hectare). The higher densities in this range should be used sparingly but are necessary to provide smaller, less expensive homes in locations dispersed throughout the community, and not all clustered in higher density areas. In theory, as one reaches the edges of any community the density should reduce dramatically as urban uses recede and rural uses dominate the landscape. However, as we well know, it is precisely these edge locations that receive most new growth pressure, and which often get swamped by a tide of new houses and apartments spread all across the landscape.

In this situation of sprawling at the edge, there are three basic strategies to manage this growth:

(a) If the proposed development doesn't meet Smart Growth criteria, and the vacant land has no water or sewer service, the municipality can stringently limit the development capacity of the land by refusing to spend public money to extend its lines or to build new ones. This option should be used more often, but many elected officials still believe their main task is to facilitate 'development' to improve their community's tax base, as noted in Chapter 2.

If it is judged sensible to allow growth at a particular edge location, or if water and sewer services are already available nearby, then the other two options come into play depending on circumstances:

(b) The new development can take the form of a higher density mixed-use 'urban village' that can create a new center for an evolving community; or

(c) It can be designed as a low density, low impact residential development that minimizes its effect on the environment and conserves as many of the site's environmental features as possible.

This discussion should make it obvious that Smart Growth isn't anti-suburb, as is often claimed by its detractors in Myth no. 3. Smart Growth is not all about cities and density at the expense of the suburbs. On the contrary, one of the aims of Smart Growth is to make *better* suburbs as part of a strategy to improve and extend the choices of urban and suburban lifestyles for homebuyers. Even the development industry in America is beginning to realize that the product they have been building for the last forty years has serious flaws. A 1998 report published by the Urban Land Institute, the developers' think tank and professional association, stated that conventional housing subdivisions, with their social isolation, segregated land use, car dependence and long commutes, did not meet consumers' needs to feel part of a real community (Warrick and Alexander, 1998). The following year the much-studied annual publication *Emerging Trends in Real Estate 1999* noted that standard suburbia may not be sustainable, with many low-density suburban communities suffering a loss of value due to poor design and increased traffic (O'Neill, 1999). Here is the paradox. Lots of Americans want to live in the suburbs, but they're fed up with problems created by standard suburban design. Smart Growth offers ways out of this dilemma with more advanced and integrated suburban design concepts.

From this brief discussion on suburban options it is easy to see that Smart Growth is not anti-car (Myth no. 4). Wanting to provide transportation choices to improve people's lifestyle is just the opposite. Smart Growth seeks to improve driving conditions by reducing the number of car trips people take every day. Road improvements and new roads have a big role to play as part of any integrated transportation strategy, but the need for public investment in new highways can be limited to everybody's advantage by reducing the amount people drive. Designing mixed-use communities to improve the balance between jobs and housing, and concentrating growth in established areas (especially if they are served by buses or trains) are two smart ways to lessen the need and the length of car trips, and to offer more choices of travel modes. By changing America's near total dependency on the car to a situation where we have more choice of how to get around our communities, we can help to reduce congestion, air pollution and save public money on new highways.

As noted in Chapter Two, the concept of more walkable communities has recently been supported by health professionals in the USA. Major research programs are underway to combat the big increases in the incidence of adult and child obesity, adult-onset diabetes and other ailments that are afflicting Americans who don't walk anywhere in their daily lives. A very small percentage of children walk to school, largely because it is impossible. New schools are generally located at the edge of communities and accessible only by car. The parents of these obese kids also don't walk. There are few places to walk to in the spread-out suburbs, and few sidewalks to walk on. The public health concept 'active living by design,' promoted by the Robert Wood Johnson Foundation in America, supports exactly the kinds of neighborhoods designed with Smart Growth and New Urbanist principles. This health initiative promotes a change of lifestyle for children and adults to one where walking becomes part of the normal daily activity. This attitude toward physical health for the general population is also extended to the elderly, and walkable neighborhoods can provide opportunities for the continued independence of older citizens when they can no longer drive.

The myth that Smart Growth doesn't work in the market place (Myth no. 5) is another common misconception that can be dispelled as easily as the other inaccuracies. One of the clearest signs of its increasing success and acceptance by the market is the increasing number of books and reports on the subject published in America by the Urban Land Institute, as noted earlier in the text. One of the ULI's missions is to lead the development industry and educate its members about new trends. ULI reports note that real estate values are expected to rise fastest in places that incorporate the attributes of successful cities, including a concentration of amenities, a mix of uses, and walkable neighborhoods (O'Neill, 1999: p. 11). People increasingly want to live in such places, whether they are city centers, or close-in neighborhoods, or in well-planned suburban fringe locations. Americans increasingly desire communities that balance new housing with places to work and shop, and preserve open space for natural beauty and environmental purposes.

The longing to live in such places is reflected in higher house prices, which is good and bad news; good that it reflects a clear market profitability, but bad as it limits affordability of housing, making the goal of a balanced, diverse and socially equitable community harder to achieve. Underlying the growing market success of Smart Growth development is a shift in demographics. Empty nesters, smaller families, married couples without children and single people are demographic groups that are growing, and looking for housing that reflects their priorities, including low-maintenance living and urban amenities. The US Census anticipates that 80% of all new households that will be formed by 2020 will comprise single people or couples with no children; already the traditional nuclear family accounts for less than one quarter of all American households. These demographic pressures will force the market to diversify, and Smart Growth developments will become increasingly profitable as they satisfy this inexorable demand. This same profitability extends to the commercial sector. Reports in *Urban Land* and the *Wharton Real Estate Review* in 2003 demonstrate that retail and office properties located as part of a mixed-use 'Main Street' type development often perform better than conventional suburban strip centers by substantial margins (Bohl, 2003; Rybczynski, 2003).

While these trends are impressive, opponents of Smart Growth and New Urbanism point to the overwhelming preponderance of conventional sprawl development in America, and ask why Smart Growth and New Urbanism didn't succeed long ago if the ideas are as good as they're claimed to be? Why don't they dominate the market place today?

The superficial reasonableness of this argument obscures the facts of history. As we have noted at some length, dispersed suburban development in America since World War II was implicitly directed by federal housing and transportation policies and subsidized by government funds, including generous tax breaks on mortgage interest payments. Low density, large lot, car-dependant suburban life has been heavily marketed as the zenith of American social achievement, and this pattern of consumption and land use has been bureaucratized by planners and engineers as the only modern way of building and developing. Developers generally have a history of following the line of least resistance to quick profits, and thus the marketplace has succumbed to years of direction, advertising and subsidies, churning out cookie-cutter subdivisions and strip shopping centers to meet the demands that have been manufactured in the minds of suburban Americans.

In short, it has not been a free market. Principles of planning and design now labeled as Smart Growth or New Urbanist were illegal under most local zoning codes across America for 40 years. In many places they still are. Until very recently, consumers have not had much of a choice. In a parody of Henry Ford's famous offer of customer choice of color for his Model T (any color so long as it's black) homebuyers and business owners during the 1950s through the 1980s could choose either conventional suburbia, or … conventional suburbia. Now that Smart Growth and New Urbanist options are becoming available, they are claiming an increasing share of the suburban market, while studies have shown that the unmet demand that exists today for compact, alternative forms of development comprises between 30 and more than 50 percent of the same market (Steuteville, 2001: pp. 1, 3–4). This consumer preference will likely grow as more and more smart developments come on line. Meanwhile there is clear evidence from developers' own costing comparisons that New Urbanist developments are more cost effective than their conventional sprawl counterpart.

The developers of a New Urbanist community in Commerce City, Colorado costed out a compact New Urbanist development and compared it in detail with an alternative conventional subdivision for the same site. The total development costs for the 171 acre (68.4 hectares) Belle Creek community came to $6.9 million for the New Urbanist scheme against $6.5 million for the conventional design. However, the conventional design yielded only 175 units, 146 single-family, and 29 townhouses. By comparison, the New Urbanist version yielded 212 units, 183 single-family, and 29 townhouses. This greater yield reduced the developers' cost per lot to $32 567 in the New Urbanist design as opposed to the more expensive $37 146 per lot in the conventional version (Schmitz: p. 183).

The last of our six myths, that Smart Growth means more government regulations that slow development and increase costs is the hardest to disprove, as there is sometimes a disconnect between theory and practice. In theory, local governments wishing to promote Smart Growth will revise their regulations to streamline the process of approval and provide incentives for developers to comply with the new rules. In practice this isn't always so. The decade of the 1990s in America is littered with examples of Smart Growth initiatives that were frustrated by city zoning ordinances and development regulations that made innovative developments based on traditional urbanism illegal. There were several other instances where the project was realized only by the persistence of the developer and his or her architects in the face of official opposition and adherence to outdated standards. Many, many more developers gave up and reverted to standard sprawl subdivisions that were approved easily. Fortunately this depressing situation is changing. The authors and their colleagues in the Lawrence Group have collectively been involved since 1994 in rewriting zoning ordinances and development regulations for nearly two dozen towns and cities in the southeastern states of America, including

model codes for the Atlanta metropolitan region. Many other architect-planners are at work on the same task across America.

The codes we write embody the Smart Growth principles noted earlier in this chapter, and also provide incentives to reward developers for embracing the more advanced ideas, including speedy approvals for complying with the more design specific rules. The codes are focused around traditional urban concepts, and in their content and graphic format, they go a long way to resolving the problems of implementing Smart Growth concepts (see Appendices III, IV and V). However, there is one further difficulty: elected officials are sometimes reluctant to give approval quickly to new schemes within their jurisdiction, thus obviating one of the main incentives to developers. Sometimes this is to avoid the impression of government being merely the handmaiden of developers. At other times, elected officials and some professional planners have trouble in reorienting their thinking toward new concepts of design and building form and away from conventional formulas based on use and generic dimensions. Progress is being made in this vitally important area, and we discuss some of our examples further in our case studies.

As we noted before, some of these myths arise from honest misconceptions about new ideas, but at other time, opponents of Smart Growth and New Urbanism spread disinformation deliberately. Most of this latter kind of opposition in America comes from groups on the conservative right of the political spectrum. At a convention in February 2003, a coalition of right-wing, libertarian and free-market organizations met to plot the downfall of Smart Growth. These groups, such as the Thoreau Institute, the Buckeye Institute, the Cascade Policy Institute, the Heartland Institute, Heritage Foundation, and the Reason Foundation, publicly despise Smart Growth and New Urbanism as intrusive government planning and 'social engineering' that tramples on Americans' 'rights' to do whatever they want with their land. Not content with spreading disinformation, the 2003 conference actively promoted smear campaigns against Smart Growth advocates and New Urbanists. Speakers at the event advised attendees to 'relentlessly' undermine the credibility of professionals like ourselves, and paint us and our colleagues in the minds of the public as 'pointy-headed intellectual fascists' out to ruin people's lives (Langdon, 2003b: p. 7). Theorists of *laissez-faire* economics view the world as inhabited only by self-focused consumers and taxpayers; the whole premise of urban design and collaborative planning is anathema to them because it's based upon public-spirited concepts of common good and integrated, long-term public interest.

It is hard to remain dispassionate in this context. Groups like this make the lives of urban designers and planners difficult because they are usually well funded, and cleverly organized. Countering their propaganda and regular attacks on Smart Growth can be almost a full-time job in itself, but we can take some comfort from the increasing fervor of the anti-Smart Growth message. The increased opposition shows that concepts of Smart Growth are successfully gaining ground in the market place, and in the mind of the American public as more and more walkable, transit-supportive developments are constructed. Ordinary Americans can increasingly see the advantages for themselves.

The extent and determination of this political opposition to progressive planning in the USA distinguishes American professional practice from its British counterpart. While democratic protest against development of all sorts has a long and venerable tradition in the UK, the organized, national campaign, focused from one end of the political spectrum on the work of architects and planners has few equivalents in Britain. For our right-wing opponents, Smart Growth and New Urbanism are combined and inflated into one single threat to 'American freedom.' But New Urbanism itself often comes under separate attacks from within the architectural profession and academia. The most common of these are the accusations of romantic nostalgia, and avoiding the 'realities' of the contemporary city. These charges appear in many critiques of traditional urbanism (Forty and Moss, 1980; Ingersoll, 1989; Sudjic, 1992; Rybczynski, 1995; Landecker, 1996; Huxtable, 1997; Chase, Crawford and Kaliski, 1999). These critics characterize New Urbanism as an escapist desire to avoid complex realities by returning to a rose-tinted imagined past, even a falsification of history (Ellis, 2002). English critics in the 1980s attacked the 'pseudo-vernacular' as promoting a false mythology of rural village life, while some American commentators accuse New Urbanists of using traditional urban forms to promote a fantasy world of small town America, where the memories of unpleasant facts like racial segregation are expunged from history. Other writers falsely identify New Urbanism with low-density suburbs, and claim its practitioners are 'dismissive of the present urban landscape' (Kaliski, 1999). This is linked with the criticism that regularly surfaces in academic and other writings is the charge that New Urbanists want to impose a sanitized, simplified

representation of reality on the complex pluralism that is the contemporary city (Safdie, 1997).

It seems to us that all these criticisms are based on a caricature of New Urbanism, either falsely constructed for the purposes of theoretical argument, or simply based on a massive misreading of the circumstances. It is as if these critics believe for their own purposes that New Urbanism begins and ends with the cute aesthetics of Seaside, instead of being a multifaceted urban and environmental movement. The reader can be the best judge of whether the work illustrated in the case studies in Chapters 7–12 is guilty as charged, or whether the critics miss their aim by a mile. When we're working with residents in a poor African-American neighborhood to bring them affordable housing and a dignified environment (Chapter 11) it's laughable (almost insulting) to accuse New Urbanism of escapism and avoiding unpleasant facts from America's history. When we work to manage the ecology of a suburban region by protecting its natural infrastructure; by setting out policies and designs for a better balance of jobs and housing to reduce commuting and improve air quality; and by integrating transit options into the future lives of all sectors of the population, (Chapter 7), it's equally galling for this kind of work to be misrepresented as the imposition of a singular, limited vision out of touch with reality and demonstrating a 'carelessness towards existing conditions' (Kaliski, 1999: p. 101).

The disdain some academic theorists have for New Urbanism is predicated on the fact that the language of traditional urbanism has been able to build a bridge between design theory and development practice. Our colleagues in academia like to argue that our ideas have merely become commodified, co-opted and transformed into shallow concepts useful to a developer in maximizing his or her profit. Academics, and some professional architects, tend to feel tainted by the association with developers, and seek to distance themselves from the 'sullied' environment of the marketplace.

We find this convergence of design theory and development practice unusual – but helpful. We are used to being in conflict with developers, and finding ourselves more in harmony with traditional adversaries can be disorienting. Only a decade ago at the beginning of the 1990s, to propose ideas of traditional urbanism in the context of American sprawl was to invite scorn and derision from developers and builders. In terms of slowing or stopping the juggernaut of sprawl this alliance between theory and practice, between design and development, embryonic though it is, is an essential bond, to be nurtured in every way possible. Now of all times is not the time to break away in search of new theoretical forms of urbanism while parts of our cities decay and our environment is degraded. As a society, we have our work cut out to improve our American habitat before these problems reach unmanageable proportions.

Urban design in America involves trying to make order out of chaos. While theoreticians and fellow academics might laud this chaos as vital and exuberant, most people who have to live and work in it just find it ugly and depressing. Believe us: it is. (See Figure 2.13). The denigration of New Urbanism, and the call to teach 'chaos theory instead of Italian hill towns' often heard in architectural schools rings hollow to those of us engaged in trying to improve this mess on the ground. Fancy theories from Europe and America that celebrate concepts of cacophony, discontinuity, fragmentation and spatial fluidity, and a disdain for traditional urban space in favor of 'zones of transition' (Koolhas and Mau, 1995: p. 1162) are fine from the luxurious context of an historic European city or an American ivory tower. But out in the spatial purgatory that comprises much of the American built landscape of the last fifty years such privileged intellectualizations have little relevance. Urban design is not about surfing chaos; it is about providing clarity and humanity in a harsh and confusing world, and saving our environment from our society's selfish depredations. Traditional urbanism – the world of the street, square and urban block – is not a quixotic effort to recreate an American past that didn't exist (Ellis, 2002: p. 267). It modernizes and retrofits historical patterns that are still relevant today, accepting the most advanced technologies, and matching the emerging new demographics in American society. It is the best weapon we have in our quest for a sustainable urban future.

# Devices and designs: sources of good urbanism

## SYNOPSIS

This chapter affirms two of our central beliefs: place matters, and places are best produced through the use of traditional urban forms. As validation of these convictions we journey to an unlikely setting, rural Mississippi, and the Neshoba County Fairgrounds, a self-made urban jewel in the heart of the countryside. From this example we can learn some basic concepts of urban design about the arrangement of buildings in space and the formation of 'urban rooms.'

The Fairgrounds also embody all three of the urban design methodologies we examine in the second section of this chapter: typology, picturesque urbanism, and designing for the social use of space. We place these concepts in a philosophical triangle of rationalism, empiricism, and pragmatism, important pillars of western thought, and illustrate how design action can draw inspiration from these philosophical bases.

Finally, we return to address a critique of traditional urbanism raised briefly in Chapter 1, namely that the streets and squares we are busy designing are nothing more than the setting for a shallow consumerist spectacle, a 'café society.' We offer a refutation to this criticism and outline a pragmatic *modus operandi* for urban designers in the face of complex and conflicting realities.

## THE AFFIRMATION OF PLACE

All the conversations in Chapter 3 have been predicated upon one fundamental point of view: place matters. The physical settings that support and enrich our daily lives matter to the extent they are functional, beautiful, and special to us in one or more ways. Richard Florida's focus on place (in Chapter 1) as an economic engine of prosperity through the emergence of a new, place-hungry 'creative class' reinforces this perspective. William J. Hudnutt III, long-time mayor of Indianapolis and now a resident fellow for public policy at the Urban Land Institute, confirms Florida's diagnosis, noting that the younger generation of wealth producers look for 'location first, jobs second' (Hudnutt, 2002). What count for the 'laptop crowd' and other creative people are the quality of life and the quality of the places where it's lived. These highly skilled young professionals take the attitude that they can work anywhere, so they look first for places that are attractive and possess the active urban lifestyle they are seeking. Generally, this combination comprises, as we have noted before, a synergy between venues of entertainment and culture and cool places to live. This means restaurants, bars and pubs, arts and music, walkable neighborhoods and districts with sidewalk cafés, streets with trees and attractive street furniture, and a variety of housing choices in a variety of price ranges.

All this energy focuses on public space, the setting for people's behavior in the world outside themselves, and the medium of their personal and community orientation. Our professional concentration on the traditional vocabularies of street and square, park and plaza, Europe's most coherent forms of public space and those most supportive of community values, will be well understood in Britain and its continental neighbors. However, in America in the early twenty-first century such spaces are still the exception rather than the rule. So we hope our British readers will forgive us if we seek once more to make this essential point regarding the relevance of traditional urban spaces. This time we use an example chosen for the dramatic impact of its odd setting. Places don't get much odder for an urbanist that rural Mississippi, but that's where we are headed to next.

That we can travel to rural Mississippi in America's Deep South and find ourselves in the midst of a sophisticated, self-made urban environment of close-packed streets and squares affirms our belief in traditional forms of urbanism. The Neshoba County Fairgrounds, a little over eight miles southwest of the small town of Philadelphia, Mississippi, demonstrate an unambiguous urge to be urban in the most unlikely setting. This Mississippi backwater is chiefly remembered in history for the brutal slaying of several civil rights activists during the early 1960s, while they were campaigning for the right to vote for American blacks. But some attitudes have changed in the last 40 years, and the Neshoba County Fairgrounds provide an odd mix of Southern conservatism and religious fervor combined with a lively sociability and ardent festivities. The cultural importance of Neshoba in the American South was illustrated when California Governor Ronald Reagan chose the Fair as the site of his announcement that he was running for President of the United States in the 1980 election.

For British readers we should explain that the annual county fairs and larger state fairs in America are very important events in the life of communities. There is a strong agricultural bias to the Neshoba event, but the festivities, which last only a week, also include fairgrounds with rides, carousels, and sideshows (called 'Midways' in America) and horse races. The closest English equivalent would be a combination of a County Show, the annual regatta week at holiday resorts around the coast, and a large village fete, but this doesn't really come close in terms of scope and activity. One of the most interesting things about these community festivals is that they often include permanent structures on site, used only for the hectic few weeks in the summer for the fair and its preparation. The Neshoba County Fairgrounds are unusual in that the community of self-built two-storey wooden cabins resembles a permanent town, laid out in a pattern of streets and squares with a consistent range of building types (Craycroft, 1989) (see Plate 1 and Figure 4.2).

The arrangement of the buildings on site, together with their details and materials of construction, have been controlled by common agreement between the families, some of whom have inhabited the settlement over several generations since the Fair's founding in 1895. Families return year after year for the one week each summer when the place is active with music, dancing, political and religious rallies, produce and craft fairs and horse racing events. For the remainder of the year family members visit the Fairgrounds occasionally to carry out maintenance and improvements to their temporary homes.

A Fair Board, acting as a sort of town council, oversees adherence to the informal zoning regulations, adopted as 'The House and Garden Rules' in 1958. These rules set out the overall size and massing of the buildings (originally 16-feet wide by 30-feet deep by two storeys high) and specify consistently tight (four feet) spacing between buildings. The only exceptions to this spacing are for existing trees; no tree can be cut without the Fair Board's approval. Where trees complicate the spacing of buildings, the extra width of space is used for ancillary elements like side porches or extra parking. Figure 4.1 illustrates how all structures have to face onto public space, respect 'build-to' lines along the streets, and are required to incorporate double-height front porches and gable roof forms for the houses (Craycroft: p. 100). The buildings and spaces produced by the application of these vernacular urban and architectural conventions blend typological consistency with many small variations bred of personal taste, preference and material choices.

The 16-feet width of the cabins has practical roots: the construction of the dwellings is generally timber balloon frame, and the longest available timber came in 16-foot lengths. Ground floors are raised two to three feet above the ground to avoid dampness and termites, and within this gable-roofed two-storey form, a common suite of secondary items such as steps, railings, posts and doorways comprise a vocabulary of details.

The Fair Board also monitors new applications for membership, and has on several occasions agreed to new 'subdivisions' of cabins built as extensions to the original 'town form'. These new areas have been constructed to regular grids, have wider cabins (24 feet), and have more enclosed, air-conditioned areas rather than open porches. These newer extensions to the Fair lack the charm of the more informal, older neighborhoods, where the specified dimensional order is warped by site circumstances like trees and gullies to provide a degree of irregular 'picturesque' urbanism unusual for most American communities (see Figure 4.2). There is a constant tension between the traditionalists and the newcomers, pitting authenticity to tradition against modern conveniences (Craycroft: p. 96). The issues concern more than just

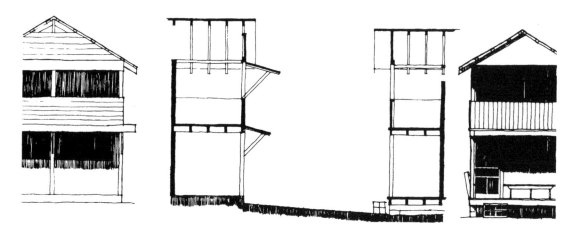

**Figure 4.1** Section Through a Typical 'Street' at Neshoba County Fair. This drawing illustrates how porches and verandas on the building façades facing the public space of the 'street' may vary in detail and size but not in their basic form and orientation. The requirement for all structures to include these spaces in their design contributes hugely to the exciting interplay of public and private spaces throughout the Fair. See also Plate 2. *(Drawing courtesy of Robert Craycroft)*

**Figure 4.2** Figure-ground Site Plan of Neshoba County Fair, 1980s. The newer neighborhoods are easily recognized by their more regular and geometric layout. Founders' Square is toward the lower left of the plan, with the community assembly pavilion slightly off-center within it. The large oval space is formed by the race track. *(Drawing courtesy of Robert Craycroft)*

aesthetics; when air-conditioned, closed spaces replace open front porches, the social dynamic changes dramatically. People have to be invited inside as opposed to the casual open neighborliness of the older parts of the Fairgrounds where the semiprivate/semipublic nature of the front porches invites a wide range of social discourse. Suburban priorities of isolation and separateness are making themselves felt even here.

Despite this suburbanization of social attitudes on the part of some residents, the design and planning concepts underlying the Neshoba County Fairgrounds are distinctly urban, even though it sits in the context of rural Mississippi. This paradox, while usefully validating our contention that certain forms of traditional urbanism have universal applicability, can be partly explained by the fact that Mississippi, although neither a prosperous nor progressive state, is blessed with many fine 'courthouse square' towns, such as Philadelphia, Oxford, and Holly Springs. In these towns, usually county seats, the neoclassical or neo-Gothic courthouse commands the middle of the town square, with a more or less regular grid of streets extending outward on all sides. This regional cultural form (it is also common in the American mid-west) provides a precedent in miniature of European urban layouts, filtered through several layers of cultural transformation, but still clearly recognizable. Figure 4.3 illustrates clearly the typological similarity between Neshoba and its grander precedent by means of a section through the courthouse and square in

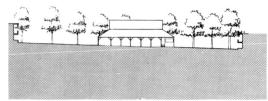

Founders Square, Neshoba County Fair

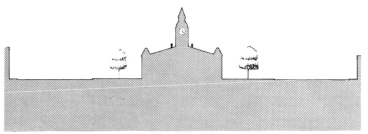

Courthouse Square, Philadelphia, Mississippi

**Figure 4.3** Founders' Square, Neshoba County Fair compared with the Courthouse Square in Neighboring Philadelphia, Mississippi. Drawn at the same scale, these two spaces clearly illustrate typological similarities. In both cases, a geometrically formal space is enclosed around a focal community building. *(Drawing courtesy of Robert Craycroft)*

Philadelphia. Mississippi, compared with a same-scale section through Founders' Square at Neshoba Fairgrounds.

It is interesting to compare the scale and density of the Fairgrounds to its urban neighbor, Philadelphia. The temporary population of the Fair is about 6500 people, the same as the nearby town. However, Philadelphia covers 370 acres (148 hectares) at a density of 17 persons per acre (42 persons per hectare) or about six dwellings per acre (15 per hectare). Neshoba, by contrast houses its 6500 people on 57 acres (23 hectares) at a density of 115 persons per acre (287 persons per hectare) or approximately 44 dwellings per acre (110 per hectare) (Craycroft: p. 130).

The plan of the Neshoba County Fairgrounds provides a fascinating organic adaptation of this recti-linear form with the community pavilion located approximately in the center of Founders' Square. The layout is full of site-specific quirks, but everywhere it's clear that traditional urban typologies are the basis for all transformations. Public streets are lined with 'houses' constructed with semiprivate porches that provide the transition from the public world of the street into the private realm of the interior (see Plate 2). Even more notable is the communal commitment to what are in effect mandatory urban design regulations for the layout and construction of the dwellings. In the region beyond the Fairgrounds, the pervading culture is one of self-assertive property rights, and individual property owners largely reject regulatory control over private land and development.

This vernacular example of urban typologies and their encoding into local custom marks an interesting intersection with New Urbanism's focus on creating urban and building codes for the development of new communities. Duany and Plater-Zyberk's code for Seaside, Florida, produced in 1983, marked the beginning of this important realization that designing the right code was as important as designing the master plan for any community. It is noteworthy in this regard to recall a visit made to the Neshoba County Fairgrounds by Andres Duany in 1985, where Professor Robert Craycroft from the School of Architecture at Mississippi State University, and a leading authority on the Fairgrounds, explained the coding of this self-regulating community to Duany. (The English author was a colleague of Professor Craycroft at that time at MSU, and also benefitted from his extensive knowledge of the Fairground's urban qualities.) The development of codes that inform and regulate the design of buildings, and how buildings relate to public space, is a central thesis of New Urbanist theory and practice, and the Neshoba example is important because it shows that using codes to control urban form is possible even in cultures unsympathetic to regulation. The central point in this instance seems to be that the codes serve the community's self-interest and maintain its unique character to the benefit of all.

It is not simply the compendium of appropriate urban design concepts – streets and squares designed as outdoor public rooms – that makes Neshoba County Fairgrounds a useful example. One of the most important points in the analysis is the way the Fairgrounds bear witness to three powerful traditions of urbanism: the typological heritage of past forms used in a contemporary context; the picturesque approach to civic design; and designing for the social use of space, rather than simply its appearance. These three traditions provide useful methodologies for contemporary urban designers, and most practitioners utilize a personal combination of all three approaches. Our own design perspective colors the analysis that follows (it's a little heavy on the picturesque) but the important lesson is to demonstrate how a clear basis of theory can directly inform how we and others work on the ground in communities.

## URBAN DESIGN METHODOLOGIES

Good urban design is important in every neighborhood and every district in every city, and the range of urban design techniques is extensive. In this section, we outline some of the most simple, yet potent concepts of urban design and hope that designers and non-designers alike will find them as useful as we do. We start with simple ideas and then relate them to a deeper level of philosophical principles. Later on, in Chapter 6, we discuss some practical extensions of these ideas and their application to everyday matters of urban design and planning.

Urban design can mean different things to different people. To architects it can simply mean designing buildings that are responsive to their urban context. To landscape architects it often means detailing the surfaces of public spaces with hard and soft landscape elements and materials. To planners, it has usually connoted some hazy notion of urban beautification (Lang, 2000). We prefer a more holistic definition as we have indicated throughout the book. For us, urban design is no more and no less than the design in three dimensions of the public infrastructure of the city and its relationship to the natural environment. Urban design is the intersection of architecture and planning, and one of its main foci is the way buildings relate to each other to create the public domain of cities, towns and villages.

At its best, urban design is the agent of transformation from abstract 'space' to humanized 'place' – and one of our favorite definitions of place is 'space enriched by the assignment of meaning' (Pocock and Hudson, 1978). It is the urban designer's responsibility to collate and synthesize the historical, physical and

historical factors that help provide such layers of meaning and emotional richness.

To realize these objectives we use a vocabulary of straightforward techniques, and the applicability of these concepts and methods of design to the profession of planning was reinforced for us when one of the authors taught a workshop about urban design for planners in North Carolina in the Spring of 2003. Over two half days, teams of experienced professionals grappled with designing developments on infill urban sites. We say designing – not planning – for a particular reason: the participants were not allowed to create their normal planners' bubble diagrams of uses linked with arrows. Instead they had to think in terms of specific building footprints and the sizes and character of public spaces. The planners were operating at or beyond the limit of their professional competence, for designing doesn't come easy to a profession that hasn't been taught concepts of form and space for several decades.

Despite the rules of the workshop, the planners started out by doing what they'd been trained to do: they 'planned' by diagraming different uses in abstract zones on a site plan without reference to building form or spatial dimension. Many of the ideas were appropriate, but the colored diagrams only scratched the surface of the given problems. Challenged to move beyond abstraction, planners eventually found they knew more than they gave themselves credit for. For example, they knew that a good depth for an apartment building was 40–50 feet. Sixty to 80 feet deep was appropriate for retail, while offices in America generally require floorplates from 90–120 feet deep. (Unlike Europe, internal, windowless offices are normal in the USA.) When the teams drew the actual dimensions and shapes of buildings, and located them specifically on the site, whole new levels of consideration opened up. Where was the front of the building? Where was the back? How were these two conditions different? Where might the front entrances be located? Where was the service and loading bay? What degree of enclosure was appropriate for public space? Where did public space begin and end? Where were the thresholds between public space and private space? And how could these transitions be handled? These issues simply don't appear at the level of colored diagrams of uses. But they are vital factors in the creation of any successful urban place.

The planners in the workshop relished this new scope and level of detail. They didn't need to draw beautifully; they just needed to commit to a layout of buildings and spaces and draw the plan with some degree of accurate scale. Then they could evaluate their outline solution, and improve it with a second, and a third drawing.

One issue stood out above all others – the relationship between the fronts and backs of buildings. It is a general rule of urban design (to be broken *very* rarely, if ever) that building fronts should face building fronts and backs should face backs. In this way, territory and patterns of activity can be identified and public spaces defined and distinguished from private. In a simple example of a typical street of houses, 'public' front gardens face each other across the sidewalks and roadway, while 'private' backyards are adjacent to similar spaces at the rear of homes. As individuals and families, we have different patterns of socially accepted behavior for each zone. It is easy to imagine the spatial and social confusion if someone's front garden and front door faced a private backyard. The cohesion of the public realm would have been breached by the intrusion of private space, and private areas compromised by excessive visibility. This simple principle applies to all scales of urban development ... or it should.

However, this was new information to many planners used to working in more or less exclusively suburban situations. In the suburbs the looser spatial pattern of buildings allows dysfunctional back-to-front relationships to be masked by distance or landscape screening with no consideration given to the design and integrity of the public realm – the spaces between buildings – especially from the point of view of the pedestrian. Structures are sited very carelessly in suburbia because the quality of the public realm is rarely an issue. The only 'public' spaces we walk across are asphalt parking lots. The concept of public space as an 'outdoor room' for shared community activities has been forgotten.

Outdoor rooms, be they long skinny ones like streets, more rectangular versions like squares and plazas, or irregular and green like neighborhood parks, all have one thing in common: a greater or lesser degree of spatial enclosure. Spatial enclosure is a function of the proportions of the space – the height of the buildings relative to the width of the space. From experience and the study of precedent, good height-to-width ratios for spaces that feel comfortable for a variety of human activities range from the tightness of 1:1 or 2:1 for pedestrian activities (a more extreme ratio of 3:1 can be pleasantly dramatic) to a more relaxed standard of 1:3 and up to a maximum of 1:6 for spaces that include cars, either

moving or parked (see Figures 4.4–4.5). Beyond the height-to-width ratio of 1:6, all sense of enclosure is lost; the width of the space is too great and the building height too low (see Figure 4.6).

The condition of enclosure generated by the height-to-width ratio of the space is related simply to the physiology of the human eye. If the width of a public space is such that the pedestrian's cone of vision encompasses more sky than building façades, then the feeling of enclosure is slight. In the reverse condition, where the building façades predominate, the feeling of enclosure is heightened.

The other important notion never to forget is that these major public rooms must be enclosed by the *fronts* of buildings, not the backs, and rarely the sides. The front façades of buildings are their public faces, and as such they must front onto public space, whether it's a street, square or a neighborood park as illustrated in Figure 4.7.

**Figure 4.4** Fosse Street, Dartmouth, Devon. The tight urban enclosure enhances the social experience of shopping for residents and visitors alike in this seaside town. Note how the vista is terminated by the tower of the parish church.

**Figure 4.5** Birkdale Village, Huntersville, NC, Shook Kelly, 2002. The more relaxed spatial enclosure of this 'urban village' accommodates the car while providing generous spaces for pedestrians (see also Plates 4–7). *(Photo courtesy of Crosland Inc., and Shook Kelly)*

**Figure 4.7** Latta Park, Dilworth, Charlotte, NC. The social space of this neighborhood park is defined by the homes (behind the trees) lining the public streets around the perimeter. Activities are supervised informally by the resident who look over the space and by pedestrians on the streets.

**Figure 4.6** Rosedale Commons, Huntersville, NC, 2000. The low scale of the buildings around the square defeats any intention of creating an inviting enclosed space for pedestrians. This weak element mars an otherwise attractive development with an integrated mixture of uses and a good pedestrian structure (see also Figure 6.37).

The design planners' workshop convinced us of the urgent need for this kind of information – fronts and backs and public rooms – as the foundation for more elaborate concepts. The participants were hungry for the knowledge and eager to develop and refine their skills. Within a few hours of intensive work these non-designers were creating some quite sophisticated designs with clear spatial ideas (see Figure 4.8). The drawings were basic but sufficient to communicate the spatial arrangements, and the important thing to grasp here is that careful drawings like these begin to deal with three dimensions in terms of anticipated building height and widths of spaces. These three-dimensional qualities can be explored further in section, a vertical slice through the buildings and site that delineates building heights and ground levels. One doesn't need to draw perspectives to design in three dimensions. Urban designers do so, either by hand or computer-generated models, to develop a design more thoroughly, but for non-designers, the section can establish many key qualities of public space, scale and building massing (see Figure 4.9).

Sometimes, basic urban design is as simple as this: size the buildings correctly and locate them in space so that public space is clearly defined. In real life it's usually more complex and subtle, and urban design isn't simply a pragmatic affair of common sense techniques. It has deeper levels of meaning and operation, and the different ways of working noted earlier can be traced back to key philosophical concepts in western thought: typology to rationalism, picturesque urbanism to empiricism and designing for the social use of space to pragmatism. We'll begin our review of urban design methods with typology, a basically simple but often misunderstood notion.

## Typology

Knowing the dimensions of various types of buildings is the first move toward working typologically,

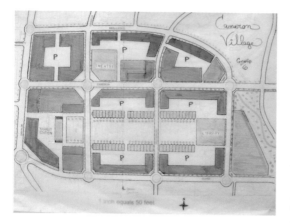

**Figure 4.8** Design for a redeveloped suburban shopping center. This quick sketch from an urban design workshop for planners was produced by professional planning officers with no formal training in design or graphics. Although a little crude, it shows a clear grasp of the spatial enclosure needed to define effective public space, with buildings fronting onto streets and a large formal lawn between two public buildings.

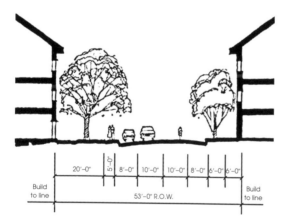

**Figure 4.9** Typical 'Street Section' Drawing. Properly proportioned sections – vertical slices through buildings and spaces – effectively engage the three-dimensional qualities of a design proposal by illustrating the heights and relative sizes of buildings, trees, people and cars.

that is, using established norms to design new projects. It's a very powerful tool, especially when it combines building mass and urban space at the same time. Clearly, the formality of the American courthouse square typology (of civic building and public space) that underlies the original layout of Neshoba County

Fairgrounds reinforces the civic attributes of a space in a direct and potent manner. The lineage of this particular typology can also be seen in an important series of Renaissance paintings of the 'Ideal City' (see Plate 3).

This makes clear what we mean when we use the term typology: consistent patterns for buildings and urban spaces that are derived from historical examples and which can be used and reused in different contemporary conditions. In some ways it's the opposite of modernist belief that 'form follows function,' or that each function has its own special form. Functionalism is derived from a biological analogy, where each species in the natural world demonstrates its own particular characteristics, but in urban terms this correspondence quickly breaks down.

We understand that the same building form can accommodate several different functions during its lifetime through a process of conversion and adaptive reuse. The form of a building can be far more permanent than its use, and this enables us to think of certain building plan types that might suit a variety of different uses. Even a cursory analysis of cities reveals the existence of some consistent patterns of buildings and urban spaces that have been utilized in different locations, conditions and times for their own merit, without a primary recourse to function. For example, the perimeter block – where buildings ring the edges of a site like a rectangular doughnut – appears in cities all over Europe and America across several centuries. The uses in the buildings may vary within the space of the block and during the life of the buildings; the basic form, however, remains the same (see Figure 4.10).

This appreciation of the longevity of form over the transience of function, the reliance on time-tested models of urbanism, and the belief in the universal (or at least wide ranging) applicability of these concepts in many different contexts, relates typological design to principles of Rationalist philosophy dating from the European Enlightenment in the seventeenth century. At that time, great thinkers like Frenchman René Descartes (1596–1650) sought universal laws and principles by which to comprehend the world, an intellectual position that was not limited by the vagaries of human experience. Typology has become a common term in architectural discourse, but not in the allied disciplines, and it's not always clearly defined. It's often confusing to nonarchitects, as it is to many architects and students of architecture raised in the Fountainhead tradition of the architect as the creator of unique and original forms.

**Figure 4.10** Perimeter Block, Charlotte, NC, LS3P Architects, 2003. Apartments line the public streets, creating a pleasant central courtyard despite the rather anaemic pseudo-classicist architecture. This space is shared by the residents but is distinct from the fully public realm of the city beyond.

**Figure 4.11** South Quadrangle, University of North Carolina at Charlotte, 2003. The typology of the academic quadrangle is alive and well, but the banal and vaguely historicist architecture stifles the development of social life in the space. The generic façades are sealed around the perimeter, providing few intermediate social spaces for sheltered gathering. Compare this courtyard with Plate 1 and Figure 4.12.

Part of this confusion is because there have been several definitions of typology during the last 200 years, and these have not always agreed with each other (Durand, 1805; Quatremere de Quincy, 1823; Argan, 1963; Rossi, 1966/1982; Colquhoun, 1967; Vidler, 1978; Moneo, 1978; Krier, 1979 et al.). While acknowledging this complex intellectual history, we choose a simple approach, and we utilize typology in our work as a practical way of learning from history and interpreting this history into the present. It helps us to establish workable patterns of urban forms and spaces quickly at the outset of a project, setting out a framework that can be enriched by the subtleties of site circumstances.

To explain this a little further, the urban perimeter block (for example) can be classified as one version of the 'courtyard' typology. The space on the interior of the block is defined by the backs of the buildings lining the street edges, is generally shared only by the users of the buildings on the block, and shielded from the fully public world of the street outside. Those readers familiar with Alfred Hitchcock's famous film *Rear Window* will recall that much of the tension in the plot comes from Jimmy Stewart's visual trespassing into the private realm of the courtyard within such a block. The academic quadrangle so typical of Oxford, Cambridge, Yale, Harvard and

many other university campuses is another version of the courtyard typology, derived in this instance from the medieval cloister where a zone of protected linear circulation is attached to the interior faces of the building. Courtyards of this type, with or without the colonnaded cloister, may be sculpted out from the mass of a larger structure or, as shown in Figure 4.11, they may be created as the space between freestanding buildings. The ubiquitous American atrium hotel is a perversion of this typology, where rooms face into a large multistorey internal volume.

Other recurring patterns of space are the circular form – for example, the Circus at Bath and the public space at Broadgate in central London (see Figure 4.12) – and the linear circulation spine with attached spaces along its length, a pattern that underlies the Greek stoa and the American Main Street.

Three final points about typology need to be made. First, it is clear from these examples that 'type' is different from 'model.' A model is something to be closely copied, an object that should be repeated exactly. Type on the other hand encapsulates the general forms and characteristics of an object that may then be interpreted differently by individual designers. This is very close to Plato's notion of an 'ideal form' that underlies the creation of each particular object, be it the ideal form of a bed that underpins a

**Figure 4.12** Broadgate Arena, London, Arup Associates, Phase I, 1985. The circular form of the main public space is lined with stores on several levels, and its shady passageways and overhanging balconies create multiple opportunities for smaller, intimate spaces around the edge of the main focal plaza.

craftsman's construction, or the ideal form of an urban square that lies at the heart of an urban designer's plan for a plaza.

Second, typology is as much about variations as it is about norms, as in the relationship between court-yard/plaza/courthouse square, and civic buildings noted earlier. It is a wonderful tool for blending 'ideal,' historic forms with specific contemporary circumstances.

Third, and we owe this to the Italian architect and urbanist Aldo Rossi, typology allows architectural and urban forms to gather validity and usefulness from the tradition of architecture itself, and not have to rely on some external justification, say from the social sciences, semiotics or chaos theory. This internalization of meaning suggests a strong thread of

historical continuity as opposed to a continual cycle of new theories and intellectual fads – such as deconstruction, which attempted during the 1980s to justify new architectural forms by reference to French linguistic theory.

We have little patience with this 'intellectual cafeteria' approach to architecture and urbanism, whereby architects can pick and choose their concepts and meanings from a menu of fashionable options. The city and its problems are too serious a venue for intellectual games, and Rossi reminds us of the value of studying our historical precedents. Here in America that means most directly the traditional forms of towns, cities and suburbs from the late nineteenth and early twentieth centuries – one of the main sources of the New Urbanist vocabulary. Typology is the opposite of superficial nostalgia; it holds the key to new buildings because it is both the repository of ideas about building and urban forms throughout history, and at the same time the genesis of new works in the city.

This simplified approach to typology lets us connect with, and be informed by, an architectural and urban legacy larger than the particular urban design problem under study; and, almost as importantly, it can render our design concepts more easily understandable to other, non-architect members of the design team. In the compressed time frame of a charrette, the intensive design workshop we use to produce our community master plans, it's especially important for members from each discipline to trust the depth and quality of ideas of their colleagues. Our forms and concepts derive a high degree of authenticity from typology, and its power to bridge from history to the present and the future: this is one important way that the traffic planner, the landscape architect and the development economist can understand where we as architects and urban designers are coming from. We are utilizing time-tested techniques, not inventing untested ideas out of the blue.

Two typologies that we use in this manner, and which appear in several of the case studies, are the Mixed-use Center and the Traditional Neighborhood. These and two others, the District and the Corridor, are explained more fully in Chapter 6, in the section on our charrette methodology, but we have already seen (in Chapter 3, Figures 3.2 and 3.3) the typological principle at work in the updating and continuity of the traditional neighborhood from Clarence Perry's version in the 1920s to the DPZ reworking of the same type in the 1990s.

## Picturesque Urbanism

In contrast to the rationalist basis of typology, the 'townscape' or picturesque approach to urban design is more 'empirical.' It's based on the specific impact particular compositions of urban form and space make on the senses and emotions of the observer, rather than relying on pre-existing, generalized concepts of form. Empiricism provides one of the other great founding principles of Western thought, articulated most clearly by Englishman John Locke. In his 1687 *Essay Concerning Human Understanding*, Locke argued (in opposition to Descartes) that everything we know about the world is amassed through sensory experience – sight, sound, smell, touch and so forth – and then from reflection upon our experience (Broadbent p. 80). This philosophical worldview translates directly into urbanism, through the work of Gordon Cullen, for example, with his principles of townscape and 'serial vision' – comprehending the city as an orchestrated sequence of visual experiences in the tradition of the English picturesque landscape garden, and orchestrating these experiences into a three-dimensional mental map of the city as a series of connected places.

The reader will recall from earlier discussions that this method of design derives specifically from the work of the Austrian urbanist Camillo Sitte at the end of the nineteenth century, and was also much used by Raymond Unwin and Barry Parker in their designs for the early Garden Cities and garden suburbs before the World War I. The illustrations of Oaklands Park, in Dawlish, on the Devon coast in southwest England, illustrate the creation of spaces as a series of vignettes, composed for pictorial or 'romantic' effect, a quality heightened by their emphasis on vernacular imagery and allusions to local building styles and materials. The spatial arrangement is specifically based on the views that a pedestrian, or a motorist at slow speed, can appreciate as a meaningful and attractive sequence (see Figures 4.13–4.15).

Sitte's 1889 text emphasized the emotional experience of being in urban spaces, and *City Building According to Artistic Principles* is an impassioned argument against one sort of typology, as manifested in the unimaginative uniformity and repetitive formulas of the nineteenth Austrian developers' architecture in Forster's heavy-handed *Ringstrasse* plan around

medieval Vienna (1859–72). But Sitte's own work, based as it was upon countless empirical visual analyses of historical European plazas, was paradoxically typological to some degree. He studied historic examples not as models to copy, but to identify underlying principles of artistic composition from earlier periods that were transferable to his time (see Figure 4.16). It's not hard to extend this search for principles into a classification of types of different arrangements for piazzas and squares, based on variables such as the relationship of major buildings to the space(s), the location of points of entry into the space, a hierarchy of major and minor spaces and their connections and so forth. Rob Krier's exhaustive typological studies in his 1979 book, *Urban Space*, follow this approach and explicitly refer to and extend the work of Sitte.

At the same time, Sitte was primarily concerned with the visual organization of spaces, and it was this attribute of his work that Unwin and especially Cullen developed further. While there is no evidence of any direct link between Sitte and Cullen (Gosling's definitive book on Cullen's work barely mentions the Viennese author [Gosling, 1996]) the townscape method of designing from eye level – based on a pedestrian's visual experience of moving around the city – is the natural three-dimensional development of Sitte's two-dimensional analyses.

The primary articulation of space in Cullen's vocabulary is the distinction between 'Here' and 'There.' 'Here' is where one stands, in a space that is known and understood, occupied at least temporarily by the user. 'There' is a different space, divided in some way from the first. It may be revealed to the observer in a direct manner as in a framed view through an arch, or it may be concealed and only hinted at by means of partial closure of the view, or the manipulation of the opening, or by a change of level. By a coherent sequence of transitions from a succession of 'heres' to a series of 'theres' Cullen builds his technique of 'serial vision,' a means of comprehending, enjoying and designing the public spaces of a city by creating memorable visual contrasts and images. He seeks to manipulate the elements of a town or city to achieve an impact on human emotion (see Figure 4.17). The urban place comes alive 'through the drama of juxtaposition' where all the elements that combine to create a particular environment, buildings, spaces, materials, trees, water, traffic and so forth, are woven together in ways that release the drama of urban experience

**Figures 4.13–4.15** Oaklands Park, Dawlish, Devon, Mervyn Seal and Associates, 1972–76. Buildings in this modest housing estate are arranged to enclose a specific series of spaces and to frame particular views as the resident or visitor moves through the development by car or on foot. The architecture is an abstracted version of the Devonshire seaside vernacular.

(Cullen, 1961: pp. 10–11). There have been several variations of Cullen's ideas, notably Ivor de Wofle and Kenneth Browne's *Civilia*, and Francis Tibbalds' *Making People-Friendly Towns* (1992). Most recently a series of articles by Andres Duany and others in *New Urban News* (2002–03) on urban composition derive directly from Cullen's seminal work.

Cullen's examples, like those of Camillo Sitte and Raymond Unwin before him, were drawn from the vernacular urbanism of European towns and cities, places where the urbanism was organic rather than monumental. These urban places had been assembled over time as a result of many individual decisions rather than laid out at a single stroke in the

S. GIMIGNANO
N   I. Piazza del Duomo.
II. Piazza della Cisterna.

S        PEROUSE
I. Piazza del Vescovato.
II. Piazza di S Lorenzo.
III. Piazza del Papa.
a. Duomo. b. Palazzo communale.

**Figure 4.16** Drawings of Piazzas after Camillo Sitte, Excerpted from 'The American Vitruvius,' by Hegemann and Peets, 1922. These two examples, San Gimignano and Perugia (Perouse), illustrate one of Sitte's main points about the asymmetrical placement of major buildings in public space, thus creating a series of varied spaces of different sizes and character. (*Illustration in the public domain*)

manner of Pierre L'Enfant's plan for Washington DC (1791), or the Beaux Arts-inspired plans of the American City Beautiful movement at the end of the nineteenth century. Townscape principles of spatial articulation are often hard to achieve in the context of American towns and cities dominated by a repetitive and uniform grid – derived from Thomas Jefferson's scheme for land division in the newly settled lands of the expanding western frontier. But we believe that these techniques are even more valid in a context where the urban fabric lacks richness and variety. By selectively, and we stress *selectively*, breaking the unforgiving monotony of American grids, and creating a more diverse palette of spaces for human activity, the urban designer can create memorability and significance (see Figure 4.18). These qualities help mediate the complex and conflicting demands, discussed later in this chapter, regarding tensions inherent in a lot of urban design and planning. Global forces that seek to unify cities with common buildings and products are contrasted with and

the desire to distinguish and enhance the local authenticity of places, and are structured around the people who inhabit them.

## The Social Use of Space

It's important to add one other qualifier to picturesque urbanism as a design method: while the social use of space was implied in the work of Cullen and his followers such as Francis Tibbalds during the 1980s and 1990s, these urban designers concentrated primarily on the visual aspects of design. By contrast, three important American urbanists – Jane Jacobs, Kevin Lynch and William H. Whyte – focused instead on what has been referred to as the 'social usage' of space (Carmona et al.: pp. 6–7). In their efforts at dealing with practical realities concerning the patterns of human activity, these three authors illustrate a third philosophical position, the uniquely American one of pragmatism.

Pragmatism is best known through the work of American philosophers Charles Sanders Pierce (1839–1914), William James (1842–1910) and John Dewey (1859–1952). Pragmatists embrace 'truths' in the plural, examining conditions in the world from the basis of their practicality and utility in the realm of concrete human experience. In the context of urban design and planning this approach has developed its theories and concepts by looking 'more closely at the practical effects of living in cities' (Broadbent: p. 86).

Jacobs, Lynch, and Whyte all stressed the importance of everyday human experience in urban design, and each in his or her own way rejected the abstraction of city life inherent in modernist values and assumptions about cities. Lynch, in his seminal work, *The Image of the City* (1960), explored people's perceptions and mental images of urban places as a way of relating the techniques of design specialists to the everyday appreciation of spaces by their users. Jacobs, most famously as we have already discussed, concentrated in *The Death and Life of American Cities* (1961) on the space of the street as a practical venue of daily life, and its role as a spatial container of social activities. Whyte extended this interest in the pragmatic use of urban space in his famous little book and accompanying video entitled *The Social Life of Small Urban Spaces* (1980), which derived common sense rules about the design of public space by watching to see what worked best in the everyday world and then using these lessons on the drawing board. This social view of habitable space and the impact of

**CASEBOOK:** SERIAL VISION

To walk from one end of the plan to another, at a uniform pace, will provide a sequence of revelations which are suggested in the serial drawings opposite, reading from left to right. Each arrow on the plan represents a drawing. The even progress of travel is illuminated by a series of sudden contrasts and so an impact is made on the eye, bringing the plan to life (like nudging a man who is going to sleep in church). My drawings bear no relation to the place itself; I chose it because it seemed an evocative plan. Note that the slightest deviation in alignment and quite small variations in projections or setbacks on plan have a disproportionally powerful effect in the third dimension.

**Figure 4.17** Gordon Cullen's 'Serial Vision,' from 'Townscape,' 1961. The sensibility to evocative qualities of irregular urban form and space in Sitte's work is taken to a higher plane of development by Cullen. While Sitte's work exists largely in two-dimensional plan form, Cullen's genius as a draughtsman brings the third dimension of urban experience vividly to life. *(Illustration courtesy of The Architectural Press)*

human behavior on design was importantly extended by Christopher Alexander and others in their compendium of design ideas, *A Pattern Language* (1977) and raised to a specifically urban level of consideration in *A New Theory of Urban Design* (1987). To show how interconnected all these different strands of urban design are, Alexander's emphasis on urban patterns also connects back to the work of Sitte, whom Alexander frequently cites.

While this American socially based approach shares many similarities and intentions with its European picturesque counterpart, it also illustrates an important difference. The townscape technique of urban design retains the viewpoint of the specialist designer. It is his or her eye that is composing the urban scene. For Lynch, Jacobs and Whyte it's the perceptions and use of space by ordinary urban residents that are paramount. This devolution of design, and a desire to construct neighborhoods and cities that are responsive to the needs and expectations of their citizens is an important tenet of contemporary urban design. It illustrates the push toward democratic populism and community activism in architecture planning, noted in Chapter 1. At the same time it indicates a third methodology of urban design. This third, pragmatic mode of operation is best categorized as 'making places for people,' and synthesizes the design of urban space as an aesthetic entity and a behavioral setting based on the realities of human use and activity (Carmona et al.: p. 7).

The place where the Americans, Lynch, Jacobs, and Whyte most clearly come together with their British counterparts, Cullen, Tibbalds and others is

**Figure 4.18** Two Rodeo Drive, Beverly Hills, California, Kaplan McLaughlin Diaz, Architects, 1990. Located at the intersection of Rodero Drive and Wilshire Boulevard, this 'upmarket theme park for adults,' as New York Times critic Paul Goldberger described it, uses a diagonal to create attractive pedestrian space in a car-dominated environment.
*(Illustration courtesy of Kaplan McLaughlin Diaz)*

the street – the connective tissue of democratic space and visual experience that structures towns and cities. But ironically we have little opportunity to celebrate this consensus. No sooner have we reached some professional agreement about the appropriateness of traditional urban spaces than other critics raise new doubts about the authenticity of our revived streets and public spaces (Sandercock, 1999). Are they not, these critics argue, just locations for a passive 'café society,' developer-driven stage sets for consumption from generic retailers like Starbucks, The Gap, and Victoria's Secret rather than places for active citizenship and democratic engagement? Are these privatized realms masquerading as public spaces? In America additional voices are raised asking if these new streets and squares are simply exclusive settings for the white middle class, places from which poorer black and Hispanic populations are excluded by income level if not by social policy. These are some of the arguments we examine in the next section.

## THE STREET AND 'CAFÉ SOCIETY'

We have seen in the earlier chapters on the history of city design how the objectives of urban design in the twentieth century have swung back and forth like a pendulum. Beginning with the street as the basic building block of urbanism at the start of the century, professional opinion has arced across to the other extreme where the development of open, continuous, modernist space marked the 'death of the street' in the decades just before and after World War II. Most recently as the century drew to a close, design theory and practice have returned to the street as the armature of contemporary, sustainable urbanism. Once again, buildings are seen today as edges to public space, defining 'urban rooms,' rather than objects adrift in open space. In Britain, this latter return to traditional urbanism was exemplified by texts such as *Responsive Environments* (Bentley et al., 1985) which still acts as an effective primer for students and practitioners alike. In America, Peter Calthorpe's *The Next American Metropolis* (1993) provided a similarly useful text at a more general level of consideration.

The urban wisdom contained within these and other publications has become enshrined in British government policy guidance notes such as *By Design: Urban Design in the Planning System: Towards Better Practice* (2000), and *By Design: Better Places to Live* (2001). In America traditional urban design principles have, as we noted in Chapter 3, been best articulated in the *Charter for the New Urbanism* (1998) and in publications by the Urban Land Institute, such as Chuck Bohl's *Placemaking: Developing Town Centers. Main Streets and Urban Villages* (2002). The differences between British and American policies about planning and urban design are examined more closely in Chapter 5, but suffice it here to say that while many design and planning objectives are similar on both sides of the Atlantic, in Britain they tend to be embedded within government policy (however flawed in application) while in America, there is a large void at the national level. Any push for good urban design is usually a function of independent professionals and pressure groups outside government.

With the help of an increasing number of texts and guidance manuals, designers in Britain and America have come to use street-oriented approaches to solve contemporary urban design and town planning problems, either retrofitting older commercial centers and corridors to become pedestrian-friendly, or by creating whole new walkable neighborhoods on greenfield sites. The dramatic increase in urban living in America has placed new demands on the public spaces of cities. Even transportation engineers now realize the function of a city street, for example, is no longer simply to move traffic. It is expected to be a place that can support several activities, movement on foot, bicycle, car or transit, and a place to meet for business or pleasure over a cup of coffee or a glass of wine. The street is once again a place of rest and relaxation, work, entertainment and recreation.

But several critics, particularly in America and Australia, have castigated traditional urbanism based on streets and squares as being retrogressive and nostalgic, preferring instead either to search for new city forms or, in some cases, to accept the existing models as indicative of consumer preference (Sudjic, 1992; Rybczynski, 1995; Safdie, 1997; Dovey, 1999; McDougall, 1999; Marshall, 2000; Sorkin, 2001). These and other critics have bemoaned the fact that traditional urbanism is by its very nature somewhat prescriptive, relying as it does upon a set of spatial types that require adherence to street alignments, build-to lines and proportional form-to-space relationships. We have argued our rebuttal to these rather tired arguments at several points throughout the text, but a more substantive critique of traditional urbanism is one that we noted briefly in Chapter 1, namely that these attempts to create walkable communities, and the use of traditional urban forms in the service of those ambitions, merely create stage sets for a sybaritic 'café society.' Such a society, it is claimed, is a venue purely for the consumption of goods rather than a place of creative cultural and democratic activities, a place where the richness and meaning of public life is reduced to a manufactured spectacle.

This criticism is easier to refute in the context of the refurbishment and adaptive reuse of buildings in central city districts, such as Quincy Market in Boston (1826, refurbished 1978), and Covent Garden in London (piazza 1631, but extensively rebuilt several times; market hall 1831, refurbished 1980) (see Figures 5.1 and 6.11). In locations like these, the urban nodes of entertainment, recreation, and retail activities have been integrated into an existing city fabric, often with dramatic improvements of urban life over a wide area. A similar rationale of social usefulness also applies to the regeneration of grayfield sites, turning old, worn-out shopping centers and commercial districts into new urban villages, but the fabrication of fresh suburban versions of these environments on peripheral greenfield sites raises more difficult questions.

We address the issue of why such developments around the urban edges of cities are unavoidable in America in some detail in Chapter 6, and make our case for turning necessity to advantage. Briefly, we believe that making new urban villages in the suburbs can be one of the most useful strategies to introduce a

hierarchy and sense of place into the otherwise sprawling periphery. They are part of a strategy to transform the suburbs into a more coherent urban fabric with discernable centers, neighborhoods and districts. One reason for the loving to death of Seaside was the lack of other places like it. Now that more new developments are being created in the form of urban villages, we believe the urbanity craved so avidly by many Americans will evolve from a consumerist spectacle into a normal setting for everyday life.

This claim is unlikely to quell the critics, but there is one point on which all can agree. Unlike the pseudo-public space of the suburban shopping mall, where the communal space is privately controlled, the streets, squares and parks in an urban village must be truly public. This is crucial, for democracy and urban life cannot flourish in privatized enclaves.

In America, the paradigm of new urban villages as the settings for middle-class urban spectacles is increasingly well ensconced in the suburban culture. Branded as 'lifestyle centers' with themed retail and entertainment venues, these developments profit from established urban typologies. They utilize urban blocks with vertical mixed uses of high-density housing and/or offices over retail stores, and traditional spatial typologies of Main Street and urban square to create pedestrian-friendly environments that encourage window shopping, browsing and sidewalk dining in decent weather.

To entice people onto the street or public square is one of an urban designer's key objectives. But all architectural and urban spaces need a program, a set of anticipated human activities that can take place in those locations, actions that can transcend passive consumerism. To meet this need in our American practice, we construct an 'ideal user,' someone we may best describe as a sort of twenty-first century *flaneur*, an updating of the famous urban dweller from the boulevards of Paris, immortalized by the French poet Charles Baudelaire.

In his essay 'The Painter of Modern Life,' first printed in the Paris newspaper *Le Figaro* in 1863, Baudelaire described the *flaneur* as someone who lived his life in the public world, strolling the boulevards, frequenting the cafés, bars and public buildings of Paris. He was anonymous in the urban crowds but drew energy from the teeming urban life all around him. (We should note in passing that this was a male role; women – apart from prostitutes – were not allowed this luxury of unaccompanied movement in the nineteenth century city.) But Baudelaire's urban wanderer was not simply a passive spectator. The French poet stressed that his pedestrian searched the city with a lofty aim. He was looking for 'modernity' in the metropolis, and in his search the *flaneur* did not merely consume urban culture. He created it by his 'passionate' activity. Multiply this individual by a population of thousands in a city, or even in a suburban center, and the possibility of an authentic public life in America is tantalizingly within reach.

One of our chief ambitions as designers is to create and maintain this public realm as a place where contemporary *flaneurs*, of both sexes, can flourish, and succeed in their quest of generating urban activity and culture. This is where the issue of truly public space is so vital. Private control over spaces that look public but aren't emasculates democratic participation in the life of the community.

One development that tries to achieve this goal of meaningful and active public space is Birkdale Village, in Huntersville, North Carolina, a suburban community just north of Charlotte. It may not succeed in every test we apply for our idealized *flaneur*, but none the less, it is a brave attempt. Located near a freeway interchange (a mark in its disfavor), Birkdale supplies urban amenities to the suburban middle class; it has gathered unto itself many aspects of the traditional center that the tiny town of Huntersville never possessed prior to its evolution into a burgeoning bedroom community of 32 000 in 2002.

Like a traditional town center, the 52-acre (20.8 hectares) Birkdale Village, with its apartments and offices over the stores, and a cinema at the end of Main Street, physically connects via a grid of walkable streets to adjacent housing developments (see Plate 4). But beneath this veneer of normality, Huntersville is a town with extraordinary social demographics. The town's population is 86 percent white and its median household income is a whopping $72 000, considerably more than the regional average. For comparison, in other Carolina communities like Winston-Salem the figures are 55 percent white with a median income of $37 000. Spartanburg's demographics are 42 percent white with a median income of $22 400. Huntersville is thus an urban area that has a limited social spectrum of users and inhabitants. Not surprisingly, the stores in Birkdale Village are upmarket, and the rents for the apartments are relatively high, but this exclusivity combined with the sense of near-genuine urbanity has bred great commercial success (see Plate 5).

The one important element that is missing is a civic presence. There is no Town Hall, no library, police station or post office. The library is isolated on the other side of the freeway, while the other civic functions remain rooted in the small downtown core, three miles away, in a brave effort to stabilize and retain that fleeting piece of history. However, on the positive side, the infrastructure of streets and public spaces in Birkdale Village has been taken over from the developer by the town and are publicly owned and maintained. They are truly public. They could, for example, be the legal site for a political demonstration, an important test. The fact that these public spaces have been created by means of private development is not an issue. The problem only occurs when the spaces that we use for public activities remain in private hands.

Despite its positive impact on the community, several local people and professionals worry that not everybody can afford to live or shop in the new *de facto* town center. This is fair criticism. It's a fact of development economics that the extra costs and complexity of creating a true mixed-use center of this type can most easily be justified in an area of high demographics and above average disposable personal income. However, this argument can easily be overstated. The construction cost of Birkdale Village averaged out to $75 per square foot (approximately £450 per square meter). Given the lower land costs for the smaller area required for this more compact development compared to a conventional development that would need a larger site to lay out all the components in separate pods, this is not an extravagant figure.

However, building the project is not the most difficult issue. Developers need the reassurance of elevated demographics and consumers with high disposable incomes to support the development risk, and to create this type of development in less wealthy locations requires some kind of public subsidy for the private development to defray costs, such as land acquisition. The market alone cannot provide this new urbanity for the working class and other, poorer sections of society unless it is part of a larger, public–private venture that tackles social equity and justice in the city. Every sector of the population deserves access to this improved urban future, not just the wealthy bourgeoisie, however important they may be in the process. This real problem of exclusion gives ammunition to the critics who complain that this is a stage set of Main Street, and makes a carnival experience of what should be the substance of everyday life. They argue that people are unaware how their public life has an unreal, sanitized and tranquilized quality. In these critics' terms, the passive café society has triumphed over an active urban reality to the detriment of all concerned.

We acknowledge this argument, but we don't quite agree. In an American suburban culture where real urbanity is not something many citizens have experienced, Birkdale's Main Street ambience is a novel condition. The development's truly public spaces, the unusual suburban presence of people living and working above the shops – sharing in the public realm of the street from their private balconies and open windows – is the nearest thing to city life that many people have ever experienced. It's imperfect, but it's a start. Surveys and empirical observations clearly show that Americans are hungry for an urban experience, and we believe it's very possible for a substantial number of Americans to grow into this lifestyle, and to gradually learn what it means to be urban dweller, a *flaneur*. If you go to Birkdale on a Friday or Saturday night you'll see plenty of genuine street life and urban activity. These people are not aware of some distant academic criticizing their behavior. The folks illustrated in Plate 6 aren't acting. They're *being*.

Our opinion is not entirely objective. In the mid-1990s the authors were instrumental in helping the town of Huntersville rewrite its zoning ordinance to ban conventional commercial strip development and to curtail residential sprawl. We did this by mandating that commercial development should be mixed in its uses and connected to adjacent residential development, and by requiring all new residential development to be laid out with a connecting network of streets and public spaces. We used examples of traditional urban design as models, and wrote the code around the attributes inherent in their design – good proportions, contextual design, compatible mixtures of uses and pedestrian-scaled townscapes which retained the convenience of the car but reduced its autonomy.

In short, high-density, mixed-use developments like Birkdale, which meet all the requirements and expectations of the code, are precisely what we had in mind (see Plate 7). We would have preferred that such a development of town center scale took place in the real town center, but the realities of the market and development economics made that impossible. The old town center, such as it is, is a mile from major highways with limited access and awkward development potential due to a straggling and diverse pattern of individual land ownership. It's a developer's nightmare with difficult and expensive land

acquisition combined with poor communications and limited visibility to passing traffic. When compared to a site near a busy freeway intersection, there is no contest.

In circumstances like this it's the urban designer's job to deal with reality and make the best places possible. It is important, we believe, not to make the quest for perfection the enemy of good design. By holding out for utopia, the urban designer runs the risk of being marginalized and neutered. We are proud of our small part in creating the Birkdale development. It's not easy to build things of higher quality on either side of the Atlantic but now that developments like Birkdale are a physical reality in America, we can put them to good purpose. We can educate the public and the development community about good urban design and, importantly, the economic practicality of creating high quality urban environments as opposed to the generic world of suburban dross.

But not all the action is in the American 'burbs'. Affluent populations from the outer and middle suburbs are returning to the city center and inner suburbs. With the departure of manufacturing and industry from the inner city, former industrial buildings become available for conversion to middle and upper income housing, and where old buildings are in short supply, developers eagerly manufacture new ones that look old to meet the need without a trace of irony (see Figure 4.19).

The rising affluence of the inner city forces out or marginalizes lower income groups, who are increasingly displaced by the middle class unless local governments intervene in the marketplace to provide affordable housing. Most service sector downtowns still provide job opportunities for lower paid workers – in the form of security staff, janitors, waiters, sales assistants and so forth. But the market provides very little in the way of housing for these workers, or indeed for the lower ranks of professional such as teachers and nurses and valued public safety employees like policemen and firemen.

One successful federal initiative in America to reduce this problem has been the HOPE VI program, whereby derelict public housing is demolished and replaced by better-designed homes in a mixture of subsidized public housing and affordable market rate dwellings. The urban and architectural design philosophy of HOPE VI has mirrored that of New Urbanism: to integrate different types of housing together in the same community, socially and visually, so that it is impossible to tell which housing is

**Figure 4.19** Camden Road, SouthEnd, Charlotte, NC, Namour Wright, Architects, 1998. Useful new urban infill development is often masked in America by a fake historicism that glorifies the past at the expense of the present. To fit in with public taste, many developers desire their buildings to look old the moment they are completed.

of which type. Charlotte has one such successful development in its downtown area, First Ward Place just two blocks from the new light rail line through the city center (see Figure 2.14). There is only one

problem with this good development. It's a drop in the ocean. Charlotte, like many American cities, has a crisis of insufficient affordable housing. First Ward Place needs to be multiplied all over the city on sites adjacent to public transit, job opportunities and services. This kind of development needs to be an integral part of the future urban villages envisaged at key nodes along the transit lines. Local authorities need to mandate the inclusions of affordable dwellings in every major development, as is required by the zoning ordinance of Davidson, North Carolina.

When affordable housing is minimal or absent from the city center altogether, the revitalized center city does become no more than the playground for the affluent classes. When this situation is combined with the economic exclusivity of suburban centers like Birkdale Village, American society is presented with a challenge of major proportions. The public spaces of cities are the only places where citizens encounter people who are different from themselves, but which some people may find daunting. Meeting strangers can be scary to a lot of people but the process is important in creating a civilized society (Sennett, 1973, 1994).

When we go out in public and encounter only people like ourselves, we are impoverished, and, most worryingly, our public life is being tranquillized. All the rough edges, odd or idiosyncratic behavior, unique individuals, any distractions that might disturb our consumption at the corporate stores, are being smoothed off and edited out, banished to parts of the city we never see. In this invidious manner we surrender our grip on the messy complex reality of city life and slip uncomplainingly into the velvet glove of a convenient simulacrum. The urban designer is in the thick of this debate. It's difficult. It's awkward. It gets confusing. But there's no other place to be.

# Practice

# Growth management, development control and the role of urban design

## SYNOPSIS

This chapter examines some of the similarities and differences between the planning systems in Britain and America. Most of the similarities occur in the professional realm, where architects, urban designers, and planners in both countries do similar tasks using similar concepts. The differences are in the political and cultural spheres, where a deep divide exists between American attitudes toward the sanctity of private property rights and the British (and European) propensity toward the communal good. We highlight some of these variations in detail to explain the different cultural contexts in which professionals have to work.

We then discuss two fundamental differences between the American and British systems: first, the American distinction between planning – establishing the future vision – and zoning – the legal means of regulating growth; and second, the fact that in America, plans are advisory and have no force in law other than to fulfil the requirement to have a plan. In Britain, by contrast, while local plans are not legally binding documents that specify precise dimensions and design parameters as they do in parts of mainland Europe, local governments, after a period of laxity during the 1980s, are once more obliged to make decisions about applications to develop land strictly in accordance with their adopted plans. Planning and development control is a unified process in which design regulation is increasingly a part.

In the final section we examine the relationship of urban design principles to the regulation of the built environment, through a brief historical discussion of design-based ordinances, particularly as they have related to American practice. We note the typological basis that underlies most design-based coding, and defend the use of urban design guidelines in contemporary practice.

## DESIGNING COMMUNITIES IN DIFFERENT CULTURES

From an American perspective, working as an urban designer in Britain seems like a rather privileged position. We know this will raise hoots of derisive laughter from British urban designers who battle daily with government intransigence and client ineptitude, but remember, one of the authors is English, with experience on both continents, so there is a basis of reality in this observation. We don't contend that urban design in the UK is easy. We are simply affirming that British professionals operate in a different world than their American counterparts. For example, there are British government policies on urban design, manifested through publications such as Planning Policy Guidance Notes issued through the 1990s. Nothing like these exist in America. There are government-backed regional centers for architectural and urban excellence in Britain. Unheard of in America. The British government's new-found wisdom on matters of urban design has been largely influenced by the professional organizations comprising the national Urban Design Alliance, including the Royal Institute of British Architects, the Royal Institution of Chartered Surveyors, the Royal Town Planning Institute, the Institution of Civil Engineers, the Landscape Institute, the Civic Trust and the Urban Design Group. No such interdisciplinary professional consensus can be found anywhere in the USA.

Before we begin a more detailed discussion of how growth and development is managed at the community level in both nations, one obvious fact has to be stated: America is a very big place, and this vast difference in scale accounts for some of the variations in government structure and focus. England and Wales, for example, will more or less fit inside the state of Oklahoma. The nation of France is about the same size as the state of Texas. America has 50 states, comprising a complex collage of cultures, climates and attitudes.

Given this disparity, it's not surprising that one of the most obvious contrasts is at the level of national policy. In Chapter 4, we noted the publication by the British government of reports entitled *By Design: Urban Design in the Planning System* (2000), and *By Design: Better Places to Live* (2001), topics close to the heart of this book. This is a level of consensus regarding policy and expectations at a national level that's not easily imaginable in America at the start of the twenty-first century. There is simply a large void of official concern and policy at national and state levels regarding the design of American towns and cities. This is not so much by neglect, but a matter of ideology: the American planning system in general works on the presumption that policies and regulation are primarily a local matter. This devolution is an excellent concept in the abstract, but in the absence of any clear guidance about national themes or priorities, or regional issues, from the federal or state governments, most planning remains introverted and local in scale, and competitive with adjacent municipalities rather than collaborative.

This competitive attitude between local governments is a crucial weakness in the American system, but it has deep roots; in large part it's based on money, particularly revenues from local taxes. Compared to Europe, where a more centralized system is the norm, a higher percentage of money to fund local government in America comes from local taxes. In American towns and cities, schools, police and fire protection, and the public infrastructure of streets, sidewalks, water and sewer are funded directly from taxes on private property in the community. To avoid always having to raise taxes to pay these costs, which continually increase due to inflation, local governments try to attract new development to expand the amount of taxable property within their borders. They often fight hard to outbid their neighbors by offering various incentives to developers and companies, including, ironically, rebates from local taxes.

However, not all growth pays for itself. For example, the taxes received from a typical American housing development generally don't pay for the services received by the homeowners, mainly due to the cost of providing schools for their children. But the taxes on a strip shopping center can create a profit for local government, as that development doesn't require the schools, libraries, community centers, swimming pools, courthouses and so forth expected by homeowners and their families. The shopping center will only need police and fire protection, water supply and sewer service. Therefore, the types of development that produce sprawl are often actively sought out by elected officials and economic development officers in American towns and cities in order to garner revenue to fund civic services.

Another important difference concerns what is taxed. In Europe, the tax structure is more heavily weighted to taxes on consumption rather than property. In other words what you use is taxed more heavily than what you own. The opposite is true in the USA, where taxes on consumption, for example, those on petrol, are only a fraction of the equivalents in Europe. As often happens, Britain hovers somewhere between the two poles.

This emphasis on taxing consumption is being extended in many European nations to so-called green taxes on pollution, particularly in Sweden, the Netherlands, Germany and Denmark. This policy can both reduce the contamination of the environment while allowing for some reductions in personal taxation. Between 1994 and 1998, for example, Denmark raised taxes on petrol, water supply, energy and waste while reducing the income tax levied on its citizens by 8 to 10 percent (Burke, 1997, in Beatley: p. 257). Any such fundamental changes in tax structure toward this kind of more centralized and use-based tax system are very unlikely in America, and local governments will therefore continue to operate in their normal, competitive, and localized manner. Many observers see nothing wrong in this; a fundamental mantra of American culture is that competition provides the best solution to most questions. In this crucial instance of municipal finance however, competition is the problem, not the solution. It is the Achilles' heel of American planning.

In addition to competing with their neighbors for sources of revenue, elected officials in almost every place we work tell us they fear the loss of their community's identity, and are thus protectively suspicious of adjacent municipalities who may have different agendas. For example, the members of several progressive town councils in the Carolinas often share few values with the County Commissioners who administer the largely rural lands beyond the towns' boundaries. For example, the leaders of the town of Mooresville, 30 miles north of Charlotte, are keen to link themselves with the big city's rail transit plans, becoming the terminus of a proposed northern line from Charlotte. However, Mooresville is located in Iredell County, an area that, apart from Mooresville and a few other towns, is predominantly rural as opposed to the urban environment of the city of Charlotte and its surrounding Mecklenburg County. It has been very hard for the Mooresville officials to make common cause with their county counterparts, who see the rail link and its associated development as symptomatic of the advancing urbanization that threatens their rural values. Mooresville's ambition to connect to Charlotte represents a major economic development opportunity for the town and fulfills some of its Smart Growth objectives. However, these priorities are driving a wedge between the town and the county, and there is no overall planning authority with the power to sort out this dispute and resolve local and regional issues. Indeed, when North Carolina set up the statutory Metropolitan Planning Organizations to manage transportation planning in the state's urban areas, it established five separate bodies for the Charlotte region, specifically so regional coordination would be difficult, and to resist the rise of regional governance.

While this might be extreme, few American states see such mediation or plan coordination between jurisdictions as part of their function; indeed, many states don't require coordinated plans for their territory. In avoiding this issue of extended governance, state government represents the opinion of many Americans who view such higher authority, whether as a regional government or, even worse, a national government policy for controlling the development of private property, as a deeply socialistic concept. Some sectors of public opinion even consider such planning initiatives as the precursor to the erosion of fundamental civil liberties.

This was certainly the case in the 1930s when the federal government first introduced legislation to create a national housing policy as part of the New Deal. Opponents destroyed the fledgling American New Towns program at that time, branding it a socialist concept, and not many attitudes have changed since then. The authors are reminded of a recent observation by a conservative Charlotte politician to the effect that if an ugly environment is the result of unplanned free enterprise, then so be it. The city councilman considered that outcome much

preferable to an attractive city brought about at the price of government regulation.

This isn't to say that there is no national legislation that affects the physical form of American towns and cities. There are and have been several examples, the urban renewal legislation discussed earlier being one dramatic postwar instance. While that set of policies has left a lingering and difficult legacy, other recent examples are more progressive. But few concern themselves with design. The shining exception is the HOPE VI program, an effort to demolish substandard public housing ghettos and replace them with more attractive mixed-income neighborhoods. While the statement of objectives does not mention design, the federal department of Housing and Urban Development (HUD) has been open to the suggestions of New Urbanist architects, including Elizabeth Plater-Zyberk, and supplementary guidance notes such as *Strategies for Providing Accessibility and Visitability for HOPE VI and Mixed Finance Homeownership*, prepared by Urban Design Associates provides exemplary design information (HUD, 2000). The HUD website http://www.designadvisor.org also provides excellent advice for the design and layout of affordable housing.

We have already noted the success of Charlotte's HOPE VI project near the city center, and this is repeated in many cities across the nation. It's thus disappointing to note that at the time of writing in 2003, the administration of President George W. Bush planned to end the whole program in October 2003 (*New Urban News*, March 2003). This intention to abandon a very successful program seems mainly ideological. It was a program much favored by the administration of President Clinton, and it succeeded in large part because central government did specify clear standards and New Urbanist design objectives that individual cities were expected to follow. But this level of federal guidance (some would say control) of local government does not sit well with many American politicians and citizens.

No federal urban program is as design based as HOPE VI, but another notably effective national initiative has been the transportation and planning legislation entitled ISTEA (1991) and its successor, TEA-21. ISTEA, widely pronounced as 'iced tea,' is an acronym for the Intermodal Surface Transportation Efficiency Act. The act explicitly linked land use and transportation planning, supported planning for public transit, highlighted the relevance of planning for bicycles and pedestrians, and promoted the idea of connecting all these modes in an integrated system. It expressly funded transportation systems that provided alternatives to the car in cities, especially in those with bad air pollution. It also included some money for historic preservation in situations where historic properties were enmeshed with transportation planning. In the context of minimal regional planning, these initiatives marked a big step forward, but there was little mention of urban design in these considerations. This is simply not an issue that enters into American thinking at a national level.

In American government, many policy initiatives on a wide range of matters originate at state level, and in an effort to improve the quality of their environment, a few states have enacted growth management legislation with some regulatory force. These include Hawaii in 1959, Vermont in 1970, (two of the smallest states in the union, where pressures of development are more obvious because of their limited size) followed by Oregon in 1973, Florida in 1985, Maine and Rhode Island in 1988, Washington in 1990 and Maryland and New Jersey in 1998. Altogether, 13 states have some form of statewide growth management control (in 2003), but even here results vary. In parts of these states a number of important natural landscapes have been preserved and some built-up areas were transformed to a more sustainable urban form, but nearby other parts of the environment is still visually and ecologically a mess.

One of the most effective techniques of regional planning at state level has been used by Maryland and New Jersey. Both states focus their spending and tax incentives to business on communities where adequate infrastructure is already in place to support infill or contiguous growth rather than new greenfield development. Smart Growth strategies like this are not designed to stop development; they simply decide on the locations for the wisest investment of public funds (Katz, 2003: p. 49).

Design is not a factor that looms large in the thinking of most state governments, but an interesting advisory document from the National Governors Association, published in 2001 and entitled *New Community Design to the Rescue: Fulfilling Another American Dream*, argues that approximately one-third of Americans have expressed preferences for living in neighborhoods which are walkable, have a mixture of uses, and provide alternatives to using the car for every household trip. In other words, it acknowledges that substantial numbers of Americans want to live in communities that embody at least some Smart Growth principles. The report goes on to note that only *1 percent* of housing in America offers such convenience and sustainability (Hudnut, 2002).

Given these progressive sentiments, it is disappointing that in many states the growth management legislation that would bring about these more sustainable urban patterns is weak. It is often well intentioned but relatively toothless, and advisory rather than regulatory. North Carolina, for example, announced in 2000 an initiative to preserve one million acres of natural open space in the state. However, it provided no funds or mechanisms to achieve this goal, leaving it up to the conscience of private developers and landowners, and relying on the inadequate powers and finances of nonprofit land trusts or individual communities to do the job.

Indeed in America it's often left to individual cities or large metropolitan areas to enact their own growth management legislation, and this often include policies on urban design. Portland, Oregon, San Diego, California, the twin cities of Minneapolis-St. Paul in Minnesota, Denver, Colorado, Chattanooga, Tennessee and Austin, Texas are notable examples. These cities have created policies with good strategic planning objectives that embody principles of Smart Growth, and San Diego made a step forward in 1992 when it adopted exemplary design guidelines for transit-oriented development (prepared by Calthorpe Associates) that embody definitive New Urbanist design principles. This example, usually for specific kinds of development like TODs, has been followed by several cities across the USA.

Atlanta, Georgia, is one such instance. The multi-county Atlanta metropolitan area was forced into regional planning and growth management by a fiscal crisis caused by the poor quality of its air; it was so polluted that the federal government cut off road building funds under the provisions of the Clean Air Act, a law dating from the presidency of Richard Nixon. This legislation explicitly tied the provision of funds to a city's maintenance of decent air quality. Stimulated by this threat to its economic growth, Atlanta, with the backing of the state governor, took a more proactive position regarding sustainable planning and urban design as a component of revamped planning guidance. The coordinating regional planning authority, the Atlanta Regional Commission, developed a 'Smart Growth Toolkit' which includes information of topics such as transit-oriented development and traditional neighborhood development. These documents, prepared by one of the authors in conjunction with the Atlanta planning firm of Jordan, Jones and Goulding, feature specific urban design guidelines and case studies and include model zoning ordinances for adoption by municipalities in the region. However, the governor's active support for regional Smart Growth legislation did not serve him well at the polls. In the 2002 election, he was defeated by an opponent who has been markedly less enthusiastic and supportive of these policies.

The most notable American successes of collaborative planning and attention to design at this metropolitan level are Portland and Minneapolis-St. Paul. In the former, an 'urban growth boundary' approximates to an English 'green belt' of preserved rural land around the urbanized area: a regional authority guides planning decisions and the urban area is well served by public transit. The regional model is more advanced in the Twin Cities. Here a Metropolitan Council has planning authority for sewer, transit and land use over a seven-county area, and guides growth in a more orderly and economical manner than if the process was left to the normal conditions of market forces and competitive municipalities. The state legislature beefed up a conventional planning agency with a budget of $40 million to a regional authority with real power and an annual budget of $600 million (Katz, 2003: p. 48). Most crucially, the Twin Cities have a tax sharing arrangement, whereby 40 per cent of the property tax revenues from commercial and industrial development are distributed across the metropolitan region. This goes a long way toward offsetting the competition for new development and its tax revenues that motivates most conventional local government in America.

Like British towns, individual cities in America usually have some form of urban design guidelines, either included within zoning legislation or as a freestanding advisory document. Sometimes such policies and guidelines are progressive, and demonstrate a deep care and concern for a city's urban environment. Other times they are nearly nonexistent, or honored mainly in the breach. Mostly, they fall in between. The city of Charlotte, for example, has in recent years enacted design provisions that place emphasis on the creation of a good pedestrian environment at street level in the downtown core. Among other things, these provisions require a certain amount of street-level retail space to be provided in new downtown development, and ban the construction of overstreet walkways that link the internal environments of office towers and deprive the street of much needed activity. Despite these regulations, in 2001 the city council approved a mid-air tunnel connecting the city's newest skyscraper to its neighbor with almost no discussion of the consequences, and waived the

street level retail requirement in a nearby large development by one of the city's powerhouse banks. Yet within a few blocks of these failures and oversights, Charlotte has developed its exemplary HOPE VI affordable housing project, embodying good urban design principles and built with decent architecture, following plans from outside consultants, Urban Design Associates (UDA) from Pittsburgh, and local architects FMK and David Furman (see Figure 2.14).

Often urban design quality is left to the development industry to enact for its own market-driven benefit. Sometimes the results are outstanding, such as the Rouse Corporation's reconstruction of the historic Faneuil Hall and Quincy Marketplace in Boston (see Figure 5.1). Other times the results fall short of excellence but still attain a high standard, such as the Birkdale Village development described in the previous chapter. But usually the results are disappointing, amounting to little more than fragments of pedestrian space with benches and decorative lighting between retail stores surrounded by huge asphalt car parks (see Figure 5.2). In cases like this, urban design is a mere fig leaf decorating the nakedness of the development team's imagination.

**Figure 5.1** Faneuil Hall Marketplace, better known as Quincy Market, Boston, Alexander Parris, 1826, Refurbished by Benjamin Thompson and Associates, 1978. The architects convinced the developers to persevere with this project at a time when redevelopment and refurbishment of historic structures was not a high priority in America. Here, new building insertions and details do not attempt to look old; there is a healthy dialogue between historic and contemporary. The public spaces are well scaled and crammed with city residents, office workers, and tourists, availing themselves of the many restaurants and stores. (*Photo by Adrian Walters*)

**Figure 5.2** Sycamore Commons Shopping center, Matthews, NC. LS3P Architects, 2002. Searching for a semblance of urbanity to use as a marketing tool, American developers increasingly commission their architects to design fragments of pedestrian space around restaurants as islands of refuge within large surface parking lots serving big-box stores.

This hands-off approach to government regulation of planning and urban design standards is indicative of the overall American cultural attitude toward private property, attitudes that are so pervasive in the USA that not all Americans realize that they are culturally determined. To some they have the status of natural law. To provide some perspective for the American reader, it's worth outlining some instances of urban planning and design in European countries, relating these to cultural attitudes in these countries, and then focusing on the British situation, which is usually the one most closely referenced by Americans. This is not to denigrate the USA, but to explain why some design and planning concepts are transferable between Europe and America, and others are not.

We have noted earlier how American cities consume land much faster than they grow in population. European cities by contrast grow more compactly at higher densities, for a number of historical and cultural reasons. Even in densely urban nations like the Netherlands, only 13 percent of the land area is urbanized. In Sweden, a far less dense country, the figure is nearer 2 percent (Beatley: p. 30). Clearly historical factors are important. Most European cities are old, with their compact form derived from a time when cities were constructed for ease of fortification

and for the convenience of pedestrian and horse traffic. But this does not explain the compact form of new settlements, like Vallingby new town outside Stockholm (1954), or Almere near Amsterdam, dating from 1977. In places like Holland a strong communal work ethic mitigates against American tendencies for hedonistic and expansive single-family lifestyles, while Swedish culture contains a very strong sense of environmentalism that promotes the conservation of rural land.

Some comparative figures of densities in European and American cities will give the reader an overview of the different levels of urban compaction on the two continents. In Amsterdam, for example, people live at nearly 49 persons per hectare (19.6 per acre). In Stockholm the figures are 53 persons per hectare (21 per acre), and London, 42 persons per hectare (17 per acre). Public transit is highly developed throughout Europe, and new developments as well as existing centers are often conveniently served by buses, trams and trains that reduce Europeans' dependence on cars and support these denser, more sustainable urban patterns. In contrast to these figures, two of the densest American cities, New York and (surprisingly) Los Angeles have densities of 19 and 22 persons per hectare, respectively (7.6 and 8.8 per acre). The figure for New York, of course covers the whole city, not just Manhattan. Houston, Texas, a city without any zoning controls and which exaggerates typical American conditions, averages a meager 9.5 persons per hectare (3.8 per acre) (Beatley: p. 30).

Amidst all the reasons why European settlements are compact and America's are sprawling, there is one important cultural difference that best explains it. It has nothing to do with the automobile. Europeans love their cars every bit as much as do Americans, and they drive them an increasing amount. No, the real difference is in how Americans think about land. Because there is so much land, and because the history of the nation was forged by quick and dramatic urban expansion across the wide-open spaces of the continent, most Americans view rural and agricultural uses of land as temporary. Despite their avowed attachment to their rural heritage, Americans' sense of value in land is driven by the concept of the highest and best use; that is, the most profitable use for the individual landowner. Land is an economic commodity and not a social resource, and thus agricultural and rural uses are expected to give way in time to urban uses. Indeed, in most American communities arable land is zoned for housing or other urban uses as a right.

**Plate 1** Founders' Square, Neshoba County Fair, Philadelphia, Mississipi. The public space is enclosed and framed by vernacular buildings that follow the community's self-generated building codes. Open, shaded porches create a whole new 'in-between' realm of semi-public social space, making a transition zone from the fully public space of the square to the private interior spaces of the cabins. (*Photo courtesy of Robert Craycroft*)

**Plate 2** A Typical 'Street' at Neshoba County Fair. The public space of the street is framed by the structured social spaces of the porches and balconies. (See also Figure 4.1.) (*Photo courtesy of Robert Craycroft*)

**Plate 3** 'Ideal City' Probably by Luciano Laurana (*c.*1420–72). The same typology that drives the design of Founders' Square and American courthouse square towns – the placement of a significant public building within a defined urban space – can be seen in this famous painting from the early Renaissance. (*Illustration courtesy of Scala Art Resource*)

**Plate 4** Birkdale Village, Huntersville, NC, Shook Kelly, Architects, 2003. Surface car parking faces the miserable environment of an eight-lane suburban highway, but the mixed-use urban core creates a new pedestrian-friendly urban center that connects to adjacent neighborhoods by a grid of walkable streets. (See Plate 7). (*Illustration courtesy of Crosland Inc., and Shook Kelley*)

**Plate 5** Main Street, Birkdale Village, Huntersville, NC. This 'town center' development crucially lacks a civic component such as a post office or town hall, but in other respects its sense of urbanity is quite convincing. The streets in the development have been taken over by the town of Huntersville as public rights-of-way. *(Illustration courtesy of Crosland Inc., and Shook Kelley)*

**Plate 6** Christmas Shoppers at Birkdale Village, Huntersville, NC. The level of urban activity in the central urban area has become so great that some retailers, and the apartment dwellers over the shops, have begun to complain about the noise in the evenings. Many suburban Americans crave an urban experience, but most have forgotten the natural rhythms and behavior patterns of authentic street life. *(Illustration courtesy of Crosland Inc., and Shook Kelley)*

**Plate 7** Plan of Birkdale Village, Huntersville, NC, 2003. The urban spaces and density of the urban core are supported by four hidden, mid-block parking decks to serve residents, office workers and shoppers. There is good connectivity in the street grid, but a design mistake in the adjacent housing means that dwellings back up to a linear park formed by a power easement instead of facing the public green as do the town homes of the central core. *(Illustration courtesy of Crosland Inc., and Shook Kelley)*

**Plate 8** Proposed Transit village at Scaleybark Light Rail Station, Charlotte, NC, Charlotte Area Transit System, 2003. Despite the potential for increased transit ridership, planners in Charlotte and other car-dominated American cities often feel they have to play safe and provide plenty of car parking at the new urban centers at the light rail stations. *(Illustration courtesy of the Charlotte Area Transit System)*

**Plate 10** Cornelius East master plan, office campus aerial perspective, The Lawrence Group, 2003. Three-dimensional drawings convey the content and future direction of an urban design master plan effectively to both lay and professional audiences. (*Illustration courtesy of The Lawrence Group*)

**Plate 9** Latta Pavilion, Dilworth, Charlotte, FMK architects, 2002. This dense, mixed-use development in a prosperous Charlotte neighborhood – the kind of infill project along major thoroughfares so crucial to any smart growth strategy – so enraged local residents that they organized to stop all future development of this type. Private selfishness triumphed over sensible public policy, and a creative developer was pilloried for his efforts.

**Plate 12** Master plan final preparation by the design team. One of the authors, second from left, works with other Lawrence Group team members on the final plan drawing during a charrette. Typically, all drawings are made by hand on site, and then digitized for immediate presentation and web site use. The plan being completed is illustrated in Plate 53.

**Plate 11** Town centre master plan, Mint Hill, NC, The Lawrence Group, 2002. The detailed vision established in the master plan by drawings like these can then be encoded into design-based zoning ordinances to ensure implementation by public policy in dialogue with private development interests. (*Illustration courtesy of The Lawrence Group*)

**Plate 13** Center Rural Village, Troutman, NC, The Lawrence Group, 2001. Small settlements require especially sensitive handling to enhance their unique qualities of scale and space. The urban fabric typically needs repair and infilling as shown in this example. (*Illustration courtesy of The Lawrence Group*)

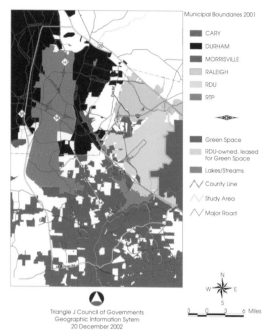

Municipal Boundaries 2001

- CARY
- DURHAM
- MORRISVILLE
- RALEIGH
- RDU
- RTP

- Green Space
- RDU-owned, leased for Green Space
- Lakes/Streams
- County Line
- Study Area
- Major Road

Triangle J Council of Governments
Geographic Information Sytem
20 December 2002

**Plate 14** CORE region Municipal Boundaries Map. This diagram clearly illustrates the circumstantial and patchy collision of political jurisdictions. (*Map courtesy of the Triangle J Council of Governments*)

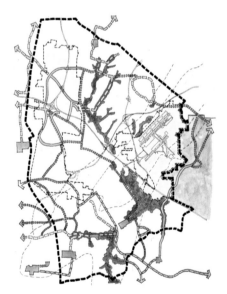

**Plate 15** Green Infrastructure Plan. The design process begins with an inventory of the environmental and ecological factors to create an interconnected framework of green spaces as a basic armature of all subsequent developments.

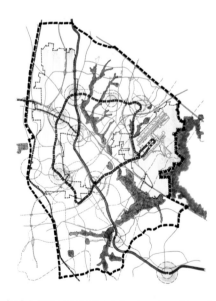

**Plate 16** Transportation Infrastructure Plan. Public transit plays a big role in any strategy of more sustainable development. In this example, public transit was the key to locating new urban and suburban centers of activity, indicated by the quarter-and half-mile concentric circles.

## Master Plan Legend

Neighborhood edge (>4 units/acre)

Neighborhood general (4–12 units/acre)

Mixed-use neighborhood center

Mixed-use village-center

Office/ employment

Civic/Institutional

Open space

Note: Blank and lightly shaded areas indicate currently developed areas

Brier Creek Village Center

Stirrup Iron Creek Center

RTP North TTA Station Area

Lowe's Grove Neighborhood Center

RTP Service Center

Triangle Metro Center

North Morrisville/Shiloh Neighborhood Center

NW Cary Center

Historic Carpenter Rural Neighborhood Center

Carpenter Neighborhood Center

**Plate 17** CORE Master Plan. The master plan combines all the various infrastructure systems and land use typologies into a holistic vision. It is then elaborated in more detail and three dimensions. See Figure 7.4 and Plate 20.

**Plate 18** Metro Center Plan. This plan establishes a benchmark and standard for future development. It embodies key design strategies for walkable and sustainable community development. See also Figure 7.4

**Plate 19** Morrisville Neighborhood Center. The complex geometries of existing roads and the airport noise contour (the light dotted line crossing the community from northeast to southwest) distort the classic pattern of transit-oriented development, pushing housing disproportionately to the north and west.

**Plate 20** RTP Service Center, as Proposed. New buildings create a street presence and sense of identity. Compare with Figure 7.5.

**Plate 21** West Raleigh Master Plan. At this smaller scale, part of city as opposed to a region, it's possible to develop more design-specific detail related to the particulars of a place. Each piece of land is considered in terms of its environmental characteristics and potential for development or conservation, and designed accordingly.

**Plate 22** Fairgrounds Station Area Plan Detail. This is one of two commuter train station sites, and we have used this opportunity to create a mixed-use urban village on underused land adjacent to the state fairgrounds (center left) and the North Carolina State University School of Veterinary Medicine (top right).

**Plate 23** Hillsborough Street Corridor Area Plan Detail. This sub-area presented an opportunity to preserve and enhance areas of open landscape for parkland and ecological storm water management while maximizing medium-density residential development along a major transportation corridor not far from either of the new train stations. New single-family residential development was extended from existing subdivisions to form the edge of the new park.

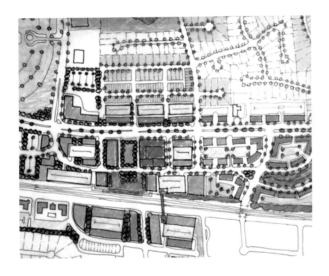

**Plate 24** West Raleigh Station Area Plan Detail. As the companion development to the Fairgrounds station transit village, we planned the West Raleigh station area with a special cultural component as part of the 'village square.' This was partly to make a polemical point about the unfortunate proposal in Raleigh at that time for a new performing arts center miles from any supporting activities and accessible only by car. There is often a huge gap to be bridged in the thinking of local government and philanthropists about the siting of cultural facilities. Far too often these facilities are conceived as stand-alone monuments rather than integral pieces of the city fabric.

**Plate 25** Village Square and Performing Arts Center. The performing arts center is seen in the middle distance on the left-hand side, forming one corner of the public square. The train station is on the far right, with other buildings comprising apartments and offices above shops.

**Plate 26** West Raleigh Main Street. Behind the buildings on the left-hand side in this drawing, residential density drops quite sharply, leading to new single-family housing that adjoins existing low-density development of that same type. The main street is designed as a multilane boulevard with on-street parking to shield pedestrians from thorough traffic.

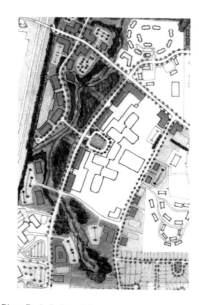

**Plate 27** Corporate Centre Drive Plan Detail. A public greenway, or small linear park, becomes the new focus of this typical suburban office park area. This landscape feature creates a new identity for the area and assists in the environmental management of storm water runoff from adjacent parking areas.

In Europe, a much higher *social* value is attached to rural land. Agricultural uses are conceived as socially important at a deep, fundamental level, having to do with aspects of national character, self-sufficiency and national security. National, and indeed continental policy through the European Union endorses this importance of farming to the economy and culture through the complex labyrinth of agricultural subsidies (Beatley: p. 58). These subsidies, particularly in continental Europe, help to maintain the countryside as a quilt of smaller working farms, stabilizing the social economies of rural communities against the rapacious economics of large-scale agribusiness.

The development pressure that promotes sprawl in America is also curtailed in Europe by different social norms regarding property rights for private land and the amount of control public authorities can exert over private property, but before exploring these in more detail, let's review the basic American position for British readers.

## Private Versus Public: The American Debate

In both nations, the concept of 'compulsory purchase' in Britain, or 'eminent domain' in America, establishes the right of governments to purchase, at fair market value, private land needed for civic improvements like building new roads. The argument between private and public interests in America stems more from other actions by government that affect land values without any compensation being paid to the landowner, and all planning is circumscribed by the concern to avoid violating the 'takings' clause of the federal constitution. The Fifth Amendment to the US Constitution reads in part 'No person shall be ... deprived of life, liberty or property without due process of law; nor shall private property be taken for public use without just compensation.'

Originally conceived by the nation's founders as a constraint upon the arbitrary power of governments (like the British crown) to take or seize land or property without payment, this precept has been extended by property rights advocates to cover changes in the zoning provisions on private land. For example, if property in a rural area on the outskirts of an American city was originally zoned for three houses to the acre, and the city wanted to reduce this classification and downzone the land to, say, one house every five acres – on the grounds that the higher level

of development would injure the environment and pollute water sources – then the elected officials may have to brace themselves for a law suit from the affected property owners. Many property owners would have little hesitation in suing the city for devaluing, or 'taking' economic value away from their property. If the city lost, it would be liable for perhaps millions of dollars in compensation to the landowners. Even if it won, it would likely have accumulated large costs in legal fees.

In cases like this cities do have the law on their side to a greater extent than one might imagine from their collective temerity. As we mentioned in the Introduction, the Supreme Court's 1978 decision in *Penn Central Transportation Company v. City of New York* established the principle that a taking does not occur unless government actions take away *all* development rights from a piece of property. Simply changing the zoning and reducing the use of land does not violate the Constitution. This ruling was endorsed by the Supreme Court's 1992 decision in *Lucas v. South Carolina Coastal Council* which affirmed that a taking occurs when all use of property is denied by government, but left open the question of whether a partial devaluation constitutes a taking. There is constant pressure from conservative groups, homebuilders' associations and property rights advocates for this decision to be revisited and for the interpretation on takings to be extended to include all downzonings, but for the moment the law stands. Polemic pamphlets arguing the property rights cause, such as *The Truth About Property Rights* published by the National Association of Homebuilders, are widely distributed to influence public opinion on this matter and to encourage conservative lawmakers to introduce new legislation that would restrict the planning powers of local government (NAHB, no date).

The American Supreme Court has also approved similar actions for the 'health, safety and welfare' of citizens under the concept of 'police powers', validated by a series of rulings over many years. These powers have nothing to do with cops and robbers, but constitute case law that makes provision for community actions to protect and enhance the public good. The key Supreme Court decision dates from a historic case in 1926, *Village of Euclid et al. v. Ambler Realty Co.*, which confirmed the general validity and legality of zoning property for the 'public welfare.' In our hypothetical example of reducing residential density to protect water supplies, there is a very good chance a city would win a court battle. However, case law is always a moving target, and this delicate balance between zoning for the good of a community and a constitutional provision for the protection of private property is a condition that's far from settled. Thus planning authorities tread very carefully, or not at all, in matters that engender such conflicts. Often many very sensible planning policies that would bring substantial benefit to the community are abandoned at the concept stage because planners don't think elected officials would uphold the policies under threat of legal challenge from aggressive property owners backed by national lobbyists. In other instances, attempts at environmental regulation are foiled by individuals.

In a celebrated case in North Carolina in 2001, property owners along the banks of the Catawba River, a waterway that supplies many communities with drinking water, faced new regulations that required them to retain a buffer of natural vegetation 50 to 100-feet wide along the water's edge. This was to enable run-off pollutants from future developments to be filtered out naturally before reaching the river. In a fit of rebellion against a county government they regarded as 'communist,' several property owners cut down every tree on their land before the regulation came into effect. By damaging their land to this draconian degree, these landowners declared they were striking a blow for individual freedom.

## Public Versus Private: The European Experience

Actions like this must seem totally bizarre to most people in Europe, where tree preservation orders are commonplace. (They appear bizarre to many Americans as well.) In Europe generally, there are no such legal constraints about devaluing land. Land ownership doesn't come with pre-packaged rights to develop it, so there is no 'taking' and no compensation payable except in the obvious cases of land purchases for public projects. For American readers we'll say that again: *Ownership of land doesn't include the rights to develop it.* These rights are generally conferred by government, acting on behalf of the public good and in accordance with a community plan that is the result of democratic debate. Patterns of growth are thus shaped far more by public authorities, and some areas around a town or city may be designated for future development, while others are not. In situations where land is required for public projects such as roads or railways, it is simply purchased by the government at the value of its existing use.

The extent to which governments plan and design such growth varies from country to country. In Germany, for example, no building can take place without a specific, detailed plan for the development, *usually prepared by government planners* (Beatley: p. 59. Authors' emphasis added). Such plans illustrate the siting and massing of buildings, building heights and densities, even tree planting. They are in effect urban design master plans. A planner from a German city visited Charlotte on a study tour a few years ago, and explained his country's system to his American hosts. A Charlotte planner asked what would happen if a landowner at the edge of town wanted to develop his open land for housing, or an office park. The German visitor didn't understand the question. 'Why would they do that?' he asked. In their turn, many of his American hosts had difficulty in comprehending a planning system that wasn't constructed around public reactions to private initiatives.

In Britain, government direction of growth is not so detailed, but it still exceeds the objectives of American planners. At a conceptual level, there is considerable similarity between the two systems, but the major differences appear in the manner of implementation, and these variations are largely a product of cultural imperatives. The function of the British planning system is to secure, in the public interest, the orderly and appropriate use and development of land. The system originated from concerns about public health and slum housing in the Victorian city, but as well as controlling and preventing abuses it has evolved to serve more positive and proactive objectives. British planners are charged with anticipating needed development and providing the necessary infrastructure. They are required to protect the natural environment and historic structures, and to stimulate economic development. During the 1990s, government guidance extended these established tasks to include meeting the objectives of sustainable development by focusing development more on brownfield sites, limiting greenfield expansion and improving public transit to limit increases in the use of private cars.

The attitudes and laws that gather the development potential of private land into the hands of European governments date largely from the era of rebuilding Europe after World War II, when towns, cities and nations had to be reconstructed from the rubble. A task of this magnitude clearly required national coordination. Attempts at national planning certainly existed in Britain during the 1930s, as they once did in America under the failed New Deal legislation, but it wasn't until the postwar planning Acts of Parliament, notably the 1947 Town and Country Planning Act, that these ambitions in Britain had any real legal power. The 1947 Act left the ownership of land in private hands, but effectively nationalized its development potential, making all land subject to planning control. Subsequent legislation from both right- and left-wing governments, with the exception of some dismantling of the planning system carried out in the 1980s by Margaret Thatcher, has followed this principle ever since.

Whereas in continental Europe much, if not most development is initiated by towns and cities in accordance with their very detailed master plans, in Britain the process has elements more recognizable to an American observer. In the UK, private landowners and developers often start the process by applying for planning permission to develop their land, usually in accordance with the precepts of the approved public plan. All communities in Britain are required to have detailed development plans that must follow national and regional planning guidance issued by the national government on matters such as urban regeneration, sustainable development, historic buildings, transportation, and so forth. As we have noted earlier, the topics for national guidance also include the quality of design, and in particular urban design. Planning procedures vary slightly between England and Scotland, and with the devolution of planning powers to the Welsh National Assembly, it is possible that further regional variations may develop. Accordingly, we'll concentrate here on the English situation; however, many of the same principles apply throughout the United Kingdom.

Planning procedures set out in a 1991 amendment to the Town and Country Planning Act require that all planning applications from landowners and developers must be determined in accordance with the municipality's development plan, unless there is some substantial 'material consideration' that may warrant some variation. This emphasis on the adopted plan was reinforced in 1999 by the government's Planning Policy Guidance Note 12 that reiterated the commitment to a 'plan-led' system. What factors might constitute a material consideration are the subject of detailed legal argument and variations to approved plans are rare and are not made lightly. (In Continental Europe there is usually even less room for variation.)

In this situation, property owners do not often make applications for developments that contradict the approved legal plan. If they do, the application is likely to be refused, and then this refusal by local government can be appealed to the national government in London. A planning inspector then adjudicates the matter and issues his or her decision, which is virtually final: the only recourse for an aggrieved party is an appeal to the British House of Lords. A relatively small proportion of planning applications are decided on appeal, and in many cases the inspector upholds the plan and disallows the appeal.

The plans on which these decisions are made are detailed and comprise three types. The first of these are 'structure plans' that cover large areas and are concerned primarily with broad-based strategies for transportation and other infrastructure, economic development, and the amount, location and type of all new development to fit these first two categories. Also of major importance are energy and environmental issues, landscape preservation, historic building conservation and concordance with national policy. These plans are based on written arguments and description and not on maps, so there is little concrete link with design at this scale. However, within the areas covered by these large plans, 'local plans' are prepared for each community which are map based. These plans focus on smaller areas and illustrate more detailed proposals for specific sites and buildings, including matters of design. Third, there are 'unitary development plans' that relate to specific large metropolitan areas, and combine the two levels of scope and detail found in structure and local plans.

All these plans are created by a lengthy process of public participation and coordination at local, regional and national levels, and are subject to continuous updating and revision. They do not have the force of law that their counterparts in European countries do, but local governments are obliged by national policy directives issued from Westminster to follow their adopted plans in adjudicating applications to develop land. During the 1990s, local authorities have revised these plans to take into account new national government guidance on sustainable development, a topic that has assumed much greater national importance. Sustainable development is defined in the British government's *Planning Policy Guidance Note 1: General Policy and Principles* (DETR, 1995), as 'development that meets the needs of the present without compromising the ability of future generation to meet their own needs.' This definition is taken from the 1987 report *Our Common Future*, by the United Nations World Commission on Environment and Development and reflects the increasing importance of sustainable development in the planning and design ethos of the British government as set out in the 1994 report *Sustainable Development: The UK Strategy* (DETR, 1994).

In addition to sustainable development, the quality of architectural and urban design has also been given greater weight in determining planning applications during the 1990s. A 1992 version of the British government's *Planning Policy Guidance Note 1* (later reissued in 1995 [DETR, 1995]) made design an explicit 'material consideration' in determining planning applications. This focus on higher design quality and sustainability came about as a reaction to the loosening of planning controls during the 1980s under the direction of the then Prime Minister, Margaret Thatcher. Thatcher's government introduced vestiges of the American system, characterized as 'planning by appeal,' where the significance of structure and local development plans was considerably reduced. Developers were implicitly encouraged by national government to initiate new proposals, often in contradiction to the plans of communities, and the government-appointed planning inspectors at that time gave favorable consideration to a wide variety of 'plan-busting' proposals. These included large out-of-town shopping malls that sucked the life out of small town centers, and new developments in the previously safeguarded green belts of agricultural land around towns and cities. For several years a purely capitalist market-driven ethos dominated planning in Britain. Planners existed to facilitate the proposals of developers, basically the American situation today.

At the same time the British government was diminishing local government authority by dismantling regional and local plans in the 1980s, it was centralizing power in national government by taking very proactive positions regarding the redevelopment of key urban sites in major cities. In many instances the national government bypassed local plans, planning staff and elected officials and set up 'Enterprise Zones,' administered by appointed officials, and based on the concept of leveraging large amounts of private investment by spending modest amounts of public money. In these zones, mainly urban areas that were deemed in need of urgent redevelopment, planning was 'streamlined' in the national or regional interest at the expense of local politics and grassroots participation. The 1980 Local Government, Planning and Land Act created these enterprise zones along with urban development corporations (UDCs), the

non-elected bodies to run them. Money to spend on cities was then taken away from local governments and given instead to these urban development corporations (Hall, 1998: p. 911). Changes were then made in 1982 to capital gains and corporate taxation that dramatically increased the attraction and profitability of property development. With the designation of 15 enterprise zones around the country, the stage was set for a new era of fast-track urban development.

London's Docklands is a case in point. Control over more than 5000 acres (2000 hectares) from Tower Bridge to the Royal Docks, several miles downstream on the River Thames, was taken from the mainly left-wing local governments by the right-wing national government and given to an urban development corporation entitled the London Docklands Development Corporation (LDDC). The main concept was one derived from American practice of the period. The development corporation had broad powers to acquire land and build buildings, and compliant public investment would provide the infrastructure that would attract private investment. The focus would be on working with the business community rather than local politicians and residents.

The theory of enterprise zones had been set forth by British planner (Sir) Peter Hall in 1969 and again in 1977. In the face of what were perceived as the failures of conventional town planning to solve problems of urban decline, Hall and others suggested that certain parts of cities should be 'thrown open to all kinds of initiative, with minimal control' (Hall, 2002: p. 387). Opinion was divided about the success of the experiment. Many critics pointed out the low quality of design of large urban projects that were pushed through on a fast track, particularly in the Canary Wharf area on the Isle of Dogs, the heart of the early phases. Others complained about the demise of local democratic control over development and the heavily North American flavor of the development and its architecture. (The main developer of Canary Wharf, before the company declared bankruptcy was the Canadian corporation Olympia and York, and the largest buildings in the first phases were designed by American architects, Cesar Pelli, HOK, and Kohn, Pederson Fox) (see Figure 5.3).

Many people decried the sacrifice of traditional community values to the boom and bust cycle of corporate capitalism. More positive interpretations argued that this process, rough and ready as it was, made old discarded brownfield sites as attractive to

**Figure 5.3** Canary Wharf, London, in 1995. For several years after its initial construction, Canary Wharf was seen by many as an unwelcome symbol of crony capitalism in league with the Thatcher government at the expense of local neighborhoods and cash-strapped London boroughs. As the architecture has matured, new buildings constructed and new transportation infrastructure (the Jubilee Line extension) provided, this image has softened and improved, along with a more constructive political climate of cooperation between the public and private sectors.

**Figure 5.4** The Lowry Center, Salford Quays, Manchester, UK, Michael Wilford, architect, 1997–2000. This project is a good example of utilizing dramatic architecture to catalyse redevelopment of decayed urban areas. Adjacent areas are slowly being filled in by a useful mixture of commercial and residential buildings but lively public spaces are still missing, despite the potential of the dockside environment.

developers as greenfield ones, and thus supported the emerging agenda for sustainable urban form. It can also be argued that the standard of architectural and urban design improved in later projects. Ironically, only after the demise of the LDDC in 1998 has the urban vision come to some level of fruition with the completion of the extension of the London Underground's Jubilee Line, which did much to improve the transportation infrastructure of the area, and provided some exemplary civic architecture in the design of the new stations.

Elsewhere in the UK, the city of Salford, part of the Greater Manchester metropolitan area, successfully revitalized its derelict docks, not least with showpiece buildings like the Lowry Center by Michael Wilford, honoring the city's most famous artist, L.S. Lowry, and the northern branch of the Imperial War Museum (see Figure 5.4). This latter building was designed by Polish American architect Daniel Libeskind, now best known for his winning competition design for the rebuilding of the World Trade Center site in New York City.

This period of 'Americanization,' of minimal planning and maximal private enterprise, drew to a close with the 1991 amendment to the Town and Country Planning Act, which established once again that planning decisions must accord with the community's development plan. Once again, at least rhetorically, the emphasis was upon the importance of local and regional development plans, and controlling suburban growth. With the departure of Margaret Thatcher, successive governments, first Conservative and subsequently Labour, gradually rebuilt parts of the planning system, with a special emphasis on the national need to increase the sustainability of urban development. Of particular note is the reintroduction of urban design concepts and criteria into planning policies, either nationally in terms of Guidance Notes, or locally by means of detailed 'planning and development briefs' for sites. These planning briefs comprise the public authority's expectations for sites deemed particularly significant in their urban setting; they establish performance requirements to be met by private development and highlight particular contextual or programmatic factors to be incorporated (see Figure 5.5).

*Planning Policy Guidance Note 1*, for example (DETR, 1995) promotes 'high-quality, mixed-use developments such as 'urban villages', characterized by compactness, mixed uses, affordable housing, employment and recreational facilities, access to public transport and open green spaces and 'high standards of

## Park Street/Moor Street

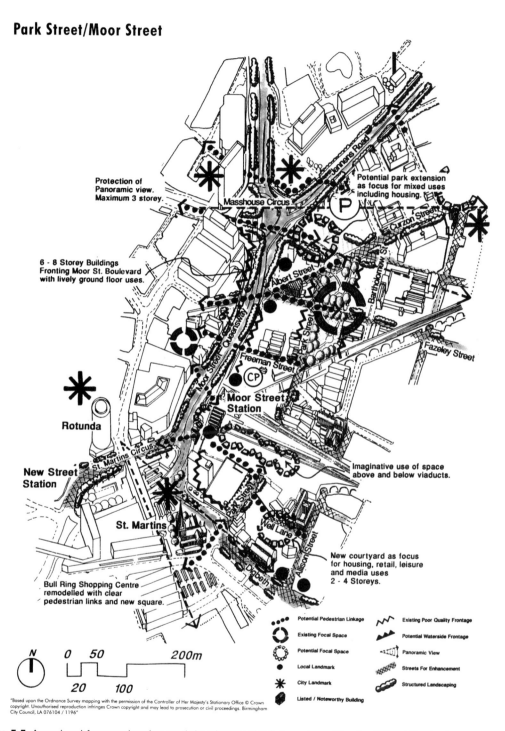

**Figure 5.5** An extract from a planning and development brief produced by the City of Birmingham, England. This document and others like it are produced to stimulate and guide new development and redevelopment of critical urban areas. Note the way the axonometric drawing is able to convey specific visual and three-dimensional criteria in additional to programmatic requirements. *(Illustration courtesy of the City of Birmingham)*

urban design.' This same Guidance Note goes on to define urban design as:

> The relationship between different buildings; the relationship between buildings and the streets, squares, parks, waterways and other spaces that make up the public domain; the nature and quality of the public domain itself; the relationship of one part of a village, town or city with other parts; and the patterns of movement and activity which are thereby established: in short, the complex relationships between all the elements of built and unbuilt space. The appearance and treatment of the spaces between and around buildings is often of comparable importance to the design of buildings themselves ...

The Guidance Note continues:

> New buildings ... have a significant effect on the character and quality of an area. They define public spaces, streets and vistas ... They are matters of proper public interest ... Good design should be ... encouraged everywhere. (It) can help promote sustainable development; improve the quality of the existing environment; attract business and investment; and reinforce civic pride and a sense of place. (DETR, 1995, available at http://www.planning. odpm.gov.uk/ppg/ppg1/02.htm.03

This brief synopsis describes a planning system that diverges considerably from the American model in many ways, and demonstrates to an American audience that there are other methods of planning for democratic societies. This is particularly relevant in the first decade of the twenty-first century because many design and planning professionals within the USA have increasingly criticized the American system for its failure to meet the challenges of suburban sprawl and regional planning during the 1990s.

Without specific reference to the planning systems of other countries, first architects in the US, and latterly their planning colleagues, have called for some major revisions to the objectives and practices of the American planning process. Most of these criticisms have focused on two main problems: the separation of planning from zoning (which we will discuss further in the next section); and controlling development through a system of zoning regulations that deal only with land use without any meaningful design content.

While critical of the American system, none of these reforming voices have called for a major redesign on a European model, however much they

may personally admire the results of those foreign systems. Such a revolution, with its necessary abridgement of the private property rights embedded in American culture, seems ideologically impossible. Instead, architects have concentrated on reforming zoning itself, making it based more on design concepts rather than use classifications, and reintegrating it with the process of making plans.

To demonstrate this trend, our case studies in Chapters 9 and 10 illustrate master plans that contain specific zoning ordinances, with the new zoning tied directly to the particulars of the plan in its design detail, and ready for adoption by the town or city. In this way the crippling divide between planning and zoning is overcome; the zoning provisions are based on design principles, and they ensure that the provisions of the master plan will be followed. For the reader to understand more easily what a major shift in policies and procedures this represents, it is necessary now to explain the workings and drawbacks of the conventional American system as practiced at the start of the twenty-first century.

## PLANNING VISIONS AND DEVELOPMENT CONTROL

With the caveat that national government in America lacks an agenda for sustainable development, the broad policy objectives in much British planning would be familiar to most American planners. The most fundamental variation resides in the relationship between planning for the future and the regulation of development to achieve that goal. In America the creation of strategies to guide development (planning) is crucially sundered from the mechanisms of development control (zoning). In Britain, and in Europe generally, the two functions are indivisible: regulation of development is carried out in accordance with the adopted plan. This is far from the case in America.

Public plans are usually generalized and advisory only; they have no force of law and are frequently ignored when influential people or wealthy developers are applying to build projects that contradict the official plan. In one famous moment of American planning democracy during the 1990s, an elected official in Charlotte, tiring of a lengthy discussion, suggested that the city council adopt a plan on which city staff and citizens had worked long and hard for many months. 'I move we adopt this plan,' she said. 'It's only a plan and we don't have to abide by it.'

Within a few months, that same council member cast a crucial vote in favor of a large development that completely contradicted the adopted plan. These cavalier sentiments and actions could be, and usually are repeated in every city across the USA.

In our home state of North Carolina, a state legislator introduced a bill in 2003 that tried, in some small way, to remedy this situation. The bill proposed that in cases where a municipality rezoned land for development that contradicted its official plan, then the public authority would have to provide detailed reasons for its decisions. Some city attorneys opposed the bill on the grounds that establishing such a legal connection between community plans and zoning decisions could mean that cities would face lawsuits from citizens who wanted the plan upheld! Many elected officials don't want to stick to the plan they've adopted on the grounds that this gives them 'flexibility.' By contrast, citizens and planners view this 'flexibility' merely as 'wiggle-room' for elected members to accommodate the ever-changing demands of developers. This inconsistency between adopted plan and permitted development brings great frustration to planning staff and to citizens who work hard in the democratic process of producing the plan. At the time of writing this book, the bill to improve the planning situation was stalled in the legislative process.

There is little interest in many state legislative bodies to deal with problems like this. Again, in North Carolina (which is no better or worse in this regard than most states) elected officials in state government receive a lot of campaign money from developers, builders and real estate agents, cash that buys these groups influence with the lawmakers. This may sound close to corruption to non-American ears, but using money to buy access to politicians is a protected right of 'free speech' under the First Amendment of the Constitution. We suspect it's not quite what the Founding Fathers had in mind, but that's how it's been interpreted by the courts in recent decades. According to a report in *The Charlotte Observer* newspaper, during the 2002 election cycle, political action committees representing real estate agents and homebuilders in North Carolina gave $255 450 and $223 159, respectively to legislative candidates, making these two organizations the largest sources of campaign funds in the state, ahead of lobbyists for health-care groups, bankers and lawyers (Hall, R., 2003). The homebuilders and real estate organizations in North Carolina are known as 'the sprawl lobby,' and the reader can safely presume

they were not asking lawmakers to tighten up planning controls or seeking Smart Growth legislation!

Beyond these legal and legislative concerns, zoning in America today is often vilified by progressive planners and urban designers for a more technical reason: it is concerned almost solely with land use rather than environmental or physical design. Zoning (as we note in more detail in the next section) was created in the early years of the twentieth century as a means of segregating uses perceived as incompatible, and protecting private residential property by excluding new uses that could encroach on and reduce the value of existing developments. However, by the latter half of the century it had morphed into the primary bargaining chip in the legal and financial game of property development: rezoning land to facilitate a more profitable use remains one of the main objectives of any developer, while neighborhood groups line up to oppose such changes.

All too often this conflict devolves into merely a squabble over numbers. Say, for example, the developer wants to raise the density on a site from four dwellings per acre to eight (10–20 units per hectare). Neighborhood activists automatically oppose the new number, suspicious from the outset that if the developer wants that density it must constitute overdevelopment of the site from the community perspective. Maybe some compromise is reached at a density of six dwellings per acre (15 per hectare). Nowhere in this process have concepts of design been introduced. Rarely does the conventional zoning process provide for a discussion about how developments at a low density might be designed well or poorly; nor how good designs of higher density development might actually be better from an urban design perspective than the low-density option. Because design is not an integral element of zoning categories, it is not something that has any legal standing. The only variables under discussion are the numbers, dwellings per acre or areas of commercial uses. This is one of the crucial problems that we try to solve with the kind of design-based zoning codes we espouse and illustrate in the case studies. Design criteria for building form, massing and public space design are embedded diagrammatically in the zoning codes (see Chapters 9 and 10).

Conventional zoning is site specific and rarely considers any criteria beyond the boundary of a specific site or project. Planning, on the other hand, concerns itself with large-scale issues and future possibilities over larger areas, and one clear illustration of the crucial American divorce of planning from zoning is that once a plan is adopted by a city, little or no action is taken to change existing zoning to conform to the new plan. Such 'corrective rezonings' are often very controversial for the reasons discussed earlier (the city 'taking' value from private property owners). Accordingly, unless there is some overriding necessity or dominant public interest, planners and elected officials usually hope (optimistically and unrealistically) that property owners will adjust their ambitions to fit with the plan without further action from the city.

Two contrasting Charlotte examples will illustrate the American planner's dilemma in these circumstances. As part of a city and countywide transportation plan, Charlotte is planning a new light rail corridor that follows a defunct railway line through old industrial and commercial areas. Train service is expected to start in 2006. Essential elements in the plans for this corridor are new urban villages clustered around the train stations along the line, but most of the land where these new communities would be constructed is zoned industrial. To assist developers create the new development on these brownfield sites, the city plans to rezone large tracts to allow the range of mixed urban uses required for a urban village – high-density housing, shops and offices. The city investment is too large, and the plans too vital to the city's future, to leave this new urban development to chance, or to require developers to bear the economic cost and political burden of major rezonings, often in the face of local opposition (see Plate 8). There has even been discussion among city officials about the city buying key parcels of land, rezoning them, and then selling them onto developers in order to stimulate the desired development.

In this instance, American planners are operating much like their British and European colleagues; the city is leading development, identifying sites, producing master plans, density requirements and urban design guidelines for private developers to follow. It is a good and professionally well-managed process that reflects credit on our city, but it is not the norm. More typical is another Charlotte example from 2002, concerning a proposed new asphalt factory in a low-income black neighborhood.

For several months, city planners worked with local residents to develop a new master plan for the small community close to the city center. The plan was a worthy effort and outlined a range of modest improvements and new opportunities for housing and small businesses. However, a lot of land in the community was zoned industrial, a relic of old zoning concepts from previous decades. These outdated ideas imagined that nobody would want to live near the city center in the future, and that the industrial classification was the highest and best use for such sites that were near major highways and contained mostly black residents. (The residents were expected eventually to move elsewhere.) In this case, having created the new plan, city planners and elected officials saw no significant public investment to protect, nor any overriding public purpose sufficient to initiate the corrective rezonings that would update the zoning plan and make sure new housing was built where the plan suggested. This was a tricky topic as the corrective rezonings would constitute a downzoning of the land from 'industrial' to 'neighborhood mixed-use,' effectively reducing the paper value of the property. Accordingly, the plan was approved with no correlation between its future proposals and the existing zoning categories. Planning staff and local residents hoped that property owners in the area would follow the plan, but they were soon disabused of that prospect.

Within only a few months of the plan being finalized, a property owner declared his intention of building a new manufacturing plant that would produce asphalt for construction projects. The residents complained angrily, concerned about fumes, noise, heavy trucks passing their houses, and above all, that this proposal was in flagrant contradiction to the plan they had worked so hard to produce and which the city council had so recently adopted. Embarrassed city planners explained that they were powerless to intervene: based on the industrial zoning of his land, the property owner was perfectly within his rights to build the factory. In effect, the plan wasn't worth the paper it was drawn and written on. Development control was, and is, a function of zoning, not planning.

In the early summer of 2003, this situation was partly resolved. The Charlotte City Council essentially bought the developer off with nearly $800 000 of public money. They gave his development company 10 acres (4 hectares) of city-owned land elsewhere in the city, valued at $194 000. The city also pledged to pay $460 000 to clean up environmental problems at the new site, and to pay $192 000 to convey an easement to prohibit future industrial use on the original site. In return, the developer agreed to pay the city a nominal $50 000 for the new site and not to protest the downzoning of the old site from industrial to neighborhood mixed-use. While this helped untangle this particular mess, many observers of the civic scene in Charlotte saw the city's actions as setting a difficult precedent – essentially paying developers to follow the city's plans. Others argued that these actions constituted an even more troublesome trend: paying money to achieve a downzoning established a *de facto* taking, with the city acknowledging the need to pay compensation to a private property owner for reducing the value of his land by a zoning change desired by city planners.

This messy story highlights the importance of zoning in American urban and suburban development, and it's worth spending a little time reviewing how it has evolved, and how it is possible to reform it by using other strands within the history of American development.

## DESIGN AND DEVELOPMENT CONTROL

While many people think of zoning in America as a twentieth-century concept, derived from the 1926 Supreme Court decision noted earlier, its origins on the continent go much further back into history, to the Spanish Laws of the Indies, codified in 1573 by King Phillip II of Castille to regulate the founding of new settlements in the New World. These Laws were a landmark in the history of urban development of the new continent, but in fact they codified earlier practices based on Royal Ordinances sent from Seville as early as 1513. The Laws specified a physical urban structure with a standardized grid plan of square blocks around a large central plaza which contained civic buildings (Broadbent: p. 43). In the same way that Roman civilization stamped symbolic geometric plans on virgin soil as urbanization expanded, so did the Spanish in what are now California, Arizona, New Mexico, Texas and Florida. This typology of civic buildings within a central square set in a rectangular grid is precisely the same as the courthouse square towns of the American South and Mid-west that we have noted earlier.

However, the Spanish town-planning codes did a lot more than set out a grid of streets around a plaza. They specified sizes, and orientations to take advantage of climatic factors such as sun, shade, and wind direction. They established street hierarchies, and promoted urban devices such as arcades. The codes also extended to regulations for the best size and mix of population, the housing of animals, the placement of hospitals, and even fines for lax clergy! (Broadbent: p. 45).

More directly pertinent to our contemporary situation are the various codes developed and employed in the nineteenth-century expansion of American suburbs, such as the one used by Frederick Law Olmsted at his Chicago suburb of Riverside (1869). Olmsted used codes to enforce the precepts of his master plan, and to maintain the desired garden suburb aesthetic recently imported from England (as we noted in Chapter 2). At Riverside, like its precedents and many successors, the houses were set back a uniform distance from the street, and a specific tree planting placement was enforced on the 'semi-public' spaces of private front yards as well as the public realm of the street to create the enfolding green canopy so typical of these suburbs. One of Olmsted's great successors, John Nolen, used similar devices in his work, a particularly fine example of which is the great, green boulevard of Queens Road, in Nolen's streetcar suburb of Myers Park (1911) in Charlotte (see Figure 5.6). For many decades during the modernist period of the twentieth century, Nolen was an obscure and neglected figure, but he was rediscovered during the 1980s and 1990s with the renewed interest in traditional neighborhood planning. He is now recognized as perhaps America's greatest town planner of the early decades of the twentieth century.

Codes like the ones for Myers Park were generally formulated as restrictive covenants, binding on all homeowners in a development, and covered a wide range of matters, including provisions that were

**Figure 5.6** Queens Road West, Myers Park, Charlotte, NC, John Nolen, 1911. Planner John Nolen created the spatial structure of his great boulevard with seven rows of identical Willow Oaks, marching across public and private space alike. The trees make the space. The buildings are secondary.

shamefully racist. The Myers Park regulations, for example, stipulated that no African-American could live or own property in the neighborhood. While such egregious examples of discrimination are long gone, zoning codes can and do still institutionalize racism by means of requiring large minimum size house lots in a residential subdivision, thus ensuring that only wealthy individuals can afford to live there. Given the fact that America in 2003 is still largely divided into more prosperous white and poorer black and Hispanic ethnic groupings, the stipulation of large lot sizes is very often synchronous with the exclusion of blacks and Hispanics.

On the positive side, the generalist scope and intent of Olmsted's and Nolen's codes enabled the regulations to deal with the overall environment, and to specify design elements that contributed to the character of the public space. This holistic design intent was in contrast to the regulations developed in England during the same period of the late nineteenth century, which were technical codes to improve the overcrowded and unsanitary urban environment of that nation's industrial cities. The Public Health Act of 1875 and subsequent legislation created standard building regulations that improved the standard of working-class housing design but which were applied literally by speculative builders without any correlation to a cohesive master plan. This resulted in what became the typical environment of working-class areas in British cities — a collection of monotonous straight streets constructed with no higher ambitions of civic design. There were no parks and few trees; these were regarded as unnecessary embellishments that reduced the developer's profits (see Figure 5.7).

This type of English regulation for urban development, based on generic formulas rather than design concepts or a specific master plan, was regrettably followed in America in the 1930s, when the Federal Housing Administration (FHA) created technical standards for subdivisions as requirements for federal insurance and mortgages (Dutton: p. 72). As we have seen in Chapter 3, it was these regulations that increased the widths of streets, enlarged the sizes of blocks by minimizing cross streets, and encouraged cul-de-sacs. Since the 1930s the holistic design intent of the earlier American codes for projects like Riverside and Myers Park was smothered by a plethora of specific requirements from an increasing range of professional specialists, each concerned with their own rules and not worrying about their place in any larger picture. For example, regulations that now

**Figure 5.7** Street in Benwell, Newcastle-upon-Tyne, 1970. Typical workers' housing on the banks of the industrial River Tyne in northeast England used the 'Tyneside flats' – terraced houses divided into upstairs and downstairs apartments – to increase density. Front gardens and setbacks were non-existent, back yards were miniscule (just large enough to hold the outside lavatories and a short clothes line) and recreational spaces such as parks or playgrounds were never considered. Every piece of space was devoted to maximizing profit for the developer.

govern much subdivision design include separate requirements from planners, transportation engineers, fire departments, utility providers of gas, water and electricity and public works departments for storm water and sewers, and lending institutions. This fragmentary nature of different sets of codes is one of the biggest hurdles New Urbanist architects and planners face in establishing new sets of regulations that return the focus of development control to design standards that embody an overall design vision.

Public discussion about sprawl and the chaotic environment that characterizes much of suburban America often refers to the mess as an 'unplanned' environment. This is simply not true. There is more planning going on than ever before. Every decision about the placement of buildings, driveways, signs, roadways and utilities is the result of conformity to one or more sets of planning, or more correctly, zoning standards. What is missing is any sense of design. Contemporary suburbia is planned to death, and more 'planning' won't improve it. The only way to rectify the situation is to return to concepts of urban design, thinking in terms of three-dimensional relationships between buildings and spaces rather than merely applying information from abstracted tables and formulas. This means a return to the examples of Riverside and its successors. This used to be the way America designed its suburbs, and these places work as well today as when they were designed one hundred or more years ago.

But there is more to the lineage of design-based codes than historic examples from early suburban America, important as they may be. The incorporation of design codes and guidelines into ordinances covering urban redevelopment has a long history. Their purpose, whether used by a public agency or a private developer, has generally been to ensure the build-out of a master development plan at a consistent level of quality and detail. An important secondary use has been to control the appearance of new development in relation to the historic urban fabric of an area. Both these ambitions are relevant to our task today.

In Paris, for example, during the reign of Louis XIV, building regulations required that all new buildings respect the street alignment, and specified details such as the solid-to-void ratio of building façades, the continuity of eaves lines from one building to the next, and the depth of courtyards in the building plans (Ellin: p. 46). While this level of aesthetic control has remained common (to varying degrees) across several European countries, American urban development has historically been far less constricted. As we have noted several times earlier, in America the powers of government to control private development have been much more limited than in European countries, and have rarely extended beyond the zoning of land according to use. Issues of what passes for design have generally been restricted to specifying the placement of buildings in relation to parking lots, the location of driveways, and tree planting requirements.

But American urban history does include some notable exceptions to this condition, and one of the earliest examples of design affecting zoning ordinances dates from 1916 in New York. These regulations followed German models in constraining the bulk of skyscrapers rising directly from the line of the street by limiting their height and mandating setbacks at specific levels above ground level, in order to ease the overshadowing of public streets and adjacent buildings. The architectural illustrator Hugh Ferris rendered these ordinances into three-dimensional forms in his famous series of drawings, 'Zoning Envelopes: First through Fourth Stages,' first published in the *New York Times* in 1922. This zoning law was

not replaced until 1961, when new ordinances were enacted based on different design ideas.

The 1961 New York ordinance was based on new modernist design concepts of a tower set back from the street and surrounded by open space. Models for this new ordinance – buildings like the Seagram Building by Mies van der Rohe and Philip Johnson (1958) – were simple vertical boxes positioned well away from the sidewalk with an intervening plaza. Residential ordinances in the city followed the same pattern, and these regulations became a prototype for similar codes in cities across the USA.

These codes virtually eliminated the traditional idea of the street as a linear public space defined by the walls of buildings, and it wasn't until the 1980s that cities like New York, Pittsburgh and San Francisco led a revisionist trend in urban design, bringing back requirements for streets and plazas defined by continuous 'street walls' of building façades. One of the stimuli for this movement was Jonathan Barnett's book *Urban Design as Public Policy* (1974) which argued a powerful (and prescient) case for urban design criteria being embedded within zoning controls. Typical of these new zoning codes, and others during the 1980s and 1990s that followed this precedent, have been a proliferation of urban design guidelines attached to, or parallel with zoning categories. Such guidelines spell out criteria for developers and their architects to follow in developing their designs, and include: street width and building height; volumetric massing; percentages and arrangements of glazed areas in building façades; entrances and storefronts at sidewalk level; and landscaping provisions to streets and sidewalks.

We have mentioned the contributions to urban design by the English urban designer Gordon Cullen on several occasions in the text, but he deserves yet another mention here as the author of one of the most innovative attempts to code the urban environment. Under the title *Notation*, Cullen developed the 'HAMS Code' (Humanity, Artifacts, Mood and Space) in the 1960s. He used a system of symbols and numeric values both to record the content and quality of an existing urban setting, and then to orchestrate future development by means of a notational system that he likened to a musical score (Cullen, 1967). In this analogy, the urban designer became the conductor, and individual architects for individual projects played the role of musicians, interpreting their parts of the melody within the overall arrangement. This approach has overtones of Camillo Sitte's view, expressed in his book *City Planning*

*According to Artistic Principles*, that architects 'should compose the city like a Beethoven symphony.'

Though unsuccessful in terms of wide acceptance, Cullen's method of coding towns and cities informed his own influential work on the reinterpretation of traditional urban forms and spaces and boosted the rise of neotraditional planning practices during the following decades. The influential design code manual, *A Design Guide for Residential Areas*, prepared for the County Council of Essex in England by Melvin Dunbar and others in 1973, is a direct descendant of Cullen's work and was a model for many similar ordinances in the UK.

While the design ordinances for the centers of American cities were being revised in the 1980s to incorporate traditional concepts of defined urban spaces, urban designers began to examine suburban environments from similar viewpoints, seeking to ameliorate the bland appearance and environmental degradation of suburban areas. But one of the main obstacles faced by New Urbanist architects and planners to the implementation of their ideas was, as we've pointed out previously, the fact that most aspects of this traditionally based urbanism were illegal under many American zoning ordinances developed after World War II. The solution of these designers has been to follow the memorable rhetoric of Andres Duany (with his Cuban American background) to 'capture the transmitters', that is, to rewrite the development ordinances that control the form of urban and suburban development.

These new codes are based intentionally on models of traditional urban design. Simplified graphic diagrams and dimensions deal explicitly with the scale, massing and placement of buildings to frame space, the organization of parking, and the design of streets, parks and squares. As we have noted earlier, this coding of development in easy-to-understand pictorial formats was first developed by Duany and Plater-Zyberk, in their design for the new town of Seaside (1981), and the 'Seaside Code' has provided a model for similar design-based ordinances across the USA. In privately controlled developments like Seaside, or Celebration, the new town near Orlando in Florida financed by the Disney Corporation (1995), these private codes can specify great detail in terms of architectural style, materials, and construction. But in normal urban and suburban contexts, where development is controlled by publicly administered zoning, state laws usually restrict the ability of municipalities to dictate this level of detail. Consequently, during the 1990s much work by architects

and progressive planners focused on marrying the concepts and practices of the New Urbanist design codes with the full complexity of public zoning ordinances for towns and cities.

This led initially to the development of 'parallel codes', where a set of design-based New Urbanist ordinances was established as the preferred option for development, but which left the old sprawl-producing regulations in place as a matter of political expediency. More radically, some communities moved to create new, replacement zoning ordinances based on New Urbanist design principles. The authors have been instrumental in developing both types of codes for communities in North Carolina. In 1994–95, we worked with the town of Davidson, North Carolina, to create a parallel code, with the intention that this would be expanded to be a full replacement ordinance after five years. In 2002 the town made that change. Meanwhile, the authors had assisted the adjacent towns of Cornelius and Huntersville to enact full replacement New Urbanist zoning ordinances in 1995 and 1996. All together these three compatible sets of regulations controlled development across an area of approximately 100 square miles. Some of this work is highlighted in Chapter 11.

Such ordinances mark a fundamental change from conventional zoning that has been based on building use as the main criterion for organizing urban development. Instead, these design-based codes operate on the principle that buildings and spaces outlast their original uses, and that regulations should be based on good design criteria rather than transient activities. Accordingly, the creators of such new regulations analyze examples of successful urbanism, either from history or from detailed design studies, and then encode these models into three-dimensional envelopes of building types, urban forms and public spaces that become the vocabulary for building towns and cities.

The primary points of reference in these codes are typological. They are constructed around established building types, such as storefront, workplace, apartment, attached house, detached house, civic building and so forth, and spatial types such as streets, parks, plazas and squares. Each building type is defined in three dimensions with sets of governing measurements and stipulations regarding scale, character and use of materials. Each zoning district is first and foremost comprised of a permitted range of building types, setting out the potential variations for that part of the community in three-dimensional form and layout. In parallel with these building types, a range of uses is then allowed within each typology, with the emphasis on mixing compatible activities rather than separating them.

Similar design-based classification systems are developed for the different types of streets (residential streets, commercial streets and special types like boulevards), and for public open spaces like playgrounds, parks and urban squares. The regulations also stress the requirements that streets and public spaces are defined by the fronts of buildings (service alleys are the only exception), and that they connect into an efficient network that is attractive, safe and convenient for pedestrians and cyclists as well as motorists. Cul-de-sacs are generally not permitted except for particular site circumstances. As we have noted previously, too many cul-de-sacs break up the connectivity of the street system and create an inefficient street layout that minimizes the choice of route and concentrates all traffic onto only a few roads. To make sure that the connected streets provide safe environments for pedestrians, street designs in residential areas focus on narrow, slow speed streets with wide sidewalks and on-street parking to protect pedestrians from moving vehicles (see Figure 5.8).

One important element of these design-based ordinances is their provision of incentives for developers and landowners. These incentives assist in the transition from conventional patterns of thinking that are based on the use of land and structures, to new ones that are founded on the design of buildings and public spaces. Such inducements usually take the form of density bonuses awarded by the regulations for either following the unfamiliar form of the regulations (if the ordinance is a parallel code in competition with conventional regulations), or for exceeding the minimum code requirements. For example, a feature of many ordinances written to deal with greenfield development concerns the protection of open space and the preservation of existing landscapes for visual or environmental reasons. Several codes of this type that we have written stipulate a minimum percentage of the site to be preserved as open space, but if the developer exceeds this amount he or she is awarded the right to build more dwellings on the remaining land. These bonuses are awarded on a sliding scale relative to the amount of land preserved over and above the minimum requirement. This typically results in clusters of compact development amid areas of preserved landscape.

These or similar incentives are needed to overcome Americans' cultural resistance to government regulation, and in particular to the perception by developers and property owners that these design-based codes are more onerous than the ones they are typically used to. We would argue that these new codes aren't more onerous in principle; rather it's the fact they're different that causes an initial negative reaction. The old suburban sprawl formulas that developers and their designers had memorized have to be unlearned and a new design ethos absorbed in its place. For this reason we strongly advocate incorporating as many incentives into the new zoning codes as possible. This provides the developer with a motive to meet the spirit as well as the letter of the new regulations. It is also a useful public relations tool for architects and planners to point out that good design provides opportunities to produce developments that are more profitable than those churned out by the old standard formulas.

The typological basis of these codes is important. We mentioned in Chapter 4 that typology was a mechanism for both analyzing the city and for producing new designs, and to these attributes we can now add a third role – controlling development. This applies to zoning ordinances, and to the last topic we want to touch on in this chapter, urban design guidelines.

When we prepare design guidelines, whether they are called 'urban design guidelines' or 'general development guidelines', our purpose is, frankly, to

**Figure 5.8** Lexington Avenue, Dilworth, Charlotte, NC. This street was laid out in the early years of the twentieth century when car ownership was very low. Its narrow dimensions mean that cars today must move slowly between parked vehicles for safety. Such narrow street designs are back in favor with designers, planners and some transportation engineers as American professionals relearn that streets are for pedestrians as well as automobiles.

minimize the chances of a bad architect or a philistine developer ruining an urban area with a poor design. In this endeavor, some of our fiercest critics are architects. Generally the complaint is one of 'restricting design freedom', as we noted earlier, but sometimes the quarrel goes deeper. This more profound attack on design guidelines was articulated by Australian architect and academic, Ian McDougall, at a conference in Melbourne in the year 2000. McDougall expressed this more abstruse antagonism against 'so-called New Urbanism', by arguing that '(w)e are sick of the urbanism of the café and the perimeter block. The city must not become the normalising environment of nostalgic guidelines … skeletal rules derived from deconstructing outmoded models of the city' (McDougall, 2000: p. 30). At the same conference, another Australian academic, Leonie Sandercock posed the question: 'Who wants to live in a city frozen in its own historical aspic?' (Sandercock, 2000: p. ix). This rhetoric was ratcheted up a notch or two with the assertion by McDougall that it was important for architects to debunk the sanctity of context, history and memory.

To us, this sounds like the worst of modernist rhetoric retooled for a new and unsuspecting audience. Only modernist doctrine considered it cool or appropriate to revel in the destruction of the past. All other periods of architecture established some relationship with history other than destroying it. The modernist city, by contrast, was a place of demolition and free composition of isolated objects in the reduced landscape of the city, and the restoration of traditional urbanism marks a return to respect for people and the public spaces they inhabit. Designing great streets that frame the public realm of the city and provide places for public life isn't recycling tired old ideas from Haussmann's Paris. It is more like waking up to a world of sanity after experiencing a nightmare. We are returning to an urbanism centered on people rather than abstract ideas, and urban space rather than architectural form. Using design guidelines isn't historicizing the city. It's implementing good urban manners and putting people first. How many more loud, boorish buildings do our cities need?

Such an approach requires architects to design once more within context, as illustrated in Figure 5.9. This means seeking continuity with context and history and rejecting idiosyncratic buildings based on contrast with their setting, except in the most particular of circumstances. Most cities can only take one Bilbao Guggenheim or Glaswegian armadillo

**Figure 5.9** Gateway Village, Charlotte, NC, Duda Paine and David Furman, Architects, 2001. Urban design guidelines by RTKL, 1997. These mixed-use buildings in Charlotte's city center all conform to detailed urban design guidelines that establish height, setbacks of top storeys, vertical rhythms and the requirement for pedestrian level 'permeability', that is, views into the ground floor uses by passing pedestrians. This communicates a sense of safety and urban activity.

**Figure 5.10** Casa Mila, Barcelona, Antonio Gaudi, 1906–10. Gaudi's building obeys the dictates of Ildefonso Cerdá's urban regulations with a simple plan that follows the required height and massing with its 45-degree corner splay. But within the apartments, Gaudi explores very sophisticated spatial rhythms, and his urban façade pulsates with idiosyncratic detail. Even greater freedom is evident on the roof, which is a riot of sculptural ornamentation. All this architectural invention occurs within a tightly controlled urban frame, and is all the more resonant because of this contrast.

conference center however wonderful each building may be as a unique object.

We like to quote the example of the Catalan architect Antonio Gaudi as an illustration of how architects can create individually compelling and idiosyncratic buildings without breaking the rules of established urban typologies and urban design guidelines. Two of Gaudi's buildings in central Barcelona, the Casa Mila apartment building (1906–10) and the nearby Casa Battlo (1904–06) demonstrate conformity with the urban design parameters established in 1859 by Ildefonso Cerdá in the Eixample, the city's massive nineteenth-century expansion. Instead of breaking the urban rules to express his own vision or to make some kind of contrasting statement to the urban pattern, Gaudi celebrated his personal architecture in the design, materials and detailing of the building façades. The vertical planes of both buildings are massively rich in forms and details, expressing in some cases profound metaphysical ideas about Catalonian nationalism, yet the ground plans are modest and subservient to the city context. This mixture of reticence and flamboyance is a model for all contemporary architects working in urban settings (see Figure 5.10).

The oft-quoted exhortation to 'employ designers of quality and trust them' reveals the very worst of outdated Fountainhead thinking, where the genius architect, preferably with a tortured and misunderstood personality, stands alone as a beacon of honor and artistic integrity against the venal idiocy of the architecture profession, clients and public at large. This is the antithesis of community design based around charrettes to gather public input. To our manner of thinking, the best designers are not those who stand apart, and feel they know better. The really best designers are talented, modest people who welcome public participation and understand that building cities is a collaborative act.

# Urban design in the real world

## SYNOPSIS

This is a long chapter, and it ranges from informed speculation about the future of American cities to the mechanics of working in community design charrettes. First we look at the circumstances that are shaping the American city, and ask the questions: what kinds of cities are American urban designers likely to be working in during the early decades of the twenty-first century, and what cultural forces are likely to shape the nation's urban areas? In answering these questions we take an optimistic view that some degree of rationality will prevail, and that at least at a local level, progress can be made toward a more sustainable urban future. We are less optimistic about the chances of improvements in national policy toward the urban and natural environments in the USA. Stewardship of America's future will likely come from individual cities and consortia of civic and business interests rather than national government, and thus these efforts will be limited in their overall effectiveness. Like our case studies in the subsequent chapters, examples of good design and planning will tend to be sporadic rather than coordinated.

If this is the case, it's all the more important that Smart Growth and New Urbanist practice must provide accessible models for other places to emulate, and thus create an extensive body of precedent and a momentum for better design nationwide. To this end, it's important that these initiatives take advantage of the full range of urban design techniques; this will improve each project's chances of success, and by demystifying these techniques we hope that they will be used extensively and often, not only by urban designers, but by planners and other parties in the development process who don't have a design background. Accordingly we extend our discussion from Chapter 4 on concepts of urban design to include more detailed practical advice.

Finally we discuss urban design master plans and the charrette process that we use to produce them. We explain our working methods as a prelude to the case studies. We discuss in detail some of the urban and development typologies that we insert into the design and planning process as catalysts for change, and we offer guidance about implementation strategies, including design-based zoning.

## THE URBAN FUTURE

The title of this chapter begs the question: what, precisely, constitutes the 'real world'? What kinds of cities are urban designers and planners going to be working in during the early decades of the twenty-first century? What are the realities of planning and development likely to be? What future forms are cities going to take? And what cultural forces are likely to shape them? We have discussed highlights from the history of Anglo-American urbanism, and these provide some clues. We have examined the relationships between center city and suburb, and considered some of the most important cultural forces at work. We have charted the (d)evolution of the urban periphery from suburbs to sprawl, and considered some of the environmental and economic issues acting in this process. We have also examined some crucial differences between American, British and continental European policies regarding the control of development and the management of growth. In considering some of the likely future circumstances that will shape the city for the next generation, and create the context within which urban designers, architects and planners will work, we will concentrate mostly on American urban futures, as frankly, the situation seems more urgent here. However, several conditions have structural similarities with British problems, and some proposed solutions use urban forms and typologies common to both cultures, so we hope some of the observations can provide a commentary on British circumstances.

We have seen that many aspects of American systems of planning and land development are constrained by conservative practices and attitudes that are resistant to change. One of the main problems with advancing the practice of community design is that many current development practices are based on repeating formulas that worked in the past with little thought for future changes in circumstances. It's not just developers and lenders who march into the future looking backward. Many planners and transportation engineers have grown comfortable administering regulations and standards that were established decades ago for a different world. Without minimizing these obstacles, we consciously base our thoughts about future planning and development on changes that might realistically be achieved in the next decades rather than circumstances that pertain today.

The crucial areas of concern that most people acknowledge – for both American and European cities – are revitalizing the center city and controlling sprawl around the urban periphery. We have seen earlier in this book that many urban ambitions and design concepts common in British and European cities are embedded in American Smart Growth policies and embraced by the professionals who espouse those policies. But the critical difference between the two continents is that European nations have, however imperfect, national systems for addressing these questions through government policies and regulations on growth management, urban design and sustainability. Moreover, most of these countries enjoy the benefits of proactive and legally enforceable public planning procedures at regional and national scales.

When we've made comparisons like this elsewhere in the book, we've imagined a variety of ribald and derisory comments from our British and European colleagues. Many of them will stand in line to recount the failings of their particular system. But the

crucial weakness that bedevils American planning and the quest for sustainable urban development is the lack of a system for dealing with these issues in any comprehensive manner. America presently lacks the political frameworks to enact the kinds of growth management policies common in Europe. There is insufficient public acceptance of the concepts of Smart Growth and little effective leadership to champion these issues at the various levels of government. (At the time of writing, North Carolina is proposing to weaken its environmental management legislation.) And as we discussed in Chapter 3, increasingly well-organized ideological opposition to the whole notion of Smart Growth has been developed by right-wing groups within American politics.

A series about the burdens of urban expansion in North Carolina in *The Charlotte Observer* newspaper in March 2003 extolled the efforts of many volunteers to promote a more sustainable agenda for managing growth in the surrounding region. But in reality there is little to show for these efforts as none of the volunteer and non-profit organizations have executive authority or large funds to support their activities. Their main achievement has been to get officials, citizens and business leaders talking about the issues. However, the progressive ideas of these pressure groups are often politely accepted and then sidelined by a power structure based largely on maintaining the status quo. Indeed, even at the grassroots level, many such growth management efforts are reactive, aimed more at stopping growth in specific local circumstances with no comprehension of any larger picture. At a larger scale, few, if any, American politicians are pushing for regional government as they know full well that voters have no liking for it. A poll in the Charlotte newspaper indicated that a large majority, nearly half of all those questioned (47 percent) believed that regional growth should be handled by citizens themselves, not government. The kind of government agency needed to enact comprehensive and enforceable regional planning received a measly 12 percent of the votes.

This general distrust of government and the hijacking of Smart Growth terminology by local organizations who want to stop growth altogether feeds opponents of Smart Growth as they gear up to roll back the few gains made in America, emboldened by the weakening of environmental laws by the Washington DC government. A March 2003 editorial in *Smart Growth Online* quoted Joel Hirschhorn, the Director of Natural Resources Policy Studies for the National Governors Association Center for

Best Practices, writing in an op-ed piece in www.planetizen.com that: 'The hatred of government and regulations by conservatives and libertarians from all over the nation is more focused. Everything they see as wrong with (America) is labeled smart growth.' Hirschhorn went on to report that Smart Growth adversaries are 'sharpening their rhetoric, reshaping their statistics, learning fast, getting more cohesive and painting smart growth as "snob growth," which reduces home and transportation choices, increases housing and transportation costs, limits affordable housing, harms minorities, stems economic growth and prosperity, and threatens "the American dream".' (Hirschhorn, 2003).

In effect, opponents are creating an Alice-in-Wonderland world where everything is the opposite of what it seems, and forging a coordinated campaign of disinformation to sway public opinion. Despite the appearance of scholarly researchers, Hirschhorn notes that conservative think tanks such as the Thoreau Institute operate as the public relations arm of the 'national sprawl industry' (ibid.). Hirschhorn warns Smart Growth organizations that they must be unequivocally pro-growth. They should absolutely disavow groups that profess Smart Growth but in reality try to stop development, and true Smart Growth advocates must stress the market advantages of this type of development.

A hostile political environment such as this raises the obvious question: why bother? The answer is simple. We must try. It's our duty. The professions of architecture and planning have a responsibility to envision a better future for our society and to assist governments, the public, and the private sector to achieve these higher goals, however Sisyphean the task may appear. Indeed, there are several small causes for optimism in the swirling debate about the future of American cities. They are scattered across the nation, and individually modest in their scope and achievements, but taken together they comprise an agenda of hope and progress.

The most progressive examples of regional planning with an eye to Smart Growth are those previously mentioned in Portland, Oregon, and the twin cities of Minneapolis-St. Paul in Minesota. Salt Lake City in Utah has also initiated a progressive regional planning process for the Salt Lake-Wasatch area which led to the passage of the Quality Growth Act by the State legislature in 1999 (Calthorpe and Fulton: p. 138). Portland is perhaps the most 'European' of all American cities in its planning strategies, which feature a regional urban growth boundary, local comprehensive plans with minimum housing densities, urban villages around rail transit stops, significant investment in the downtown core, and a regional open space plan – all with a strong regional government to back it up (Beatley: p. 67).

For Smart Growth planners and urban designers this situation represents as close to utopia as it's possible to get in contemporary America, but to many in the development and real estate industries, the comprehensiveness and regional scope of this planning system is ideologically repugnant. It's almost routine at homebuilders' or Realtors' conferences to hear speakers lampoon Portland's regional cooperation as 'The People's Republic of Portland,' and in the minds of many passive observers, this title tars the progressive model with the dreaded brush of socialism and anti-Americanism. However loopy this may seem to British readers (and it's pretty daft to lots of Americans, too) it's a political reality that has a lot of impact on development decisions in many cities all across the country. In our work in the American South, we've learned to use very few examples from Portland as it can be counterproductive, and generates as much negative reaction as positive support.

There must be something special about the American northwest, for the neighboring west coast city of Seattle in Washington State also demonstrates progressive planning around the concepts of urban mixed-use village centers served by public transit within an urban area growth boundary. The foundation for these initiatives was laid by Seattle's 2002 Vision Plan dating from 1987, which stimulated the passage of a statewide growth management law, the 1991 Washington Growth Management Act. The concept of transit supported mixed-use urban centers as a growth management tool is gathering momentum in many other American cities. Other North American cities currently operating or planning new light rail or commuter rail systems include Dallas, Texas; Sacramento, San Diego, San Jose and Los Angeles, all in California; Charlotte and Raleigh, North Carolina; St. Louis, Missouri; Baltimore, Maryland; Washington, DC; Denver, Colorado; and Toronto, in Canada. Even Phoenix, Arizona, by many measures the most sprawling city in the USA is building its first light rail line. However, few are considering the more difficult, but equally necessary growth boundary legislation.

Our home city of Charlotte is a classic case. It is spending a lot of money and effort in planning and constructing a good transit system with a necklace of urban villages along the lines. At the same time it's constructing a massive outerbelt freeway that is spreading growth into surrounding counties at a faster rate than planning can manage. In Charlotte, and many other American cities using the same rail-based planning concepts, there is a vocal debate about the relevance of rail transit as the catalyst for reshaping the city. Critics describe it as a 'nineteenth century technology' unsuited to the car-dominated American landscape. The fact that passenger trains are almost extinct in America has consigned rail technology to the museum in the minds of many citizens and policy makers alike, and blinded them to the fact that modern rail transit is a very effective and advanced technology. This is a strikingly different attitude to Europe's, where train service has remained an integral part of life.

The companion piece to public transit in these first efforts at creating a sustainable urban strategy is the much-touted mixed-use urban village. At its root, this development type represents our best chance at meeting what is perhaps the most crucial challenge in American urbanism at the start of the new century: how can we re-embed real and meaningful public space into the sprawling new developments of the urban periphery?

However, the urban village has many detractors from the conservative end of the political spectrum, and opposition also arises from residents of existing neighborhoods. American conservative opinion decries the concept as social engineering, by which they suggest that elitist planners and architects are 'forcing Americans to live like Europeans' – a step backward to people of this jingoistic mindset. The opposition from residents of existing neighborhoods is less ideological. It's generally the classic Not In My Backyard (NIMBY) variety, where residents erroneously equate density with crime, traffic and lower property values. While these NIMBYs drive us mad in practice, we have to sympathize with them to some (small) degree. Examples of this kind of urban village development have been so sparse in American suburbs for the last 50 years that public opinion has few positive models to relate to. Only in the past five years have decent developments of this type begun to appear in American cities (see Plate 9).

Despite this combined opposition, urban villages have one very powerful ally – national demographics. The number of American households that conform to the conventional profile of a married couple with children, typical consumers of single-family housing in suburbia, fell to less than one quarter (24.3 percent) of the total number of households as recorded in the 2000 census, and is expected to keep falling for the next several decades. By contrast, the numbers of aging 'baby boomers' who are 'downsizing' to urban dwellings in more compact, walkable urban areas is increasing, as is the number of 'echo boomers,' the generation that comprises the children of baby-boomers. Both generations are seeking an urban setting that supports their changing lifestyle expectations as an alternative to conventional suburbia.

The urban village typology meets the needs of the younger group of residents, workers and consumers, who desire a vibrant urban environment replete with street life, bars, restaurants, an art and music scene, and social diversity – the sort of places discussed by Richard Florida in *The Creative Class* and summarized here in Chapter 1. At the same time, their elders are seeking locations that will support them as they get older, where they can 'age in place' rather than be cut off from community life in suburbia as their mobility and independence decreases. The American author watched her parents suffering this undignified decline in their last years, and this sad family experience is shared by millions of Americans. As a consequence, many baby boomers now approaching retirement are urgently seeking alternative and more sustaining urban settings.

Aging in place is really a public health issue, and this connection between public health and urban form has also been made in relation to children and younger adult segments of the American population, particularly linking the lack of walkable environments to obesity and its consequent health problems. In America, the prestigious Robert Wood Johnson Foundation has funded research about 'Active Living by Design' to the tune of $16.5 million. This is a program that explores the links between obesity and the design of cities and neighborhoods, and focuses on ways the layout of urban areas can allow and encourage physical activity as a normal part of all citizens' daily routines. Promotion of a healthy lifestyle means opportunities for children to walk to school on safe pedestrian-friendly streets with sidewalks, or cycle on local streets without recourse to arterial highways. It means having a balance of jobs and housing in each neighborhood to increase the opportunities for residents to live near enough to their work so walking is a realistic option. It means having parks for passive and active recreation that are accessible safely on foot or by bicycle within each neighborhood. And it means having a mixture of uses, including shops and civic buildings that people of all ages, including older residents, can reach conveniently by walking. This provides healthy exercise and a means for the elderly to stay involved with the general life of the community.

If this sounds a lot like New Urbanism, it is. There is a direct match between the objectives of Active Living by Design and the principles of New Urbanism and Smart Growth. The demographic trends, coupled with the explicit linking of urban design with public health, promise a radical shift in planning and development policies in the years ahead. In 2003, the number of new developments in America that satisfied this kind of lifestyle comprised only a very small percentage of residential construction, but future market demand as much as any planning policies will stimulate a major increase in this type of urban neighborhood.

To these demographic and market forces for change can be added the growing sense among Americans that the physical environment is a precious resource to be preserved, or at least not totally subjugated to urban uses. As we discussed in Chapter 2, the loss of natural landscape and open space, coupled with increasing levels of pollution in America's air and water are problems understood by an increasing proportion of public opinion. The aggregation of all these various trends and attitudes, combined with the awesome projections for population growth in the USA over the next two decades (an increase of 50–60 million people to a total population figure of approximately 340 million in 2020) allows us to make forecasts about the future form of American cities based on solid realities.

Some commentators see sufficient evidence to anticipate that American cities will develop a more concentrated urban form with more intensive uses surrounded by protected natural areas (McIlwain, 2002). We are not so optimistic. This sounds too much like Europe to be practical in America. We expect American cities to continue to sprawl to the point of dysfunction before any radical change occurs, and by that time cities will have extended into surrounding areas past the point of efficient restructuring without massive government redirection of policies and resources. Whether American society will evolve to permit such action is a question too large for the scope of this book, but we see little sign of this major redirection of national objectives. However, within the large-scale inefficiency of sprawling, market-driven metropolitan urbanism, we do expect small-scale efficiencies to take root – examples of micro-sustainability sufficient to form the basis of a more rational urban form should one emerge over a longer time frame. Our case studies illustrate such micro examples in the hope that they can be repeated enough times in enough places, and improved upon in the process, so that a critical mass of good practice can be established. In this way, sufficient momentum may be generated to offset the worst excesses of the mega-sprawl that's just over the American horizon.

These small-scale successes build on four progressive trends in American urbanism. The first, but not the dominant one, is the continued regeneration of city centers, whereby central business districts are transforming themselves into central cultural and entertainment districts with a strong residential component. Charlotte is an excellent example of this trend, with 50 000 daily employees in its office towers, and nearly 8000 residents living downtown in medium and high-density housing. City streets that in 1990 were arid corridors deserted of pedestrians are now home to a vibrant street life, with museums, art galleries, performing arts venues, bars, restaurants, and even the occasional political demonstration enlivening the urban scene (see Figure 6.1). However, not all cities will be able to achieve this transformation, and those that fail are likely to be ones that face the most precipitous decline in economic fortune.

This process of urban regeneration is shared by Britain and America, with British cities like

**Figure 6.1** Public space in downtown Charlotte, NC. A controversial street exhibition promoting vegetarianism took over the center city sidewalk at lunchtime in the summer of 2003, mingling with hot-dog stands. Many people were upset by these images, but the demonstrators were exercising their democratic rights in public space.

Manchester, Liverpool, Birmingham and Bristol using public–private partnerships to revitalize, and in some cases rebuild inner city areas (see Figure 6.2). These redevelopment efforts utilize the same formula of high-density mixed-use projects, often with a major emphasis on housing, set out on traditional urban block patterns. Sometimes the projects involve the demolition or major restructuring of 1960s era urban highways to return lost civic space to pedestrian use.

The second progressive trend in America concerns the sites of old and out-of-date shopping malls and commercial areas that are reinventing themselves as new mixed-use districts, even town centers in miniature (see Figure 6.3). As this process continues, the emphasis will still be on shops and offices, but these new centers will include a wider range of uses including civic buildings like libraries and police stations, plus a lot of residential units. A recent book published by the Urban Land Institute (ULI), *Transforming Suburban Business Districts*, sets out the parameters and opportunities for this suburban restructuring (Booth et al., 2002). Similar issues are examined in *Grayfields into Goldfields* published by the Congress for the New Urbanism (2002). The Lindberg Center in Atlanta illustrated in Figure 2.15 is one good example of this increasingly common trend.

Third, and the most extensive trend of the four in America, will be the creation of new centers in the so-called 'edge-burbs,' the newest frontiers of suburban expansion (McIlwain, 2002: p. 41). A report by the Brookings Institution illustrated how the population of edge-burbs grew at more than 21 percent during the 1990s. In comparison, existing suburbs enlarged their populations by about 14 percent, and center cities by about 7 percent (Lucy and Phillips, 2001, in McIlwain: p. 43). The trend for retrofitting older suburban centers to meet the lifestyle expectations of residents is extending to the design of new centers around the periphery. Examples can be found around the edges of most large cities, and our previous example of Birkdale Village in Huntersville, North Carolina, 15 miles north of Charlotte is a case in point (see Plate 5). Even in Portland, Oregon, where an urban growth boundary was established to direct growth to infill and city center sites, most development is occurring at the urban periphery.

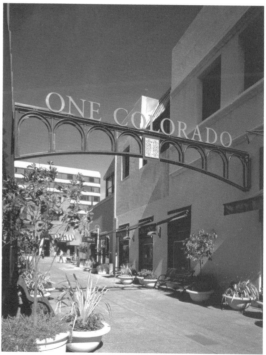

**Figure 6.3** One Colorado, Pasadena, California, Kaplan McLaughlin Diaz, architects, 1992. A decayed commercial area in Pasadena has been revived into a mixed-use complex, drawing people to a previously blighted part of town. (Photo credit Kaplan, McLaughlin, Diaz).

**Figure 6.2** Central square, Brindleyplace, Birmingham, UK. Urban design master plan by John Chatwin, 1993. Decayed canalside land has been reclaimed as an exciting, productive mixture of uses though a comprehensive urban design master plan, good contemporary architecture and the careful design of the public spaces.

The multiple market opportunities represented by the growing urban desires of increasing numbers of the baby-boom and echo-boom generations has boosted the economic profile of urban villages in America considerably, whether on recycled grayfield or new greenfield sites. In May 2003, the Charlotte developers of Birkdale Village announced they had sold the majority share in the development to a national Real Estate Investment Trust (REIT). This purchase is significant because REITs comprise large and powerful investors at the end of the development chain. At the outset of any development process, all developers try to establish their exit strategy, that is, who will they be able to sell the development on to? Until recently, urban villages were regarded as unproven in the marketplace, and large investors were skittish about their long-term value as investment property. This in turn made the initial developers nervous about making the original investments in these kinds of projects. The decision by the cautious, conservative end of the financial markets to put increasingly large investments into urban village developments does a great deal to establish the credibility of the mixed-use center as a stable development type.

We have specifically left the fourth factor, the preservation of open space, till last because we want to highlight a common American misconception about this objective. In many ways, this is the most prolific of the positive trends; it certainly has the most public support. Between 1998 and 2002, 679 proposals to conserve open space were placed on local election ballots across the USA, and 565 passed, setting aside a total of $21.5 billion (in US terms) for purchasing open land (http://experts.uli.org/Content/PressRoom/press_release/ 2003/PR_009.htm).

The conservation of open land highlights the greatest difference between American and British practice. In the UK, despite many instances of urban encroachments into the protected greenbelts around cities, the overall concept of a clear distinction between urban and rural still holds. A conversation in the Spring of 2003 between the authors and Mary Newsom, a Charlotte journalist and advocate of Smart Growth, who was giving a talk on open space conservation to a rural county in the Charlotte region highlighted the cultural gulf between the two nations.

We loaned Ms Newsom slides of the small English town of Ashburton, in South Devon, to use in her presentation (see Figure 6.4). The images showed the compact form of the historic town in its landscape, with clear edges between the urban areas and the surrounding countryside. We apologized for the slightly faded quality of the slides, as they were 25-years old, but assured our friend that they were still accurate, as we often revisit the town (where the English author lived in the late 1970s). Our American colleague was astonished that development could be organized in such a way as to preserve this natural beauty and historic character over a quarter of a century. We explained that the local and regional plans that regulate development directed new building to take place on infill sites and reclaimed land from other, defunct uses. New greenfield expansion was not permitted as the town was not designated as a high growth area. Other, nearby towns in the region fulfilled that role, with some new peripheral development being allowed in each of those communities. Ashburton's economy depends on tourism and farming, so the landscape is a prime economic resource, as is the charming historic character of the town itself. A freeway bypasses the town taking all through traffic away from the medieval center, but no development is allowed at the interchanges. All commerce is kept in the center of town, to ensure a vibrant urban area, and to allow new subdivisions to sprawl into the precious landscape, and stores and gas stations to clutter the highway would be unthinkable to the town's citizens and to business and civic leaders. Such development would compromise the economic prosperity of the town. Conservation is good for business.

**Figure 6.4** Ashburton, Devon, UK. The physical expansion of the town is strictly limited to preserve the working farmland around its edges. A modest new development of townhomes is just visible in the middle of the photograph (a white gable and two long parallel roofs) fitting in between adjacent buildings and backing up to the fields.

American readers will remember that the British planning system operates on the principle that private ownership of land does not automatically convey development rights. These rights are conferred on certain properties according to the provisions of the communally agreed development plans, and the democratically open process of plan development and revision enables all viewpoints to be heard and priorities agreed upon. In the case of many communities in South Devon, the agreed priorities have everything to do with conserving the natural beauty of the area for environmental and economic benefit.

Ironically, the rural county outside Charlotte where Mary Newsom gave her talk also contains much beautiful scenery and productive farmland sprinkled with pleasant small towns. But new freeways are bringing this rural idyll within easy commuting reach of Charlotte, and developers are lining up greenfield sites for conventional suburban development. Local politicians are getting ready to compete for new strip centers and gas stations and big-box stores to boost their tax revenues to meet the financial costs of new schools, water and sewer lines, and police and fire protection services for the new residential subdivisions that will inevitably appear. Many of the qualities that make the area so delightful are headed for extinction as development paves over the landscape, substituting rural beauty with urban mediocrity.

The county authorities are unprepared to deal with these formidable challenges and have few public policy tools to allow them much control over the patterns of development other than assisting non-profit land conservation organizations to purchase some small parcels of land that are most threatened by new building. In contrast to places like Ashburton, small towns in the countryside outside Charlotte have little chance of retaining their residual historic character, or of protecting their rural heritage in any meaningful way. Without some unforeseen civic miracle, they are doomed to be smothered in sprawl.

The natural reaction to this gloomy future is to preserve as much open space as possible, and in the minds of many Americans, citizens and elected officials alike, there is a false assumption that preserving open space is a panacea for sprawl. This is far from the case, for in many instances preserved open spaces exist as unconnected pockets surrounded by development. Saving open space is too often a reactive gesture to stop development, rather than the enactment of a coherent rural vision. Preserving open space must be part of such a comprehensive conservation

vision for a protected or enhanced countryside, and this rural vision must be complemented by an equivalent *urban* vision. We can't make better towns and cities just by preserving woodlands and meadows. We are delighted when citizens and their elected officials want to preserve farmland, or protect natural habitat. But we are dismayed when those same folks demonstrate no corresponding passion about urban areas. Our case studies try to remedy that omission by presenting a compelling vision of urbanity to complement preserved countryside.

These visions of urbanity usually coalesce around some sort of urban village, the idea that keeps cropping up throughout this book. The regeneration of city centers is one congruency between British and American urbanism in the early years of the twenty-first century, and the urban village is the second. While the physical settings of British and American cities are markedly dissimilar, except for their reviving central areas, the urban village concept has assumed considerable relevance in both countries (Darley et al., 1991; Aldous, 1992; Sucher, 1995). This type of development satisfies European objectives of sustainability as well as American lifestyle and demographic trends; as we've already noted, it's becoming the strategy of choice in the USA for redeveloping out-of-date shopping centers as mixed-use centers, and for building new mixed-use 'town centres' in the far flung suburbs.

These same lifestyle-related demographics are also present in Europe, where the same quest for active, trendy urban living emerged in the 1990s as a powerful ally of environmental goals for sustainable urbanism, which increasingly became a matter of public policy in Europe during the 1990s. Sustainability isn't totally absent from the American agenda (witness Peter Calthorpe's original Pedestrian Pockets of the late 1980s and the subsequent emphasis on transit-oriented development) but movements toward higher goals of urban sustainability and energy efficiency remain objectives of dedicated professionals rather than a matter of public policy.

A key study in the quest for a usable definition of sustainable urban form came from Australia in 1989, where two planners, Peter Newman and Jeffrey Kenworthy compared the use of energy by urban Australians, Americans and Europeans (Hall, 2002: p. 414). Not surpisingly, Americans used most energy, the Australians came in second and the Europeans were the most frugal of the three study groups. The researchers related this energy use to the spatial character of cities and the availability of public transport, and concluded that the compactness of European cities combined with the high standard of public transport accounted for the lower figures of energy consumption. From this conclusion came the oft-repeated wisdom that the most sustainable form of urban development was one that restricted the geographical spread to a defined area and then served this area with good public transportation. The corollary to this was that cities and neighborhoods should be denser, and have a mixture of uses within walking distance. Bingo! The urban village was born.

The twin typologies of New Urbanism, Calthorpe's Transit-Oriented Development (TOD) and Duany and Plater-Zyberk's Traditional Neighborhood Development (TND), were paralleled in Britain by the urban villages promoted by the Urban Villages Group (Aldous, 1992, 1995). Explicit connections were drawn in America to traditional urban types of the small town and streetcar suburb, as well as to Ebenezer Howard's Garden City and the Anglo-American Garden Suburb. In the UK, British market towns and their architecture substituted for American models, but the other sources were the same. It appeared as if avant-garde architect-planners on both sides of the Atlantic had reinvented the wheel (Hall, 2002: p. 415).

The demographic shifts evident in Britain and America that help generate the need for 'new' solutions like the urban village are most easily categorized as a move away from conventional nuclear families into more and smaller households. Especially notable in both countries is the growth in single person households. Adults of all ages are living alone with the compensatory expectation of a richer and more sociable public life. In America this demand is being partly met by the market-driven distribution of these new households in all three locations noted earlier, the city center, revitalized suburban centers in the older suburbs, and new suburban centers at the metropolitan periphery. In Britain, government policy since the late 1990s has explicitly required that the majority of such new development take place on existing, reconditioned brownfield sites to minimize suburban extensions into the green belts around cities. While this makes good sense in terms of sustainable city form, this formula also had more pragmatic roots. It was partly a victory for the powerful countryside lobby in the UK, and the policy helps to assuage deep resentment by rural communities at the thought of newcomers encroaching on their countryside amenities and way of life.

In practice, the British Labour government has backtracked on some of its goals for sustainable urban growth, simply because there were not enough brownfield sites available to handle the population explosion, estimated in 1996 at an extra 4.4 million households in England over a 25 year period (Hall, 2002: p 418). New expansions of urban areas are accordingly planned around London and in the south-east of the country, where the situation is most acute. A government statement in February 2003 specified extensions to the city of Milton Keynes (300 000 new homes), development along the corridor of the M11 motorway between London and Cambridge (250 000–500 000 new homes) and 70 000 new homes in the county of Kent, including the Thames Gateway project, a 50-mile development corridor along the River Thames related to the Channel Tunnel high-speed rail link (http://news.bbc.co.uk/2/hi/uk-news/england/2727399.stm).

Despite these compromises, the British government's overall policy for more sustainable urban form retains the concept of higher density, active urban places, with more house types that suit the multitude of smaller, childless households in the population projections. American readers will note the great difference to their country: British government agencies act strategically in the long-term interest of the community as a whole, as opposed to the American system of allowing the 'free' market, acting for the short-term profit of a few, to establish where and when this new development will take place. In America, the biggest environmental challenge is the hurdle of creating national or regional policies for sustainable growth that are enforceable, and not just a wish list of concepts with no mechanisms for implementing them. Such a regulatory framework is a concept that flies in the face of profound cultural beliefs about the sanctity of private property rights, and few people in America believe it's even a remote possibility. Moves in a few states, like New Jersey and Maryland to support growth with public resources in existing urban areas rather than greenfield sites are good steps in this direction, but even these policies can't stop development in places that may cause harm to a community's long-term environmental and cultural sustainability.

The second most difficult design and development challenge for America's urban areas is to find a way that the new and reviving urban villages do not become isolated middle-class playgrounds supporting a lifestyle unavailable to the poorer sections of society. This is a very real problem in a market-driven

**129**

development process, where the lower economic potential of poorer communities cannot provide the return on investment most developers desire in their financial equations for higher-density mixed-use urban villages. This effectively puts whole sections of cities off-limits to this kind of development, and even when poorer communities have the infrastructure (albeit decayed) and are in a good location near the city center, new development in their neighborhoods tend to displace low wage earners and renters.

These are the people who have to move as property is purchased house by house by middle-class gentrifiers, or by developers who are scooping out territory ahead of the market mainstream. It doesn't take large-scale development projects to cause this exodus. Overall, the city benefits by this process of gentrification, but without social policies and financial subsidies that support enough existing residents to stay in place and benefit from the improvements in their neighborhoods, poorer working-class areas will simply transform into tomorrow's cool new venues for the bourgeoisie. This gentrification has a lot of benefits, but this urban improvement shouldn't come at the expense of the urban poor.

This issue of social equity applies to new developments as well. Few local governments in America practice what is called 'inclusionary zoning,' whereby a certain proportion of units in a new housing development are 'set aside' as affordable for lower income home buyers. American conservatives oppose this concept as yet another instance of social engineering and interference by government in private development. It takes a brave and progressive local government to enact and carry through such a policy, to ensure that a wider range of income groups shares the benefits of growth and well-designed new neighborhoods. One such American town is Davidson, North Carolina, where the zoning ordinance requires 12.5 percent of all new dwellings to be affordable to individuals and families earning only 60–80 percent of the national median income.

In our work with towns and cities in North and South Carolina, we try wherever possible to bring good design within reach of all sections of those communities. There is no national or state policy to bring this about, so it happens only as a result of detailed work with each community, incorporating the 'set aside' provisions for affordable housing in the zoning code and establishing uniform design guidelines so that lower-cost homes share the design and aesthetic character of their more expensive counterparts. We worked with the town of Davidson on its progressive

zoning ordinance, and with the City of Greenville, S.C., to upgrade a run-down and poor, African-American neighborhood south of downtown without displacing existing residents. This latter project forms the case study examined in Chapter 10. These are successful projects, but they need to be emulated (and improved upon) in towns and cities all across America.

## URBAN DESIGN TECHNIQUES

In this section we want to outline a vocabulary of urban design techniques that will build on these basic concepts described in Chapter 4, and enable non-design professionals, elected officials and citizens to enter into a more effective and deeper dialogue with designers. We also aim to sharpen the awareness of trained designers about important issues of spatial enclosure, scale and proportion, and building façade design. The evidence of our cities shows that these lessons have not always been well understood during the last several decades.

The decision on whether or not to recap and extend some of the ideas we have previously discussed in Chapter 4 was resolved for us one day in the early spring of 2003. One of the authors was sitting in a design review for architecture graduate students at a multi-university symposium held in Charlotte, and a visiting student was explaining his final thesis work. It was a promising project involving the redevelopment of a part of Charleston, South Carolina, that was being reclaimed for the city by the demolition of an urban expressway. But despite the student's earnestness to do the right thing for the city and its inhabitants, the scheme was very poor, comprising out-of-date concepts of raised walkways above streets, with isolated single-use buildings disposed like abstract shapes in a first-year basic design exercise. In short it was the antithesis of everything good about Charleston and a reprise of all the mistakes of urban renewal from the 1950s and 1960s.

Of most concern to the author was not a weak student project, but the fact that this unfortunate young man had been led seriously astray by teachers and experienced professionals who should know better. The fact that such (well-intentioned but disastrous) urban vandalism continues to be taught in reputable American colleges of architecture in the early years of the twenty-first century demonstrated to us just how much education the architectural profession still needs! Hence our decision to go over once more some key points about urban design.

# BUILDING 2

## OBJECTIVES & CONTROLS

Opportunities

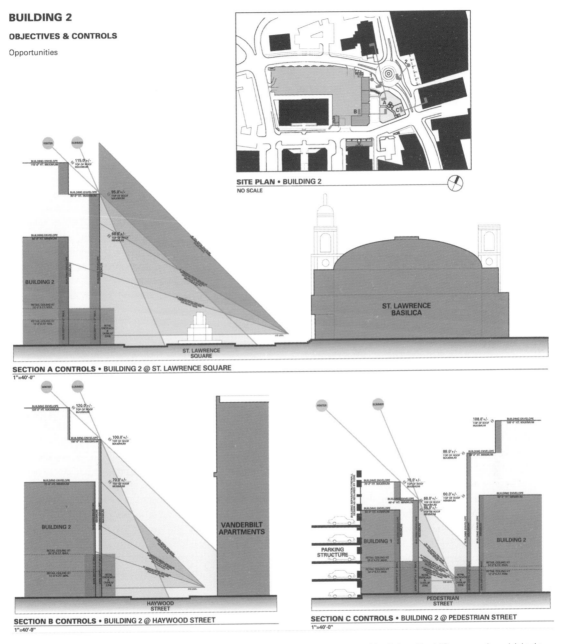

**Figure 6.5** Diagram of sun angles in urban space. This infill development in Asheville, NC, around an historic church benefits from careful study of sun penetration and shading of public space. (*Illustration courtesy of Shook Kelly, architects*)

We also think it's worth reprising some of the key attributes of urban design to clarify them in the mind of the reader, especially if that reader isn't a design professional. As educators, we know firsthand the difficulty even architects and planners have in visualizing and designing the voids of urban space rather than the solid form of objects. All too often urban space is the residual area left over between buildings, rather than a positive entity in its own right that affects the buildings around it.

Urban designers use a vocabulary of straightforward techniques to design and define space, and we have discussed several of them in Chapter 4, but here we want to expand on three of them a little more. The first, and most important, objective is to create spatial enclosure, designing public space as a series of 'urban rooms' for pedestrians – and, when appropriate, for vehicles also. Second, and intimately related to spatial enclosure is the architectural design of the building façades that combine to create the walls of these urban rooms, be they plazas or streets. Third is a set of concepts for controlling the car, so that neighborhoods and districts are conveniently accessible but not overrun by vehicles. Some designers would put this first in the hierarchy of issues to resolve, for if the cars aren't handled efficiently and conveniently, all other efforts at making urban places for people are likely to be unsuccessful. But we put people first. It's a matter of principle.

## Spatial Enclosure

Spatial enclosure is a function of two main factors, the proportions of the space – the height of the buildings relative to the width of the space – and the architectural scale and character of the building façades that form the walls to the urban room. We set out some simple rules of thumb for spatial proportions in Chapter 4 (2 : 1 and 1 : 1 for intimate pedestrian space; 1 : 3 for more relaxed enclosure, up to a maximum of 1 : 6 for spaces with people and cars), but climatic factors can affect decisions on urban proportions differently in Britain and America. In Britain, it is normal to orientate outdoor public space to receive as much sun as possible. In the southern states of America it is necessary to create shade to seek relief from the harsh summer sun and temperatures regularly above 90 degrees Fahrenheit (32 degrees Centigrade). Charlotte is located at 35 degrees north of the equator on a Mediterranean latitude, level with Malta and Cyprus, as opposed to London at approximately 52 degrees north, the same as Nova Scotia in Canada.

Calculating the shading of space by buildings with graphic sun studies – projecting sun angles into the space for different times of year – is always a good idea (see Figure 6.5). Better still is studying the space in three-dimensional model form on a heliodon, where actual shadows can be observed in model form, or with special computer programs. We also advise wind tunnel studies for key public spaces if at all possible. These are harder to achieve in practice, and impossible in a charrette format, but many windswept plazas have defeated the efforts of urban designers to create activity because of increased wind speeds due to the untested massing and arrangement of buildings and spaces.

Like any room, a public square or the linear space of a street has points of entry and exit, and views to and from the space. The more points of entry and exit – such as building entrances – the more lively the space will be. Major openings in the enclosing walls of an urban space by streets will reduce the feeling of enclosure, and accordingly these large openings should be limited. The sense of enclosure is heightened if views into the space can be terminated by buildings, rather than the viewer's line of sight passing straight through the space (see Figures 6.6 and 6.7). Congruently, views out of the space to other parts of the city enable the user of the space to feel connected to a larger urban area. If there are no views out (perhaps the entry was achieved by means of a curved street so that the view back is limited) then the sense of enclosure is heightened. However, this must be balanced with a potential sense of being isolated and shut off from the rest of the urban scene.

The character of these views into and out of any public space are important in forming a sense of place and urban character, but equally necessary is attention to the architectural, landscape and artistic elements within the space. Many historic squares contain public art, often in the form of statues of kings, dukes, generals and other male worthies, and public art of all types can play an important role in establishing the personality of a public space. Urban design should be intimately responsive to this dimension of community identity and sense of place. Artwork may be freestanding, like a statue or a fountain, or it may be integrated into its surroundings as an architectural element. Urban spaces always benefit more from the inclusion of public art at the design stage, rather than as an add-on element afterwards (see Figure 6.8).

**Figures 6.6 and 6.7** Ashburton 'Bull Ring,' Devon. These two views of the same urban space illustrate the markedly different spatial character derived from open and closed views. The open view, on the left, pulls the viewer onwards, while the closed view, on the right, suggests a destination. The name 'Bull Ring' owes its origin to the cruel practice of baiting bulls (and bears) during the medieval fairs held in this location.

**Figure 6.8** Victoria Square, Birmingham, UK. Public art and fountains are integral elements of this important and attractive and well-used public square.

**Figure 6.9** Urban square in Savannah, Georgia. One of twenty-one surviving squares from James Oglethorpe's original 1735 town plan, this delightful mini-park epitomizes the urban shade generated by the native evergreen live oak trees in the hot and humid American South. The lush planting, however, was a Victorian development. Originally the squares were hard surfaced for everyday urban uses, including drilling the town's militia.

The use of trees within an urban setting will vary depending on the location of the space. In general, American cities use more trees in plazas and along streets than British or European equivalents. In part this is cultural; Americans are historically suspicious of cities and urbanity in general (refer back to Chapter 5 for a discussion on this point) and prefer to soften the urban ambience of a public square with greenery. In part, certainly in the American South, this preference for a large number of trees in urban settings is climatic; trees play a vital role in providing much-needed summer shade (see Figure 6.9). Europeans tend to distinguish squares and plazas as 'hardscape' areas distinct from urban parks, which are green oases in the city.

It is not easy to imagine a public square in Arezzo, or the Piazza Navona in Rome dotted with trees. In these situations, the edges of the buildings, lined with steps, arcades or outdoor cafés with umbrellas provide sufficient softening and scale to the formality and hardness of the pedestrian environment (see Figure 6.10).

William H. Whyte's classic analysis of *The Social Life of Small Urban Spaces* (1980) explains the basic principles of plaza design with elegant simplicity. This slim

**Figure 6.10** Piazza Grande, Arezzo, Tuscany; Loggia by Giorgio Vasari, 1511–74. Like many European plazas, the Piazza Grande functions as the urban living room for the community, the setting for informal gathering and large communal events like the antique market.

**Figure 6.11** Covent Garden, London, Inigo Jones 1631; market buildings by Charles Fowler, 1832. This refurbished space is now the most European (and lively) of London's public squares, with arcaded edges, 18-hour-a-day activity and a complete lack of greenery (except for imported Christmas trees).

volume is a massive indictment of blank walls, bare concrete paving and barren open space and provides a compendium of good details about intimate scale, multiple places to sit, and habitable edges as places to meet and watch the passing urban theater. Ultimately, the design of the edges of the space and its location are more important than whether it has trees or not.

British attitudes to nature in the city, predictably, fall somewhere between the American and European extremes. On the one hand, a public space like Covent Garden (see Figure 6.11) follows continental European precedent – not surprisingly as Inigo Jones designed it in 1631 based on an Italian model, the piazza at Livorno. On the other hand, the green squares of London, although originally hardscaped, now integrate nature into the city in a way that is far more comfortable to American sensibilities (see Figure 6.12).

Historically, American cities have included few urban squares in their plans, although Philadelphia and Savannah (see Figure 6.9) are two notable exceptions. Whereas Italian cities, for example, are best known for their public piazzas, London by its tree-filled urban squares, the iconic American urban space, as we have noted before, is the street. The commercial typology is the classic 'Main Street' lined with stores, wide sidewalks and on-street parking (see Figure 6.13). Its residential equivalent is 'Elm Street' (or a similar tree name) which can be found in the

**Figure 6.12** St. James' Square, London. Although this handsome square is now surrounded mainly by modern offices and nineteenth-century residences, there are traces of some early dwellings built on this site in the 1670s, and a couple of notable Georgian town houses still remain. The square itself is a typical London oasis, intimate, public and green.

older residential quarters of almost every American town (see Figure 6.14). This focus on streets as the primary type of public space in America partly explains the emphasis on proper street design typical of New Urbanism, for without a street design that encourages and enhances walking in residential neighborhoods and mixed-use commercial districts,

**Figure 6.13** Main Street, Salisbury, NC. The iconic American space of Main Street has declined in stature and character since the 1950s with the development of suburban shopping centers. However, the renewed interest in urban living since the 1990s has stimulated downtown refurbishment and two of these buildings (far left and far right) in this small North Carolina town now boast apartments above active stores.

**Figure 6.15** Newberry Street, Boston. What were once the front gardens of mass-produced town homes in this Boston neighborhood have become thriving places of recreation and commerce, creating one of the most dynamic and enjoyable streets in North America. (*Photo by Adrian Walters*)

**Figure 6.14** Residential street in Dilworth, Charlotte, NC. Many streets in American 'streetcar suburbs' devolved to slum conditions in the 1960s and 1970s as residents moved out to new houses in the new suburbs. Urban pioneers reclaimed these older neighborhoods during the late 1970s and by the end of the 1990s houses on streets like this example were selling for several hundred thousand dollars as inner-city living became desirable once again. Pedestrian-friendly streets like this now form one of the public space models for New Urbanist designs.

few Smart Growth objectives can be achieved. Figure 10.13 illustrates a typical street design for a commercial street that balances pedestrian priority with car parking and circulation.

## Building Façades

The second element in our design vocabulary is the design of the building façades that enclose and define urban space to create the sensation of an outdoor room. This is especially crucial at the ground floor pedestrian level. Here the entrances into the buildings should be obvious and they should be accessed directly from the public space, be it a sidewalk along a street or a plaza. The edges of an urban space should consist wherever possible of active uses such as retail, cafés and restaurants and high-density housing with entrances directly off the public space, as illustrated in Figure 6.15. These uses provide the pedestrian traffic that energizes the space and renders it safe and attractive. Arcades and colonnades are especially useful design devices for the edges of public space. They provide a sheltered intermediate zone that further protects and enhances activities along the edges of public spaces (see Figure 6.16).

For residential buildings, this intermediate zone is best created by the use of porches or stoops, raised semi-public spaces that create a threshold between the public realm of the street or square and the private realm of the home. These spaces (and the lowest residential floors that they provide access to) should be elevated at least three feet above the public areas outside the dwelling where pedestrians walk close by (see Figure 6.17). This safeguards visual privacy within the dwelling.

**Figure 6.16** The Loggia, Piazza Grande, Arezzo. Arcades and colonnades provide a handsome and sheltered setting for casual dining and social interaction. These half-indoor, half-outdoor spaces are valuable urban design tools for creating lively urban places.

**Figure 6.17** Residential stoops at 400, North Church Street, Charlotte, NC, FMK architects, 1997. The steps tumbling to the street from the elevated first floor apartments serve to connect the public and private realms, while the difference in level maintains the necessary detachment for private living spaces. The porches and steps provide visual interest to the streetscape, while the ground floor walls mask private car parking.

**Figure 6.18** Townhouses, Mint Street, Charlotte, NC, 1998. The repetitive rooflines are dramatic, and bring a sense of appropriate scale to the row of houses without being fussy and over-ornamental.

We always maintain that new buildings should be designed with close reference to their context. This does *not* mean a historicist approach, attaching historical elements like columns and pediments to building façades in an attempt to 'blend in,' but rather one that is sensitive to the underlying rhythms in the surrounding urban and natural conditions. In practice we have found it useful to examine the cityscape by means of 10 design elements that can reveal the orchestration of the context. Working in harmony with these contextual factors can establish a deeper level of visual connection between new buildings and existing contexts than can ever be achieved by simply copying façade details. New projects do not necessarily have to address all 10 criteria, but they should rarely disrupt these contextual patterns.

The 10 design elements to look for in the context surrounding any new project in an urban location are:

1. Building Silhouette: The pitch and scale of rooflines [Figure 6.18. Mint Street housing].
2. Spacing between Building Façades: Gaps or notches between primary façades [Figure 6.19. Dilworth Crescent].
3. Setback from the Property Line: Consistency of spacing [Figure 6.20. Dilworth 'Victorians'].
4. Proportion of Windows, Bays and Doorways: Vertical and horizontal integration of elements across façade [Figure 6.21. The Radcliffe].

5. Proportion of Solid to Void: Permeability of façade created by the ratio of windows and doors to solid walls [Figure 6.22. Atherton Heights].

6. Location and Treatment of Entryways: Rhythms, scale and spacing [Figure 6.23. 5th and Poplar].

7. Exterior Materials: Range of materials of adjacent buildings [Figure 6.24. Hearst Plaza].

8. Building Scale: Compatible size and configuration [Figure 6.25. Infill housing, London].

9. Shadow Patterns: Visual interest created by projections and setbacks [Figure 6.26. 400 N. Church Street].

10. Landscaping: Defines space and ties buildings together [Figure 6.27. Gateway Village plaza].

Large buildings create special problems for the urban designer, but if their massing and façades are handled properly, buildings bigger than those in the surrounding context can be successfully integrated into the townscape. The key is to break down the bulk of the new building into a composition of vertical and horizontal elements. A rhythm of vertical bays is especially useful in this regard. The design of building façades usually means creating more vertical rhythms rather than horizontal ones, and articulating the façade vertically (by projecting or inset bays, design detail or color) creates the sense of human scale we want in the streetscape – especially when viewed in perspective (see Figure 6.28).

**Figure 6.19** Dilworth Crescent, Charlotte, NC, 1992. The setbacks between each townhouse effectively screen garage doors from view and establish a separate architectural identity for each house in the terrace.

**Figure 6.20** Houses on Park Avenue, Dilworth, Charlotte, NC, late 1980s. These modern reproductions of Victorian houses fit into the neighborhood by maintaining a consistent setback from the street.

**Figure 6.21** Radcliffe on the Green, Charlotte, NC, FMK architects, 2002. This block of luxury downtown housing above offices and restaurants creates complex rhythms and relationships to integrate a wide range of architectural elements across the façade.

**Figure 6.22** Atherton Heights, Dilworth, Charlotte, NC, David Furman, architect, 1998. This low cost housing organizes the proportions of its façade by tying together different sized openings with patterned brickwork on a predominantly solid wall.

**Figure 6.23** Fifth and Poplar apartments, Charlotte city centre, LS3P architects, 2003 The projecting entryways to the ground floor dwellings of this perimeter block contrast with recessed balconies on the floor above to create a lively street scene while protecting residential privacy.

**Figure 6.24** Hearst Plaza, Charlotte city centre, Shook Kelley architects, 2003. This plaza has been inserted into the existing city fabric as a new public urban space at the foot of a large office tower. The walls of the new low-rise buildings enclosing the space provide a dynamic contrast with the older architecture without overpowering the scale of the existing buildings.

**Figure 6.25** Infill housing, Victoria, London. This infill housing from the late 1980s/early 1990s manages to insert a new, larger building into its context by carefully matching the ground floor proportions and cornice heights.

Our work in practice has taught us that some kind of vertical articulation needs to happen approximately every 60 feet along a façade to create this desired scale and human reference. The streetscapes in older towns and cities that so many people admire for their urban character and beauty follow this pattern: they were usually constructed as a series of individual buildings on relatively narrow and deep lots that were similar in size, setting up a repetitive rhythm of entrances and building mass. The buildings could differ in detailed respects but the ensemble

**Figure 6.26** Urban housing, 400, North Church Street, Charlotte, NC, FMK architects, 1997. The repetitive rhythms of projections and recessions in this façade create multiple shadow patterns and sources of visual interest.

**Figure 6.28** Gateway Village / Trade Street condominiums, Charlotte, NC, David Furman architect, 2001. The dominant vertical rhythms of the street façade are enhanced by the pedestrian's perspective, giving a sense of urban compaction and activity. In the distance is the Bank of America tower by Cesar Pelli (1992).

**Figure 6.27** Gateway Village, Charlotte, NC, Duda Paine architects; Cole Jenest and Stone, landscape architects, 2001–02. Innovative fountain and landscape design enrich and unify the main public space between office buildings to right and left, and apartments in the distance.

was broadly harmonious in aggregate. This does not mean that designers should force a series of false façades onto large buildings (far from it!) but that the building wall should be carefully articulated. This sense of balance between order and variation is more easily achieved through vertical proportions and rhythms than through horizontal, and even when urban areas are built in large increments, like the squares and terraces of eighteenth- and nineteenth-century London, the use of repetitive vertical porches projecting from a uniform façade serves to communicate scale and human presence (see Figure 6.29).

This London example offers a multitude of building entrances, but in situations where entrances are less frequent, every attempt should be made to locate them no further than 150 feet apart. This enables pedestrians to move in and out of the buildings at several points, thus generating the activity that helps to energize an area, and also humanizes an otherwise

**Figure 6.29** Nineteenth-century terrace in Belgravia, London. This view illustrates the power of repetition. Flat façades, so typical of nineteenth-century developers' architecture, reduce construction costs, but their potential boredom is relieved by the bold projection of entrance porches. Although identical, their vertical rhythms satisfy the eye and break the terrace down into identifiable units.

**Figure 6.30** Eleventh Street, Atlanta, Georgia. Within the constraints of cheap modern construction, the new apartments on the left use projecting entrances, balconies, cornice lines and roof overhangs to harmonize with the bold architecture of the 1920s apartments on the right-hand side of the street.

long and potentially bland façade. Figure 6.30 illustrates how the designers of an apartment building in Atlanta have organized the entrances to acknowledge the powerful rhythms of the older apartment house across the street. Note that we recommend *subtle* articulations to create vertical rhythms. It is not necessary to push and pull the plan into fancy geometries to achieve this effect. In fact, the more simple

**Figure 6.31** Gateway Village, Charlotte, NC, Duda Paine, architects, 2001, detail. The façade of this large office building is enriched by the subtle details of the brick and tile cladding, where small projections and recessions combine with changes of material to break down the surface into a complex grid of regulating lines.

and regular the plan, the more effective are the smaller scale design moves. Small scale elements such as pilasters, cornices, string courses (a row of bricks laid vertically), lintels, projecting window sills, drainage pipes and awnings are all useful devices to achieve the necessary articulation (see Figure 6.31).

## Controlling the Car

Despite all the good ideas and techniques discussed earlier, none of these efforts at placemaking will work effectively if private cars dominate spaces used by pedestrians. In America, almost everybody depends on automobiles for almost every aspect of daily and family life, and while light rail transit is changing some patterns of personal mobility, no development can succeed in the marketplace if it doesn't design for the car. This is one major difference from European cities: in those locations, despite increasing use of cars in urban areas, large percentages of people still organize their daily lives around convenient public transit, and private cars are effectively banned from large parts of towns and cities (see Figure 6.32). Two cities, London and Oslo, now charge motorists for using the streets of the city center, a controversial practice that has worked far better than expected to reduce congestion. But in America the car still rules, and all urban design is constrained by designing facilities for accommodating the private automobile. This means designing the parking so that it is convenient but unobtrusive.

**Figure 6.32** Town center, Kingston-upon-Thames, London. Many European cities have pedestrianized their main shopping streets to great effect, whereas American efforts to do the same have failed miserably. The key factor is the availability of efficient public transit, used by all socio-economic groups, that reduces the need for every trip to be taken in private automobiles.

**Figure 6.33** Parking lot, South Boulevard, Charlotte, NC. The standard American formula of large parking lots in front of stores created spaces for cars but nowhere that a normal human being could ever find hospitable. When the retail businesses fail, there is no other reason to be in these spaces, and the cycle of decline increases.

There are two types of car parking – on-street and on site. From the 1950s through the 1980s, most American design and planning practice was based on two objectives: eliminating on-street parking as an impediment to free-flowing traffic, and creating of large car parks in front of buildings to maximize customer convenience. Parking lots were hugely over-sized for the convenience of one-time Christmas crowds; no consideration was given to the aesthetic effects of these huge areas of asphalt, or to their environmental consequences of polluted surface water run-off into streams, or of their complete obliteration of any environmental qualities that were pleasant to the pedestrian (see Figure 6.33).

It wasn't until the 1990s that New Urbanism offered Americans the opportunity to relearn what most Europeans in their older, more compact cities never quite forgot (although there are plenty of cases in Britain and elsewhere of selective amnesia, where car-dominated planning oppresses the pedestrian). The best urban places are structured around human beings, not their cars, and while vehicle access and parking should be ample and convenient, the most attractive and prosperous places in urban America are now those where cars on site are subservient to pedestrians. Car parking is still an essential component however; only in the densest of American cities like

Boston and New York where there is good public transit, is it feasible to build developments without integral parking. Elsewhere, in lower density cities, we are always working out the car parking plan while pursuing our townscape aims and larger urban design objectives for any particular development.

In conventional suburbia, each separate use requires its own parking provision. When driving and parking patterns are analyzed, figures show it takes five parking spaces to accommodate each vehicle in a community on a daily basis. There is one at home, one at work, and three others scattered around at stores, health clubs, at the doctor's office, parks, schools, churches and so forth. This means that each car requires 1600 square feet (148.6 square meters) of concrete or asphalt just for parking (Schmitz: p. 18). It is imperative to reduce this figure, by sharing parking between uses, by linking parking lots within the block for easier access, and by providing on-street parking.

We try to provide on-street parking in every possible location. This doesn't do a whole lot to solve the numerical problems of the parking requirements, but cars parked along streets provide protection for the pedestrian from moving traffic. They slow down the speed of vehicles and, importantly, they signify activity. People are parked there for a reason, popping into to the store, going to a meeting in the office or visiting friends. The potential availability of finding on-street parking in a development is a vital psychological factor in the success of street level retail space. All drivers hope that they are going to be lucky and slip into a spot just as it opens up. For the majority who are unsuccessful in this quest, off-street parking must be immediately and easily accessible from the street but at the same time screened by buildings (see Figure 10.12). Nothing harms pedestrian street life more than having to walk directly past large parking lots or parking decks. Car parks and parking decks should ideally be placed in the interior of the block, but if a deck has a street frontage, the ground level should include retail or office spaces to promote pedestrian use. Any street façade of a parking deck should always be clad in high quality materials and given some proportional articulation – usually vertical bays – to fit into the rhythm of the streetscape (see Figure 6.34).

While designing for adequate and convenient parking is an almost universal preoccupation, it's no exaggeration to say that in America, the parking provision drives the design. The other complication is the cost of parking structures. In American terms, a surface level parking space costs about $1000–$1500 at 2003 prices. The equivalent space in a deck costs between $10 000 and 15 000, and in an underground structure over $20 000. These costs provide

another reason to reduce parking areas by sharing spaces between uses. Ideally, customers or workers should arrive by car, park once, and then be able to reach their other destinations in the area on foot or by transit within a walkable, mixed-use environment. In this way, separate parking spaces for each different use are replaced by one or two centralized facilities.

Even with these economies, parking costs are hard for most developments to bear, and the development economics of high-density, mixed-use infill schemes are often balanced on a knife-edge if there is no public financing as part of the deal. The climate of American political and public opinion often makes it difficult for a city to inject public tax dollars into a development project for facilities such as parking structures. This is often viewed by politicians and the public as an unnecessary subsidy to private companies, and a negative sign that 'the market' won't support such a development in its 'pure,' private form.

Public funding of major downtown developments such as sports stadiums and museums is increasingly common in American cities, but these blockbuster projects often have more to do with a city's image-making agenda rather than a truly Smart Growth vision. There is some residual reluctance on the part of many US cities to initiate or partner in more progressive development, such as high-density mixed-use developments – despite the desire of forward-looking sectors of the private development industry for such partnerships. This hesitancy means that American cities are not as proactive as their European counterparts in directing growth in ways that suit their long-term interests, preferring to allow city form to follow market forces. This factor, and its consequent result of *ad hoc* sprawl, remain two of the more structural differences between American and European urbanism.

In this confusing and fluctuating American political context, the opportunities for design and planning professionals to have profound influence on the form of communities are limited. For this reason it's all the more important to pursue Smart Growth objectives with a sharpened sense of urban design that can promote three-dimensional thinking. Just as important as these objectives are the means of achieving them, and in practice we have found the charrette process by far the best method of providing a vigorous democratic forum for the production of detailed master plans and implementation strategies. Therefore, before presenting the case studies, we describe the concept of the urban design master plan and our charrette process in some detail.

**Figure 6.34** Seventh Street parking deck, Charlotte, NC. This parking deck, located on a new light rail line through the city center, features a grocery store and two restaurants on its lower floor. Its walls are enlivened by public art.

## MASTER PLANS AND MASTER-PLANNING: THE CHARRETTE PROCESS

The urban design and Smart Growth planning concepts described earlier are most usefully brought together by the creation of 'urbanistic' master plans that focus on three-dimensional urban form instead of two-dimensional plan diagrams that indicate land use only. This is one of the key messages of the whole book: *three dimensions are better than two*. These plans are public documents that must be understood easily. Clear and attractive graphics that deal with form and space as well as use facilitate the production of the plans and their implementation (see Plates 10 and 11). Moreover, this three-dimensional infrastructure of form and space allows long-term flexibility of use and operation; it maps out the physical future of the community in ways that enable change to be monitored effectively over time.

A strong urban form – a robust and connected pattern of public and private spaces defined by coherent building masses – can provide an armature for resolving many potentially conflicting concerns of community design. These issues include the impacts of changes in technology, social structures, economics, uses, architectural styles, and development practices. The detail study inherent in the kind of urban design master plans illustrated in Plate 11 establishes the physical framework for growth and change, and a guide for public policy and investment strategies. This practice is reinforced when the master plan and its detail design vignettes are encoded by means of a regulating plan, a design-based zoning ordinance, urban design guidelines or general development guidelines.

The reason for encoding detailed community design proposals into regulatory form allows communities to mediate potentially major changes in patterns of use within an urban framework of building forms and spaces that is clear and communally understood. In particular, the design-based zoning codes ensure a typological fit between the new buildings and spaces and the existing urban fabric. This allows for more continuous and less disruptive patterns of human occupation; new buildings, and conversions of old ones, are subject to physical standards of scale and arrangement that are clearly depicted.

The master plan therefore provides a detailed vision of the conceptual 'build-out' of the plan area under the relevant market conditions. The plan, like the one illustrated in Plate 21, lays out major roads, public squares and parks, local streets and greenways; it sets out the infrastructure of public transit; it plans residential subdivisions by drawing all the individual house lots; it locates all major buildings, and it defines areas for environmental protection or landscape conservation. In our practice we do this on very large colored drawings, often larger than 6 feet (2 meters) square, combined with perspective views, dimensioned sections through streets, and any other specific details that might be appropriate to each plan area (see Plate 12). We work this way even on large-scale regional projects, (for example, the 60 square mile area described in the first case study in Chapter 7). At this scale this level of detail is necessarily illustrative of key development types and projects rather than comprehensive.

We know that no master plan we produce during a charrette will ever be built exactly as we suggest, even though our recommendations are always based on developmental realities. However, we specifically work at this level of detail for three reasons:

- First, clear, detailed design of specific places establishes a lucid pictorial image of the proposals much more effectively than any two-dimensional colored map of generic land uses can ever do. The extra levels of specific information enable the community to understand what is being proposed and to share the vision more easily.
- Second, the projection of the future at this level of detail enables the community to handle future alternatives and changes in a realistic and rational manner. The impact of new buildings and patterns of use can be evaluated visually in three dimensions to supplement and modify conventional planning abstractions of traffic flow and trip generation statistics.
- Third, we design the master plan area in detail to see what makes sense under various scenarios, and generally select one set of proposals as the most appropriate for our final recommendations. We do however, often include alternative design and development proposals for important or controversial sites as noted in the second case study in Chapter 8.

Accordingly, the urban design master plan works out and illustrates this high level of detail not to establish the exact template for future development, but to put firmly in place the potential character of new buildings and spaces, with clear guidelines for the future implementation, and *variation*, of the plan by others. Changes are much easier to deal with if there is a yardstick against which to measure new alternatives. Clear plans, three-dimensional illustrations and graphic zoning regulations provide this clear standard for comparison and judgment much more effectively than the conventional method of abstract plans and legal language.

Hand-in-hand with the detailed master plan go the various sets of regulating documents. These most usually comprise a Regulating Plan – a diagram of zoning classifications derived from the master plan detail, and a Zoning Code specific to the plan area under study that will enable the plan's recommendations to be implemented with consistency and predictability. The code, samples of which are included in Appendix III, and discussed in detail in Chapter 10, sets out in graphic detail the legally enforceable design and development standards. British readers will recall the discussion in Chapter 5 about this disconnection in conventional American planning between creating a community plan and not changing the existing zoning to comply with the new plan. This fusion of the master plan and zoning codes derived from the design concepts of the plan is specifically intended to bridge this American gap between plan formulation and development control.

The product of our charrettes thus always includes specific new zoning regulations, urban design guidelines or development guidelines to ensure that new development complies with the plan. These documents are described schematically at the end of the charrette, and worked up into fully detailed documents in the subsequent weeks. So far, over a period of several years, no public body has declined the new zoning provisions or guidelines as part of the overall plan. We believe this is partly because the visual detail of the master plan enables local elected officials to understand more fully the implications of the proposal, and thus feel more comfortable than usual about changing the zoning classification on private property. The local officials also know that the owners of property in contentious or difficult locations have usually been sought out during the charrette process to participate in the discussions about the future of their land and their community.

At the level below the legally enforceable Regulating Plan and Zoning Code come the advisory Urban Design Guidelines that establish the specific levels of design deemed appropriate for the community. These cover a wide range of matters concerning the functionality and aesthetic character of the shared public realm, and can be broken down into four main categories:

1. The Criteria for Mixed-Use Centers. These define the content of mixed-use centers at various scales and relate them to their urban context.

2. Site Design Issues. These comprise the placement and arrangement of buildings to define and enclose public space; the relationship of new buildings to their context; vehicle circulation, parking provision and preferred layouts; the integration of public transit, pedestrian and bicycle amenities; techniques for environmental protection; and provisions for public art.

3. Street Design Standards. These include functional cross sections for a pedestrian-friendly connected street network and principles of proportion for appropriate spatial enclosure.

4. Building Design Recommendations. This section discusses building massing, scale, façade treatment, the relationship of buildings to public streets, the placement and character of building entrances and the organization of service functions such as deliveries and rubbish collection. Some of these guiding principles – 10 elements of contextual design, for example – were discussed and illustrated earlier in this chapter, and serve to illustrate an important point. The design guidelines do not mandate building *style*; they concentrate on principles and techniques derived from good practice.

These guidelines are advisory only, but they're specific in their articulation of good practice to be followed. As in Britain, they are used by American planners to lead developers and their architects, engineers and surveyors toward the communally agreed standards of community design.

At a more general level, Development Guidelines are intended, as the name suggests, to guide the development of property according to standards of good practice for Smart Growth. Development guidelines are even less prescriptive than urban design guidelines, but they do define the key typologies that are the building blocks of the master plan and illustrate criteria and recommendations for good sustainable design practice.

These factors comprise:

1. The different typologies of neighborhoods and districts within the plan area, for example, traditional neighborhoods, employment districts and various scales of mixed-use centers. These provide models of walkable developments that can define and reinforce a sense of place within a community.

2. Typologies of open space, from undisturbed stream buffers and watersheds to urban parks and plazas. These open space guidelines aim to protect the natural habitat and to improve the human habitat with spaces that satisfy the daily needs of social interaction.

3. Criteria for a sustainable transportation network. These include a connectivity index, to ensure adequate street connections in every neighborhood, general street design principles and the integration of public transit. Also very important is the delineation of regional connectors and corridors, which can range from highways, boulevards, and rail lines to rivers, parkways and greenways.

4. Recommendations for site and building design. This section covers some of the same ground as the Urban Design Guidelines, having to do with design elements that promote contextual site planning and architectural design. Our two basic premises are that all buildings should reinforce a sense of place; and the preservation and renewal of historic buildings, districts and landscapes affirms the continuity and evolution of civic life. A third topic for American practice is that buildings should comply with the current US Green Building Council's LEED (Leadership in Energy and Environmental Design) standard for reduced energy use.

Typical extracts from our General Development Guidelines and Urban Design Guidelines are included as Appendices IV and V, respectively. Both sets of guidelines establish a clear framework that assists designers and developers to understand the goals and criteria of public policy, and to enable the decisions of elected and officials and city staff to be consistent for different projects. We structure the provisions and the wording specifically to influence future zoning codes; much of the text of the guidelines uses 'suggestive' language such as 'should and 'may,' but this terminology can easily be replaced with 'required' language such as 'shall' and 'must.'

We write these standards and guidelines to complement the master plans, and to guide development as it may extend beyond the original scope and time-frame of the plan itself. The guidelines are detailed because the master plan is detailed, and for one further reason: buildings often outlive their original uses. An old industrial structure, for example, can become new offices, shops and restaurants, live–work units or trendy apartments, and the blending of old and new adds to the character of the building and the neighborhood. Buildings are more stable benchmarks of community and catalysts of urban quality than the transient uses that fill them. Therefore we place more emphasis on getting the arrangement of buildings and spaces right rather than fixing the patterns of use by geographic location. What we deem a suitable use at the present time may, and probably will change

over the next decade or two. In this situation of flux, we want to create a physical environment that will handle change and retain its basic quality beyond the next investment cycle of five to ten years.

To this end, most buildings in a neighborhood or district will be 'background' buildings, providing the backdrop to public life rather than seizing center stage for themselves. We know from experience that designing 'backdrop' buildings is every bit as difficult, and satisfying, as creating landmark structures, but the mythology of the architect as form-giving hero is hard to overcome. In the absence of enlightened design humility from architects, urban design regulations are a necessary fact of life.

Within this regulatory framework, architectural invention is welcomed at the level of detail, but the overall form and massing of buildings should comply with the specifics of the community guidelines (see Figure 5.10). The only exceptions to this premise are special civic and community buildings, like churches, town halls and museums. Here architectural invention can have a free rein; if there are enough competent background buildings to establish a coherent context, the occasional bold and innovative structure for a special purpose can become a defining landmark in the community. Daniel Libeskind's Jewish Museum in Berlin is a case in point.

However, idiosyncratic buildings should still respect the public spaces within which they sit, for ultimately the quality and integrity of public space are more important than any individual building. While unique, innovative and eccentric structures can enhance a neighborhood, these need to be in the minority, counterpoints to the general continuum of the urban fabric. We have found from experience that it's usually the less talented architects that complain the loudest about restrictions on their 'design freedom.' We have no doubt that the best architects can interpret our regulations creatively, while we hope to stop the worst from foisting their poor designs on the public realm.

## Charrettes

These master plans and their subsequent codes and guidelines are produced most effectively using the charrette format – intensive design workshops usually lasting four, six or eight days. The term 'charrette' is derived from the French word for the 'little cart' used to collect the final architectural drawings prepared by students at the nineteenth century Parisian École des Beaux Arts. The students worked in different locations around the city, usually in the ateliers of their professors, and when they heard the sound of the little cart's iron-rimmed wheels echoing on the cobblestone streets, they knew their design time was almost up. The sound and the imminent arrival of the cart induced frantic, last-minute efforts by the students to complete the drawings. The term has since evolved to mean any fast-paced design activity which is brought to a conclusion at a fixed time.

But a word of warning! The term 'charrette' is misused extensively by planners who tend to call all manner of public meetings, even those of only a few hours duration, a 'charrette'. A true charrette, by contrast, lasts at least a few days, and is defined by reaching a definite conclusion, marked by the production of a complete set of drawings. The charrettes that produced all but two of the case studies, lasted between four and eight days. This emphasis on the production of definitive detail drawings in a short timeframe also distinguishes our charrette process from the British Action Planning format described in such excellent publications as *The Community Planning Handbook* (Wates, 2000). The way we organize a charrette shares some characteristics of the 'Design Fest' described by Wates, but we structure the event to include aspects of several other methods outlined as alternative and parallel activities under the British model.

The concentrated focus and definitive end product of a true charrette is invaluable, and provides a much better method than the slow drip feed of community meetings once a week for several months. These lengthy enterprises, though worthy, drag the process out, lose momentum and end up being a burden on all involved. By contrast, an eight- or nine-person design team, working 12–14 hours a day for four days, can rack up the equivalent man-hours for one single planner laboring on the problem all day, every day for three months. And the brainpower increases exponentially!

With this level of intensity, and by working out in design detail the most awkward and hotly debated problems, we get as close as we can to common agreement about contentious issues. But not everyone is going to be happy. Our aim is not necessarily consensus; in every development or redevelopment scenario there are going to be some winners and some losers. Our main objective is always to minimize the disadvantages to individuals and groups within the community while capitalizing on the potential for overall civic improvement. Therefore one of the main features of the charrette process, as we illustrate further

in Chapters 7–11, is the synchronous process of debate, design and demonstration.

The charrette also has an important educational function in this regard. Many revered urban places across the western world were created by order of a king, duke, Pope or some other autocratic ruler. Creating good design in a democracy is much harder, for while everybody's opinion is valued, not all citizens may be equally informed, or fully understand the true circumstances concerning a community. The open forum of the charrette, with all its drawings and plans, provides a good, condensed learning opportunity for citizens about important issues affecting their community.

Our case studies illustrate what is achievable by using design charrettes to stimulate public involvement, and we would restate our conviction that democratic debate is vital in all types of design processes about making urban places. Design done in secret, carried out behind closed doors by experts who are happy in their conviction that they know best, has proved a recipe for much bad urbanism, from ubiquitous and faceless urban renewal schemes in cities worldwide to London's high-profile Canary Wharf in the Isle of Dogs (see Figure 5.3). In our process, the only work not carried out in public are those tasks required as preparation for a charrette, such as economic analyses of existing development and statistical projections about future growth, an environmental analysis of a fragile area of landscape, or the collation of demographic data. Before we start, our charrette team also works with each municipality to produce full and accurate mapping of the area to a large scale, showing all roads and streets, large and small structures, topography, tree mass, and property boundaries.

Even when being fully committed to public participation, it's easy to overly romanticize the positive role of the public in these processes. In our experience, several people come to these public events to complain, and in a few extreme cases to stop the process from even taking place. These folk are from the ranks of the NIMBYs and BANANAs (Build Absolutely Nothing Anywhere Near Anything) brigades; they come to talk, not to listen and least of all to hear. Many have made up their mind about issues usually on the basis of half-truths, myths and downright falsehoods circulating about the particular project in question. Often public opinion is in direct opposition to good planning and design sense, and we work to overcome these obstacles of ignorance.

Several key Smart Growth principles are almost guaranteed to generate opposition from community groups and neighborhood associations. As we have noted earlier, these usually involve higher-density mixed-use and infill developments that introduce new buildings, new residents and visitors into an existing neighborhood. Citizen groups often pay lip service to such Smart Growth ideas in general, but maintain that they're not right for *their* particular area. It's a well-known paradox in American social attitudes that citizens complain loudly against sprawl and the loss of open space, and equally loudly about the higher-density development that is the most effective solution to the problem (see Plate 9).

Nevertheless, a good professional must strive to garner public input, and as noted earlier, a lot of this work involves public education. The best way to educate the public is in public – to allow them to see the design process in action, and learn how variables are balanced, priorities assessed, and the various criteria established. Our working method allows the public to watch us at work, and to give daily, even hourly feedback on the ideas taking shape. At its best, the floodlight of public design dialogue can illuminate many murky corners of private prejudice and misunderstanding, and provide opportunities for a more honest and productive debate. In the majority of instances some accord can be reached, but we've never been able to please all participants.

But we try, and to this end we have four guiding principles for every charrette.

1. Involve everyone from the start.
2. Work concurrently and cross-functionally.
3. Work in short feedback loops.
4. Work in detail.

First, we get all the points of view into the open for vigorous discussion so that elected officials, planning and design professionals and concerned citizens can understand the full scope of the problem. Anyone who might have an opinion or be affected by the plan should be involved from the very beginning. We arrange specific consultation times with various stakeholder groups, while design activity is running constantly in the background, accessible to all on the other side of the room. By making people roll up their sleeves and work with the design team, the process gains mutual authorship and benefits from a shared vision.

Second, we operate with a multi-disciplinary design team that usually includes architects, urban designers, planners, landscape architects, traffic plan-

ners, and real estate experts. Sometimes we add other environmental specialists if the task demands it, and we particularly welcome the advice of local artists, who often have a unique perspective to contribute. During the charrette all these specialists become generalists, assimilating each other's expertise and working across professional boundaries on problems and opportunities that arise as the charrette progresses.

Third, we work quickly, getting tentative solutions to problems pinned up on the wall for discussion as soon as possible, often after only a few hours. Members of the public need to be able to propose ideas and see them designed briskly for their review and comment by others. We hold pin-up sessions every evening to gather public input on the preferred direction(s) for development based upon what we heard during the day.

Fourth, working in detail has all the advantages we've mentioned previously. Only by designing to a level of detail that includes building types, urban blocks and public spaces as well as the big picture issues of circulation, transportation land use, landscape preservation and other major public amenities can opportunities be revealed and fatal flaws reduced or eliminated. This level of detail is achievable in the compressed timeframe because of our typological framework. We bring with us to the process development and spatial typologies that we believe have very wide applicability. This general base of information enables us to move quickly into site specific detail. We introduced the four typological categories earlier in Chapter 4: they are Traditional Neighborhoods, Mixed-Use Centers, Districts and Corridors.

### Traditional Neighborhoods

The traditional neighborhoods typology comprises a compact residential area with a variety of housing types and some supporting service and civic uses like small shops, libraries and churches. It is designed to accommodate pedestrians and public transit as well as travel by car, and like most New Urbanist designers, and New York sociologist Clarence Perry before us, we base the size of neighborhoods on the 1/4-mile measurement as the distance the typical adult can walk from center to edge in approximately five minutes. Completing the circle with this radius creates an area of approximately 125 acres (50 hectares) and comprises about 1000 homes at an average density of 8 dwellings per acre (52 persons per hectare). This figure anticipates a range of dwelling types from some single-family houses on medium-sized lots (1/3-acre), a larger proportion of single-family dwellings on smaller lots (1/4–1/8-acre), plus town-homes and apartments, and computes to an average population of about 2600 residents. These are densities similar to those of typical European cities noted in Chapter 5, and thus mark a significant break with current American practice. Figures 3.2 and 3.3 illustrate the typologically similar neighborhood design concepts of Clarence Perry from the 1920s and Duany and Plater-Zyberk from the 1990s, and it's interesting to note that Perry envisioned 5000 residents living in his neighborhood, nearly twice as many as our contemporary total.

However, this increase in density is not such a radical shift as it might first appear. As twenty-first century demographics in the USA move rapidly towards more, smaller households, developers' organizations expect the demand for homes on smaller lots to increase. Surveys of American homebuyers have indicated that residents are as satisfied with housing in developments averaging six or seven units per acre (39–45 persons per hectare) as they are with densities of three or four dwellings per acre (19–26 persons per hectare) *if* the smaller lots are balanced by good amenities and public spaces (Ewing, in Schmitz: p. 11).

Smaller lot size also helps in the important quest for dwellings that are more affordable not only to lower paid workers but also to the middle class, who are increasingly being priced out of markets in several parts of America. In some parts of California, for example, the average cost of a new home is $500 000 (!) and only 27 percent of Californians can afford a median-priced home (O'Connell and Johnson: p. 32).

Studies of housing affordability across the USA have shown how market-rate housing stimulates commercial and service sector employment as retail, offices and other urban services follow rooftops, and these new commercial enterprises offer jobs which, in part, are filled by workers from low and moderate income households. In other words, the wealthier middle classes need working-class people to service their needs. Ensuring adequate workforce housing in the right place – to avoid long trips between home and workplace – requires special effort, and close cooperation between communities and specialized developers. It's one of our bedrock principles that a complete community encompasses a variety of household types at various levels of income. Planning new development to include such less expensive housing from the outset will enhance the ability of public and non-profit agencies to provide such housing at an orderly and necessary pace, and decent affordable housing can enhance the livability and profitability of market-rate housing in the community (see Figure 6.35). We recommend that between 10 and 15 percent of all new housing in neighborhoods should be affordable under the criteria of the US Department of Housing and Urban Development, that is, it's accessible to people earning 80 percent of the national median income. As incentives to developers to construct this housing, we further recommend that the 'affordable' units not be counted in the density calculations for the project,

**Figure 6.35** Affordable housing, Davidson, NC, John Burgess, architect, 2000. All affordable housing should utilize the same architectural styles and attention to detail as typical market-rate housing in the same neighborhood.

**148**

effectively providing the developer with a substantial density bonus.

In the USA there is often pressure from existing communities to lower densities and include a greater proportion of larger lot single-family homes, on the mistaken belief that higher densities bring crime and other problems. However, if one accedes to this pressure, the critical advantage of having enough people in a walkable area to support local services like small businesses and public transit is lost, and social equity is sacrificed on the altar of prejudice. Pursuing lower densities at the expense of community services and diversity of housing opportunities quickly ends up with developments that are simply another version of sprawl. No structural environmental or socio-economic problems are solved. One of the advantages of the charrette process is that several of these doubts and fears about density can be quelled by illustrating the design detail of such new developments.

Developments larger than 125 acres (50 hectares) should be divided into separate, walkable neighborhoods interconnected by a street network that balances the needs of the automobile, the transit rider, the bicyclist and the pedestrian. This connectivity is essential for improved access, and neighborhoods should eventually form contiguous development rather than separated pods. In this way facilities can be more easily shared, spreading value among adjacent neighborhoods, reducing traffic on arterial roads, and lessening the pressure for continual widening. As these neighborhoods cohere, they create the new structure of towns and villages (see Figure 6.36). Natural landscapes should also be extended through adjacent developments, creating linear habitats for wildlife, and protecting scenic features and views for the benefit of many people.

To this end, each neighborhood should contain a minimum of 10 percent open space and possibly as much as 50 percent if circumstances permit. This latter figure is particularly appropriate in areas of landscape beauty or environmental sensitivity, where open land can be permanently preserved by means of conservation easements (with potential tax advantages) or dedicated public open space as shown in Figure 2.16. Some additional details about neighborhood design are included in the first case study illustrated in Chapter 7.

## Mixed-Use Centers

Mixed-Use Centers are areas of concentrated activity involving multiple uses – living, working, learning,

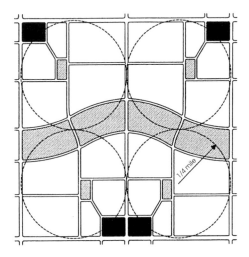

**Figure 6.36** Traditional neighborhood combination diagram. Each neighborhood can combine to form a larger structure of streets and open spaces. Individual site characteristics will engender local variations within this unified structure. (*Drawing courtesy of Duany Plater-Zyberk and Company*).

playing, eating, shopping and so on. – designed to accommodate pedestrians and transit use in addition to auto travel. Centers can be of several different scales from high urban in the central city to rural in outlying areas, but the three most usual scales outside the urban core are: urban village center, neighborhood center and rural village center. (It seems nearly every development type has to have the term 'village' appended to it in the early years of the twenty-first century. In America the word is often used to attach a romantic gloss to urban development and to ameliorate consumer concerns about the density and urbanity of high-intensity mixed-use development. There are few precedents for using the more European term of 'quarter.' 'Urban village' is something of an oxymoron, but it's become the accepted term in development parlance, so we'll accept it and move on!)

*Urban Village Centers* Urban Village Centers are mixed-use activity centers scaled to serve a trade area with a radius between five to fifteen miles. This area comprises 50–75 residential neighborhoods, or 40 000–60 000 homes using a slightly lower average density figure of 800 homes per neighborhood for conventional suburbia rather than the figure of 1000 for New Urbanist traditional neighborhoods.

Typically they have a core area between 30 acres (12 hectares) and 125 acres (50 hectares). Thirty acres approximates to the area contained within a 1/8-mile walking radius, and 125 acres fits inside a circle with 1/4-mile radius. These centers include retail or other commercial uses totalling between 150 000–300 000 square feet (13 940–27 820 square meters), and shopfronts are built to the street with offices or apartments above. Parking is provided on-street and behind the buildings, possibly in decks in larger developments. Residential densities are normally between 7–50 dwellings per acre (45–325 persons per hectare) except in transit-oriented centers where the minimum density should be 16 dwellings per acre (104 persons per hectare). Urban open space should be designed as 'urban rooms' – squares, greens or small parks – with their edges defined by buildings. The oft-cited Birkdale Village in Huntersville (see Plates 4, 5, 6 and 7) illustrates a prototypical urban village at this scale.

*Neighborhood Centers* Neighborhood Centers are mixed-use activity centers scaled to serve a trade area with a radius less than three miles. The core area is typically between 8 and 30 acres (3–12 hectares) and a retail component is sized between 15 000-150 000 square meter (1394–13 940 square meters). Smaller neighborhood centers typically offer 'convenience' scale retail shops with no large anchor tenants, and

require a minimum of four to five neighborhoods (about 3200–4000 homes at the slightly lower density figure) for viable support. Larger neighborhood centers typically include a full-service supermarket or grocery store and serve no less than six neighborhoods (roughly 4800 homes). Parking is provided on-street and behind the buildings, usually in surface car parks. As with the larger centers, residential densities are normally between 7 and 50 dwellings per acre (45–325 persons per hectare) except in transit-oriented centers where the minimum density should again be 16 dwellings per acre (104 persons per hectare). Urban open space, as always, should be designed as 'urban rooms' – squares, greens or small parks – with their edges defined by buildings. While vertical mixed-use (offices or housing over retail) is encouraged, it is likely that the different uses in a neighborhood center will be mixed horizontally, that is, located on adjacent parcels of land within the development. Figure 6.37 illustrates a typical small-scale urban village.

*Rural Village Centers* Rural Village Centers comprise mixed-use activity centers in rural settings, consisting of scattered, small buildings – typically less than 6000 square feet (557 square meters) each – with retail and other commercial components totaling not more than 25 000 square feet (2323 square meters). The buildings, like those illustrated in Plate 13, are most usefully clustered around a central public space or prominent intersection to create a focus for community events such as a farmers market. This space should be informal in layout and generally not exceed one acre in size. If appropriate, new housing at between two to six dwellings per acre (13–39 persons per hectare) should be constructed in the vicinity of rural village centers.

### Districts

Districts generally comprise a special, single use like large industrial facilities and airports, which, because of their technical requirements and impacts, must stand apart from the urban fabric. They should however be connected to the network of other city elements. This category also includes large office and research campuses, which may evolve over time into more pedestrian-friendly setting. The North Carolina State Centennial Campus in Raleigh (see Figure 6.38) shows how this might be achieved.

To achieve this greater integration into a walkable and transit-supportive environment, offices and light

**Figure 6.37** Rosedale Commons, Huntersville, NC. This lower density development mixes uses horizontally in adjacent buildings rather than vertically within the same structure. Although not ideal, this kind of development is easier to build and finance than the more complex vertical mixing of uses. To function properly, the various uses – housing, offices and shops – must be linked together by pedestrian-friendly streets and urban spaces.

**Figure 6.38** North Carolina State University 'Centennial Campus, Raleigh, NC.' Instead of following the standard suburban office park formula, this research campus of a large university has been planned around a more pedestrian-orientated network of streets and spaces and linked to the main university by regular transit service.

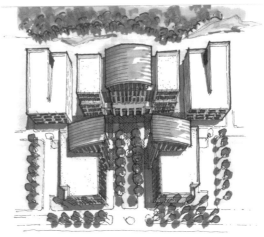

**Figure 6.39** Transit-supportive office typology, The Lawrence Group, 2002. The arrangement of typical large office buildings can be improved by screening the parking and creating entrance courtyards close to the street that can be used by transit vehicles and pedestrians. (*Illustration courtesy of The Lawrence Group*)

industrial buildings should be placed close to the public street, or at a minimum, they should reduce the amount of parking in front of the primary entrance. Figure 6.39 depicts a transit-supportive arrangement of large office buildings that achieves this goal and creates a formal pedestrian plaza entrance to the buildings. New buildings should be designed with pedestrian-friendly building façades (even for light industrial buildings, there is usually an office area that can accomplish this goal) and pedestrian entrances should be easily visible and accessible from the street and potential future transit stops. In addition, buildings should be aligned on a network of streets that include sidewalks and street trees. Where practical, other uses should be planned at street intersections to define these spaces and create pedestrian destinations in these locations.

## Corridors

Corridors are regional connectors of neighborhoods, centers and districts: they range from freeways, boulevards and rail lines to streams and greenways, and the character and location of these corridors is determined by the intensities of their use. Freeways and busy freight rail corridors should remain tangential to neighborhoods and towns; at the local level they are barriers, not connectors. Light rail and bus corridors can be incorporated into boulevards at the edges of neighborhoods or provide access to the cen-

ter of neighborhoods at pedestrian-friendly stops. Watercourses can function as boundaries for cities and towns, and streams can enter and connect neighborhoods through greenways.

During charrettes, these four typologies – traditional neighborhoods, mixed-use centers, districts, and corridors – form the basis of many detailed design decisions. Using them, we can quickly evaluate alternatives, and at the end of the charrette process, we can demonstrate the advantages of the preferred design by clearly communicating its purpose, content and appearance to the audience by reference not only to our drawings, but photographs of other examples of the relevant typologies. To see these ideas manifest in buildings and developments already completed is a very persuasive argument, particularly for elected officials whose job it will be to implement the plan's recommendations, sometimes in the face of citizen opposition. We maintain a massive digital image bank for this purpose.

All the drawings from the charrette, which are all done by hand, are digitized on the spot – by scanning or by means of digital photography for the large drawings – for inclusion into a closing PowerPoint presentation and for posting on the community's web site the following day. Most of the drawings included in the following chapters where produced during the charrettes, and indicate the level of design investigation and production it's possible to achieve in a properly organized event. The specifics of the zoning codes and other regulations are developed usually within 60 days subsequent to the charrette. During that time the design content of the master plan is encoded and any other relevant circumstances are covered by reference to appropriate urban design standards or development guidelines.

The visual power of the charrette – its capacity to produce compelling graphics that capture the public's imagination – has helped it become the dominant methodology of New Urbanist architects and planners. Creating visual images in two and three dimensions is the most effective way we know to get to a very important issue in the making of public space – the role of public debate in forming public places. We have discussed at some length the importance of public space for a free and democratic society, but the involvement of the public in that space should not be simply as users, but also as makers. Urban design is fundamentally a language of democracy, and it connects individuals to the larger worlds of their neighborhood, town, city and region.

This connection to democratic action further reinforces the lineage of public design charrettes. They are direct descendants of the anarchist philosophy of radical thinkers like Peter Kropotkin (1842–1921), who argued that the built form of towns and cities should be derived from the work of their citizens. This same anarchist ideology lies at the root of many major movements in modern planning, including Ebenezer Howard's Garden Cities, Patrick Geddes' rehabilitation strategies, The American Regional Planning Association, F.L. Wright's Broadacre City and the work of John Turner in South America during the 1950s and 1960s. The activism of people like Brian Anson and Colin Ward in the United Kingdom, and the intellectual pattern languages and urban design methods described by the Anglo-America mathematician-architect Christopher Alexander, have continued this paradigm in the 1970s through the 1990s.

The full glare of public and media scrutiny – sometimes hostile – make charrettes exhausting for designers. It's commonplace to have to explain concepts over and over again to individuals and interest groups who don't stay within the allotted workshop schedule. But it's imperative never to turn away members of the public; a friendly conversation with someone may turn them into an ally. To this end we always have at least one member of the team specifically on watch for newcomers, and whose role is to involve them creatively in the process. Equally so, an offhand remark can create an opponent, and we try hard to avoid unscripted comments, or disparaging remarks. It's much easier to change a drawing than to take back something we've said.

Within these caveats, our experience shows that most people who involve themselves in the charrette process begin to understand the relevant issues more fully – and people who came simply to complain can become constructive participants on complex planning, traffic, environmental or whatever kinds of problems are under discussion. With good public involvement, in a four–to-eight day period, the design team can analyze the most important issues, create a planning framework for the area under discussion, develop the master plan with buildings, streets and open spaces, and depict specific design details in three dimensions for key areas. This combination produces a document that establishes and illustrates a holistic vision combined with implementation strategies as the basis for future political action. This might sound a grand claim, but it works. We do it in practice, as do many other professionals in Britain and America. The following chapters illustrate the results of this process at five scales of operation – the region, the city, the town, the neighborhood and the urban block.

# Preamble to
# case studies

## PREAMBLE TO CASE STUDIES

Design professionals in Britain will recognize most, if not all the design and planning concepts contained in these American case studies, and this commonality highlights a paradox of working within the two different cultures. The design concepts are nearly identical, but the political systems within which American and British professionals work vary considerably.

We saw in Chapter 5 some of the important and substantial differences between American zoning techniques of 'growth management' and English procedures of 'development control.' British readers will thus notice important differences in the implementation strategies and tactics of these American plans. All these projects have been initiated by American local governments, which work within the system described in Chapter 5 that separates planning for the future from development control in the present. With frustrating frequency, the plans produced by American towns and cities are simply regarded as 'vision documents' or 'road maps' to guide future decisions, without any regulatory teeth. There are plenty of good ideas and good intentions, but no requirement that private development proposals and public decisions follow the approved plans. As with any road map, the plan is subservient to the driver, who is free to change destination or direction at any time. In Britain, by contrast, government policy requires that all decisions on development must follow the provisions of the appropriate publicly adopted plan with only very limited exceptions.

The following case studies differ from much conventional American practice, because they try to bridge the problematic divide between planning and zoning. As we discussed in Chapter 6, detailed, design-based zoning codes for these projects are almost always included in our planning and design process, irrespective of scale, and these zoning ordinances are prepared as part of the master-planning package to give the plan legal weight. This is important because in American law the design plans themselves lack legal authority, other than fulfilling a statutory requirement to have a community plan on file as the benchmark for other regulatory instruments.

Integrating design-based zoning regulations with the master plan that's developed and approved in the full light of public debate and scrutiny means that these changes to local zoning laws can be adopted when the plan is approved, or very shortly thereafter. This goes a long way toward healing the American breach between planning and zoning; under this system, the community's development plan that establishes the future vision is directly linked with the zoning ordinance that regulates the build-out of the plan over time. However, there is still no legal requirement for American elected officials to follow the plan and zoning they've so carefully constructed. On an *ad hoc* basis, governments can rezone parcels of land against the provisions of their plans at any time in the future if a developer or other interest group can persuade them to do so. This lack of civic backbone brings the plans into public disrepute, but in only a couple of our projects has this unfortunate circumstance occurred. We include one example in the case studies where firmer action was needed to reinforce the importance of maintaining the integrity of adopted community plans in the face of development pressure and bureaucratic inertia.

One of the most compelling attributes of the Charter of the New Urbanism is its common commitment to good urban design and planning at a wide variety of different scales, from the region to an individual urban block. Accordingly, we have organized our own work to reflect this hierarchy and commonality. Like many designers, we believe passionately that what we plan should relate to the physical qualities of the particular place, be it an area of 60 square miles covering several political jurisdictions or a single town center site of 10 acres. We want our work to stand as a critical practice, countering the throwaway attitudes of American culture – making haste and making waste. Our work tries to re-imbue our sites, whether they be cities or suburbs, with a sense of history, to create memories for the future where none existed.

Each case study begins with a project description and identification of the key issues and goals. This is followed by a brief summary of the particular charrette process and the explanation of the full master plan, replete with its recommendations and illustrative drawings. Our intent is to demonstrate the level of design detail that can be achieved in charrettes, and in consequence, the sophisticated level of planning attainable with this process. Nearly all the drawings illustrated were produced during the charrette; they have *not* been touched up or redrawn for publication. (Where graphics were produced or modified after the charrette, usually for the project report, we have noted

these accordingly.) Unless otherwise noted on the plans, north is orientated to the top of the page.

Each master plan is complemented by various strategies for implementation and development control. In larger projects, these usually take the form of development and design guidelines and zoning recommendations; smaller scale projects typically include studies of economic viability, an evaluation of public funding strategies, project timetables, and of course design-based zoning codes keyed to the master plan. Finally, we present a short, critical evaluation of the case study, highlighting its successes and disappointments. All five case studies have been necessarily abridged from their full complexity concerning fine scale project locations and details in order to render them accessible to the general reader.

One final point of clarification: up to this point we have used the personal pronoun 'we' to indicate the two authors. Henceforth, in all the case studies with the exception of Chapter 11, 'we' means the design team of the Lawrence Group, architects, and town planners, who carried out this work for the relevant public authorities. Accordingly, the 'voice' and style of writing changes slightly as we move inside our urban design practice and retell some stories of community planning by design. Describing these case studies involves recapitulating past events, describing things and places that exist, recounting values and beliefs held in the present, and projecting implementation into the future. This shifting between tenses can be confusing to the reader, and so we have negotiated this obstacle using the simple criterion of what sounds clearest rather than absolute academic consistency. We trust our colleagues will forgive us this vernacular preference.

# The region

## Case Study 1: CORE, North Carolina

### PROJECT AND CONTEXT DESCRIPTION

The acronym CORE stands for 'Center of the Region Enterprise,' a collaborative planning effort involving 12 different local governments and quasi-public authorities covering an area of 60 square miles approximately in the geographic center of the state of North Carolina. It is close to, or includes within its boundaries, several important focal points: the center of state government – the city of Raleigh (named after Sir Walter); a center of technological innovation – the Research Triangle Park (RTP); and an international transportation center – the Raleigh-Durham International Airport.

The larger region that surrounds the CORE is generally known as 'The Research Triangle,' so named because it's defined by a geographic area whose three cardinal points comprise the great research universities of the University of North Carolina at Chapel Hill; North Carolina State University, and Duke University. Within this region, the study area is bisected from east to west by Interstate 40, the main transportation artery, and by the anticipated regional rail system being designed by the Triangle Transit Authority (TTA) that will travel through it from north to south.

The study area straddles the ridge line between two of North Carolina's major, but environmentally fragile river basins – the Neuse and the Cape Fear – and is also home to one of the state's most notable green spaces, Umstead State Park, a fine wildlife preserve and environmental resource. Within this context, the CORE boundaries define a place where the borders of six municipalities meet: Cary, Durham City, Morrisville, Raleigh, Durham County and Wake

County (See Plate 14). Although at the center of the region, the project area is on the edge of most communities and, because of this multi-jurisdictional nexus, the area has not received as much care and study as it deserves. This has led to several serious planning and environmental problems.

The prevailing themes we were asked to address in the charrette, in April 2002, were the mismatch between jobs, homes and services, and the related challenges to mobility caused by this disparity. The 60 square mile area supports more than 90 000 jobs but only 8200 homes, most of them in the town of Cary to the south. Local planners forecast that over the next 10 to 20 years, 35 percent more jobs and four times more residents will locate in this area. The daytime population of the study area swells to a thousand percent during working hours, resulting in heavy congestion caused by peak hour commuter traffic. This is comprised largely of employees traveling between homes outside the study area to jobs in the RTP and other key employment nodes such as airport.

Because most workers leave the area at the end of the day, taking their purchasing power elsewhere, residents who do live in the CORE area have few services available locally, requiring them to drive to other locations. This lack of convenient restaurants and shops also means that daytime employees who wish to run errands or eat lunch somewhere other than the office cafeteria often must travel long distances by car, thereby increasing frustration, congestion and automobile emissions.

Despite these current problems, the RTP has been an enormous boon to the area, both within its boundaries and throughout the region. Since its founding in 1959, the RTP has acted as a magnetic force for brainpower and innovation in biotechnology, communications, and related research. The entire region has benefited from substantial investments in land and buildings inside and outside the Park by a wide range of companies and their support services. Firms that moved to RTP in the early days found easy access (by car and plane) to a beautiful, park-like campus setting within a region with a highly educated work force.

Yet this success, combined with insufficient collaborative planning in the region as a whole, has spawned the unforeseen current problems of congestion and pollution. In the 1970s and 1980s it was simply assumed that building more and bigger roads would solve future problems. But now, with extensive freeways in place and congestion getting worse, it has dawned on all parties that the achievements of the past could soon become a liability as the quality of life in the region declines. It has become clear that yesterday's models of development cannot answer all of today's and tomorrow's needs; a more sustainable model is needed.

However, it's not as easy as simply allowing residential development in the RTP. This wouldn't necessarily improve overall sustainability. Even if housing were permitted in the research office area (which it isn't at present, kept at bay by restrictive covenants and concerns about security), the long distances and gated entrances from public streets to many of the research buildings are barriers to pedestrian activity. In order for housing to pass the sustainability test, it must be sited in neighborhoods that promote walking and alternative transportation choices as means of reducing automobile use. Fundamental changes in the design of many sites and buildings in the RTP would be needed.

At the time of the study, there were minimal transportation alternatives in the project area. A regional rail system was in the final engineering stages and some bus services were provided, but planners have found it difficult to serve the sprawling, disconnected suburban office campuses and low-density residential development with public transit. This is because of the distances employees must walk from bus stops at the street to the front doors of offices sometimes located hundreds of yards away. There are sidewalks and multiuse paths within many research and office campuses, but few extend beyond the employment centers to residential developments and retail services.

The market and locations for housing in the area are also constrained by a number of factors including airport noise contours, freeway rights-of-way and incompatible zoning. In addressing this housing challenge, we recognized it was important to focus not just on the amount of housing, but its diversity as well, providing affordable homes for the wide range of people who work in the CORE area.

Additionally, the current design of most development outside the RTP discourages pedestrians. Even the nearby hotels, retail centers and the higher density residential developments that do exist have been developed with minimal sidewalks, substantial building setbacks covered by expansive parking lots, and long distances between buildings. Taken together, these factors make it unpleasant, dangerous or impossible to walk to many potential destinations. This means that cars are used for every trip for every purpose, often burdening the interstate system with local traffic that exacerbates congestion. On a positive note, however, the beginnings of a regional greenway system are evident along stream corridors and other public open spaces. The team recognized it would be important to connect these corridors to employment centers, retail services, community facilities and housing so they could be used for convenient access to a variety of places and not just for recreational activities.

Over and above physical improvements and new plans, the region needs a better collaborative structure to address common planning concerns and development impacts in the CORE area. This is a common challenge throughout the United States, but here the confluence of six political jurisdictions, two transportation planning organizations, one regional public transit authority (the TTA), two quasi-public organizations with substantial decision-making authority (the RTP and the Airport), together with one advisory planning body for the overall area (the Triangle J Council of Governments – the commissioning body of the CORE study) makes addressing this challenge particularly important.

Several development decisions taken by various municipalities have caused problems for neighboring communities. For example, land-use decisions that appeared sensible to individual local authorities do not necessarily make sense when looked at systematically in terms of the overall region. A good example is the large amount of land zoned for office and industrial use by nearly every jurisdiction in the CORE area. These large areas zoned for single uses appear to each jurisdiction as opportunities to build their tax base and take advantage of their proximity to the airport and RTP. However, the cumulative result is a

60 square mile area devoted to employment with no thought given to convenient and affordable housing for workers. The net effect of these disparate policies is a workforce that must commute increasingly long distances, giving rise to the troubling congestion and pollution at the heart of the region's problems.

## KEY ISSUES AND GOALS

The key issues facing the design team during the charrette could therefore be summarized as follows:

1. The CORE area had an imbalance between employment, homes and services.
2. There were few housing opportunities in the RTP.
3. The thoroughfare system was heavily congested.
4. There were minimal transportation alternatives to the car.
5. The existing patterns of development were heavily auto-dependent.
6. To meet the future challenges of economic development the CORE area needed a stronger physical identity, and a sense of place.
7. The region needed a stronger collaborative planning structure to address common concerns and development impacts.

In turn these issues led to the statement of two main goals for the overall project.

1. *Short-term goal*: Demonstrate how local governments, regional organizations and the private sector could collaborate to match new patterns of development more efficiently with the public infrastructure and its planned extensions.
2. *Long-term goal*: Plant the seeds of commitment among local governments, regional organizations, and land development interests to produce a pattern of development that is more balanced and sustainable.

## THE CHARRETTE

The CORE project had three phases:

1. An introductory period of citizens' meetings to define key issues.
2. Focus group interviews, a market study and the four-day design charrette.
3. Production of the Planning and Design Charrette Report and a General Development Guidelines Manual.

The pre-charrette meetings, carried out by planners in the region over a period of several weeks, highlighted some of the key issues and goals noted above and laid the groundwork for the main element of the process, the four-day charrette in April 2002. The opening presentation at the charrette included the findings from these background interviews and meetings and our team's overview of market conditions and trends. Then town planners, urban designers, architects, transportation planners and real estate market analysts worked for four days, and some nights with hundreds of residents, property owners, elected and appointed officials, local and regional agency staff, developers and business leaders to identify opportunities for the CORE area over the next generation (See Figure 7.1). The charrette tackled the key issues by addressing the following questions:

1. Was the current development pattern in the study area a sustainable model? If not, what changes would need to be made?
2. Were there other models of development such as traditional neighborhoods, transit-oriented employment centers, transit-oriented village centers and neighborhood centers that could be incorporated in future planning decisions?
3. Could these other models have enough impact to affect the required change?

It was clear to most charrette participants that conventional land-use planning strategies were not effective in dealing with the challenges facing the region. Accordingly, instead of conventional categories of land use, we introduced four new development typologies into the debate to structure the master plan: *the Neighborhood, the Mixed-use Center, the District* and *the Corridor*. (These four typologies were defined in detail in Chapter 6.) We wanted to shift the thinking of the CORE partners away from the hackneyed planning of large, single-use housing subdivisions, office parks, apartment complexes and shopping centers, and instead base all future planning on these interlinked components that comprise the building blocks of a sustainable city. During the charrette, these spatial and development typologies formed the basis of planning and design discussions, and the results culminated in the production of the overall master plan.

## THE MASTER PLAN

The CORE charrette concluded with a full digital presentation of the strategies and solutions generated by

| April 2002 | Charrette Schedule |
|---|---|

| Monday, April 8 | | Wednesday, April 10 | |
|---|---|---|---|
| 6:30 p.m. | Sponsor reception | 8:30 a.m. | Developers' and focus area owners' plans and advice |
| 7:00–9:00 p.m. | Opening presentation | 10:00 a.m. | All interested participants |
| | | 1:00 p.m. | All interested participants |
| Tuesday, April 9 | | 5:30–6:00 p.m. | Pin-up sesssion/update |
| 8:30 a.m. | Water resources and environment focus | Thursday, April 11 | |
| 10:00 a.m. | Transportation focus – roads | 7:00–9:00 p.m. | Closing presentation |
| 11:00 a.m. | Transportation focus – transit | | |
| 1:00 p.m. | Open space, trails and parks focus | Friday, April 12 | |
| 2:30 p.m. | Community facilities focus | 8:00 a.m. | Closing presentation summary |
| 5:30–6.00 p.m. | Pin-up session/update | | |
| 7:00–9.00 p.m. | Participatory design | | |

**Figure 7.1** CORE Charrette Schedule. Meetings are prearranged with key individuals and groups, but design work begins on the first morning and continues all day, each day, with a public discussion of each day's design ideas at 5.30 pm.

the many participants. We presented the master plan in four main graphic components dealing with the main environmental, mobility and development patterns of the area – *Green Infrastructure, Transit Infrastructure Street Infrastructure* and *Mixed-use Activity Centers* – plus another two sections, *Neighborhoods* and *Districts* that featured urban design recommendations for prototypical developments. These are discussed in the next section.

## Green Infrastructure (see Plate 15)

As part of our development of the Corridor typology, we made two main recommendations regarding environmental issues.

*Recommendation 1: Develop a detailed green space network that links and completes entire corridors and protected open spaces.*

We stressed that a 'green' network must be established as a complement and alternative to the regional transportation network of roads and planned rail lines. This network should consist of a combination of the following green elements:

- *Greenway trails*: Conventional multi-use paths along creeks and floodplains.
- *Multi-use paths*: Pathways for pedestrians and bicyclists that run parallel to main roads or rail lines at a safe distance.
- *Green streets*: Sidewalks and bicycle lanes along well-landscaped streets in Mixed-use Centers, Districts and Neighborhoods.

- *Public parks*: Areas with universal access for passive or active recreation that are owned and maintained by a public authority.
- *Conservation areas*: Open spaces that are protected by contracts, deeds or covenants that protect sensitive environmental features.

This network of linked green spaces would create a valuable local and regional amenity, and it should be designed to allow greenways to cross under major new or expanded highways and rail lines. These crossings should be wide and high enough to permit passage of pedestrians, bicyclists and wildlife, and should be included as the road or rail corridors are designed and built.

*Recommendation 2: Coordinate stream buffer standards across jurisdictional boundaries.* Buffer widths for undisturbed vegetation along the banks of streams vary widely among the participating jurisdictions in the CORE, from as little as 35 feet to 100 feet (10.6 to 130.5 meters). Coordinated standards should be established at the high end of the scale to ensure clear and consistent protection of the local ecosystem.

## Transit Infrastructure (see Plate 16)

This section comprised the second element of our Corridor typology, for as the core area continues to urbanize, public transportation must play a more important role in providing mobility choices for residents as well as workers. The regional transit corridors currently comprise the planned TTA Phase I commuter rail project through the study area, a future connector branching off west to the university town of Chapel Hill, and a long-term future north–south corridor running along a freight rail line that parallels the western boundary of the study area.

We proposed one major addition to this transit system, shown in purple in Plate 16. Other recommendations regarding types of development that are more supportive of transit are included in the sections on Mixed-use Centers, Neighborhoods and Districts below.

### Main Transit Recommendation

*Create a transit loop for the CORE that connects the TTA Phase 1 corridor with the RTP and the airport.*

To complement the first phase of the commuter rail line, we mapped a new high-frequency circulating service that would cover a large portion of the CORE study area, connecting many of our proposed mixed-use centers with RTP office campuses and the airport. The success this loop would depend on high-density development in the proposed mixed-use centers as well as convenient connections at the commuter train stations.

Many leaders in the Triangle expressed the belief that in order for the commuter rail system to be successful, it had to be connected to the airport, otherwise business customers wouldn't use the train. Yet, transit studies of journeys to and from airports across the U.S. by bus and train have indicated that most trips were made not by people who were travelling somewhere else, but by people who worked at the airport. While the number of business travellers using transit might be expected to rise in the coming years, this mixed ridership reinforced our concern that the CORE loop must connect not only the airport, but all the new mixed-use activity centers and the RTP. To succeed, the transit service must serve as wide a spectrum of customers as possible to maximize its ridership.

Our CORE transit loop intersected the rail line at the already planned RTP North/IBM Station and at a new North Morrisville Station proposed in our plan. We also proposed an additional connection to the future transit line to Chapel Hill – located at the RTP Service Center just west of the Triangle Metro Center. In the long term, we envisioned this loop as a 'fixed guideway system' such as rapid bus, streetcar or light rail, but the service could begin as more conventional bus service and expand as future demand makes more advanced technologies financially

feasible. As real estate and infrastructure development projects move forward, a corridor for the CORE loop must be preserved.

## Street Infrastructure

In this third subset of the Corridor typology, we considered all types of streets and roads, from freeways to local neighborhood streets. This hierarchy is shown in red in Plate 16.

We recommended four actions:

1. *Eliminate a portion of planned freeway that dumped traffic into the center of Morrisville for no apparent reason.*
2. *Improve east-west connections by extending three local main roads to form a more coherent network for the study area.*
3. *Create greater connectivity of neighborhood streets.*
4. *Establish design criteria for streets that include pedestrian and bicycle facilities.*

Of most interest to the reader will be the connectivity index and the street designs. One of the fundamental principles of New Urbanist design is that all neighborhood streets be multifunctional, that is, safe and attractive for pedestrians and cyclists as well as for cars, and that they connect to form a network with multiple choices of routes. This connectivity spreads out traffic more evenly and reduces congestion, but this pattern contrasts markedly with most new development in the CORE area, which has been designed with few points of access, often with only one way in or out. This is true of office and industrial parks as well as residential neighborhoods.

It's hard to overstate the importance of connecting streets into a network. Mobility for vehicles, bicyclists, and pedestrians increases and costs of civic services (public transit, school buses, police, fire and ambulance services) are decreased by having more convenient choices of routes around any neighborhood or district. This same flexibility increases the efficiency of these emergency services as they're able to respond faster to emergencies. Street connectivity can even lead to improved water pressure and easier maintenance of the underground pipes by looping lines through a development rather than creating dead ends in cul-de-sacs.

In projects covering a smaller area, we normally plan out the entire street network, but here we amended the larger regional framework of arterials, established guidelines for the street pattern in the multiuse centers, and set our performance standards for all future neighborhood street connectivity. In this way a connected network of streets will grow in step with new development.

We based our connectivity index on one already implemented in the study area by the town of Cary. This index measures the number of 'links' (defined as street intersections and cul-de-sac dead ends) and the number of 'nodes' (segments of streets between links, and street stubs that end at property lines for future connections) (see Figure 7.2). In this figure, links are represented by black circles and nodes by stars. In the diagram there are 11 links and 9 nodes. Dividing the number of links by the number of nodes results in a connectivity index of 1.22.

A perfect grid has a connectivity index of 2.5. Most conventional cul-de-sac subdivisions yield an average connectivity index of only 1.0. We recommended a connectivity index of at least 1.4–1.5, though variations could be granted in a few cases where severe topographic conditions make connections very difficult and expensive. In these situations, cul-de-sacs may be used, but these dead-end streets

must be strictly limited to preserve the integrity and performance of the connected street system.

The connectivity of streets is not the only important issue in their design. The correct design details to accommodate pedestrians and cyclists are also very necessary for the network to be attractive and function well. Though the RTP and several of the municipalities in the area have installed sidewalks and bicycle paths, or have recently begun requiring them, such facilities are noticeably absent on many of the area's local streets and thoroughfares. This omission is compounded by the fact that even where sidewalks and bicycle facilities exist, there are often gaps between segments, significant barriers to their use (such as major thoroughfares, or wide intersections on roads without islands for pedestrian refuge) or pedestrian-unfriendly developments that discourage walking and cycling.

To help remedy these deficiencies, we recommended that new streets and improvements to existing streets should, at a minimum, have five-foot wide sidewalks on both sides to permit two adults to walk comfortably next to one another. Collector streets and thoroughfares should also be retrofitted with wide outside lanes for cyclists. Alternatively, multiuse paths at least 10-feet wide that can be safely used by both pedestrians and bicyclists should be constructed alongside roadways. Figure 7.3 illustrates an appropriate design for a multiuse path in cross section. In addition to pedestrian and bicycle facilities along

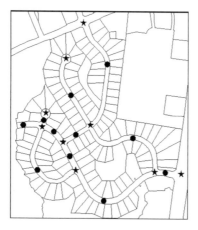

**Figure 7.2** Connectivity Index Diagram. Street connectivity is vital for efficient and sustainable neighborhood design, and is measured by the ration of 'links' to 'nodes'. Links are represented by black circles and nodes by stars. This example gives a connectivity index of 1.22 (dividing 11 links by 9 nodes). This is barely sufficient. An index ratio of 1.4 or 1.5 is much preferred. For example, if the two cul-de-sacs were eliminated and the streets extended in a 'north–east' direction to connect to adjacent streets, the number of nodes (stars), would not increase, but there would be two extra links (circles) created between the new intersections. This would give a connectivity index of 1.44 (13 links divided by 9 nodes).

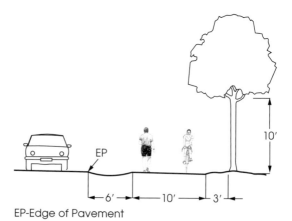

EP-Edge of Pavement

**Figure 7.3** Cross-section of a Multi-use Path. Where sidewalks adjacent to busy roads are not formed by buildings, multiuse paths can provide valuable connections for cyclists and pedestrians.

streets, we recommended that selected greenway corridors could also provide bicycling commuter routes.

## Mixed-use Activity Centers
(see Plate 17)

We made several detailed recommendations regarding the location and design of mixed-use activity centers throughout the study area, but we established one overall principle: *The Center of the Region should be anchored by a series of neighborhoods and villages, each with a defineable, coherent mixed-use core at the appropriate scale.*

This recommendation marked a significant shift from the current development pattern of single-use office parks, apartment complexes and large-lot single family subdivisions, and as such it was one of the most important components of the plan. It is inherently more sustainable to build the region around a series of neighborhood or village centers linked by a transportation network that promotes walking, bicycling, and public transit as alternatives to driving everywhere. This new typology provides opportunities to live, work, play and shop without long commutes, and supports a wider range of lifestyles and different types of households.

These mixed-use centers comprise the most important urban building blocks of the whole plan, providing focal points of activity and neighborhood structure throughout the study area. Plate 17 indicates the location of each of the 10 proposed centers, and we illustrate three of them – the Triangle Metro Center, the North Morrisville Neighborhood Center and the RTP Service Center – in more detail, each differing in scale and character. As stressed earlier in this chapter and elsewhere, each type of center typically includes some residential development and also has direct, pedestrian connections to surrounding neighborhoods. This residential element is essential. Good restaurants, for example, will never survive by depending on lunchtime traffic alone; they must attract the dinner crowd as well. Therefore, wherever it's practical, residential development needs to accompany new retail and office development to provide both a daytime and night-time market. The amount of office development in each center, and its residential mix, depend on its particular location and character.

*Triangle Metro Center (see Plate 18 and Figure 7.4)*

We made one major recommendation for this key site, positioned at a future commuter rail station

at the edge of the RTP: *The Triangle Metro Center should be developed as a transit-oriented development (TOD).*

This area around the transit station planned at the south end of the RTP has great potential for private development. The Triangle Transit Authority has envisaged this location as a main transfer point for passengers to change between trains and local buses, and we indicated how our amendments to the design of a previously proposed Triangle Metro Center project next to the station could build on this level of activity by creating the hub of a new high-density urban village (see Figure 7.4). The original project, which predated the charrette, proposed significant investment in offices, shops and housing, and we were able to complement this effort by creating an urban neighborhood on two large tracts of open property to the south (see Plate 18). The land immediately to the north of the Center is part of an existing large office campus, and unavailable for development, although at some future date connections between the research buildings and the Center could be provided.

On the land to the south, we were able to create an urban neighborhood that provided a variety of housing types for employees in the RTP and surrounding office developments. Our design concept in Plate 18 shows development around the station area stretching for approximately 3/4-mile, but the intensity of development tapers off beyond the five-minute walk (1/4-mile). Within 1/4-mile of the station we

**Figure 7.4** Aerial perspective of Metro Center. We were able to refine and develop a project that was already in the planning stages to maximize its potential as a catalyst for adjacent transit-friendly and sustainable development.

illustrated higher density residential development in the form of three- and four-story apartments. On the east side of the tracks we redesigned an existing retail center along an adjacent major north–south street as a three- and four-story mixed-use development of offices and shops, with the potential also for some live-work unit and adjacent high-density apartments. A new street beneath the tracks improves connectivity and leads to a new civic building, possibly a YMCA fitness facility or a small school, indicated in purple in Plate 18.

Between 1/4-mile and 1/2-mile from the station area, we scaled down development to a mix of townhomes and narrow-lot, single-family homes. We laid out the remaining property beyond the 1/2-mile radius with similar development, backing it up to and screening it from revitalized small commercial buildings fronting adjacent streets. This development pattern provides the necessary variety of housing options for a successful urban village, while respecting the topography and natural features on the site, in particular the creek that traverses the site. By enhancing the required environmental buffers along the creek, we created a small linear park for the neighborhood and the Center. It's important to note that houses *front* onto this park, providing visual security. It is rarely a good idea to back houses up to public green space, unless it is a publicly maintained greenway or a large area. The lessons about buildings facing onto public space that were discussed in Chapter 4 apply here. This park would also make an excellent corridor for a greenway that could tie trails in the RTP to the train station area.

### North Morrisville Neighborhood Center (see Plate 19)

Morrisville is the only town wholly within the study area. It has suffered from being under the flight path to and from the Raleigh-Durham International Airport as well as being sandwiched directly between the wealthy community of Cary to the south and the RTP to the north. As a consequence of airport noise, development has been limited, and the town has had to cope with a lot of commuting traffic. Overall, Morrisville has not been able to turn its location next to the major employment center of the RTP to its advantage, and we saw this new regional plan as providing the town with the vision and means to overcome these difficulties.

The area is complex. Morrisville's jurisdiction includes the future extension of a regional interstate highway, the TTA rail corridor and the 65 DNL (average day/night noise level) contour line from the airport. The town is home to the small but historic African-American community of Shiloh, which is left undeveloped just to the west of the five-minute walk radius from the train station shown in Plate 19.

This area's proximity to major employment centers and new road and rail connections suggests that redevelopment is very likely over the next 10–20 years. To structure this growth, we recommended that: *A new Neighborhood Center should be created in the north Morrisville area that includes a new transit station for commuter rail and the CORE transit loop.*

Where our new transit loop crosses the proposed rail line is an excellent location for another TOD that would create a focal point and hierarchy to the development in the southern part of the study area. The location of this new multimodal station would enable the southern portion of the RTP to be served efficiently with high-quality, secure transit service from the employers' front doors or parking areas to the airport and to other destinations on the commuter rail line, including downtown Raleigh and N.C. State University. This would require a new grade-separated bridge for extending a new major road across the rail corridor, as the route for buses or streetcars on the transit loop. The transit station is located, as always, at the center of the five and 10-minute walking radii.

The southeastern portion of this new urban village falls within the airport noise contour that restricts residential development due to decibel levels, and so we designed this area as a mixed-commercial Village Center based around offices and some neighborhood retail (blue and red buildings in Plate 19). We located residential development (shown in yellow and orange) to the north of this area (beyond the 65 dB noise contour) as well as on the west side of the area.

The land squeezed between the north–south road and rail corridors provided the opportunity for higher density housing close to the transit station with apartments and townhomes. These have smaller footprints than commercial buildings and can take better advantage of the narrow sites. Because of the ownership pattern and larger tracts of land on the west side of the tracks, we laid out the residential development there as a medium-density traditional neighborhood with a predominately single-family character, though we included some townhomes and condominiums (not more than 30 percent of the total number of units) in order to maintain the density figures best suited for the TOD.

A general rule of TOD design requires the highest densities of the development be located within 1/4-mile of the station platform, but here we made an exception due to the lopsided nature of the area, constrained in the eastern and southern quadrants by the airport noise contour that largely eliminated residential development in those locations. We therefore allowed higher density residential development to stretch further north adjacent to the main road and rail line, and we took advantage of a new linear park opportunity to the northwest, where an existing creek could be enhanced and framed with town homes. The increased density of the townhomes would be needed to pay for the two-single frontage streets that run along the park's edges.

*RTP Service Center (see Figure 7.5 and Plate 20)*

This is our third example of a mixed-use activity center, and illustrates a smaller scale intervention into the loose suburban form of the study area. The dispersed campus development pattern of the RTP presented only a few opportunities to inject mixed-use development close to the large office and research buildings. One such opportunity was the Triangle Metro Center described earlier. Another is the RTP Service Center near a large hotel, the Governor's Inn, a location that was intended to provide retail and support services for the initial tenants of the RTP. The RTP has grown significantly since this local site was first planned, and it

presented us with an opportunity to upgrade the Service Center to promote new development that would meet the changing needs of RTP employees.

Our recommendation therefore was: *Redevelop the RTP Service Center as a small scale mixed-use Neighborhood Center, providing an improved 'front door' for the Governor's Inn.*

Our simple concept for redevelopment is shown in Plate 20, illustrating new multistorey, mixed-use buildings for retail, restaurants and offices. The buildings screen their parking and front directly onto the main road to create an improved streetscape together with a new formalized front lawn and visual gateway to the Governor's Inn (compare to Figure 7.5). One or more of the office buildings could easily be replaced by apartments if the market conditions were favorable. Our proposed CORE transit loop would cross through this area with a stop that could serve the Governor's Inn, the new mixed-use buildings, and some existing office buildings to the west of the Service Center.

## Neighborhoods

On smaller projects we normally design each neighborhood, laying out streets and major buildings, and plotting the lots as indicated on the two Mixed-use Center plans (Plates 18 and 19), but in this 60 square mile area, such detail was not possible in a four-day period. Accordingly, we made the following seven general recommendations regarding residential development in the CORE area following the typology of

**Figure 7.5** RTP Service Center, as existing. This photo-collage illustrates an undistinguished collection of buildings with no spatial cohesion or sense of place. Compare with Plate 20.

traditional neighborhood design introduced during the charrette.

1. *New neighborhoods should be developed using the Traditional Neighborhood typology.*

   This typology was described in detail in Chapter 6. The following recommendations add detail to the main attributes previously noted.

2. *The design of new buildings should be responsive to regional building typologies, climate and traditions common throughout the Triangle.*

   Architects and builders should be encouraged to design structures that are compatible with the character of the communities in which they are located. Durable materials such as brick, stone, clapboard, cementacious fiberboard, and cedar shingles should be considered in lieu of vinyl and exterior insulated finishing systems (EIFS). For residential buildings, porches and stoops should form the predominant architectural motif of the façade, providing good climatic modification and a useful transition space from the public realm of the street to the private interior of the home (see Figure 7.6).

3. *Buildings should be close to the street to encourage social interaction and pedestrian scale.*

   Locating buildings close to the street as shown in Figures 7.6 through 7.8 encourages contact between neighbors, and the street is also self-policed by residents observing the public space from their porches or front rooms. It also improves the overall aesthetics of the street by minimizing the visibility of car parking (the garages are recessed) and highlighting the architectural design. In addition, siting the home closer to the front of the lot creates a more useable rear yard. As an example, a typical suburban home has a 35-foot (10.6 meters) front yard setback and a 30-foot (9.1 meters) rear yard setback. By moving the home forward to within 10–15 feet (3–4.5 meters) of the sidewalk, 15–20 feet (4.5–6 meters) of private backyard can be gained, providing enough space on even a modestly sized lot for amenities like a small pool.

4. *A mix of housing types should be integrated into the design of all new neighborhoods* (Figures 7.7 and 7.8) As we noted in Chapter 6, it's one of our core beliefs that a complete community encompasses a variety of household types at various levels of income. Figure 7.7 illustrates how medium-density townhomes can be designed to fit elegantly with adjacent single-family homes and other uses, and thus reduce the stigma often associated with

**Figure 7.6** Houses with Porches, Davidson, NC. These new houses, although a bit too traditional for the authors' tastes, provide an excellent illustration of the rich streetscape and semi-public social spaces provided by generous front porches located within talking distance of the sidewalk.

**Figure 7.7** Townhomes, Baxter, Fort Mill, SC. These townhomes use the same design motifs, albeit very traditional, of adjacent single-family homes, allowing them to blend seamlessly with their more expensive neighbors and achieving some measure of residential diversity.

lower-cost housing. To this end, we maintained our standard recommendation that approximately 15 percent of all new housing should be affordable under the criteria of the US Department of Housing and Urban Development (HUD). Apart from providing a range of different types of smaller, less expensive housing, it will always be necessary to find creative ways of funding such developments to keep housing affordable over time. Some mechanisms for achieving this are discussed in more detail in a subsequent case study in Chapter 10.

5. *Reduce the impact of parking and garages in all site planning.*

   Particularly on smaller lots, the garage and related parking areas tend to dominate the streetscape if not considered in the initial design. Residential design should emphasize indoor and outdoor living spaces and de-emphasize car storage. To that end, no garage should extend beyond the frontage line of the house and should be designed as a secondary volume. Figures 7.6 and 7.7 illustrate this technique for single-family houses and townhomes, and indicate how different types can be integrated together by hiding the parking areas from the street by insetting the garages or servicing them from a rear alley.

   Multi-family developments in particular need to consider carefully the design of parking areas. Lots of cars on asphalt in front of the buildings can render this housing type incompatible with other residential uses. For apartments and condominiums, off-street parking should not be visible from the street. It should be screened by the buildings which must face and define the street's public space as shown in Figure 7.8. For commercial buildings, parking should be to the side or rear of all buildings. While on-street parking should be provided wherever possible, off-street parking in front of the building should be generally discouraged. Encouraging the use of shared parking can reduce the size of parking areas and minimize the impact on the environment.

6. *All neighborhoods should provide public, useable open spaces.*

   Neighborhoods should include small parks within their curtilage, generally no more than a five-minute walk from any dwelling. Instead of the amorphous term 'open space,' we have found that it's always a good idea to name the open space for what it is – ball fields, parks, squares, plazas, community gardens or playgrounds. Naming identifies the purpose of the open space, and

**Figure 7.8** Apartment Building, Davidson, NC. These apartments screen their parking at the rear and provide good definition to the public space of the street. It is important that some entrances into the building are accessible directly from the sidewalk. These connect the private spaces of the building visually and socially to the public space of the street.

provides the outline program for its design and use. 'Green space' or 'open space' are vague and indefinite terms, and often lead to poor design.

Parks, playgrounds, squares and gardens are designed for daily use and enjoyment. These kinds of 'domesticated' public open space are distinct from those areas that are environmentally significant and must be protected in their pristine state. They are also significantly different from the open space that has been grudgingly provided in conventional sprawl development, which has often been defined only in quantitative terms, as a function of population or land area. In many subdivisions developers have simply designated leftover or otherwise unusable land as open space irrespective of its location.

To improve this sorry state of affairs and to be truly public, parks, squares and other types of open space should be lined by the front façades of buildings and by public streets (see Figures 2.16 and 4.7). Safety in public open spaces is provided by the visual supervision of people on their porches, at their windows, or walking, jogging and driving.

7. *The jurisdictions in the CORE area should adopt a compatible set of standards for Traditional Neighborhood Development (TND).*

   To eliminate confusion in the marketplace and to encourage more Traditional Neighborhood Development, we suggested that a common TND ordinance should be adopted by all CORE partners. Approvals for TNDs should also be streamlined to permit them by right with administrative approval by planning staff if the design criteria are met. This avoids a lengthy, drawn out debate by elected officials about policy that has already been decided. Additional consideration should be given to restructuring various fees and requirements (impact fees, development fees, etc.) as incentives for TND. Street design standards should be common across the different jurisdictions within the CORE area. The recommendations of the Institute of Transportation Engineers in *Traffic Engineering for NeoTraditional Neighborhood Design* (1994) and the *TND Guidelines*, adopted by the North Carolina Department of Transportation in August 2000, are excellent resources for street design standards and should be locally adopted by each jurisdiction and incorporated into their TND Ordinance (ITE, 1994; NCDOT, 2000).

## Districts

As noted in Chapter 6, districts are relatively low-density areas with a dominant single use designed primarily for automobile access. Though the RTP currently employs 42 000 people, there are 48 000 additional jobs outside its boundary but within the rest of the CORE area. Much of this development has occurred in sprawling flex-warehouse buildings, though multi-tenant office buildings are also prevalent. Many of these facilities outside the Park have traditionally housed back-office operations of RTP companies including call centers, distribution, and sales. Numerous service providers for RTP companies have also found a place in these areas with the proximity to the Park at a much lower lease rate.

In this context, we made three principle recommendations:

1. *While Office and Industrial Districts generally emphasize a special, single use they should follow the principles of neighborhood design when possible.* These criteria were outlined in Chapter 6.
2. *Encourage more mixed-use development in areas currently zoned for office and industrial development.* According to our market study, the CORE area is over-zoned for office and industrial uses. Many opportunities exist to inject housing of all forms and types throughout this area and these should be encouraged. We included housing in nearly all the detailed designs produced during the charrette.
3. *Develop new transit-supportive types of office development to provide workers with more transportation choices.*

Office developments have conventionally been designed with isolation, rather than integration in mind. This makes them nearly impossible to serve with transit. Because the foundation of every successful transit network is its local bus routes, neither the commuter rail nor our new transit loop will work efficiently without local buses carrying passengers to and from the stations and office buildings where thousands of people work. It's thus very important to encourage office workers to use transit by making it easy and convenient. The office design typology shown in Figure 6.39 depicts a much more transit-friendly arrangement that moves the buildings and their entrances closer to the street and creates a formal pedestrian plaza. We urged the RTP management to encourage larger employers with expansion plans to pursue designs like this to encourage higher use of transit.

## IMPLEMENTATION

As part of our recommendations for implementing the master plan, we developed a matrix of all recommendations prioritized for levels of urgency, and identifying the parties responsible for taking action. The full details of this matrix are too detailed for this abbreviated case study, but typical extracts are shown in Table 7.1.

We determined priorities by considering the following factors:

- The relative severity of the problem.
- The availability of personnel and financial resources necessary to implement the specific proposals.
- The interdependence of the various implementation tasks, in particular, the degree to which implementing one item depended on the successful completion of another item.

In view of the above factors, we felt we could not put forward a precise timetable for every recommendation, but listed the levels of priority as follows:

*High*: Short time frame (6 months – 1 year). Resources should be immediately allocated to address these tasks.

*Medium*: Tasks should be completed in a 1–5-year time frame as resources allow.

*Low*: No urgency required. Task may be completed when resources and timing allow.

**Table 7.1** Implementation Matrix (Extract). Master plans are incomplete without clear implementation strategies that identify project content, priority and responsible parties.

| Studies and plans | | |
|---|---|---|
| Recommendations and Implementation tasks | Priority | Responsible party |
| R11 — Investigate the feasibility of a demand response/point-deviation transit system for the RTP and surrounding employment areas<br><br>*Develop a plan for providing CORE area-wide transit services that connects the RTP, TTA commuter rail system, and the Airport using a system of high frequency circulator buses* | Medium | TTA, RTP |
| R12 — Evaluate terminating the Durham Freeway at I-540 and providing any access road from Davis Drive<br><br>*Work with NCDOT, the MPOs, and RTP to explore this alternative for the extension of the Durham Freeway* | High | CAMPO, DCHC MPO, NC DOT, Morrisville |
| R13 — Extend Airport Boulevard to Davis Drive<br><br>*Develop and adopt an alignment and cross-section for the extension of Airport Blvd to Davis Drive with a grade separation at the TTA corridor* | Medium | CAMPO, DCHC MPO, NC DOT, Cary, Morrisville |
| R14 — Extend McCrimmon Parkway across the rail line toward the Airport<br><br>*Develop and adopt an alignment and cross-section consistent with a neighborhood center* | Medium | CAMPO, DCHC MPO, NC DOT, Cary, Morrisville |
| R15 — Extend Evans Road parallel to NC 54 and reconnect to NC 54 beyond I-540<br>*Develop and adopt an alignment and cross-section for the extension of Evans Rood to NC 54* | Medium | CAMPO, DCHC MPO, NC DOT, Cary, Morrisville |
| R17 — Complete the collector street plan for the CORE area<br><br>*Develop and adopt a collector street plan for the portion of the CORE south of I-540 and adopt the collector street plan previously proposed for the area north of I-540* | High | CAMPO, DCHC MPO, NC DOT, Durham, Raleigh, Cary, Morrisville, TJCOG |
| R29 — Study the feasibility of creating an intermodal transit station and Neighborhood Center in the north Morrisville/Shiloh area<br><br>*Develop a schematic development plan for this area that includes detailed street, block, open space, and building type patterns for adoption as an amendment to the Town's Comprehensive Plan. Complete the Preliminary Engineering for the traffic operations and transportation improvements necessary in this area* | Medium | Morrisville, CAMPO, TTA |

The other main component of the implementation strategies comprised a detailed document setting out General Development Guidelines to be used by all parties in the CORE to rewrite their own regulations around the common themes of the master plan. In this instance, we made these development guidelines nearly as detailed as a full set of urban design guidelines to make up for the fact that new zoning codes were not part of this contract. (These two types of guidelines are discussed in Chapter 6.) The multi-jurisdictional complexity of this project made uniform zoning codes politically impossible, although a more modest example of common design-based coding across three municipalities is included in Chapter 11. A typical extract from the General Development Guidelines is illustrated in Appendix IV.

## CONCLUSIONS

At the conclusion of the process, we evaluated the charrette results against the three important questions identified at the beginning of the project. The first question asked: *Is the current development pattern in the study area a sustainable model? If not, to what degree will changes need to be made?*

Our clear response was no, the pattern is not sustainable. While the RTP continues to provide economic development to the region, the lack of balance in the study area between the various components of daily life – homes, jobs, shops, schools, churches and parks – will seriously hinder the chances of long-term community, economic and environmental sustainability. Change needs to occur, and for this to happen, a shift in development practices is needed. There is enough land and plenty of opportunities in the study area for new development to take place in strategic locations, but this will take some significant intervention in planning policies and the marketplace before such a change occurs.

We argued that change needed to begin immediately, but it would also need to be strategic and carefully managed. To British eyes, solutions might seem simple. We know the right kinds of policies and design standards that are needed; just go ahead and make the shift. For example, a regional planning authority could require all future development to be built in appropriate locations following the established typologies of mixed-use centers, traditional neighborhoods, districts and corridors that are consistent with UK practice. Unfortunately, in this American context there is no single authority with any mandate to initiate and monitor such bold changes in the face of resistance

and inertia from the private sector and divided local governments. The regional planning organization called the Triangle J Council of Governments, is only an advisory body, and the six municipalities do not have much history of effective collaboration. In true American fashion, their relationship has been competitive, not collaborative. Without some dynamic top-down leadership, for which there is little precedent and less expectation, this collaboration is going to be slow in coming. Even if the public bodies did coalesce around a single set of policies, requiring higher standards could be counterproductive, creating antagonism amongst private developers who would (the planners fear) turn their attentions elsewhere, taking money and energy out of the region. We think this fear is overstated, but it is very real in the minds of public officials.

The private sector is unlikely to initiate this kind of structural change on its own. Developers and their lenders are inherently conservative, evaluating future actions and risks based on what has worked in the past. In other words, under a somewhat pessimistic scenario, the market will likely keep churning out yesterday's developments until the regional system breaks down and business energy transfers to another place. The best way to break this cycle, and to affect change in a dramatic manner, would be to focus on a few early model developments, probably created by public–private partnerships. The urban village at the Triangle Metro Center (see Plate 18) is an obvious place to start, linking large offices as the basis of the urban village with transit and new housing. Most of the pieces of the puzzle are included in this one project, which already has some momentum. The most effective way of changing the attitudes of public officials and private developers is for them to see working examples of these more sustainable types of development, and to see them succeeding economically on the ground, in the region.

Our second question asked: *Are there other models of development such as traditional neighborhoods, transit-oriented employment centers, transit-oriented village centers and neighborhood centers that can be incorporated in future planning decisions?*

This question answers itself. Yes, these are the best models for promoting sustainable communities. In particular, properly designed village and neighborhood centers are inherently transit-supportive, and should therefore be planned and developed early, irrespective of the current modes of transit that can serve them, or even if no transit is currently available. As the market matures and urbanizes, transit can serve these centers efficiently when it's practical to do so with little need of retrofitting for rights of way. Ways to promote these changes were discussed in the answer to question 1.

The third question inquired: *Given the existing level of public and private investment, can these other models have enough impact to affect the required change?*

There is no doubt that the money invested in and earmarked for the suburban pattern of large separated single-use developments, coupled with new freeways to serve this dispersed pattern represents a substantial commitment to the status quo. However, the planned commuter rail lines in the region will begin to change people's perceptions, and this more sustainable transportation option is the vital catalyst for new patterns of development.

It would only take three or four traditional neighborhoods with their accompanying neighborhood or village centers to make a significant difference to this area. Following the criteria for neighborhood design set out in Chapter 6, four new neighborhoods could house the next 10 000 residents in a more sustainable pattern

1 neighborhood = 125 acres (50 ha) × 8 dwellings per acre (average) × 2.6 persons per dwelling × 4 = **10 400 residents**

These compact patterns of development would take up only a small proportion of the available land in the CORE, allowing for several times this amount of residential growth, while still enhancing the framework of regional green space for environmental purposes.

## CRITICAL EVALUATION OF CASE STUDY

This 2002 contract was the largest project we have attempted using the charrette format, and it proved to us that the method works for a big site area just as effectively as it does for a small one. There was one main difference: for the first time we didn't plan out the entire study area and depict it graphically. Instead, our conceptual strategy for sustainable development – more compact development around mixed-use centers as the foci for new and existing neighborhoods and districts – allowed us to concentrate on key sites as illustrations backed up by detailed performance specifications for the remaining land area.

A secondary difference was the lack of a definitive new zoning ordinance to regulate future development. At smaller scales of project with a single

municipality, this is our normal way of working, making as sure as we can that the conventional gap in American planning between development plans and zoning controls is eradicated, or at least minimized. Three of the subsequent case studies illustrate this process, but here, with the participation to varying degrees of six different municipalities plus the other quasi-public organizations there was no opportunity for such a document to be produced; in fact it was contractually excluded from our scope of services. It was not politically viable for each different, and quite fiercely independent jurisdiction to accept the overlay of common regulations.

Accordingly, with the CORE project, we had to be satisfied with recommending particular types and examples of zoning for transit-supportive and sustainable development that the partnering cities and counties could adopt individually, at their own pace. The implementation of these recommendations is therefore likely to be inconsistent and patchy. As noted above under 'Implementation,' the one overarching document we did produce subsequent to the charrette was a manual of General Development Guidelines for all municipalities in the CORE region to use as a model for amending their own regulations. We packed the guidelines with more detail than normal to make up in part for the lack of clear new zoning regulations, turning them into a 'lite' version of urban design guidelines in all but name. Detailed aesthetic guidance was omitted, but site planning strategies, public space design, and environmental practices were highlighted. If followed closely, these guidelines would lead development along a clear path toward greater long-term sustainability. The obvious problem is that these are only guidelines that recommend; they are not regulations that require. Once again, implementation might not be consistent across the different jurisdictions initially. But it's a start.

The obvious and positive lesson to be learned from this multi-jurisdictional exercise is simply that it brought all the regional parties together in a focused debate about vital issues of community planning and design. The format encouraged a level of interaction that was above the norm for the parties themselves and the general public. By designing prototypical developments in detail, we were able to allow the participants to see the real-life implications of various options and decisions, and the exciting opportunities for action. Most participants were converted to the charrette process and detailed design as an effective community planning tool. The feedback we received from the project was that this charrette has become the model for future collaborative planning efforts in the CORE. At this scale of working, consensus around a common process is as important as agreement on the detailed proposals.

We were very pleased at this new level of collaboration and the success of the charrette format, as there was some skepticism among the parties at the outset. We were expressly forbidden to use the word 'charrette'; perhaps this was considered to be a strange and suspicious foreign term. In all the project documentation the word 'workshop' was used exclusively, and only in *this text* have we changed workshop to 'charrette' for consistency.

From our perspective the downside of the CORE project is obvious. The large scope over multiple jurisdictions meant that we were not able to exert as much influence over future development as we usually are able to with a smaller compass. This was frustrating in an area where much change is needed. We feel we have laid the groundwork for others to carry forward, but we're not entirely sure the challenges will be met with equal vigor by all participants.

# The City

## Case Study 2: City of Raleigh, NC, Arena Small Area Plan

### PROJECT AND CONTEXT DESCRIPTION

For this case study carried out in 2000, we stay in the central region of North Carolina and focus on the city of Raleigh, the state capital. The site for this Small Area Plan lies just a couple miles east of the previous CORE project, and comprises approximately four square miles, bounded on the west, north and east sides by freeways, and on the south by a local arterial street that connects directly with the city center, four miles to the east. This southern edge of the project area also includes the proposed Triangle Transit Authority's (TTAs) future commuter rail line, the same one that was featured in the previous case study. The line is used for freight and Amtrak, and will continue to be so, but two passenger rail stations on the new commuter tracks are planned within this study area. The western edge of the site marks the border between Raleigh and its neighbor, the city of Cary (see Figure 8.1).

The study area includes a wide variety of uses. These range from large recreational facilities (the Entertainment and Sports Arena, the NC State University football stadium, an equestrian complex, and the State Fairground) to a corporate office park, large educational institutions (a local high school and the NC State School of Veterinary Medicine) and small residential neighborhoods plus a smattering of local businesses. Large undeveloped areas that are ripe for development exist within the plan area; however, these same properties include landscapes and environmental systems that have been damaged by previous suburban construction and need environment protection.

The two sports facilities and the Fairground bring tens, even hundreds of thousands of visitors and fans to

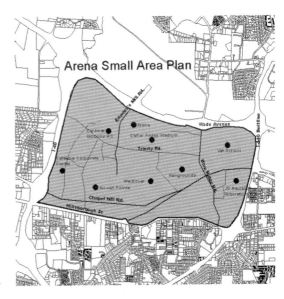

**Figure 8.1** West Raleigh Location Map. The east–west dimension of the master plan area is a little over three miles, and the north–south distance just over a mile on average.

the site at various times of the year. These intermittent uses put a strain on the transportation infrastructure, and on the quality of life of residents and workers in the adjacent neighborhoods and office parks. In addition, the overall project area serves as a gateway to Raleigh from many points west including Cary, the Research Triangle, Durham, Chapel Hill and beyond. Its access to interstate freeways is excellent, but the current transportation system surrounding the site depends almost exclusively on large, limited access thoroughfares. These roads move a high volume of regional traffic through this area between downtown Raleigh and the Research Triangle. As a result, the infrastructure is heavily dependent upon a few connecting highways to serve both regional and local traffic. There is not a very good network of local streets, and the planned extension of a north–south highway across the site linking populous areas to the south with a shopping mall to the north will increase regional traffic around and through the site. Planned street improvements and extensions along the southern boundary will help to relieve the stress on that east–west corridor and create a new southern edge for the study area.

The main objective of the Small Area Plan was to provide a coherent framework for development that achieved three things:

1. Resolved the dichotomies of large-scale and small-scale uses;
2. Avoided the kind of uncoordinated piecemeal development of the type that had taken place to date; and
3. Established a balance between development and environmental protection.

A parallel requirement was to prepare a set of urban design guidelines that would orchestrate development in the future mixed-use centers proposed in the plan, and that would be extended to cover all such village and neighborhood centers within the city of Raleigh.

## KEY ISSUES AND GOALS

Within this overarching objective, we established four main issues to be examined by the plan. These were:

1. Achieving a balance between development and environmental protection;
2. Improving the transportation infrastructure through the site and capitalizing on the proposed new commuter rail service;
3. Creating new types of transit-oriented development (TOD) around the rail stations that illustrated principles of good urban design and development economics;
4. Resolving the difficult relationships of scale between the major state and civic operations and adjacent new and existing neighborhoods.

### Development and Environmental Protection

In general terms, the study area poses a classic dichotomy between the conservation of natural landscape for water quality protection and open space amenity on the one hand, and the pattern of suburban growth that has spread haphazardly throughout the area on the other. These issues are relevant across the site in general, but they come into sharp focus in the northwest corner of the site, where a large 159-acre (63.6 hectares) tract of rolling and wooded land owned by the state of North Carolina was actively listed for sale at the time of the charrette. Two environmentally fragile streams that are in danger of further degradation traverse this parcel of land, which needs very sensitive handling. However, it is located at the junction of two freeways with excellent visibility and good accessibility through nearby interchanges, making it a prime site for development.

### Transit and Transportation

One of the key strategic opportunities for this area is the development of a commuter rail transit system. In the throes of advanced planning and preliminary engineering at the time of the charrette in December 2001, the system is anticipated to begin service in 2008. We were convinced that the presence of this transportation alternative would become the primary catalyst for development and redevelopment throughout the area.

This pattern of Transit-oriented Development has been widely established and proven in other parts of America with similar growth and development conditions. Denver, Dallas, St. Louis, San Diego, Salt Lake City and other cities have seen a tremendous response to 'new start' rail systems with ridership estimates exceeded in the first year of service. The area around Raleigh is no exception, and we wanted to use this plan to support the credibility and attractiveness of this rail operation. The system, as we noted in the first case study, is planned to serve Durham, Research Triangle Park (RTP), Morrisville, Cary, Raleigh and other destinations with a convenient, clean and efficient means for travel throughout the region.

The TTA proposes to use Diesel Multiple Units (DMUs) as the mode of technology along the corridor, running on their own dedicated double tracks. The DMU is a lightweight, self-propelled train that combines the long distance capability of heavy commuter rail, similar to Amtrak service, with the flexibility to stop more frequently. Stations spaced one to three miles apart, and the system can be built for a fraction of the price of light rail. This technology, used in Europe for years, is now being adapted for use in the United States. We are strong supporters of commuter rail service wherever it is feasible, and we believe in this instance that the service proposed by TTA is a logical and cost effective start to providing a true alternative to the automobile-dependent society in central North Carolina. We felt that by integrating development around the train stations as we did in the CORE study, this Raleigh Small Area Plan could establish this typology as the preferred pattern of development for other stops on the line.

In terms of road and street infrastructure, the main issues focused on resolving key points of traffic congestion that would be exacerbated by the frequent passenger trains at some crossing points, especially adjacent to the Fairground and the School of Veterinary Medicine toward the east end of the study area. In addition it was important to create a network of connected streets within the study area to serve the internal needs of residents and workers without always having to rely on the major peripheral highways to move around.

## New Types of Transit-Oriented Development

High and medium density developments centered around train stations are a new phenomenon in the Raleigh region, and we wanted to use this opportunity (the charrette was carried out 16 months earlier than the CORE project in Chapter 7) to explain and illustrate the potential of TODs. Accordingly, we set out the four specific design criteria that need to be met in any TOD design:

- A centrally located transit station or transit stop;
- A shopping street or streets immediately adjacent to the station;
- A network of connected streets that branch out into the surrounding neighborhood(s); and
- A variety of housing types, including multifamily.

Beyond these fairly obvious principles, important questions needed to be answered about the character and development potential of the site. Will the TODs be 'residentially-led,' that is, designed primarily around different types of housing, including detached single-family dwellings, and with only a small amount of service retail; or will they be 'employment-led,' designed mainly with office buildings supported by medium to higher density housing? Answers to these questions would be predicated on the site's location, its context and market studies for the area. When a TOD is based on employment opportunities, we utilize types of office buildings that typically provide workspace for 40 to 80 workers on

each acre of developable land (100–200 workers per hectare). This intensity of occupation works well for suburban and infill sites that aren't located in the city center; in central urban areas the figures would be higher.

These discussions about TODs automatically cross-reference with the typology of mixed-use centers outlined in Chapter 6, and in addition to the criteria listed there, TODs outside the center city can best be classified under three headings:

- *Specialized urban center* – high intensity development with some specialized retail or employment focus;
- *Urban village center* – a medium to high intensity development serving a mixed-use district and surrounding area;
- *Neighborhood center* – a medium to low intensity development serving a particular neighborhood.

The 'urban village center' and the 'neighborhood center' match the same categories of mixed-use activity centers described in Chapter 6. The 'rural village center' from Chapter 6 is generally not associated with Transit-oriented Development because the densities involved are too low, and the 'specialized urban center' is simply a higher density version of the urban village with the addition of some particular transit-supportive characteristic of use or location.

These three types generate different development intensities of residential density and 'floor area ratios' (FARs). FARs measure the density of commercial space in an equivalent way that 'dwellings per acre', or 'persons per hectare' gauge residential density. The floor area ratio is the total floor area of the building or buildings on a site divided by the gross area of the parcel of land.

For example, if a site of 40 000 square feet (3716 square meters) had an FAR of 0.5, the developer could construct 20 000 square feet (1858 square meters) of building. If this building area was organized as two floors of 10 000 square feet each (929 square meters), 30 000 square feet (2787 square meters) of site area would be left open for landscaping and car parking. Parking standards for typical suburban offices require four spaces per 1000 square feet (92.9 square meters) at approximate 350 square feet (32.5 square meters) per (American) car. (This figure per car includes an averaged allowance for driveways, circulation, disabled spaces, landscaping areas and so forth; it is not the actual measurement of the parking space.) Thus our 20 000 square foot office building requires 80 parking spaces at 350 square feet each, giving a parking area of 28 000 square feet (2601 square meters).

**177**

This area fits within the 30 000 square feet available, with some space left over for pedestrian areas at building entrances, dumpster locations, and other miscellaneous items. It's also worth noting that the area for car parking in this typical suburban example is greater than the area of the building. If our hypothetical building had been designed as a single-storey structure, the building and parking would not have fitted on the site. Thus FARs are increased in key locations not only to allow more development, but to force buildings into more urban, multi-story configurations.

In employment-led TODs the parking ratios are often drastically reduced, from four spaces per 1000 square feet (92.9 square meters) to three or even 2.5, in the expectation that many workers will arrive by train or live within walking distance. Architects and planners, and even some developers would like to see these figures reduced further, but the conservatism of lending organizations means that finance is not easily available for developments that do not include the conventional (i.e. suburban) amount of car parking, or something close to it.

With all this in mind, the minimum densities we design to for each of the different types of TOD are set out below. The 'core' refers to development within the 1/4-mile radius, and the 'neighborhood' that part of the site between 1/4-mile and 1/2-mile from the train station.

### Specialized Urban Center

*Core*: Residential – 22 dwellings per acre (143 persons per hectare)
Commercial – FAR 0.75

*Neighborhood*: Residential – 10 dwellings per acre (65 persons per hectare)
Commercial – FAR 0.3

### Village Center

*Core*: Residential – 15 dwellings per acre (97 persons per hectare)
Commercial – FAR 0.5

*Neighborhood*: Residential – 10 dwellings per acre (65 persons per hectare)
Commercial – FAR 0.25

### Neighborhood Center

*Core*: Residential – 10 dwellings per acre (65 persons per hectare)
Commercial – FAR 0.35

*Neighborhood*: Residential 6 dwellings per acre (39 persons per hectare)
Commercial – FAR 0.15

(To put these FARs of 0.15–0.75 in perspective, a typical floor area ratio for development in midtown Manhattan, New York, is between 12 and 15.)

## Relationships Between the Major State Functions and Adjacent Smaller Scale Developments

The State Fairground has been well established over many decades, and it needs large land areas for its activities, ranging from agricultural shows and competitions to funfair rides and concerts. (The scale of the operation is many times that of the Neshoba County Fair described in Chapter 4.) There are no permanent residential buildings, but several large communal structures for commercial and educational purposes do exist. Indeed, one of these, the Dorton Arena, dating from the 1950s is protected as a historic structure on account of its advanced reinforced concrete shell roof design. At the time of the State Fairground's original construction, the site was fully rural as befitted its purpose. Now it sits uncomfortably with a variety of suburban uses that have surrounded it on many sides. Only to the east, where the fields and campus of the N.C. State University School of Veterinary Medicine are located, does any remnant exist of the original open landscape that once characterized this area. Other fields to the west of the main Fairground site are used to accommodate peak car parking demands, but these sit awkwardly next to established low-to-middle income residential neighborhoods.

The adjacent large sports facilities represent typical suburban planning of the pre-Smart Growth era: that is, locate a piece of open land near a freeway, construct a large building with all its requisite car parking, and make everybody drive to and from the events. One of the main issues in this case study was to seek alternative patterns of land use and transit that could reduce this complete car dependency. Even with the extensive freeway network that surrounds the study area, the traffic congestion before and after major sporting events creates substantial problems. This in turn burdens residents and workers with considerable difficulty travelling to and from homes and workplace.

## THE CHARRETTE

This master plan was developed during a highly intensive, public design charrette over a four-day period in December 2000 (see Figure 8.2). The charrette was

|  | Monday – Dec. 11 | Tuesday – Dec. 12 | Wednesday – Dec. 13 | Thursday – Dec. 14 |
|---|---|---|---|---|
| 8:00 |  | Breakfast | Breakfast | Breakfast |
| 9:00 |  | 8:30 Fairgrounds and Agricultural Complex | 9:00 Centennial arena authority | DESIGN |
| 10:00 |  | | | |
| 11:00 | 11:00 Team arrives and studio set-up | 9:30 NC State (Surplus Property, Carter-Finley, Centennial Campus) | 10:30 NC dot | |
| 12:00 | 12:00 Overview by local staff during lunch and bus tour of area (Planning, Transportation, Parks and Rec, TTA) | Lunch | Lunch | Lunch |
| 1:00 | | 1:00 Environmental interest groups lunch meeting | DESIGN | DESIGN |
| 2:00 | | | DESIGN | DESIGN |
| 3:00 | 4:00 Market study presentation by Karnes Research | 3:00 Developers (Corporate Center Dr, etc.) | | |
| 4:00 | | | | |
| 5:00 | Dinner with Planning Commission | 5:30 Pin-up session and project update | 5:30 Pin-up session and project update | Close-up studio |
| 6:00 | | Dinner | Dinner | Dinner |
| 7:00 | Opening presentation | 7:00 Neighborhood Associations (Westover, Nowell Point, LincolnVille) | DESIGN | Closing presentation |

**Figure 8.2** Charrette Schedule. Four-day charrettes are typically the minimum period we will accept to deal with the complexity of a community master plan. Five or six days produce better results, but at around $15 000 to $20 000 a day, plus the costs of preparation and producing the subsequent reports and zoning documents, some municipalities opt for the shorter period.

conducted at a temporary design studio set up in bowels of the Entertainment and Sports Arena (not an easily accessible space for the public to find), where the multidisciplinary design team consisting of planners, urban designers, architects, landscape architects, transportation planners, traffic engineers and market analysts conducted a series of meetings with the interested stakeholder groups. According to our standard practice, each day we developed design alternatives that directly reflected the public input.

These stakeholder groups included representatives from the Raleigh Planning Commission, the Raleigh Appearance Commission, the Raleigh Department of Transportation, the NC Department of Transportation, NC State University, NC State Surplus Property Office, the Centennial Authority that operated the arena, the TTA, environmental interest groups, business owners and residents. The resultant plan was truly a collaborative effort balancing, to the extent practical in a market-driven context, the various and diverse visions and desires of the participants. The master plan maintained our commitment to the construction of places as one of our four typologies. Neighborhoods, Centers, Districts, and Corridors, where every area recognizes some level of mixed-use, organized by a coherent, interconnected, multi-modal transportation network. This includes facilities for transit, vehicles, bicycles and pedestrians.

Our initial analysis broke the large area down into five sub-areas:

1. The State Fair Transit Station Neighborhood;
2. The Hillsborough Street Corridor;
3. The West Raleigh Transit Station Neighborhood;
4. The Corporate District, comprising Corporate Center Drive and the '159 acres' (63.6 hectares) a wooded site being offered for development by the State of North Carolina;
5. The Entertainment, Sports, and Cultural (ESC) District.

**179**

Our detailed market analysis study of the area indicated a very firm market for residential and office space, with relatively weak expectations for retail development. During the charrette, we examined these five areas in detail, and formulated the master plan by the cohesive reassembly of these distinct subareas.

## THE MASTER PLAN

The reader will see from Plate 21 that working at this smaller scale, we were able to design everything within the study area to a hypothetical build-out. This approach is one of our standard procedures to investigate the best use of each parcel of land, and to examine its full potential for development or environmental conservation. We complement these detailed plans with perspectives and aerial views to explain our design concepts to professionals and laypersons alike.

### The State Fair Transit Station Neighborhood (See Plate 22)

#### Current Conditions

The land around the North Carolina State Fair is highly used during times of operation, but is otherwise very underdeveloped. The roads have no curbs, gutters or sidewalks, and small single-story buildings are clustered around the intersections of adjacent main streets. Two of these streets run east-west, parallel to the train tracks on either side, while a major north-south highway crosses both streets and the rail line, creating a confused muddle of intersections. Some highway commercial development has encroached around these intersections along with a significant number of 'flex-warehouse' buildings. The NC State School of Veterinary Medicine, with its large tract of open land, is located to the northeast of these important intersections.

The intersections required significant improvements. The efficiency of operation, measured by grades 'A'–'F' by transportation engineers, was already significantly impaired due to difficult dual traffic signal requirements. This complex intersection was expected to receive a grade of 'F' in the next few years due to increased traffic, and when the commuter trains begin to run at frequent intervals in 2008, things would only get worse.

In addition, while the State Fairground hosts various events year-round, the two-week period devoted to the State Fair itself, attracts as many as 130 000 attendees per day. During this period, traffic exceeds the capacities of all the streets, and parking within a mile of the Fairground is at a premium.

The TTA had planned a station to serve the State Fairground on their commuter rail system. The proposal called for a standard 400-foot (122 meters) platform with a pedestrian tunnel under Hillsborough Street to bring people from the train directly to a main ticket gate at the Fairground. The freight rail lines directly south of the commuter tracks would remain in operation, but there were no plans to provide pedestrian access across the freight lines at this location to developable land on the south side of the tracks.

### Plan Recommendations

Our master plan called for the establishment of Hillsborough Street as a true gateway into downtown Raleigh (four miles to the east), converting it to a landscaped boulevard with multi-use paths and street trees. The intersection of this improved street with Blue Ridge Road however, caused us considerable difficulty. After much consideration and study of alternatives, including a tunnel, we felt the severe traffic congestion at this location could best be solved by the construction of a bridge to facilitate through traffic, with a new access road for local drivers connecting to adjacent streets on the north side of the tracks (see Figure 8.3). Connections on the south side could be made through the new street network that would be developed as part of the transit-oriented development on that part of the site. This rearrangement would dramatically improve movement in the entire area. The fall of the land to the south facilitated this bridge construction by requiring little in the way of ramping up north of Hillsborough Street. This would enable satisfactory pedestrian connections to be made from the expanded School of Veterinary Medicine campus to the new commuter rail station and associated developments.

The current master plan for the School of Veterinary Medicine created approximately 2 000 000 square feet (185 800 square meters) of high-technology, research and development space around an expanded Veterinary Medicine Hospital. We worked very hard with the campus architect and city and state highway engineers to facilitate a compromise that changed the campus plan without destroying its concept

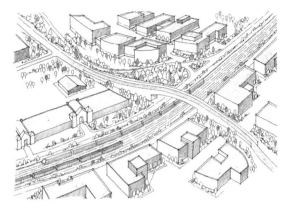

**Figure 8.3** Axonometric View of the New Road Bridge at the Fairgrounds Station. This three-dimensional sketch was crucial in obtaining agreement between the city highway engineers and the university administrators regarding new road construction to relieve congestion at this busy intersection.

while configuring the specially designed new access road on the north side. All parties had to be flexible to achieve the compromise solution, and final agreement was reached only hours before the final presentation to the public. The final drawing was nearly complete, with only this quadrant missing, and in true charrette tradition, the solution was drawn in and colored with only minutes to spare! We are certain that the high-intensity design pressure of the charrette contributed to this dramatic breakthrough in a dispute between two parties who had previously adopted somewhat intransigent positions about their own needs.

As part of the Triangle Transit Authority train station, we proposed a new pedestrian bridge across Hillsborough Street and the freight line, connecting the Dorton Arena to a new signature office building on a site owned by the city of Raleigh. Around this focus of the station and major new building, we designed a medium-rise (4–5 storys) mixed-use urban village to capitalize on the TOD opportunity, with direct links to downtown Raleigh and good connections to nearby interstate highways. This TOD fell somewhere in between the 'Specialized Urban Center' and the 'Urban Village' typologies noted earlier, and we interpolated between the appropriate density figures for a building layout that best suited the site. We designed our new pedestrian bridge as a gateway element to the new urban village and the Fairground, particularly for those who travel to the

Fair by commuter rail. The connection of this new urban village to the Fairground and its year-round program of events would also help support the restaurants and cafés so important to authentic street life.

Within its hybrid typology, we organized the village as an 'employment-led TOD,' meaning that we concentrated on office development as the main economic generator, backed by medium to high-density housing in three- to four-story apartment buildings with some small-lot single family housing at the periphery of the site. Along the eastern boundary, this housing faces onto a wonderful arboretum of trees and lawns operated by NC State University.

## The Hillsborough Street Corridor
(See Plate 23)

### Current Conditions

This second sub-area is bordered by the State Fairground to the east and north, and includes open land owned by the State Fair. The area contains the Westover community that predates most of the development in this area; the neighborhood, mostly single-family bungalows built on a grid of streets, is one of the few residential populations in the vicinity. It enjoys a small commercial center on the adjacent main road that consists of service stations, scattered convenience stores, and some small offices. A long-established hardware store serves as the neighborhood's landmark. In spite of the lack of pedestrian amenities, the corridor maintains a human scale, due in large part to the placement of a number of buildings close to the street.

A planned and funded extension of a north–south arterial road through the undeveloped land would open up this area to regional traffic from the north in addition to the current east–west patterns. This road would also create a view corridor through property that is currently forested and traversed by a number of small streams (see Figure 8.4).

### Plan Recommendations

This was clearly an area in transition. The potential for development and redevelopment could help this area evolve into a true urban mixed-use corridor surrounded by thriving, interconnected neighborhoods with protected green space in the form of parks and recreation areas. The key to this transformation lay in few large parcels of land, paramount of which was the

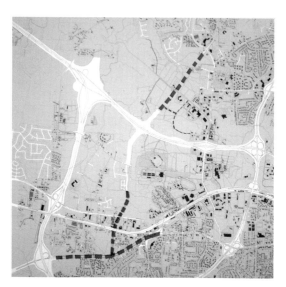

**Figure 8.4** Main Road Extensions Plan. This drawing illustrates the new highway planned by the city and state to improve north–south connectivity. We suggested substantial design revisions to turn this road into a pedestrian-friendly boulevard to serve adjacent neighborhoods as well as moving traffic from other parts of the city.

tract currently owned by the NC State Fair that would contain the future north–south road connection. The section of this road already constructed further north on the site is hostile to pedestrians, and pods of existing development, quite understandably, back away from it in self-imposed seclusion.

It was important to change the character of this road as it passes through this sub-area into a pedestrian-friendly boulevard with multi-use paths on either side. Large canopy trees should be planted in the median and between the curb and the multi-use path. With this design, we felt it would be possible to create some strong and attractive connections with new and existing neighborhoods.

In this part of the site, we also recommended changes to the long-term destination and alignment of the north–south roadway. Instead of the proposed freeway-style flyover spanning the existing east–west roads and the railway, and its traumatic extension through the mature neighborhoods to the south of the study area, we recommended an extension south of our site only as far as an adjacent east–west arterial highway, tunneling under a street and the rail

corridor in the process. This east–west artery takes traffic directly to the freeway at the western edge of the study area, thus serving the transportation needs on the long-term thoroughfare plan without causing major harm to existing residential neighborhoods (see Figure 8.4). Open land exists in appropriate locations for this more modest alignment with a minimum of disruption to existing and proposed development.

The plan in Plate 23 shows the expansion of the adjacent single-family residential neighborhood on the west edge of the site into the State Fair property. Our layout permits neighborhood connections to the thoroughfare and to our vision of a new city park and playing fields that we located on either side of the new boulevard. Some of these playing fields could be used as overflow parking during the peak weeks of the State Fair. We specified that this neighborhood expansion should meet and exceed the current construction standards of the existing community. In other words, house lots similar in size to the existing neighborhood should be placed along narrow, landscaped streets, containing curbs and sidewalks on both sides of the street, and lit by pedestrian-scaled lamps. In addition, numerous streams traverse the property, creating a wonderful opportunity for recreation trails and greenways. This preserves stands of trees serving as significant buffers from the traffic on the boulevard. We also recommended that these streams should be protected from all development activity by a minimum of 100 feet (30.5 meters) of undisturbed landscape buffers on either side.

We designed the land between the existing east–west street and the rail line along the southern edge of the site as a higher density residential development with traditional block sizes of 400–600 feet (122–183 meters). This layout increased the residential density along the transit line at a location midway between two stations, both reasonably close by. This new development also contained opportunities for small retail or office components on the first floors of corner buildings.

The final piece in this section of the planning jigsaw was a linear park extending from the streams on the State Fair property beneath the upgraded east–west boulevard, and leading ultimately to the West Raleigh transit station described in the next section. This linear park, lined by public streets and three-storey apartments, would provide safe and convenient pedestrian and bicycle paths to the proposed new urban village centered around this second train

**Plate 28** `159 acres,' Option A. This alternative plan limits development to the part of the site that extends the theme of the Corporate Drive linear park immediately to the south. It preserves the majority of sensitive landscaped areas as a community resource. The single access point, however, creates a significant problem of adequate access.

**Plate 29** `159 acres,' Option B. This plan is based on more conventional assumptions about development priorities, but tries to salvage as much open space to aesthetic and environmental purposes as possible.

**Plate 30** `159 acres,' Option C. This option accepts a large amount of development as inevitable, given the state's firm intent to raise money by selling the land for commercial use. The design sacrificed the visual beauty of the meadow, leaving a fragment as a small, but attractive park framed by buildings in order to leave undeveloped the more environmentally sensitive land around the stream corridor.

**Plate 31** Entertainment, Sports and Cultural District Plan Detail. This area was the least susceptible to coherent urbanization due to the random placement of the large entertainment facilities isolated in acres of car parking. Only modest improvements could be made to the infrastructure by adding pedestrian sidewalks and street trees, while at the eastern edge of this sub-area, new hotels and conference facilities could provide compatible patterns of use without competing with other, more urban developments in adjacent sections of the master plan.

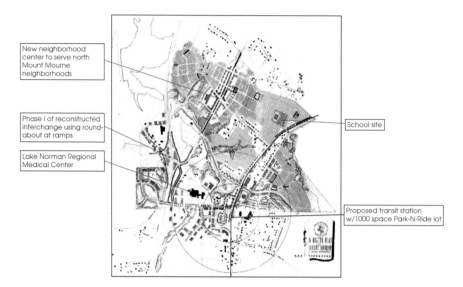

New neighborhood center to serve north Mount Mourne neighborhoods

Phase I of reconstructed interchange using round-about at ramps

Lake Norman Regional Medical Center

School site

Proposed transit station w/1000 space Park-N-Ride lot

**Plate 32** Mount Mourne Master Plan. The master plan divides the site into four main geographical areas:
1. The Transit Village within the 1/4-mile radius of the train station and the areas immediately to the northeast within the half-mile radius;
2. The Hospital District to the west of the station within the half-mile radius;
3. The Interstate and 'Hospital West', comprising the land to the west of the interstate; and
4. The North Neighborhood – the largely residential areas north of the transit village and hospital.

**Plate 33** Transit Village Plan Detail. The existing community of Mount Mourne can be seen in the undeveloped southeast quadrant of the plan. The train station is located at the center of the 1/4-mile circle.

**Plate 34** Hospital District Detail Plan. We intended that the area around the hospital and adjacent to the transit village would develop with primarily medical office buildings for services supporting the hospital. These uses could extend into the undeveloped land in the southwest quadrant of the plan, just outside our study area. We had expected that larger office development would also take place nearby, adjacent to the freeway interchange. See Plate 36.

**Plate 35** Revised Master Plan with Lowes Headquarters. As it turned out, the land south of our study area opened up for development sooner than expected, and the Lowes Corporation master planned that site to take advantage of the opportunities noted in our charrette report. With other consultants, notably the landscape architecture firm of Land Design in Charlotte, the Lawrence Group helped revise the master plan to connect the Lowes campus directly to the future transit village and to increase the density of office development between the campus and the hospital to accommodate some of the many vendors who are expected to relocate near their major customer.

**Plate 36** The Interstate and 'Hospital West' Detail Plan. A planned new bridge over the interstate will provide excellent access to land in the west of our study area. We considered this area a prime site for new corporate offices (at a scale smaller than Lowes). Now this site is likely to be developed for smaller companies who provide Lowes with products and materials.

**Plate 37** North Neighborhood Detail Plan. Development of this land between downtown Mooresville and Mount Mourne can provide a wide range of housing types to accommodate substantial portions of Mooresville's growth without radically extending the town limits into new greenfield areas. The plan sets out housing, retail and commercial sub-centers, parks, greenways and a local school to allow some measure of self-sufficiency for the neighborhood.

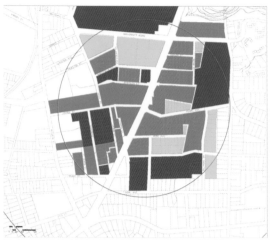

**Plate 38** Haynie-Sirrine Property Values Map. An accurate assessment of economic conditions is a very important factor in the analysis phase of the charrette. It directly informs preliminary design decisions.

**Plate 39** Redevelopment Potential Map. The physical and economic analysis allowed the design team to establish three categories of redevelopment potential: Blue indicates major redevelopment opportunities due to factors such as vacant land, multiple properties under common ownership, or areas of excessive housing blight. Green identifies locations for moderate redevelopment, land characterized mainly as multiple rental properties under common ownership and areas of moderate infrastructure degradation where infill development could occur using the existing block structure. Yellow areas are those slated for minimal redevelopment, predominately owner-occupied housing or well-maintained rental housing where only minor repairs are needed to the housing and/or infrastructure.

**Plate 40** Master Plan for the Haynie-Sirrine Neighborhood. At full size, this drawing is approximately six feet (1.8 meters) square, all drawn by hand. We then take a digital photograph in the last hours before the public presentation and build the graphic image into the final Powerpoint presentation.

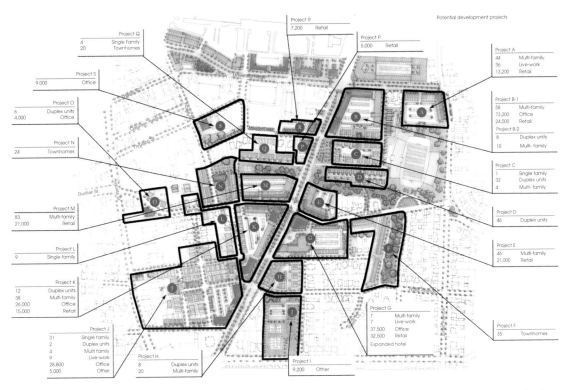

Potential development projects

Project Q
4   Single Family
20   Townhomes

Project R
7,200   Retail

Project P
5,000   Retail

Project A
44   Multi-family
36   Live-work
13,200   Retail

Project S
9,000   Office

Project B-1
58   Multi-family
73,200   Office
24,000   Retail

Project O
6   Duplex units
4,000   Office

Project B-2
8   Duplex units
10   Multi-family

Project N
24   Townhomes

Project C
1   Single family
32   Duplex units
4   Multi-family

Dunbar St.

Project M
83   Multi-family
21,000   Retail

Project D
46   Duplex units

Project L
9   Single family

Project E
46   Multi-family
21,000   Retail

Project K
12   Duplex units
38   Multi-family
26,000   Office
15,000   Retail

Project G
7   Multi-family
7   Live-work
37,500   Office
32,500   Retail
Expanded hotel

Project F
35   Townhomes

Project J
31   Single family
2   Duplex units
4   Multi family
9   Live-work
28,800   Office
5,000   Other

Project H
8   Duplex units
20   Multi-family

Project I
9,200   Other

**Plate 41** Potential Redevelopment Projects. The master plan is broken down into smaller, definable projects as the basis for implementation strategies.

**Plate 42** Church Street Neighborhood Center, as proposed (compare with Figure 10.11). Watercolour perspective renderings are very effective tools in creating images of proposed development. The richness of the medium adds depth and luster that is rarely present in pencil or colored marker drawings. Two design team members began working on a series of perspectives from about the halfway point in the schedule. This means identifying key sites and projects early in the process (See also Plates 43, 44, 47 and 49).

**Plate 43** Church Street North as proposed. This part of the site, at the ridge overlooking downtown Greenville has the greatest redevelopment potential for upmarket mixed-use development. Accordingly, the buildings here are larger and denser than elsewhere on the site. Compare with Figure 10.15.

**Plate 44** Proposed Biltmore Park and Townhomes. In this illustration, the squalid duplexes have been demolished and the stream that ran beneath them in a culvert opened up to the daylight as the main feature of a neighborhood park. New townhomes along the rear of the site provide more dwellings than were demolished, and face onto the park, enclosing the space and providing informal neighborhoods security. Compare with Figure 10.17.

**Plate 45** Section through New Townhomes and Biltmore Park. Existing dwellings (far left and far right) frame the new development. Note the graphic consistency of pencil stroke and angle of application. Such precision pays handsome dividends in the quality of the final graphics.

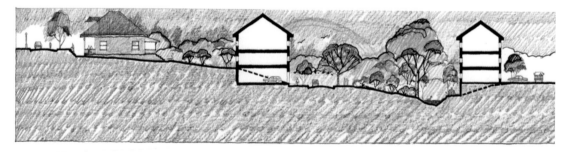

**Plate 46** Section through Springer Street and New Park. Affordable townhomes and apartments are fitted onto tight sites framing a new neighborhood park.

**Plate 47** Sirrine Neighborhood Center as proposed. New live-work units screen a new parking deck and provide the much-needed spatial enclosure for the street and local neighborhood center. Compare with Figure 10.19.

**Plate 48** Section through Sirrine Stadium and New Parking Deck. This a prime example of multi-use shared parking facilities.

**Plate 49** Redesigned Springer Street Tunnel. The city of Greenville selected this design as the first public project to be constructed. Compare with Figure 10.3.

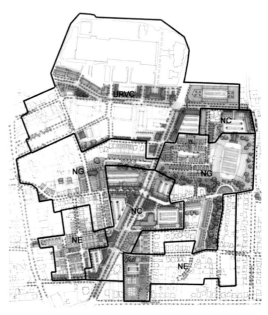

**Plate 50** Zoning or 'Regulating' Plan. Within the new Zoning District, four sub-zones regulate the form and intensity of development. These four categories, in ascending order, are defined as Neighborhood Edge (NE), Neighborhood General (NG), Neighborhood Center (NC), and University Ridge Village Center (URVC). These are geographic areas defined according to their urban character and are mapped directly over the urban design master plan.

**Plate 51** North Mecklenburg Map. This large map covering approximately 80 square miles was created by the authors over a period of two years working with the three north Mecklenburg towns of Huntersville, Cornelius, and Davidson. It illustrated the hypothetical 'build-out' of the full land area, including new urban village centers, transportation infrastructure and areas of landscape conservation, and formed the basis of the region's coordinated establishment of New Urbanist design-based zoning ordinances.

**Plate 53** Cornelius East Master Plan, The Lawrence Group, 2003. This master plan sits to the south of the Cole Jenest and Stone TOD plan shown in Figure 11.7. It links Cornelius with the adjacent communities of Davidson to the northeast and Huntersville to the south, and strikes a balance between extensive preservation of rural land, some low-density development, and focal areas of increased density. This last category includes an employment-led TOD at the next stop south on the commuter line from Cornelius town center.

**Plate 52** Cornelius Town Center Master Plan, Shook Kelley, Architects, 1997. Many elements in common with Campbell's thesis are visible in this plan (see Figure 11.2). The main difference is the location of the town hall away from the corner paired with a new police station in Beaux-Arts symmetry. (*Drawing courtesy of Shook Kelley architects*).

station. The park space with its small stream would also provide natural drainage from this urban core.

## The West Raleigh Transit Station Neighborhood (See Plates 24–26)

### Current Conditions

The east–west road through this third sub-area is a low-scale commercial strip corridor with office, retail, and service uses in single-storey buildings generally set back from the road. The area north of the road is a mixture of some low-density residential neighborhoods and small office-flex buildings. The TTAs had proposed to site their West Raleigh commuter rail station on land occupied by the North Carolina State Surplus Property office and storage yard, a site with good frontage onto adjacent roads that made it suitable for the park and ride lot planned by the TTA as the initial station development. However, this sub-area demonstrated to us great potential for a more intensive urban use as a function of the new train service.

There is also a freeway interchange immediately to the west of this subarea, providing excellent accessibility by car. To take advantage of this, the area to the northwest has been developed as an office park, but plenty of land remains undeveloped in this quadrant.

### Plan Recommendations

Our master plan proposed that the West Raleigh transit station area develop as a residentially-led mixed-use urban village to balance the employment-led TOD designed for the State Fairground station area, but with one important amendment. We suggested that a distinctive aspect of this TOD could be the presence of a regionally significant civic building such as a performing arts center. We didn't pluck this idea out of thin air, but recast an existing proposal by the city of Raleigh to place such an arts center in a nearby suburban location, isolated from any other uses and accessible only by car. We believed that proposal was shortsighted and likely to lead to increased traffic congestion in a system that is already overloaded at peak times.

As a provocative alternative, we illustrated how the performing arts center could fit on the State Surplus Property yard in the midst of a new urban village (see Plate 25). This site, located across the street from the train station, also has excellent access from nearby thoroughfares and the interstate immediately to the west. Failing this specific proposal, we recommended strongly that this site be reserved for some similarly important civic and public building. These community facilities should be integrated into pedestrian-scaled districts that offer complimentary amenities such as restaurants and public transportation. They should not be strung out on a highway only accessible by car. We also added slightly more office development than normal for this typology on account of the adjacent office park and the site's excellent freeway access.

This special intensity of development would need several parking decks, financed by public–private partnerships, to serve the mixed-use retail, office, and residential core, along with some park-and-ride spaces. We located the decks within the blocks adjacent to the transit station and the main boulevard through the site, upgraded from its previous condition as a semirural road. Other development was accommodated with surface parking, and if this TOD was reduced in scale, most parking could be provided without decks.

As designed, the proposed urban village comprised three and four-story mixed-use buildings on its Main Street, the east–west boulevard that bisected the site, and the buildings tapered down in scale block by block to two-story residential development integrated into the existing neighborhoods (see Plate 26). The plan in Plate 26 proposed new single-family homes backing up to existing single-family lots. It's a good tactic wherever possible to match like with like when bringing new development up to existing neighborhoods. (We couldn't manage this on the south side due to narrow strips of developable land. To the east, we transitioned to apartment buildings around the end of the linear park that enters the station area from the sub-area described in the previous section.)

At the station, we recommended the construction of a pedestrian bridge over the freight line and an adjacent street. This bridge connection would open up the properties on the south side of the tracks for transit-friendly development. Just as with the State Fair Station, the bridge would be visually significant and serve as a gateway to the area. The plan also encouraged the placement of a conference hotel on a prominent corner two blocks west of the train station and adjacent to the existing office park with its large corporate users (shown in pink in Plate 24). This would be one of the first buildings seen when driving into this area from the interstate exit immediately to the west, and because of its prominence, the building should be designed to create a strong gateway by framing the street edge and providing a good pedestrian environment. Elsewhere we planned smaller 'boutique' office buildings with typical floorplates of 6000–8000 square feet (557–743 square meters). The only exception was a large corporate building visible from the interstate at the western edge of the site with its parking tiered down into the fall of the land (Bottom left in Plate 21).

We continued the existing street from the office park southwards across our upgraded east–west boulevard to link directly with the train station so that office workers in the northern campus could reach the station easily by a small shuttle bus. On our plan, this connecting street continued to the east to link up with the end of the linear park, which in its turn provided bicycle and pedestrian access between the station and the adjacent neighborhoods and playing fields described in the previous section.

## The Corporate District and the '159 acres' (See Plates 27–30)

### Current Conditions

Containing just a few large tenants, the existing corporate office park is a surprisingly underdeveloped business campus. It is home to a large bank's mortgage center and a training facility for a technology company. The main north–south drive is constructed to a greater width than is required, with a cross section measuring an amazing 41 feet wide (12.5 meters). There are no sidewalks anywhere.

The headwaters of another stream system traverse the business park, making development on the west side of the property difficult. The stream that flows north remains in relatively pristine condition, and has not yet been damaged by the environmental degradation that development has caused to other streams in the area. At the time of the plan, late in 2000, new apartments were being constructed in the northern part of the site in a typical suburban configuration of buildings placed amidst parking lots. This development abuts the state-owned tract of 159 acres (63.6 hectares), known locally as 'The Swine Education Unit' on account of its previous university use for agricultural programs in pig farming. This publicaly owned site has a tremendous amount of potential as a corporate campus, with good interstate visibility and access, and the state had offered the land for sale on the open market prior to the charrette. The pristine stream noted above divides the western one-third of the property and another

stream, already impaired by development, crosses the northeast corner. Environmental protection of these stream systems was of paramount importance on this property. A beautiful sylvan meadow lies at the heart of the property.

### Plan Recommendations

*Corporate District (See Plate 27)* The axis of the plan for this area was the construction of a public greenway along the pristine stream through the office park, bounded by streets and visually overlooked by new buildings on both sides. This visual supervision would ensure the safety and use of this landscaped amenity. People want to see other people using open spaces; empty open spaces are more hostile to human activity than poorly landscaped ones. This section of the greenway would connect the existing and proposed large employment uses, including the '159 acres,' to the West Raleigh train station to the south. If an underpass could be engineered beneath the interstate immediately to the north, the greenway could link regionally to extensive existing forest preserves. Even with existing large-scale office buildings, a substantial amount of land remained undeveloped, or partially developed with only parking lots and front lawns.

To accomplish the degree of urbanism necessary to frame the stream properly, we strongly recommended the construction of new mixed-use buildings (small service retail on the ground floor, offices on the upper floors) along the street edge of the bank mortgage office site. This replaced the previously approved, but unbuilt, suburban pattern of buildings scattered amidst extensive areas of parking. No floor area would be lost, it would simply be reconfigured into a more urban arrangement. On the west side of the stream, new office buildings could be constructed to complete the framing of the space. The height of the buildings, two to three storys, would be limited by the amount of parking that could be provided.

*The 159 Acres* We developed three alternatives for the 159-acre (63.6 hectare) site, as this was the focus of intense debate during the charrette. On one side were environmental groups who wanted to protect the stream systems from further damage, and to save some open landscape as an antidote to the creeping suburban sprawl evident in surrounding areas. On the other were city and state officials who wished to realize the full development value of this property in order to purchase other areas of open space in the region. In preparing these options, we followed the findings of our detailed market analysis that showed a strong need for residential and office space, but relatively weak demand for retail. The published master plan drawing illustrated Option A as the preferred alternative for this area; we had decided to take the most environmentally conscious viewpoint. However we then came under late pressure from civic officials to illustrate more 'development-friendly' alternatives. We developed Options B and C in time for the final presentation, but not in time to include them on the full master plan drawing.

*Option A (See Plate 28; 159 acres plan A)*   Option A was the most environmentally sensitive of the three options. It clustered development to the west side of the stream in order to preserve the woodlands and beautiful open meadow that lies within the eastern portion of the property. Access was from a long single drive that extended the street pattern proposed for the greenway development immediately to the south, and there were no expensive stream crossings. Under this alternative, the property could support approximately 1 000 000 square feet (92 900 square meters) of development in a series of four-story buildings with parking accommodated in one very large four-story deck with additional surface car parks. It also avoided putting any development near the already fragile stream at the eastern edge of the site. While this alternative preserved nearly 70 percent of the site and gave some interstate visibility above the treetops, we were forced to admit that serving this amount of office development from one access point was impractical.

*Option B (See Plate 29; 159 acres plan B)*   Option B illustrated the opposite point of view, opening the site up for more intensive development while preserving a smaller percentage of open space. This plan spread the development across the site, but still preserved part of the meadow as one end of a large neighborhood park framed by offices, apartments, and a hotel. The main stream was also protected as a greenway within and beyond this park, but parking lots backed up to the other stream on the eastern edge, compounding its environmental problems. Parking was provided in surface lots only, but the parking was terraced into the landscape behind the buildings. The placement and smaller size of buildings, generally two to three-storys, was dictated by providing cheaper but lower capacity surface parking in lieu of expensive parking decks.

Because of the more extensive street layout (with two expensive stream crossings) and a direct connection to the road leading to the adjacent freeway interchange, there was a greater opportunity for a mixed-use development. This alternative illustrated opportunities for a 300-room conference hotel (in pink) fronting on the park, numerous restaurants and specialty shops ((in red) nearest the interchange) with apartments and corporate offices lining the streets.

*Option C (See Plate 30; 159 acres plan C)*   Option C was a compromise and a blend of A and B. It included nearly as much development as Option B, but kept the development activity on the southern and eastern parts of the site and maintained the northwestern part of the site including the main-stream corridor as open space. To address the parking requirements for this type of clustering, parking decks would be needed for the offices on the west side of the site to permit construction of two four-story, 100 000 square foot (9290 square meters) buildings. The remaining five office buildings in this cluster were proposed as two storys, though taller buildings could be built with additional structured parking.

Surface parking was provided for all the other buildings. If practicable, parking decks could be constructed instead of surface parking on the east side of the site to minimize grading and cluster the development more tightly to preserve a larger proportion of the meadow, which was almost completely lost in this alternative. The main stream however was left in its natural state, except for one bridge crossing at the southern part of the site to connect with the office development on the west side.

We made the four office buildings on the east side four or five storys – hence the expansive fields of surface parking to avoid the cost of decks while still providing parking at four spaces per 1000 square feet (92.9 square meters). The mixed-use buildings comprised three blocks of ground floor shops and restaurants with two to four stories of offices and apartments above. On-street parking was provided on all the streets along with a pedestrian-scaled streetscape of curb and gutter, street trees and sidewalks. Sidewalks in front of shops should be at least 15 feet (4.6 meters) wide (see Figure 10.16), while all other locations should be 6–8 feet (1.8–2.4 meters) wide. It was also important to us to retain 'green connections' through the site and beneath the freeway to link with the nearby forest preserves (located on the edge of the CORE area of the previous case study) for walking and bicycling trails.

While there were trade-offs for each scenario, by the conclusion of the charrette, and in the light of the state's firm intention to sell the site for its maximum development potential, we generally supported the development of the property under Option C with the hope that more parking decks could enable several office buildings to be resited to preserve more of the original meadow as illustrated in Option B.

## The Entertainment, Sports, and Cultural (ESC) District (See Plate 31)

### Current Conditions

Clearly some of the most important elements of this entire planning study were the four regional entertainment and sports venues located in the middle of the master plan. The arena, the adjacent NC State University football stadium, an equestrian complex to the south of the stadium and the extensive State Fairground together form a complex that is a state-wide destination, and where events occur nearly every day of the year.

This sub-area of the plan comprises approximately 460 acres (184 hectares) and includes thousands of temporary and permanent parking spaces, although at the time of the charrette, no official parking capacity numbers were available. There has been an informal agreement to share parking during peak events such as football games and the State Fair; in addition, the arena relies heavily on the football stadium parking on a regular basis, and to meet their own needs, NC State University had recently purchased land adjacent to the stadium for additional parking and practice fields. There was no comprehensive marketing strategy for all the facilities, and with the exception of some banners at the stadium and the arena, no coordinated signage or streetscape program. The one local road that bisects the area from east to west completely lacks any pedestrian amenities. The tens of thousands of fans and spectators at the various events walk in the road or along grass verges.

### Plan Recommendations

Other than two key hotel and office sites near the intersection of the existing roads at the eastern edge of the site, no substantial development opportunities were identified during the charrette for this fifth and last sub-area of the Small Area Plan. One hotel could be a major conference facility, and both would

provide much needed accommodation in an underserved market area. The charrette team entertained the idea of developing a larger shopping and restaurant complex near the stadium that would be a citywide destination, but we decided it was not feasible. A development of this type would be too isolated in that location, not visible from the freeway, not easily accessible by transit, and would be overwhelmed by traffic and parking from the State Fair, football games, and other major events. In addition, we considered it would generate unwanted competition for the potential mixed-use urban village around the State Fair train station to the south.

We did, however, believe there was a great need for general infrastructure improvements in the area including coordinated lighting and streetscape amenities. We recommended that the east–west street be widened to a four-lane boulevard with a landscaped median, curb and gutter, street trees and eight feet (2.4 meters) wide sidewalks. This type of streetscape design would permit and encourage pedestrian movement much more safely than existing conditions allowed.

In addition to the basic streetscape improvements, we strongly encouraged the arena, the stadium and the State Fairground to develop a coordinated, formal strategy for parking. We were concerned that no actual count of parking spaces could be readily provided, and that parking was creeping throughout the area on an *ad hoc* basis. This coordination could ultimately take the form of a Parking Authority charged with the maintenance of all the parking available to the main venues and construction of any new facilities.

We also encouraged all the venues to coordinate marketing and events better. Their close proximity should entice larger national and international events that require such large facilities. If nothing else, this coordination would assist all the venues to plan traffic and parking properly, avoiding the annual issue of whether NC State will have a home football game during the State Fair. We also strongly suggested the improvement of an existing lane along the east side of the adjacent residential westover neighborhood with curb and gutter, street trees and wide sidewalks to permit pedestrian and shuttle bus circulation from the State Fair train station to the arena and football stadium. During events, this street could be closed to automobile traffic and opened to frequent transit shuttles. There were only a few homes in the neighborhood with direct access from this existing lane that would need some modification to accommodate these improvements. This could take the form of a limited access rear lane along the boundaries of the properties, utilizing land within the street right-of-way.

## IMPLEMENTATION

This project was unusual for us because we were not asked to produce any implementation strategies as part of the plan other than citywide Urban Design Guidelines that dealt in passing with the two urban transit villages in the master plan. These guidelines, extracts of which are included in Appendix V, were subsequently adopted by the city of Raleigh to cover all mixed-use centers within their jurisdiction after extensive debate and several public presentations.

Subsequent to our involvement in the planning process, the state sold the '159 acres' to a developer from Birmingham, Alabama, for a modified mixed-use development, somewhat similar to our Options B and C. Detailed negotiations between the city and the developer ensued, with the master plan as the focus of debate. City staff expressed themselves very pleased with the detail of the master plan, as it enabled discussions with the developer to get right down to meaningful detail, and they credited the master plan for elevating the design of the new development above and beyond the normative suburban commercial centre.

## CONCLUSIONS

The fundamental impulse of the plan was to pull together several conflicting patterns of development into one coherent vision that took into account market, development, and environmental realities. From all these variables, we highlighted the importance of focusing urban development around the two train stations on the site. We felt we could not overstate the importance of proactive planning for commuter rail transit. This important transportation choice for citizens should give rise to Transit-oriented Developments around each of the two stations that would provide models for similar projects in the region. For transit to maximize its impact under any Smart Growth scenario, it must transcend issues relating purely to transportation and have a direct influence on adjacent land use decisions. The initial planning by the Triangle Transit Authority for simple park-and-ride lots at both stations should represent only a first stage in the active promotion, perhaps through public–private partnerships, of a

pair of mixed-use urban villages that would invigorate and enrich the whole plan area.

We were also concerned about the lack of a coordinated parking strategy between the main event organizers on site. We felt such a strategy was essential, for without this, valuable and attractive land would become marginalized as low-grade fields of temporary parking, unsuitable for other, more productive uses. This would be poor stewardship of public land.

Existing neighborhoods presented another delicate issue. They had recently focused their community energies on withdrawing defensively from future development, and instead we wanted to encourage them to join in a more positive vision for the future. We accomplished some of this during the charrette as we showed residents that their property values could benefit from upgrading the plan area into a showcase of integrated mixed uses. Our drawings convinced several key participants that their single-family neighborhoods could be sensitively enlarged and connected to a lively and attractive mix of workplaces, shops and entertainment opportunities. However, this selective densification could only work environmentally, and in terms of neighborhood politics, if substantial areas of the study area were maintained as compensatory public open space, as parks, nature trails and other opportunities for active and passive recreation in green and attractive natural surroundings. The stewardship of the remaining natural landscape needed to extend beyond the protection of the stream buffers. Well-planned and maintained open spaces as parks and greenways are the necessary corollary to urban density, providing a contrast with, and clear boundaries to the proposed new urban villages.

We argued that developing this managed gradient between open space and natural surrounding and urban neighborhoods and centers was the most important strategic objective for this plan area as it transformed itself from an undifferentiated suburban mélange to an orchestrated series of urban villages and parks.

## CRITICAL EVALUATION OF CASE STUDY

The outcome of this project was mixed. On the positive side, we were able to demonstrate to a planning authority somewhat unfamiliar with the potential of the charrette process just how much more could be achieved that with the conventional drip-feed 'one meeting a month' planning process. Another substantial achievement was the illustration of the

**187**

opportunities for medium to high-density transit villages at the train stations locations, as opposed to the previously rather minimal vision of simple park and ride facilities put forth as the first stage by the TTA. In doing so we were able to build some bridges between the transportation planners of the transit authority and the city land use planners.

Our biggest regret with this project was not being able to create any strategies for implementing the plan other than the urban design guidelines that only applied to the proposed transit villages. With so many different players operating at so many different scales, a prioritized list of actions could have committed the parties to build on the collaborative success of the plan's vision. As a result, even though the plan was adopted enthusiastically by the city of Raleigh, and received the political backing of two elected officials who represented the area, it functioned purely as a vision document. The plan stood alone, with no reinforcement in the form of new design-based zoning codes for the project area or even recommendations for changes to the existing zoning classifications to bring them in line with the plan vision.

However, the plan withstood its first big test (more or less) with the proposed development of the 159-acre site. Planning staff worked long and hard with the developer and the community to achieve an acceptable design, and while the development wasn't as good as the planners themselves would have liked, it was a lot better than average because of the master plan. We can only imagine how many further improvements could have been achieved with design-based zoning regulations in place. Like many American cities of its size and type, Raleigh has talented planners but a very complex and unwieldy zoning code, assembled bit by bit over many years, and we sensed resistance to major changes in the document. There is no doubt the process to affect changes on a citywide basis would be complex and highly politicized. However, to adopt zoning amendments keyed directly to a local plan everyone supported should not have been too difficult. But large cities are like supertankers; they have a lot of momentum and can't easily change course to a dramatic new heading. Smaller towns are different. They are politically more flexible and mobile, and the weakness evident in this second case study was avoided by the commitment to change on the part of a smaller local authority in the third case study, the town of Mooresville, NC.

# The Town

## Case Study 3: Mooresville, North Carolina

### PROJECT AND CONTEXT DESCRIPTION

Mooresville is a town of approximately 20 000 people, located on the urban periphery of Charlotte, North Carolina. Charlotte, named for the wife of King George III, is the hub city of the largest urban region in the Carolinas with an overall population of some two million people, and is located within Mecklenburg County, designated in honor of Queen Charlotte's birthplace in northern Germany. Mooresville sits in southern Iredell County, 30 miles north of central Charlotte and just over the county line that separates Iredell from Mecklenburg. The town is the northern terminus of a proposed commuter rail line (the North Transit Corridor) linking Mooresville and three towns in northern Mecklenburg County with Charlotte city center. Interstate 77, one of the main north–south arteries in the state passes through the town's incorporated area to the west of the downtown and through the project area, providing the town and the project site with good freeway access from a number of interchanges. This transportation infrastructure will be enhanced when the proposed commuter rail line begins operation in 2008.

The project area comprises 1200 acres (480 hectares) of predominantly greenfield land located three miles south of Mooresville's downtown. The topography is generally flat and gently rolling with few dramatic slopes or other features. Our master plan provided a framework to manage the growth around a new regional hospital (the Lake Norman Regional Medical Centre) and an aging interstate interchange (Exit 33). The new growth fuelled by this large hospital, the extensive suburban expansion of Charlotte around the nearby Lake Norman, and the potential for future transit-oriented development

around a station planned near the hospital have combined to bring considerable pressure to bear on this area (see Figure 9.1).

The social heart of the project area is the small historic settlement of Mount Mourne, located toward the southeast of the site, and adjacent to the existing, lightly used freight railroad that will be transformed in the near future to a commuter train service utilizing the same kind of Diesel Multiple Units (DMUs) planned for the central area of North Carolina and featured in the first two case studies. With a post office, school, fire station and several churches, Mount Mourne possesses as much civic fabric as many small towns, and thus provides a solid foundation for the master plan.

This plan represents the second and third phases of a detailed study process that lasted two years with plenty of public input and participation, and which examined transportation, environmental, land use and zoning issues in the Mooresville area. As part of the first phase, before we were involved, the town had employed a separate traffic consultant to establish a new roadway plan and redesign elements of the freeway interchange (Exit 33) on the site.

Since the completion of our first version of the master plan in 2000 (phase two in the overall process), we and other consultants reworked it in 2001 (phase three) following the relocation of a major corporate headquarters to the site. The Lowes corporation (a major 'do-it-yourself' and home improvement retail chain) was attracted to the site by the accommodating provisions of the original plan and its synchronised zoning ordinance that made relocation of their large facility relatively straightforward. This major new complex has affected the area so much that a second revision of the master

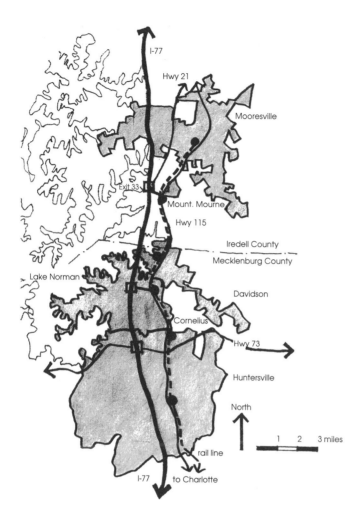

**Figure 9.1** Location Map. Mount Mourne is located south of downtown Mooresville and north of the three Mecklenburg county towns of Huntersville, Cornelius and Davidson. These communities all embrace New Urbanist and Smart Growth concepts in their zoning ordinances and land use plans (see Chapter 11).

plan (phase four) has been scheduled for 2003–2004. This aims to ensure that a new wave of subsidiary office development, providing space for companies that supply Lowes with goods and services, does not overturn some of the founding principles of the 2000 master plan.

## KEY ISSUES AND GOALS

The overall goal of the master plan was to create a development scenario for the 1200 acres (480 hectares) that balanced the area's economic development potential with principles of Smart Growth, and capitalized on the site's transportation advantages while maintaining an appropriate urban scale

and environmental protections. The plan thus included detailed provisions for residential, office, and retail buildings, public parks and areas of preserved landscape, and an interconnected street network.

The key issues were:

1. Establishing a distinct identity for the location.
2. Creating a southern gateway into Mooresville.
3. Creating a plan that blended the walkability of a mixed-use urban village around the train station with vehicle accessibility from the freeway interchange for commercial and healthcare development.
4. Ensuring housing affordability in the new neighborhoods.
5. Safeguarding environmental protection and open space provision.

## THE CHARRETTE

We held a charrette at a local church on the site for three days in March, 2000 during which neighbors, property owners, developers, real estate agents, church groups and town officials expressed their views in a candid, public environment that aired a long list of issues and opportunities. The town's original intention was to focus on the growing area at freeway Exit 33, and create an attractive southern gateway into the town, leaving Mount Mourne on the fringe of consideration. While not diminishing the importance of this objective, we quickly came to understand the importance of the Mount Mourne community and its history. Accordingly, our first action was to retitle the process 'the Mount Mourne charrette,' and establish this identity for the area instead of simply calling it 'Exit 33.' This shift of emphasis was enthusiastically endorsed by all participants, and created a positive atmosphere where local people felt more ownership of the project. It helped turn some initial skepticism into a collaborative attitude.

## THE MASTER PLAN (See Plate 32)

Our site analysis and understanding of the local dynamics led us quickly to divide the master plan into four main geographic areas:

1. The Transit Village
2. The Hospital District
3. The Interstate and 'Hospital West'
4. The North Neighborhood.

Additionally, we set out policies on three specific topics:

5. Open Space Design and Environmental Protection
6. Housing
7. A new Development code.

### The Transit Village (see Plate 33)

After a number of discussions with the Charlotte Area Transit System (CATS), Mooresville town leaders, and local residents, we determined that the most logical placement for a train station was near the existing Mount Mourne community where the rail line runs north–south and parallel to a local main road, Highway 115, that connects Mooresville's downtown area with the neighboring town of Davidson in Mecklenburg County to the south. This location also has a good existing east–west street connection to the hospital area and the interstate, just

over half-a-mile to the west. This location is also three miles north of the Davidson station and three miles south of the terminus in the center of Mooresville. Three miles between stations is an ideal distance for the DMU technology as it enables the trains to reach and maintain efficient high speeds for a reasonable distance between slowing down and starting up again at the stops.

Charlotte transit officials required this station to be a park-and-ride facility to serve a wide cachement area in southern Iredell County (a 10-minute drive defines a five-mile radius around the station). While agreeing with this proposal, we realized that a typical park-and-ride stop with its large areas of asphalt parking, would do considerable damage to the environment and character of the existing Mount Mourne community. Accordingly, we developed the station as a hybrid, a park-and-ride facility combined with a pedestrian-oriented TOD.

We believed that due to its unique location, this park-and-ride lot could mature into something altogether more interesting, and we designed the required parking area for 1000 cars on a rectangular block structure with a green square at the center, preserving an existing grove of mature trees. This square is the same dimension as a typical square in Savannah, Georgia (see Figure 6.9). Initially providing as many as 1000 surface parking spaces, as development pressure expands over time, these 400 feet × 400 feet (122 meters × 122 meters) urban sized blocks could be redeveloped with two- to three-story mixed-use buildings served by mid-block parking decks should the land value grow sufficiently to support that cost. These parking structures would be sized to provide enough spaces for continued park-and-ride service.

Placing the station midway between the parking areas and land available for higher density development enabled us to plan a small mixed-use urban village on a grid of streets within 1/4-mile of this proposed transit stop. As the DMU technology for commuter rail is not as pedestrian-friendly as light rail (it's heavier and noisier) the immediate 'on street' relationship between the urban village and the light rail station cannot be replicated. Some extra safety distances are required, and for the station to be in a separate block from the core of the urban village is quite satisfactory in this condition. We recommended in this instance that the village be developed as an 'employment-led TOD,' with a combination of office and housing rather than retail, which should be limited to smaller neighborhood service stores and restaurants. Large, car-dependent shopping centers would be counterproductive to the transit efficiencies gained by walk-up ridership from offices and housing and we recommended firmly that nothing larger than a neighborhood grocery store should be permitted in this location.

Within 1/4-mile radius of the train station, an area of 125 acres (50 hectares), we planned 635 residential units, workspace for over 1000 employees and a park-and-ride lot with 1000 parking spaces. Within 1/2-mile of the train station, an area of 400 acres (160 hectares) these figures increased to 887 residential units and workspace for nearly 3000 new employees, not counting the existing hospital. For this kind of hybrid development to work, it's important that connections between the uses are convenient and attractive. In this particular example, a strong pedestrian and bicycle connection needed to be made between the station, the urban village and the medical center. To achieve this, we redesigned the east–west connecting street (Fairview Road) as an urban boulevard with four travel lanes, two outside parallel parking lanes, kerb and gutter, street trees and wide sidewalks. The plan illustrated how other street connections could be established as a loose grid as development expands.

Rail crossings are an important issue with the kind of high-speed commuter rail service envisaged on this line. In principle, at-grade crossings have to be kept to a minimum, and we limited them to three within the plan area plus one grade-separated crossing where an important east–west street and a creek could pass underneath the rail tracks and Highway 115. Two of the three at-grade crossings occur within the 1/2 mile radius of the transit village, and support easy pedestrian and bicycle access between the new village and the existing nucleus of Mount Mourne.

Focusing the development of the urban village around one of these at-grade crossings, the intersection of Fairview Road and Highway 115, the natural junction of north–south and east–west traffic, enabled us to build on the rich heritage of the Mount Mourne historic settlement. The prominence of the existing churches, school, post office and fire station served to anchor this village and gave it the civic elements necessary to produce a viable mixed-use center for the southern areas of Mooresville. To support this evolution, we found a suitable site for a local grocery store on Highway 115, just on the edge of the five-minute walking radius from the train station.

One of the factors that makes this plan unique is the presence of a large medical facility in its core, and

**Figure 9.2** Morehead Street, Charlotte, NC. This street served as a model for the new and upgraded streets in the areas around the hospital. Offices, apartments, churches, shops and medical facilities all line the street to create a well-balanced and attractive public realm. Parking is screened behind buildings.

we wanted the hospital to integrate itself into the community and not remain an island unto itself. For this to happen it was critical that new buildings engage the streets; not only must they provide convenient services for hospital staff, they must also create spaces along the streets that are attractive places to walk in their own right. Our model for this kind of environment was a street in Charlotte near a major hospital that featured disciplined street tree plantings, wide sidewalks and a mixture of buildings with different uses, all facing the street (see Figure 9.2).

## The Hospital District (See Plate 34)

We wrote the following two paragraphs in the 2000 project report:

> Currently, the hospital provides a large amount of leasable office space to its physicians and the building was designed with the ability to rise an additional story. Still, there is clearly a demand for off-site medical practices and a number of other complimentary professional services associated with a hospital. In short, areas surrounding hospitals have the greatest potential in most markets to be viable Class A office locations. With the added premium of its proximity to the proposed commuter transit station, this area has the potential to be the largest employment centre in the North Transit Corridor.

(However) the propensity to overbuild this area must be tempered with other long-term needs including convenience retail (banks, restaurants, dry cleaners, convenience goods) and more importantly, residential development. The failure of most office parks in today's marketplace is their disconnection from these quality-of-life enhancements. The requirement that every employee own a car and commute to work serves only as an impediment to attracting employees, particularly in this low unemployment market. The suburban office market, particularly in the Charlotte Region, is now taking steps to offer transit service to . . . buildings, simply to attract new employees who either do not own a car or are disillusioned with the commuting traffic.

**Figure 9.3** The new Lowes Corporate Headquarters under construction, 2003, Calloway Johnson Moore and West, architects. This refreshingly contemporary design is free from the needless neoclassical ornamentation so beloved by other North Carolina architects.

In 2001, the Lowes corporation recognized these same locational advantages, and with our master plan in place, Mooresville was able to forge agreements quickly for the relocation of this company's national headquarters. As a result of this major economic boost to the town, we and other consultants revisited the master plan in 2001, to integrate the very large facilty (more extensive than we had imagined in our original work) into the area. Plate 35 illustrates the revised master plan.

Although the architecture of the new offices was attractive (see Figure. 9.3) the new corporate site layout was not a particularly urban-friendly form. However, we were able to avoid some of the issues of segregated campus design that were so problematic in the CORE study discussed in Chapter 7. We relocated the train station a block south of its original location to bring it within half-a-mile of the center of the new office complex, and redesigned the streets and block pattern between the campus and the hospital on a more formal, urban layout, especially to provide a new north–south street that linked the campus with the hospital and areas to the north. We relocated the convenience retail stores onto the new streets that linked the corporate headquarters with the hospital, and we reduced the amount of parking at the station. With 8000 new employees working at the Lowes headquarters, we felt this area would increasingly become a destination as much as a point of departure, and the master plan for the corporate campus also included extensive car parking.

While the emphasis of property within the 1/2-mile radius of the train station was still primarily office, we increased the residential presence in the redesigned village center in the form of apartments, townhomes, and mixed-use buildings with flats above the shops. Residential development in these locations will help to boost transit ridership and provide places for employees to live near their workplace. We recommended that Mooresville be proactive in ensuring adequate affordable housing, and in this location we recommended that the town require developers to build a certain number of units affordable to citizens earning the equivalent of the (relatively low) median income for the Mooresville area. We did not specifiy a number, but in practice 10–15 percent of the total units is usually a workable minimum.

Within this hospital and employment district, two churches inside the half-mile radius from the train station serve both as sanctuaries of tranquility and connections to the natural environment. One of the most significant undisturbed woodlands in this master plan area surrounds a stream that runs behind the churches and the hospital on their north side. We included this as part of a continuous greenway traversing the site from east to northwest, connecting the neighborhoods to the north while at the same time serving as a natural transition from the transit village to new lower density neighborhoods on the northern acreage of the site. We noted that to comply with watershed protection requirements, this existing vegetation should be vigorously preserved.

### The Interstate and 'Hospital West' (see Plate 36)

Part of the traffic study that preceded the charrette proposed the innovative idea of converting the existing confused traffic pattern around Exit 33 into a double-roundabout interchange that provided a short-term solution to the burgeoning issue of east–west movement across the freeway to expanding residential areas around the adjacent Lake Norman to the west. We believed that the ultimate remedy for this interchange must be a complete redesign into an 'urban diamond;' this would be especially appropriate with increased traffic after the completion of the new corporate headquarters.

Of particular importance from the earlier traffic study was the proposal to construct a new bridge over the interstate on the line of an extended Fairview Road, the main east–west street which we upgraded to a boulevard in our plan. East–west movements were already very difficult in this area, and we endorsed a simple bridge crossing (without access ramps to the freeway) that would extend the Hospital District over the interstate and open up another premium office site immediately to the west of the freeway with access to the hospital and Exit 33 immediately the north. This was the site we had originally envisaged for a corporate headquarters. It falls within a stringent environmental protection zone, but a water detention system that was properly disguised as a lake would add an attractive landscape feature, just like the one constructed as part of the Lowes master plan.

The area around the west side of the freeway exit featured a mixture of low-intensity uses, and we laid this segment out for small offices or light manufacturing on an improved grid of streets, with a small additional amount of retail to complement an existing grocery store in that location. This did not change in our master plan revision.

## The North Neighborhood (see Plate 37)

We designed the area to the north of the hospital and transit village as a series of interconnected traditional neighborhoods with a range of housing types, small scale commercial uses and a series of formal and informal open spaces. Because much of the land had been cleared for farming, there were few significant stands of trees to be preserved. To make up for this, we proposed a program of disciplined tree planting along streets and in the new neighborhood parks to revive significant vegetation in areas that had not seen large trees in over a hundred years.

The farmland north of the stream 'fingers' that branch off the main creek is mainly flat, without major topographic features, and so we designed the layout in this area as a tight street grid with a variety of lot sizes,

and we laid out the open spaces as formal parks. Smaller house lots were sited around or near these neighborhood parks as the communal open space compensates for smaller private gardens. The flat topography of this northen section also made it an ideal place for a small elementary school and associated playing fields to be integrated into the neighborhood.

As part of this new street pattern we organized east–west streets to provide connections between the two existing north–south streets leading to and from Mooresville town center, and we concentrated commercial and higher density residential development along the westernmost of this pair, Highway 21, leading north into town from Exit 33. This created the template for a new neighborhood mixed-use center at the junction of this highway and the main east–west cross street to serve the population as it grows in future years.

As a contrast to the formality and tight grid of the northernmost section of the residential layout, in the areas bordering the streams we used the irregular geometries of the stream beds to create more 'organic' parks fronted by public streets and single-family homes. In other locations we laid out greenways on an informal pattern. By protecting and enhancing these stream corridors, we were able to create an important alternative transportation network that connected the northern neighborhoods to the Village Center. Where possible, we lined these greenways with public streets on at least one side to ensure their safety and encourage their use.

In addition to these four geographic areas, we highlighted three special topics in the master plan that deserved of their own particular policies. As noted earlier, these were: open space design and environmental protection; housing; and a new development code.

## Open Space Design and Environmental Protection

The benefits of usable open spaces have long been touted by environmental groups such as the Sierra Club and the Natural Resources Defense Council, and even by developers' organizations from the late 1990s onward (Santos, 2003). In all towns, and even at the neighborhood scale if possible, we believe there should always be a balance between natural open space that is preserved, and 'improved' open spaces like parks that are celebrated and utilized.

Accordingly, we recommended to the town of Mooresville that it consider greenways as an important part of the overall transportation network, with walking and biking paths extending along their length, and connecting residential neighborhoods without recourse to cars. In addition to this greenway network, we strongly recommended the preservation of as much of the existing tree canopy as possible. The majority of this area was cleared for farming in the late nineteenth century which left clumps of trees rather than large wooded areas. It's especially important therefore that all existing tree stands be preserved and new trees planted in both the public realm (streets and squares) and in private spaces (yards and parking lots). The 1913 example of John Nolen in Myers Park, Charlotte, illustrated in Figure 5.6, shows how disciplined planting links the public and private realms can turn a former cotton field into an urban forest.

Along with the establishment of a greenway system to bind the neighborhoods to the Village Centre and the Hospital District, it is important that both passive and active recreation opportunities be provided within neighborhoods to serve as focal points for the community. We therefore recommended the implementation of rules requiring parks and playgrounds for all new neighborhoods. The current ordinances of the town only required that certain open space be improved, but fell short of making them usable with any design criteria. Our new zoning regulations (see New Development Code below) required all homes to be within 1/8-mile (660 feet/201 meters) of a park, playground, greenway or playing field.

The open space in this master plan serves as a 'green' network for the Mount Mourne area. Under the new zoning, as property is developed according to this master plan, developers would be required to provide open space designed for the needs of the nearby residents. Though the ratio of open space drawn in Plate 32 is approximately 15 percent, we believe that the long-term provision of all types of usable open space should eventually exceed 25 percent of land area.

Because a majority of the plan area is within a protected watershed basin, the impervious surface areas of individual projects are limited to a maximum of 50 percent in areas dubbed 'Critical,' or 74 percent of the site in the higher risk 'Protected' areas. These ratios apply if engineered, stormwater detention devices are used in the site layout. Without the use of ponds, sand filters or other such devices, development (impervious area) would be limited to 24 percent of the total project area. These criteria give the design of open space an important ecological dimension as well as social and aesthetic ones. In combination with the protection of water supplies, it is also important to protect the habitats and ecosystems of the creeks and wetlands in this area. We therefore strongly recommended that the town of Mooresville adopt strong Stream Buffer Policies to protect the natural environments of plants and aquatic life.

## Housing

As should be clear by now, we believe all neighborhoods should be diverse and provide a variety of housing opportunities. Accordingly, new neighborhoods should be encouraged, if not required, to provide a variety of housing to avoid cookie-cutter subdivisions with a limited range of price points. We have found that a ratio of 70 single-family homes to 30 multi-family homes, with the latter in the form of duplexes/semi-detached, townhomes, condominiums, and apartments, is a mix that works in most markets. In this specific case, we recommended that the pressure by developers to build large apartment complexes should be resisted except within 1/4-mile of the proposed transit station, or in relation to the potential mixed-use center in the North Neighborhood area. Higher density housing in close proximity to commercial development provides a market for retailers and ensures a more sustainable environment for residents and merchants alike. From the municipal viewpoint, only in these areas can this type of development be efficiently supported with services and their traffic impacts mitigated.

Requiring a range of housing types in all large developments is an efficient way of providing affordable housing in the appropriate ratio with market-rate dwellings. Affordable housing does not have to mean lower quality, but it usually requires intervention by a governmental or non-profit agency to ensure its affordability over the long term. When developers provide decent quality affordable housing in a good location, the market tends to drive up the price beyond what is affordable. To deal with this issue, we recommended the formation of a non-profit housing agency to works with the town and developers to ensure an adequate supply of affordable housing as was the case in the neighboring town of Davidson (see Figure 6.35). This is discussed further in Chapter 10.

## New Development Code

Our primary recommendation for implementing the plan was a new development code of design-based regulations keyed directly to the plan's design provisions. This type of code is discussed briefly in 'Implementation,' below, and in more detail in Chapter 10.

## IMPLEMENTATION

In order to implement many of the recommendations of the Mooresville master plan, it was important to establish a new regulatory framework in which appropriate future development could occur. The current zoning regulations were insufficient to enforce many of the recommendations, and we therefore wrote and drew a new design-based zoning ordinance for the town to cover the master plan area, and which could be extended to other parts of town as needed. This zoning code was adopted by the town in 2001 shortly after the acceptance of the master plan.

The new code for Mooresville is very similar to the one described in detail in the next chapter, developed for our neighborhood-scaled master plan for Greenville, South Carolina. The Mooresville version was an early example of the more developed format we now use as standard. Accordingly, we will defer detailed explanation of design-based zoning until Chapter 10, where the more evolved effort can best be described (see also Appendix III for typical pages from the Greenville code). Suffice it here to say that the whole code for Mount Mourne comprised only 19 pages, of which six were full-page diagrams and drawings.

## CONCLUSIONS

From the outset, this plan was a hybrid, collaging together a transit-oriented urban village, a park-and-ride facility, a more conventional scenario of office development around a freeway interchange and the opportunities for large-scale residential development on adjacent sites. An additional complexity was the presence of the small community of Mount Mourne.

With so much potential development activity adjacent to the existing community, we decided from the outset to follow the clearly stated wishes of the existing residents and curtail any redevelopment within the small settlement. Instead, we concentrated new buildings in the other three quadrants around the train station. This led to a distortion of the classic TOD model with the transit stop in the center of an evenly developed, circumferential neighborhood. This asymmetry,

**Figure 9.4** New Townhomes at 'Station View.' These new homes, constructed in 2003 in locations indicated by the master plan were the first new residential buildings to capitalize on the location of the future commuter train station.

combined with the need to accommodate the extensive car parking for the train station, were important factors in deciding to design the urban village as an employment-led development rather than basing it primarily on residential uses. This decision reinforced the potential for office development around the hospital and the freeway interchange and created a critical mass of future employment. Our prognosis that the Mount Mourne area could become the primary workplace destination on the North Transit Corridor was handsomely fulfilled with the selection of the site by the Lowes Corporation for its national headquarters.

While most development within the plan area since its adoption by the town has been offices, some new residential buildings have also been constructed. Figure 9.4 illustrates a development of modest townhomes that have been built exactly where we drew them on the plan near the future site of the train station.

## CRITICAL EVALUATION OF CASE STUDY

This is a project with several phases, and very much a work in progress at the time of writing this book in the late spring of 2003. This plan is a living organism that is adapting to change in an exciting manner. We have revised it once, in 2001, to accommodate the specifics of the new corporate headquarters, and expect to do so again in 2004. At that time we will examine how the multitude of smaller companies who supply Lowes with equipment and products, and who wish to relocate close to the new headquarters, can be accomodated without compromising the intent of the original plan concepts.

The dynamic nature of this master plan is a working testament to our thesis that designing communities in detail provides the best means of managing change. In this Mooresville example, developments of a scale not imagined in our first version of the plan have evolved, but the original detailed design enabled us to establish a spatial framework that could absorb and even direct this change. The detail indicated on the master plan went a long way to calming the fears and concerns of Mount Mourne residents in ways that conventional colored bubble diagrams of land uses never could. The clarity of the plan and its new zoning was also a major factor affecting the decision of Lowes to relocate its headquarters to this site, with great economic benefits to Mooresville and the surrounding region.

All too often, promoting development as a means of economic growth and job creation has meant getting rid of the zoning provisions and environmental controls that were designed, however imperfectly, to protect American communities. These environmental and community safeguards were usually seen as impediments to economic efficiency by developers and business lobbyists. Indeed, in their typical, generic form, conventional planning and zoning practices do often fail to facilitate development or enhance community liveability. This master plan succeeded in both aspects by means of its detail. It was able to communicate clearly and effectively the development potential of property and the design character of new neighborhoods, centers and districts. It was able to bridge the gap between external development interests and the local community, groups that are usually adversarial in growth and development debates. In 2003, three years after we produced the first version of the plan, we had the pleasure of sitting in a meeting with representatives of local business groups, traditional opponents of government planning and zoning, and hearing the master plan praised as the town's most effective tool in economic development.

This was one of our earliest yet most successful master-planning projects. At that time we were still refining our charrette techniques and graphic repetoire, and this leads to our one caveat: three days is too short a time to undertake projects of this scope and complexity. Although the three-day time period enabled us to identify quickly the complexities of this area, it was not long enough to deal satisfactorily with all the issues, and as a principle we now never undertake charrettes of less than four days' duration. This shortness of time resulted in, amongst other things, a lower quality of drawn finished product. (Compare the plan graphics in Plates 32 and 40). Because some drawings lacked sufficient graphic discipline, we instituted a progressively more rigorous regime of standard graphic colors, conventions and techniques for subsequent charrettes.

# The neighborhood

*Case Study 4: Haynie-Sirrine Neighborhood, Greenville, South Carolina*

## PROJECT AND CONTEXT DESCRIPTION

This is most usefully explained by briefly relating the history of the site and describing its key physical characteristics of centers, edges and streets.

### History

In August 2001, the City of Greenville, in partnership with a joint venture of local property owners, real estate agents and developers, commissioned a public design charrette to create a master plan for the redevelopment of the Haynie-Sirrine neighborhood, a low-income African-American community just one mile south of Greenville city center. The ideas of residents, property owners, merchants, government agencies, and interested investors were aired and collected during an intensive six-day process.

The history the Haynie-Sirrine neighborhood is one of transition from its original farmland, to the commercial use in the 1890s of the site's mineral springs for the cure of illnesses caused by 'improper habits of living', to one of the first black urban communities within the city of Greenville. Settlement began around 1900 when the neighborhood became home to domestic servants, blacksmiths, hostlers, factory workers, hotel maids and cooks, chauffeurs and preachers.

By the second half of the twentieth century, most of the original springs had been culverted under new streets and the playing field for a local high school, and the neighborhood had stabilized into an active black working-class community of several hundred people. However, in the 1950s, a major road-widening project fractured the community into two halves when Church Street, the main road that passes through the community from southwest

to northeast on its way to the city center, was transformed into what the traffic engineers of the time called a six-lane 'superhighway'. In the adjacent middle-class white neighborhoods to the south it remained only four lanes wide, and it was widened to six lanes just for its length through the black community before reducing back to four lanes to cross a bridge over the Reedy River gorge that separates Haynie-Sirrine from downtown Greenville. For nearly 50 years this road has created a difficult and dangerous barrier to community life and accessibility (see Figure 10.1).

In the 1960s land immediately to the north of the community was developed as a standard strip shopping center, also with widened access roads. By the 1990s this had been abandoned, but was then adaptively reused by county government as offices. The old strip center has been put to good use, but no improvements have been made to the physical environment. Wide roads and seas of asphalt parking still dominate the townscape.

During the 1980s and 1990s the neighborhood suffered a further decline, characterized predominately by substandard housing, vacant property, deteriorating infrastructure and crime (see Figure 10.2). Yet many residents continued to make significant contributions, not just to their neighborhood, but also to the larger Greenville community. By their civic activism and quest for social equity, these individuals provided the foundation for the resurgence of the Haynie-Sirrine neighborhood. White neighborhoods to the south and west have retained their character and value due in large measure to the proximity to downtown and we shared the residents' conviction that there was no reason why Haynie-Sirrine could not enjoy its own renaissance.

**Figure 10.1** Members of the design team need the help of the local police to cross Church Street, the six-lane highway that divides the Haynie-Sirrine community.

**Figure 10.2** Urban decay in the Haynie-Sirrine neighborhood. Despite the depressing environment in some parts of the neighborhood, members of the community remained optimistic about the area's potential. This photograph illustrates the lack of care and maintenance by both the public and private sectors.

The crucial challenge was to stimulate new market rate development in parts of the neighborhood by capitalizing on its location while retaining affordable housing for the existing community elsewhere on site. Large portions of the study area were held by a few property owners who lived in the city, were the landlords for many residents and, significantly, were co-sponsors of the charrette. These individuals were

keen to take advantage of the increased demand for higher density living near the town center and to realize the development value of those parts of their properties most suitable for this kind of up-market development. At the same time, these property owners made a public commitment to the neighborhood and the city that they would strive to maintain affordable housing on the land within the community.

## Site Analysis and Community Patterns

We analyzed the site under two main headings – 'Centers, Streets and Edges' and 'Building Forms and Configurations.'

### Centers, Streets and Edges

The intersection of Church Street with two east–west cross streets, Haynie and Pearl, forms the physical center of the neighborhood. From this point nearly all property is contained within a 1/4-mile radius (see Plate 39). However, from a community perspective, this location is not a center at all. Because of its extreme width and high-speed traffic, Church Street here presents a hostile barrier to pedestrians. Instead of being a place to gather, the center of the neighborhood had become a place to avoid. One positive attribute of this location is its high visibility to commuters, and because of this a Ramada Inn remains operational at this key intersection. Another factor in its favor is the position of this potential center in relation to its context: within one mile of the intersection of Haynie and Pearl with Church Street are a number of very stable neighborhoods, Greenville's vibrant downtown core, and the beautiful Reedy River and its greenway parks.

There is only one other crossing point of this highway as it passes through the neighborhood, the Springer Street Tunnel, a dark, narrow divided passage under Church Street that connects Haynie on the west with Sirrine on the east. A minimal set of stairs leads up from the tunnel to Church Street. There is potential here for a convenient pedestrian connection across the neighborhood avoiding Church Street traffic, but as Figure 10.3 illustrates, the location does not feel safe. It is gloomy with hardly enough room for one car in each lane of the tunnel, let alone a car and a pedestrian. Additionally, there are few homes along adjacent streets, creating a feeling of isolation and potential menace. There are not enough 'eyes on the street' for a feeling of comfort and safety.

**Figure 10.3** The Springer Street Tunnel. This is not a place you would like to walk through alone.

**Figure 10.4** Neighborhood Street. While the houses need maintenance and the street needs sidewalks, several local streets like Chicora Drive (shown here) provide a potentially very decent environment.

The northern boundary of the community is a five-minute walk from the geographic center, and is marked by the University Ridge highway, so named in part for Furman University that was founded in that location in the late 1800s before moving to the suburbs, and for the ridge of land that forms the high point of the neighborhood. From this vantage point one gains extensive views northward over downtown Greenville and the river in its valley below. While the ugly sheds, large plastic signs and extensive surface parking lots render the University Ridge area unattractive in its current form (see Figure 10.15) the geography has great potential for high-density mixed-use development: it is only 3/4-mile from downtown with great views and immediate accessibility to the Reedy River park. At the northeastern boundary of the study area, a more pedestrian-friendly environment exists, with viable neighborhood retail activity. The setting would be more appealing if the shops actually lined the street instead of being set back behind parking, but the modest proportions and friendly character of the buildings help to offset that deficiency (see Figure 10.19).

Streets in the Haynie-Sirrine neighborhood are typically narrow and lined with beautiful, mature oak trees that help the neighborhood stay cool, even during the hottest days of August. The ecological advantage augments the aesthetic effect of these enormous specimens. Street widths serve as positive design elements, creating a 'village feeling' and contributing to the 'front porch character' of the neighborhood. The narrow width also serves as an effective traffic-calming measure (see Figure 10.4).

The western boundary of the neighborhood is formed by Augusta Street, a successful, yet congested commercial corridor that serves as the primary shopping district for the downtown area. The eastern boundary shares its edge with the McDaniel Avenue neighborhood, one of the most affluent neighborhoods in the city.

### Building Forms and Configurations

As noted earlier, in its better areas, Haynie-Sirrine can be described as a 'front-porch community'. Most of the homes in this neighborhood are placed close together and close to the street. During our summer study period, many neighbors spent time on their porches, creating a warm and welcome feeling of community (see Figure 10.5). There were other locations however, where people lurking on the street gave us cause for concern, and a brooding sense of menace and despair were evident in the most run-down areas.

The 'shotgun house' is a common housing type in the neighborhood, usually one-room wide and three-rooms deep, with a front porch and circulation that passes straight through the rooms (see Figure 10.6). Although many consider this traditional Southern housing type obsolete, its long and narrow configuration allows excellent cross ventilation for the local hot, humid summers. This form of energy efficiency should not be underestimated when planning affordable housing in this climate. The narrow width of these vernacular homes also allows a higher density, increasing affordability and contribute to a feeling of community. Unfortunately, conditions of severe

**203**

**Figure 10.5** Children on the Front Porch. Local residents described their neighborhood as a 'front porch' community. Here, local children collaborated on their homework until disturbed by the design team.

**Figure 10.7** Traditional Bungalow. This common American house type is a staple of single-family housing in towns across the nation. Several good examples remained in the study area.

**Figure 10.6** Traditional Southern 'Shotgun' Houses. Although some of these houses were too decayed to be rehabilitated, others could be saved. This modest housing type can usefully serve as a model for new affordable housing in the community.

disrepair and dereliction required that most of these homes in the neighborhood be replaced. However, we noted in our recommendations that future designers could usefully incorporate the advantages of this vernacular type into new affordable housing designs.

The 'bungalow cottage' is another housing type well represented in the study area. Although these homes are wider and more substantially built than the shotguns, many fit into the affordable range. Most are one-storey frame homes with low-slung rooflines, front-facing gables and wide front porches. Again, the relatively narrow width allows a higher density appropriate for an urban village (see Figure 10.7).

The third type of housing in the neighborhood is much less promising. A series of single-storey brick duplexes were constructed in the 1970s along the streets in the eastern part of the area, and this housing type is markedly out of character with the rest of the neighborhood. Its building footprint is wide; setbacks from the street are deep; it is built flat on the ground rather than with a raised ground floor, and the crude, uncovered patios contrast sharply with the protected, cozy feeling offered by the covered porches of the other homes in the area. Gables face the side of the house instead of the front, and the suburban-looking brick ranch style does not blend well with the adjacent traditional housing types (see Figure 10.17).

There are two small, white frame churches in the community, indicated in purple on the master plan shown in Plate 40. These buildings are tiny in scale, traditional in shape with wood frame steeples, and they nestle neatly into the urban fabric to provide a community focus, add character, and help the neighborhood feel like a small village.

One other building stands out in the neighborhood – the football stadium for the nearby Greenville High School. Despite its large scale, this structure blends reasonably well into its context, and plans were underway to renovate the facility at the time of the charrette. Parking and crowds can create problems for local residents during game nights, and we wanted to find solutions to these challenges so the neighbors will welcome more community events at this site.

## KEY ISSUES AND GOALS

As a result of pre-charrette discussions and a series of site analyses carried out during the early stages of the charrette, we formulated five key objectives:

1. Capitalize on the market value of available property located near University Ridge for major new development. (This would provide property owners with a high return on their investments to offset the lower profitability of affordable housing developments elsewhere on the project site.)
2. Upgrade and increase the stock of affordable housing for existing residents.
3. Enhance neighborhood identity and character.
4. Facilitate the expansion of the Sirrine football stadium without disrupting the neighborhood scale.
5. Recognize and protect historic landmarks in the neighborhood.

## THE CHARRETTE

We developed the master plan during a six-day charrette in August 2001. We had helped orchestrate a lot of local publicity prior to the event, and over 350 people participated (see Figure 10.8). The team set up its temporary design studio at the Ramada Inn in the heart of the neighborhood, a location that

enabled a large number of residents and other interested people to contribute throughout the week. The charrette began with a walking tour of the neighborhood: over 25 design team members, advisory committee members, interested developers, city staff, residents and community police officers walked every street in the study area, photographing key elements, measuring spaces, and talking to people on the streets and porches. That evening, our opening presentation was heard by a standing room-only crowd.

Throughout the week, we held numerous interviews with interest groups including transportation planners and engineers, developers, public safety officials, stormwater engineers, housing groups, and residents. Meetings continued throughout the day as well as in the evening to give everyone an opportunity to join in the public discussion. Each evening before dinner, we pinned up the day's drawings on the wall and invited all participants to join the designers in a discussion of the day's developments. The schedule was an extended version of the one illustrated in Figure 8.2, and as always, we followed our key charrette principles as noted in Chapter 6:

- Involve everyone from the start;
- Work concurrently and cross-functionally;
- Work in short feedback loops:
- Work in detail.

Because of the publicity campaign, most residents were aware of the charrette and frequently spoke with designers both at the hotel and around the neighborhood. On Sunday morning, a local church member even took the time to show the team the parking problems of her church, a pattern repeated time and again as interested residents articulated their needs

**Figure 10.8** Local newspaper front page. Active engagement with the local media is essential in any charrette process. We spoke extensively with newspapers and television reporters, and were rewarded with good and sympathetic coverage (see also Figure 10.10).

and their vision for the neighborhood. This over-whelming participation from citizens, public officials and staff was the foundation for the highly successful charrette. In addition, we held two more meetings after the charrette to give residents, property owners and interested citizens the opportunity to learn more about the plans and the proposed new zoning code for the area.

On the first day, we completed a series of analyses, including the current zoning, a survey of vacant property and owner-occupied housing and an assess-ment of site values and redevelopment potential (see Plate 38, Figure 10.9, and Plate 39). The current zoning for this part of the city reflected a familiar bias against a coherent neighborhood structure. The zon-ing on the west side of Church Street was predomi-nately Office/Institutional, further facilitating the influx of generic commercial development along the northwestern edges, where single-family homes faced large expanses of surface parking and dumpsters directly across the street. The east side was a patch-work of higher density residential classifications, set out in a manner that did little to consider the current or historic neighborhood structure. Zoning districts ran along street lines, rather than mid-block, causing different kinds of development to occur on either side of the street and creating badly defined public spaces. (Wherever possible, we try to change zoning districts at mid-block, thus enabling a more coherent streetscape to be achieved with similar building types facing each other to define the public space.)

Using a combination of market value analysis, owner-occupant/rental housing locations and maps of vacant land, the charrette team developed an overall assessment of the redevelopment potential of each parcel of property in the neighborhood, ranging from those that required minimal assistance to others needing complete redevelopment. These diagrams, which were refined during the course of the charrette, formed the basis for all development proposals put forth in the master plan In our overall assessment of redevelopment potential, we divided all properties into one of three categories:

### Major Redevelopment Potential

This comprised vacant land, multiple properties under common ownership or areas of excessive hous-ing blight. We also included in this category places where the street infrastructure was so degraded that any improvements were likely to reconfigure the

**Figure 10.9** Vacant Land and Homeowners Map. This analysis enabled us to clarify which areas were available for major redevelopment and which other parts (the pockets of homeownership) should be protected and nourished.

existing blocks into a new urban pattern. As noted earlier, we were excited by the redevelopment poten-tial of property along University Ridge (at the top of the diagrams in Plate 38, Figure 10.9 and Plate 39). However, as much of this land to the north was owned by the county, it was politically off-limits for a city-sponsored charrette to 'interfere' with county property. We were therefore forced to be modest in our recommendations for this area, focusing mainly on the northeast segment around the football sta-dium. But in this case study we illustrate the full master plan showing major redevelopment of the old shopping mall site, revealing its potential for reclama-tion to a thriving mixed-use area (see Plate 40).

### Moderate Redevelopment Potential

In this classification we placed multiple rental proper-ties under common ownership, scattered-site owner-occupied housing and areas of moderate infrastructure degradation where infill development could occur using the existing block structure

### Minimal Redevelopment Requirement

This third section consisted of areas of predominately owner-occupied housing or well-maintained rental

**Figure 10.10** Newspaper Coverage of the Charrette. Worth its weight in gold.

housing where only minor repairs were needed to the housing and/or infrastructure.

From this analysis, we identified a large number of properties as requiring major redevelopment or providing superior opportunities in that regard. Yet, complete blocks of solid, stable housing that required only minor building repairs or infrastructure improvement were also identified. These areas provided anchors for the final master plan, and when we presented our final recommendations nearly 200 people, mostly local residents attended the closing reception and presentation to view the plan. This participation remained high partly because we maintained television and newspaper coverage of the charrette during the six-day period (see Figure 10.10).

## THE MASTER PLAN (See Plate 40).

Our key recommendations were as follows:

1. *Concentrate the greatest intensity of use in a new neighborhood center at the intersection of Church Street and Haynie Street/Pearl Avenue to create a vibrant environment for living, working, and shopping.*
2. *Upgrade Church Street by reducing it to a four-lane, median-divided boulevard with street trees and wide sidewalks. Improve the street design of Haynie and Pearl Streets to support this pedestrian activity.*
3. *Encourage the construction of a wide variety of housing throughout the neighborhood. Ensure long-term*

*affordable housing using a variety of strategies including public investment, land-trust, and non-profit involvement.*
4. *Leverage private funding with key public infrastructure investments including street improvements and parking facilities.*
5. *Use natural features including historic springs and streams as amenities for the entire neighborhood to enjoy. Create public spaces including parks, greenways and plazas that are accessible to all residents.*
6. *Adopt a new zoning ordinance developed directly from the urban design details of the master plan.*

Based on these principles we identified 19 redevelopment opportunities, some large, some small, and we assembled the master plan from these individual projects. These projects together comprised 50 new single-family dwellings, 100 duplexes (semi-detached homes), 393 apartments, 52 live/work units, 178 500 square feet (16 586 square meters) of commercial space and 118 900 square feet (11 047 square meters) of retail space. Over 1900 parking spaces were provided. We did not impose any singular grand plan vision, but sought instead to promote a collage of separate projects that could be accomplished individually by private property owners on their own or in partnership with public authorities, in an incremental manner (see Plate 41).

We worked out schematic development pro-formas to validate the economic viability of each proposal, and also costed out the public expenditure associated with the necessary infrastructure improvements. From these calculations we showed how approximately $10 million of public money for street improvements and two parking decks (one in conjunction with a developer at the Neighborhood Center and the other with the city's school system at the football stadium) could leverage $90 million in private investment in redevelopment. Approximately $40 million of new development was tied to the Church Street improvements noted later, but even if these crucial modifications did not take place, other viable private development projects worth $50 million still existed in the community.

This case study illustrates a sample of these 19 redevelopment opportunities at a range of economic scales. These are:

1. The Church Street Neighborhood Center, a cluster of four projects on the four quadrants of the Church Street – Haynie/Pearl Street intersection.

2. The mixed-use development at the junction of Church Street with University Ridge (Church Street North).

3. The development of replacement housing for the shoddy brick duplexes and the creation of a neighborhood park by opening up a culverted stream (Biltmore Park).

4. New townhomes and a greenway inserted in left-over land (Springer Street East).

5. The redevelopment of the football stadium and adjacent mixed-use development (Sirrine Neighborhood Center). Projects ('E', 'G', 'M' and 'K' in Plate 41.)

## The Church Street Neighborhood Center

Two factors spurred the development of this center-piece of the plan. First, was its central location at the logical crossroads of the community where local residents could meet people from outside the area. Second, this location was distinguished by the presence of the functioning Ramada Inn, which a developer (and co-sponsor of the charrette) proposed to upgrade and redevelop with new conference and fitness facilities. The developer planned to support this redevelopment, together with adjacent mixed-use buildings by a parking deck constructed as a public–private joint venture with the city (project 'G' on Plate 41).

Building off this redevelopment of the southeast quadrant of the intersection, we designed a series of mainly three-storey mixed-use buildings, predominantly, housing over retail and restaurants, interspersed with offices.

Because of the odd block configurations created by the diagonal alignment of Church Street, it was difficult to create typical building floorplates for the intensity of development usually found in a Neighborhood Center and still fit sufficient parking on each site. As a result, the center will need the centralized parking deck in the Ramada Inn redevelopment to achieve its optimum building densities. This facility will provide an opportunity to 'park once and walk' to other retail stores and restaurants in the area. Residential apartments and townhomes would line the structure to provide a visual screen to the cars and an active street edge along its public perimeter. Figure 10.12 illustrates a typical example of this arrangement from Charlotte. Shared parking arrangements with staggered peak and off-peak timing between uses will also facilitate the success of this center. We also recommended that the local bus route, which currently runs down the western edge of the neighborhood, be re-routed to pass directly through the center, thus making the new activity center accessible by means other than the car.

**Figure 10.12** Apartments screening parking deck. Park Avenue, Charlotte, NC, 2002. David Furman, Architect. The parking deck is shared with an adjacent office building and street level stores. This is a standard, but highly effective urban typology. The only drawback is that the apartments are single aspect, that is, they face only one way and are accessed off an internal corridor. The consequent lack of natural cross-ventilation means that most climate control has to be mechanical even under benign external conditions.

**Figure 10.11** Site of Church Street Neighborhood Center, as existing (Compare with Plate 42).

We took care to preserve the 60-year old willow oak trees along the north side of Haynie Street with their capacious tree canopy. We set our new buildings back from the street to protect the trees' root system, and recessed the upper floors still further to make room for the canopy branches (see Figure 10.13).

We knew that most of this development, and the regeneration of the neighborhood's core area, was contingent upon the improvement of Church Street, transforming it from a hostile thoroughfare to a pedestrian-friendly boulevard: the street needed to change from a barrier into a seam that reconnected both sides of the neighborhood and reinvigorated the area with pedestrian activity. The team's preliminary traffic analysis indicated that four lanes would be sufficient to carry thorough traffic, and we accordingly recommended the following changes to the roadway as shown in Figure 10.14.

- *A landscaped median taking over the center two lanes with protected turn lanes at key locations.*
- *Improvements to the pedestrian environment with wide sidewalks separated from the kerb by a generous planting strip and geometrically ordered street trees.*
- *Lighting in the median for automobiles and along sidewalks for pedestrians.*
- *Buried and relocated overhead wiring within the vicinity of the Neighborhood Center. The wiring in the remainder of the corridor should first be consolidated to one side and placed on decorative poles in an orderly manner, or if finances allow, buried*

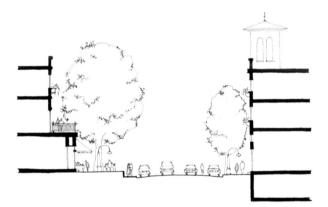

**Figure 10.13** Haynie Street Section. At this urban focus, the spatial enclosure on the neighborhood streets is tightened. Here the height-to-width ratio is approximately 1:1.5. The mature trees enhance the enclosure and sense of a central place.

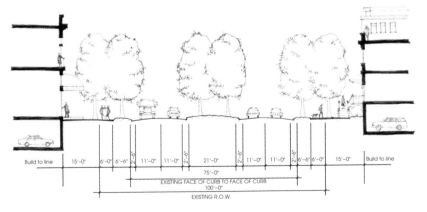

Build to line | 15'–0" | 6'–0" | 6'–6" | 11'–0" | 11'–0" | 21'–0" | 11'–0" | 11'–0" | 6'–6" | 6'–0" | 15'–0" | Build to line
75'–0"
EXISTING FACE OF CURB TO FACE OF CURB
100'–0"
EXISTING R.O.W.

**Figure 10.14** Church Street Section. This section is taken at a 'typical' point along the length of the street rather than at the neighborhood center in order to demonstrate the generic condition. With a street width of 130 feet (39 meters), the buildings can rarely be tall enough to create the desired spatial enclosure. Disciplined tree planting helps to break down the width and create zones of enclosure within the overall space.

*underground in duct banks and conduits. All new lateral utility services from the mains into the buildings should be underground.*

We knew that the negotiations to achieve these improvements to a main city thoroughfare would be difficult. The transformation involved a paradigm shift from thinking about roads as a means of mobility (getting everywhere as fast as possible) to a framework of accessibility (providing connections to a range of users). We asked all parties to remember a number of key points during the discussions:

- Redesigning Church Street in this manner would be a proactive reparation for the African-American community consistent with federal environmental justice policies that protect neighborhoods, particularly minority neighborhoods, against intrusions by large traffic projects.
- The proposed Church Street changes would be necessary to promote and retain a mix of land uses, a walkable urban environment and increased residential density within close proximity to downtown Greenville, one of the city's own Smart Growth agenda items.
- Given the large right-of-way that existed, and the excess capacity of the six lanes, all our proposed modifications could be accomplished within Church Street's existing kerb lines, offering significant cost savings. We estimated the costs for this project at approximately $3 million, but this public investment has the potential to leverage $40 million in new private development.

## Church Street North: Mixed-use Development at the Junction of Church Street and University Ridge
(project 'B' on Plate 41)

This site, located at the southeast corner of the University Ridge and Church Street intersection, is perhaps the most visible site in the entire neighborhood. It is located at the busiest intersection, and its prominence on the ridge gives it an outstanding view of the downtown skyline and the Reedy River greenway. This site also forms the gateway for pedestrians and vehicles to Sirrine Stadium to the east and the proposed new neighborhood center to the south. In addition to this obvious potential, nearly all the land is held in a single ownership, permitting relatively easy redevelopment.

To take maximum advantage of this location, we proposed a mid-rise block (4–5 storys in height)

**Figure 10.15** Church Street North as existing and proposed. This part of the site, at the ridge overlooking downtown Greenville has the greatest redevelopment potential for upmarket mixed-use development. (Compare with Plate 43.)

including up to 73 200 square feet (6799 square meters) of office and/or residential condominiums built generally to the street frontage (see Figure 10.15 and Plate 43). In addition, these mixed-use buildings could accommodate up to 24 000 square feet (2230 square meters) of ground-level shops. Parking would be provided in a 460 space, two-level, parking structure to the rear of the buildings, constructed in two trays fitted into the fall of the land. This relatively economical parking deck would be privately financed as part of the development package.

In order for ground-level offices or shops to succeed in this location, improvements to both Church Street and University Ridge would be necessary to enhance the pedestrian environment. We therefore recommended that the sidewalks should be 12–16 feet (3.6–4.9 meters) wide in this location creating a sufficient setback from traffic, and providing space for planting sizeable street trees. Figure 10.16 illustrates a typical example of this condition. In the remainder of the block we brought the scale of buildings down to two- and three-story residential buildings to blend in with new duplexes and apartments on adjacent properties. As a complementary project, we arranged a small courtyard block of apartments opposite one of the small wood-frame churches so that an intimate urban space aligned with the church entrance to honor the existing structure (Project 'C' in Plate 41). The church's parking requirements

**Figure 10.16** Wide Sidewalk for Outdoor Dining. If the detailing is right, outdoor dining can be pleasant even near a busy street. The street trees help to provide spatial definition to the area and separation from the street.

**Figure 10.17** Existing Biltmore Avenue duplexes. These badly designed buildings are only 25 years old, but are already slums. Their unlovely, squat design is a large factor in this sorry state of affairs (Compare with Plate 44).

could now be solved easily by sharing the parking deck less than a block away.

## Biltmore Park: Replacing the Duplexes and Opening the Stream (project 'F' in Plate 41)

This project replaced ugly, substandard duplex housing with a greater number of affordable townhome units, while capitalizing on the potential of the neighborhood's natural heritage, its springs and streams. The site is located along Biltmore Avenue across the street from an economically stable section of the neighborhood, and has direct access to Sirrine Stadium and the proposed enhancement of an existing small neighborhood center. Figure 10.17 and Plates 44 and 45 illustrate this proposed improvement.

The project removed the 11 existing duplexes (22 total units) and redeveloped the site with 35 townhomes. Using the topography of the site, we set out the main row of buildings at the higher grade of existing streets at the rear of the site, with a bonus room built into the lower level in lieu of a retaining wall. Service access is from the rear, with front doors facing the park with entrance off a small access drive (see Plate 45). A front porch and staircase provide primary access to the main level. Figure 10.18 illustrates a similar condition found throughout Savannah where the lower level is often a rental unit and the primary entrance on the second floor (British first floor) is reached by stairs from the street. An alternative but

**Figure 10.18** Entrance Staircase in Savannah, Georgia. Stairs and porches to the front doors at the elevated main entrance level provide visual interest to the street as well as establishing visual privacy to the main rooms. Compare with Figures 6.17 and 6.23.

less striking design would simply place the front entrance on the lower level directly into the bonus room with an internal stair.

The companion improvement to this new housing created a new neighborhood park along the banks of the existing spring-fed stream that had been trapped in a culvert for many years. From here the water is channelled under Sirrine Stadium and University Ridge, at which point it re-emerges to flow into the Reedy River. By removing the stream from its pipe, a linear park can be created, thereby enhancing the values of the properties around it. The stream and related park would become a wonderful amenity shared by the townhomes and the larger community.

Clearly the park and the recuperated stream would substantially enhance the redevelopment value of the site, and create an incentive for the developer to assist in the restoration of the stream, but the expected costs for such an environmental project would require additional assistance to make it feasible. The public benefits of the restoration of a natural stream channel would include greater groundwater infiltration, improving capacity as well as water quality, and of course, the creation of a wonderful public space. We calculated that simply to restore the stream to daylight and open air (without the surrounding park improvements) would cost approximately $170 000. If this cost was borne by the city, the private developer could then develop the park as part of his project by preserving the mature trees and adding simple landscaping and then transfer it to the city for maintenance and upkeep. This project was important as it represented a redevelopment opportunity that was not contingent on the improvement of Church Street, and could proceed independently.

### Springer Street West: New Townhomes and a Greenway Inserted in Leftover Land (project 'Q' in Plate 41).

In most master-planning efforts a small nook or leftover parcel of land usually surfaces that could be utilized for an innovative infill project. Such a piece of property existed along Springer Street on the west side of the aforementioned tunnel. The lots on the north side of the street have their primary frontage on Wakefield Street immediately to the north, and they are unusually deep. If these lots were to be subdivided, the master plan suggested that

townhomes could be built on the Springer Street side of these long, thin properties. Because of the minimal lot depth of the proposed dwellings, parking could be provided on-street, in combination with some garages or carports on the lowest storey (see Plate 46). Because of the minimal land costs involved with this residual land, this would be a good opportunity for affordable housing.

To improve the view of these lots and add an additional amenity to the neighborhood, we showed the creek on the south side of Springer Street cleared of underbrush and debris and its channel stabilized. This small park connected with a redesigned park and community garden immediately to the west, and via an improved Springer Street Tunnel (see the section 'Implementation,') to a greenway leading to the new Biltmore Park and Sirrine Stadium. This green east–west axis across the site thus provided park space accessible to all residents. To complete the new Springer Street Park we framed its southern edge by townhomes and apartments that looked over the park and backed up to parking lots for the adjacent Neighborhood Center. This location offered another opportunity for new affordable housing.

### Sirrine Neighborhood Center: The redevelopment of the football stadium and adjacent mixed-use development (project 'A' in Plate 41).

Immediately to the east of the stadium in the northeast corner of the site, a small, local neighborhood center contains a few thriving businesses in an area graced with mature trees and sidewalks (see Figure 10.19). What this location lacks are buildings close enough to the street to engage the pedestrian and create an urban character. Opposite these local shops is the existing parking lot in front of the stadium, which remains largely unused except during Friday evening high school football games, when every available space within walking distance in the surrounding neighborhood is taken over by spectators' cars. In order to meet the parking objectives for Sirrine Stadium, as well as provide additional development opportunities to complete the urban design of this neighborhood center, the master plan proposed development along the existing street edges using two- or three-story live-work buildings. These buildings could provide significant income for the school authorities through the sale of the land, and

**Figure 10.19** Sirrine neighborhood center as existing (Compare with Plate 47).

serve to screen the parking lot from pedestrians on the street. Given the demographics of the surrounding neighborhoods, our experience suggested there was likely to be an underserved market for small boutique retail/office opportunities as well as urban residential units (see Plate 47).

Plate 48 illustrates how the construction of another parking structure in two simple trays fitted into the fall of the land allows access to both levels without the use of expensive ramps, and provides additional on-site parking for Sirrine Stadium events. We estimated construction costs for this deck to be $1.6 million. The additional parking on-site, combined with the deck for the nearby North Church Street development should help to relieve the neighborhood during football games and permit additional activities to occur at the Stadium without adverse impact.

## IMPLEMENTATION

As part of the follow-up to any charrette, it is vital to describe realistic implementation strategies. Without these the master plan cannot be taken seriously, and our implementation strategies for Haynie-Sirrine covered:

- Public finance
- Affordable housing strategies.
- A detailed implementation project schedule
- A design-based zoning ordinance tailored to the master plan.

## Public Finance

In order to implement this master plan, a number of strategic public investments would be needed to improve and expand the infrastructure for the neighborhood. These investments comprise:

- Basic Street Improvements: We estimated repairs and upgrades to the existing infrastructure to a level consistent with the surrounding neighborhoods would cost approximately $552 000.
- *Church Street Improvements.* Approximately 45 percent of the redevelopment for this neighborhood is dependent upon the improvement and upgrading of this thoroughfare to a true boulevard. Not only does this improvement directly impact the neighborhood, but also its prominence as a gateway to the downtown makes this a highly visible aesthetic improvement for the entire city. We estimated the approximate cost for this work at nearly $3 000 000.
- *Haynie Street and Pearl Avenue Streetscape Improvements.* After the improvements have been completed for Church Street, a similar streetscaping treatment should be applied to Haynie Street and Pearl Avenue at an estimated cost of $275 000.
- *New Street Construction.* Our master plan included nearly 2000 linear feet (609 meters) of new streets. This would cost approximately $420 000.
- *New Parking Decks.* The large deck to support the Church Street Neighborhood Center would cost about $4 000 000, and the smaller one for the Sirrine Stadium about $1 600 000. (The third deck to serve the commercial and residential development at the north end of Church Street would be privately financed.)
- Biltmore Park Stream Restoration: We estimated this project, not including the development of the park, would cost about $170 000.

These investments total approximately to $10 million, but as we noted earlier, they have the capacity to leverage as much as $90 million in private investment. And herein lies one of the keys to financing these necessary improvements – a Tax Increment Financing (TIF) district. TIF works by using the future tax revenues from new developments to pay for capital improvements that support and promote them, most usually by covering the repayments on municipal bonds floated to finance the projects at the outset. As part of our final charrette presentation, we illustrated that if one estimated that building out the master plan would take 10 years, the increasing amount of taxes paid on new development during that period could total $6 million at the end of the decade. The years after 'build-out' would each generate approximately $1.5 million in taxes, amounting to $15 million over the following 10 years, adding up to a total of $21 million in tax revenues to cover the original $10 million public investment.

Additional funds to help cover the initial outlay could also be sought from TEA-21 and TEA-3 federal funds (the successors to the ISTEA legislation described in Chapter 5) for pedestrian-friendly transportation improvements.

## Affordable Housing

The primary concern expressed during the entire charrette process by the existing residents was the issue of housing affordability and their fears of being displaced by gentrifying newcomers and upscale development. This was not the premise of the proposed master plan. While demolition and redevelopment would occur in several areas, it was our strong intention that affordable housing should remain a primary component of the neighborhood. To assist this objective we offered the following three observations.

First, good quality design should not be sacrificed for affordability. Our dwellings are a mirror of ourselves and are therefore linked to our individual self-esteem and community pride. We can build less expensively, but not at the cost of good architecture and craftsmanship. If housing is poorly designed it will always remain 'affordable' because it is unloved and unlovely. Such was the case with the substandard housing present in the neighborhood at the time of the charrette. This is not the kind of affordability that nurtures community, and simply to build new homes that are cheap because they are badly designed and badly built is a short-term, shortsighted approach. By contrast, affordable housing should be spread throughout the neighborhood and should be indistinguishable from market-rate housing (see Figure 6.35 Affordable Housing in Davidson, NC).

Second, long-term affordability can be assured only through direct intervention in the marketplace by governments and nonprofit agencies, often in partnership. We urged the city of Greenville to make a commitment to build housing efficiently, and to participate in maintaining long-term affordability. This would ensure that the city's service workers, teachers, and police officers have the opportunity to live in the neighborhoods they serve, along with

senior citizens who can 'age in place'. Using a variety of techniques, including tax credits, housing vouchers and land trusts, new moderately priced homes can be made affordable to people whose need is urgent. Communities can also leverage federal and state dollars to provide the infrastructure of streets, utilities, trees and sidewalks, thus reducing the direct cost of the home because these costs don't have to be passed on to the purchaser.

Third, in addition to the usual sources of funds and action for affordable housing such as Community Development Block Grants and HOME funds (both from the US Department of Housing and Urban Development) along with volunteer organizations like Habitat for Humanity, we specifically recommended that the city and its partners investigate Community Land Trusts (CLTs).

A land trust is a mechanism for balancing community equity and individual ownership by separating the cost of land from the resale value of a privately owned home. A separate entity, typically a nonprofit housing organization, owns title to the land underneath a house, similar to an American condominium arrangement or a British leasehold. In this instance, the land is not included in the original sale or resale cost of the home, thereby reducing the overall housing costs by 20 to 25 percent. CLTs help communities to:

- Gain local control over land and reduce absentee ownership;
- Promote resident ownership and control of housing;
- Keep housing affordable for future residents;
- Capture the value of public investment in land for long-term community benefit; and
- Build a strong base for community action.

Community Land Trusts can acquire vacant land and develop housing or other structures on it; at other times, CLTs may acquire land and buildings together. In both cases, CLTs treat land and buildings differently. The land is held permanently by the land trust so that it will benefit the community: buildings (known as improvements) can be owned by those who use them. When a CLT sells homes, it leases the underlying land to the homeowners through a long-term (usually 99-year) renewable lease, which gives the residents and their descendants the right to use the land for as long as they wish to live there. When a CLT homeowner decides to move out of his or her home, he or she can sell it. However, the land lease requires that the home be sold either back to the CLT or to another low-income household for an affordable price. As the land value is not part of the house price, this means that the home remains affordable for the next homeowner. The affordable housing illustrated in Figure 6.35 was developed by this kind of organization.

## Implementation Project Schedule

As part of the charrette report, we created a detailed schedule for implementing projects in priority over a period of 10–20 years, the anticipated build-out of the whole neighborhood. The charrette was completed in August 2001, just a few days before the traumatic events of September 11, 2001, which displaced all our estimates. Like most of America, the city of Greenville and the local community were thrown into a state of shock, and in the economic slump exacerbated by the attack on the World Trade Center, little work was done on neighborhood revitalization projects for several months. During that time, the developer of the Ramada Inn project pulled out, putting the Neighborhood Center on hold and dealing a blow to the heart of the scheme. Without this impetus, negotiations between city officials and highway engineers on the redesign of Church Street continued slowly.

However, the master plan was adopted by the city council in January 2003, and the zoning code implemented on a case-by-case basis. In the spring of 2003, the city authorities decided on a bold demonstration project to reinforce their commitment to the neighborhood and to the master plan. For this illustration, city officials chose the refurbishment of the Springer Street Tunnel, illustrated in its former dark and dank state in Figure 10.3. Plate 49 illustrates our redesign, with a new stairway and rearranged traffic flow.

We recommended improving bicycle and pedestrian access through the tunnel by converting one side to one-way traffic that would yield to oncoming vehicles as befits a slow-speed neighborhood street. This left the other side exclusively for cyclists and pedestrians. We suggested that a light well be formed in the median of Church Street to allow natural light to flood into the tunnel midway along its length. Combined with new lighting inside and around the tunnel entrances, this would go a long way to offsetting the forbidding character of the space. Springer Street would be further enhanced by new wide stairways leading up to Church Street on either side. This improves accessibility, opens up the space and provides an opportunity for civic design and public art to enhance the neighborhood.

## Design-based Zoning Ordinance Tailored to the Master Plan

Because the master plan is a realistic build-out study rather than a firm development proposal, it is necessary to enact a new zoning code tied to the specific design principles of the plan in order to guide actual development projects as they are prepared. Our Neighborhood Code was written to provide for the development of property as shown in the master plan, but it has the inherent flexibility to adapt to future market conditions and more site-specific studies. In addition, the code provides predictability and assurance to potential investors that any future development will be consistent with the master plan.

The Code is implemented by a new Zoning District entitled 'Haynie-Sirrine Neighborhood' with four sub-zones that regulate the form and intensity of development. These four categories are defined as Neighborhood Edge (NE), Neighborhood General (NG), Neighborhood Center (NC) and University Ridge Village Center (URVC). These are geographic areas defined *according to their urban character rather than their use*, and are mapped directly over the urban design master plan which forms the basic frame of reference for design and functional criteria (see Plate 50). This type of zoning plan is often referred to as a 'regulating plan', so-called because it regulates development in accordance with the urban design master plan. Our zoning areas that classify urban character are similar in concept to the urban zones of the 'transect', an environmental ordering system conceptualized as a long section through an idealized landscape from rural edge to city center (DPZ, 2002: page A.4.1). Derived in the late 1990s by Duany and Plater-Zyberk, this transect in turn owes a debt to the classic valley section of Scottish geographer Patrick Geddes (1854–1932), which set the various sectors of urbanization in their regional geographic context.

The principles of design-based zoning are very simple. The concept is based on a series of typologies classifying the urban variables as follows:

1. Type of urban area (e.g. Neighborhood Center, Neighborhood Edge, etc.) This urban typology dealing with overall character becomes the defining zoning classification.
2. Building type (e.g. Detached House, Civic Building, etc.)
3. Open space types (e.g. Greenway, Park, Square, etc.)
4. Street types (e.g. Boulevard, Local Street, Parkside Drive, etc.)

Into this framework of physical form, space and character are fitted details of uses, architectural requirements, parking layout, environmental protection, signage and so forth. The fundamentally important point here is this: *Design-based zoning begins with urban form, not with use.*

The code thus begins by dividing the community into geographic areas, based on a simple typological gradient: Village Center (the most urban); Neighborhood Center; Neighborhood General; and Neighborhood Edge (least urban) (see Plate 50). These four urban typologies cover most circumstances, but others can be added to cover more rural situations or higher density urban conditions as necessary. Each typology is characterized by a particular scale of buildings, illustrated in the simple section drawings on page 238 in Appendix III. These drawings also identify the range of applicable uses, which are amplified in the columns of text on page 239 in Appendix III.

The next set of governing criteria comprises a range of Building Types, typically Detached House, Townhouse, Apartment Building, Shopfront Building, Workplace Building and Civic Building. Each building type is described and dimensioned on a single sheet with three-dimensional diagrams, photographs, and text (see pages 240–241 in Appendix III). Note that while the Shopfront type is based on the traditional model of main street stores, it also accommodates large-scale uses such as grocery stores with only minor amendments, and can be extended to cover 'big-box' stores as well, disciplining them into a more urban configuration. Uses are implied in the naming of the building type, but they are specified in detail on the main pages of the code illustrated by the diagrams and text on pages one and two.

The Open Space Types are defined and illustrated in a spectrum of urban to more rural conditions – Squares and Plazas to Greens, Parks and Playgrounds, to Meadows and Greenways. Street Types are illustrated in dimensioned section and plan drawings, supplemented by a page of notes providing design and engineering standards. Other sections of the code deal with parking placement and standards, and requirements for commercial signs, outdoor lighting, environmental protection and landscaping (see pages 242–243 in Appendix III).

The first two pages of the zoning ordinance extracts depicted in Appendix III can be printed together as one large poster sized wallchart that provides at-a-glance information of all key topics regarding zoning district, building type and building use. This poster is the companion piece to the zoning map or regulating plan, and these two pieces of paper contain the answers to most of the strategic questions concerning development opportunities in the community. More detail is provided on the pages describing the individual building types and the one page parking information sheet. The complete document, more evolved and detailed than its Mooresville equivalent outlined in Chapter 9, is still only 22 pages long. One point of note in the section diagrams of the permitted buildings is that ancillary accommodation over detached garages is allowed as a right, creating a potential supply of affordable rental apartments. This provision of small, cheap rental units makes a modest contribution to solving America's affordable housing crisis, while providing extra income to the homeowner. A flat in this location could also function as a separate home for an elderly relative to remain within the family circle while retaining a measure of independence.

## CONCLUSIONS

This master plan was constructed around a series of 19 different redevelopment opportunities in the community, ranging from high-end market rate mixed-use development to affordable housing infill on scattered sites. We calculated that $10 million of public investment in infrastructure could leverage $90 million in private investment, about half of which was dependent on the upgrading of Church Street, with the other half spread around the neighborhood in a variety of projects. At the core was the creation of a lively mixed-use neighborhood center where people from within and outside the community could meet in the shops, offices and housing focused around that location.

A central component of the plan was the preservation of affordable housing in the area. A number of different strategies would need to be employed to ensure long-term affordability, including public investment, land trusts and non-profit housing agency involvement. Though implementation of the plan would primarily be market-driven, the city would need to develop programs and incentives to ensure long-term affordability. The final master plan also included a new zoning overlay code with standards for the design of buildings, streets and open spaces keyed specifically to the master plan.

## CRITICAL EVALUATION OF CASE STUDY

This was one of our most successful charrettes, and also one of the least typologically driven of our master plans. With the exception of some fragmentary typologies of the perimeter block with buildings lining the streets and wrapping around parking, most redevelopment opportunities were based on detailed circumstantial responses to particular site conditions. In part, this reflects the great level of individual site appraisal that was possible on a project of this neighborhood scale and scope. In larger city or regional plans, greater reliance has to be placed on typological solutions that hold within themselves the seeds of subsequent detail development. This level of detail design was also a function of the longer time period, six days instead of our more usual four. In many ways, six days is ideal, but the extra expense usually militates against this arrangement. In this instance the city of Greenville had creatively tapped a number of sources in the public and private sectors to finance the longer period.

At the time of writing the book in the spring of 2003, the city had adopted the plan and was implementing the zoning code. While detailed discussions were still continuing on the Church Street improvements, the city's decision to proceed with the Springer Street tunnel improvements was a welcome pledge of commitment to the master plan and the Haynie-Sirrine neighborhood. City staff were also using the plan to convince the school board not to condemn land around the stadium for new high school playing fields. This would be a bad decision for the neighborhood and the city. It would take valuable land off the tax rolls, as the school board, a public body, does not pay property taxes, and it would seriously disturb the balance of the plan in its carefully constructed relationships of economic diversity. From conversations with city officials, it appeared at the time of writing that they were confident the plan would remain intact and that the wide consensus and commitment developed through the design process between the city, the neighborhood, and the private sponsors would endure.

The only disappointing note in the process and its aftermath was the withdrawal of the hotel developer. He dropped out as the market declined during the economic recession that followed the attacks of September 11. Despite this setback, the prognosis for the neighborhood is good, and local observers expect private developments to begin on site as the overall economy slowly improves.

# The block

## Case Study 5: Town Center, Cornelius, North Carolina

### PROJECT AND CONTEXT DESCRIPTION

Our final case study is dramatically different from those that have preceded it in many ways. This difference is not simply a matter of scale; the personnel and the procedure varied, too. The authors and other professional colleagues featured in previous case studies were heavily involved, but all played very different roles. And this project was not produced by a charrette; rather it evolved over a decade, beginning in 1993 as a series of academic projects by architectural students. For a few years it lay fallow while the property at the heart of the town of Cornelius was enmeshed in a legal dispute and the focus of the authors and others was elsewhere, helping to reformulate the town's development plans and zoning ordinance on New Urbanist principles. Finally, the project re-emerged in 1997 as an innovative public–private partnership between the town and a private developer.

The particulars of the Cornelius town center project are relatively localized but the site is enmeshed in a much larger tale of regional collaborative planning. We'll briefly describe the planning context as the prelude to the story of the block's dramatic redevelopment, but first, the site itself. It comprises a 10-acre (4 hectares) urban block in the historic center of Cornelius, a small town 20 miles north of Charlotte. The site is located at the intersection of a major north–south regional road, Highway 115, and Main Street, which until the mid-1990s was a main connector to points west. For decades, the block was occupied by a textile mill, housed in a random series of brick and tin sheds of no architectural quality. These industrial buildings were served by a long-defunct rail spur from the nearby freight line, and they lined one side of Main Street with a long, blank

brick wall. In 1990, manufacturing ceased on the site, and the vacant buildings soon became a derelict eyesore at the center of the old town, casting a shroud over the development potential of the surrounding area. Partly as a consequence of this blighted environment, extensive suburban growth sprouted a couple miles away on more pleasing property along the shores of Lake Norman, a very large man-made lake formed for the generation of electricity. Figure 11.1 shows the site with the demolition of the old industrial buildings in progress.

This new development was separated from the old town by Interstate-77, which acted as a barrier between the two parts of the community. This is the same interstate that played a key role in the Mooresville case study in Chapter 9, and Cornelius is situated

**Figure 11.1** Aerial Photo of Cornelius Old Mill Site. This photo from 1997 records the early stages of demolishing the old mill buildings, ugly sheds of no architectural quality. (*Photograph courtesy of Shook Kelley architects*)

only five miles south of the Mount Mourne area (see Figure 9.1). These and two other towns noted below are linked not only by the interstate but also by Highway 115 and the same future high-speed commuter rail line, all three transportation corridors paralleling each other in a north–south direction.

Cornelius is one of three contiguous towns that together comprise the northern portion of Mecklenburg County in North Carolina, the other two being Huntersville immediately to the south and Davidson sharing a boundary to the north. Together, the three towns cover a combined territory of approximately 80 square miles. At the heart of Mecklenburg County sits big city Charlotte, the heart of a Metropolitan Statistical Area (MSA) of approximately two million people, of which, in 2003, about 55 000 lived in the three north Mecklenburg towns.

This case study documents the saga of the rebirth of this decrepit urban block into an active mixed-use center – the catalyst for the creation of a real town center where none had ever existed. But it also tells a larger story of regional collaborations between three towns in forging an unique example of Smart Growth and New Urbanist development that has gone largely unheralded in contemporary American town planning. This story also demonstrates, once again if proof were needed, the relevance and continuity of New Urbanist concepts of town planning from the scale of a region to a single urban block located at its core.

## Forging a Regional Vision

In 1994, one of the authors received a phone call from a concerned citizen in the town of Davidson about a major thoroughfare that was planned to rip through the edge of town and disturb the quaint, small town character of that community. This was a familiar enough beginning – on either side of the Atlantic – for citizen activism to rise against thoughtless transportation planning that had little regard to adjacent patterns of land use or community character. A series of public protest meetings followed, where it became clear that the proposed road was only the symptom of a larger problem. The town of Davidson, a pleasant community 25 miles outside the major regional city of Charlotte simply had no effective means to manage the suburban sprawl that was heading inexorably its way.

All that the town possessed prior to 1994 was a standard zoning ordinance compiled from regulations dating from the 1970s and which, if implemented, was guaranteed to produce sprawl. Davidson did however employ a dynamic young planner, Timothy Keane, who was acutely aware of the problem. Keane (who moved onward and upward a few years later to become Planning Director of Charleston, SC) persuaded the Town Board to appoint the architect author as town planning consultant, and together the pair explored the application of traditional town planning principles (in 1994 New Urbansim had not yet become the term of choice) to the town's development problems. In particular, we investigated how best to adapt coding examples like DPZ's famous Seaside Code to the challenges of managing growth in a full, public municipal context. An intensive, 12-month public process led to the adoption in 1995 of a new Land Plan for the town combined with a design-based code, pages from which were illustrated in Figure 3.4.

The same author was then appointed as town-planning consultant to neighboring Cornelius, with the charge of leading the town toward a similar growth management strategy. Work on a new town plan and zoning ordinance led to the appointment of two new staff members, Timothy Brown as Planning Director (now Planning Director of neighboring Mooresville, NC) and Craig Lewis as Assistant Town Manager (now a colleague of the authors in private practice). Between them these two newly appointed planners wrote the new Cornelius neotraditional zoning ordinance (adopted in 1996) while the author moved one town south to become planning consultant to the town of Huntersville. Working this time with Planning Director Ann Hammond (now Planning Director of Nashville and Davidson County, TN) the author helped craft a similar new town plan and zoning ordinance for that town, both of which were adopted late in 1996.

As part of this multi-year public process, the authors, working with community groups in all three towns, developed a large hand-drawn map of the anticipated build-out scenario for the whole of the northern part of Mecklenburg County covered by the jurisdictions of the three towns. Conceived originally as a public participation tool to educate the public and developers into the advantages of New Urbanist concepts by designing typical or contentious sites in detail, this map grew to a comprehensive vision of collaborative growth management. It featured extensive interconnected street and open space networks, transit village centers along the proposed commuter rail line to and from Charlotte, and was backed up by compatible design-based and transit-supportive zoning across all three jurisdictions (see Plate 51). This collaborative civic regionalism was hailed in *The Charlotte Observer* as 'the Mecklenburg Miracle,' (Newsom, 1996) and featured briefly in an American PBS television documentary and companion book (Hylton, 2000).

As part of the detailed design exercises for key sites in the three towns, several students at the College of Architecture at the University of North Carolina worked with the architect author on illustrative projects, and one fifth-year student, Mick Campbell, produced a detailed urban design master plan for the old center of Cornelius in 1996. This plan showed the old manufacturing site redeveloped as a mixed-use town center with a new town hall, grocery store, retail shops and live-work units. In accordance with the early plans for transit in north Mecklenburg County, Campbell sited a new commuter train station directly adjacent to this town center, and on vacant land on the other side of the tracks laid out a transit-oriented development following New Urbanist guidelines (see Figure 11.2). This prescient scheme paralleled moves being made by the town for the redevelopment of its historic center.

## The Town Center and the Old Mill Site

The old town center of Cornelius was first identified as a potential commuter rail stop in Charlotte and Mecklenburg County's 2025 Land Use and Transportation Plan, adopted in 1994. The previous year, architecture students from UNC Charlotte had responded to the town's request by presenting development alternatives for the old mill site. Building on these twin initiatives, town officials, with guidance from the architect author, began more advanced conceptual studies for the redevelopment of the old town center and adjacent land as a transit-oriented urban village in 1995.

To advance its vision, and to stop heavy trucks from further degrading the old town center, the town had already rezoned the old mill property in 1993 to avoid its continued use for manufacturing or as a warehouse. The town also tried to purchase the 10-acre industrial site and in 1995, but were unsuccessful, and the civic plans were further thwarted by a private businessman who outbid the town and refurbished some of the buildings as warehouses in direct opposition to the town's wishes. A complex legal battle ensued, which was initially won, against the odds, by the private owner on a zoning technicality. At one

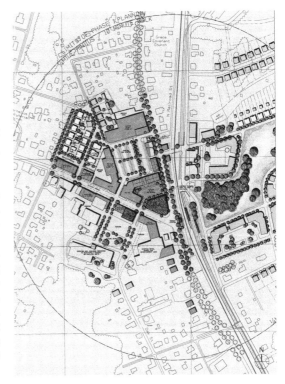

**Figure 11.2** Cornelius Town Center, Student Thesis Project, 1996. As part of a continuing dialogue between the town of Cornelius and students at the UNC Charlotte College of Architecture, this design by Mick Campbell identified key themes for the redevelopment of the block: the main retail stores organized around a parking piazza within the block; smaller shops and apartments lining the streets; and a new town hall on the main corner opposite the future train station. Compare with Plate 52. *(Drawing courtesy of Mick Campbell)*

point the owner even grazed goats on the property to establish some legal point! Despite this setback, Cornelius officials immediately threatened to appeal, and the consensus of legal opinion agreed the aberrant decision of the lower court jury would not likely be upheld under the more informed scrutiny of the appeal court. Accordingly, the owner settled out of court with the town and early in 1997, Cornelius eventually achieved ownership of the property (Brown, 2002).

During the ownership struggle, the town, with the architect author acting as planning consultant, had laid the planning groundwork for a new town center. Accordingly, in June 1997, a few months after the adoption of New Urbanist zoning ordinance, the town, under the guidance of Tim Brown and Craig Lewis, was able to enter into a public–private partnership with a local developer to redevelop the site with a mixture of commercial and residential uses, and a new town hall.

## KEY ISSUES AND OBJECTIVES

The main objective of the mill site redevelopment was to lay the foundation of what would, over a 10–20-year period, become a thriving town center focused on the commuter rail station.

Subsidiary objectives for the site and its immediately surrounding area were:

- Build a new grocery store to serve the older, eastern half of the community bisected by Interstate 77.
- Revive the civic heart of the community by constructing a new town hall to replace the miserable, windowless brick shed that city staff had worked in since the 1930s, together with a new police station, and nearby on a separate site, a new town library.
- Create a new residential population in the historic core by including market-rate and affordable housing on the town center site.
- Redevelop the site to increase the town's tax revenues.
- Stimulate new development in the older eastern part of town to balance the extensive suburban sprawl in the western parts of town on the other side of the interstate.
- Design the site layout to link with a future train station on adjacent land immediately to the east and future transit-oriented residential development on the other side of the tracks.

## THE MASTER PLAN (PLATE 52)

The master plan for the block was designed by the Charlotte architects Shook Design Group (later Shook Kelly), who worked with town officials and the McAdams Company, the private developer. Highway 115 runs south to north along the eastern edge of the property, paralleled by the rail line that will provide the future commuter service between Mooresville and Charlotte. Main Street runs east to west along the bottom of the plan. The design process began in November 1997, construction documents were finalized in May 1998, and the first phase was completed by December of that same year.

Phase I comprised the 33 000 square feet (3066 square meters) grocery store plus 10 000 square feet (929 square meters) of ancillary retail shops on 4.47 acres (1.79 hectares).

This grocery store was visible from Main Street, with its required parking lot directly in front of the store's entrance to conform to the established suburban stereotype, but this conventional arrangement would later be screened by subsequent phases of development along the street edge (see Figure 11.3). This was a neat solution (presaged in Campbell's plan in Figure 11.2) to the problem of fixed attitudes by grocery and other 'big-box' retailers regarding what is to them a mandatory requirement for parking in front of their stores. This design provided parking where it was needed to satisfy this expectation (and those of the conservative lenders who finance such projects), but it established a larger pedestrian-friendly urban frame around the conventional solution. (Also see Figure 11.5).

Phase II comprised the construction of the new town hall, at 27 000 square feet (2508 square meters) nine times the size of the old civic building. While some thought was given to locating this important structure on the southeastern corner, at the junction of two main roads – for visual and symbolic significance – the town and the designers opted for a Main Street location that could be paired with the future police station in a formal, symmetrical arrangement to give a

**Figure 11.3** Grocery store viewed from Main Street. Two rows of three-storey live-work units line the new Cornelius Main Street, creating a space between them through which the grocery store and its parking are clearly visible and accessible. In this way the large parking area does not dominate the townscape.

sense of civic scale and grandeur to the composition. The town hall was also designed by the Shook Kelly to be reminiscent of older courthouses and municipal buildings, with enhanced vertical scale and massive neo-classical symmetry, in order to stamp its civic presence on what could otherwise appear a normative commercial development. Design of the town hall was begun in October 1997, and the building completed in August 1999 (see Figure 11.4).

Phase III, the most important urban design element of the master plan, comprised the construction of two terraces of three-story live–work units along the northern side of Main Street (see Figure 11.5). Designed by Charlotte architect David Furman, these 25 live-work units illustrate some of the complexities of building regulations designed for suburban situations where every building has its own separate use, and stands apart in its own space. These terraces were constructed as three-story residential townhomes because of the difficulty under state-building codes of dealing with the simple mixed-use arrangement of living above the store – the condition that characterized Main Street America for nearly two centuries. To make these buildings suitable for their true use, Furman made the footprint of the building's plan deeper than normal townhomes to accommodate ground floor business uses. The town's zoning code then circum-vented the limitations of the state building code by allowing the street level 'living room' to be used as an office or shop as a 'home occupation.'

These units were marketed in February 2000 for between $142 000–$255 000 and quickly sold out, illustrating the impact of America's fastest growing business sector, the small entrepreneur working from home (Brown: p. 56). Similar buildings have been designed for the eastern frontage of the site along Highway 115, but these constitute a later phase, tied more to the construction of the future train station on the opposite side of the road than to Main Street's revitalization. This timing and orientation also applies to the remaining buildings planned at the important intersection of Main Street and Highway 115.

Main Street was also redesigned to allow angled parking, a boon for street level businesses, but even this improvement necessitated the town arguing with higher state authorities. As a state-maintained highway, diagonal parking was not allowed under out-of-date regulations that regarded the parking and backing out of cars to be an impediment to the smooth and speedy flow of vehicles. To achieve the pedestrian-friendly improvements necessary for the success of the overall project, the town had to agree to take over maintenance of the street from the state, adding a cost to its municipal budget. Once the

**Figure 11.4** Cornelius Town Hall, Shook Kelley Architects, 1999. The monumental scale of the new town hall was a shock to many local residents, used to paying their taxes and going to meetings in a single-storey shed for several decades. While this building works well and provides excellent facilities for the town, the authors can't help but wish the architecture had made a more contemporary statement rather than retreating into historicism.

**Figure 11.5** Live-work units on Cornelius Main Street, David Furman, Architect, 2001. These buildings illustrate a common American quandary: progressive urban design constructed with historicist aesthetics. American taste at the beginning of the twenty-first century has little affinity with crisp, modern aesthetics to match the advances in urbanism. Compare this architecture with that illustrated in Figure 3.9.

**223**

street was taken over by the town, it assumed authority over the space, and could re-classify it as a town street with angled parking.

The fourth phase of the town center consisted of the new 18 000 square foot (1672 square meters) police station, completed in late 2002 to the designs of Charlotte architects LS3P, who also designed the nearby branch library opposite the town's elementary school two blocks away in 1998. Both these buildings demonstrate good urban design sensitivity to the public street, but manifest a conservative, brick and stone neo-classicism in their external appearance, echoing the 'retro' character of all the architecture in the new town center (see Figure 11.6).

A fifth phase, comprising the vital component of affordable housing in the form of small townhomes around the west and north of the site, completed the construction to date at the time of writing in the late spring of 2003. The master plan also sketched in further terraces of mixed-use development along the south side of Main Street to mirror those on the north. This redevelopment on land not owned by the town is not likely to come to fruition for several years, but on other nearby properties a considerable amount refurbishment and infill development has materialized in response to the town's commitment to reviving its historic core. As a result, the 1996 assessed tax valuation of $800 000 for the town center area had increased by 2003 to several million dollars.

**Figure 11.6** Aerial View of partly completed development showing Police Station, LS3P Architects, 2002. The police station is visible on the left-hand side of the photograph, opposite the town hall. Like the town hall it contributes to good urban design but its tepid neo-classicism is disappointing.

## IMPLEMENTATION

North Carolina state law allows public–private partnership ventures to occur for downtown revitalization, but this town center project tested the legal boundaries of the statute as the first instance of its use. The town had optioned the site while negotiating with the developer, and upon agreement of terms, assigned the option to the development company. The town then spent $500 000 to clear and clean up the site, and $250 000 to bury all the power and telephone lines along Main Street. As part of the clever legal agreement, the town bought back the site of the town hall for $800 000 and entered into a 'build-to-suit' contract with the developer for the construction of the new building. This enabled the town to save money, benefit from the economies of scale by being part of the larger, overall development with more competitive pricing, and, importantly, enjoy a faster design and development schedule afforded by the private sector compared to conventional process of separate design and competitive bidding for publicly financed municipal buildings (Brown: p. 55). All this innovative manoeuvering necessitated detailed negotiations between the town and the state commission for local government in order to approve the methods of financing.

We noted earlier that Professor Walters' work with the town in the mid-1990s had established the principle of a transit-oriented town center on this site and adjacent properties, with the redevelopment of the old mill as the foundation for this vision. With the economic and critical success of this town center block (it received awards for its detailed design from the American Institute of Architects and the American Planning Association) Cornelius took another bold step in January 2000. Following its innovative precedent on the old mill site, the town contracted to purchase 128 acres (51 hectares) of land immediately on the opposite side of the rail line from the town center, where Campbell's 1996 student thesis had explored a transit-oriented residential development. The town did so 'as a catalyst to support and facilitate the successful development of this property, (but) with no desire to own or develop the property themselves' (Brown, 60). It was their intention to produce a design for a TOD while the property was under their option to buy, and then 'flip' the site, with its design and full zoning in place, to a developer, who would be the actual one to purchase the land and proceed with construction. This strategy kept the town's financial commitment low, while leveraging extensive private investment to complete the project.

The town employed Duany Plater-Zyberk & Company to prepare a master plan and assessments of development feasibility, which they completed through a public design charrette in December 2000. With the plan in place, elected officials and staff interviewed several development companies before selecting one to implement the project. The DPZ plan created an attractive blueprint for the transit-oriented development, and established a viable framework, but some difficult topographic and implementation issues remained unresolved. As a result of some disagreements between the consultants and the town, Charlotte landscape architects Cole Jenest and Stone (members of the original design team) were hired to revise the plan to meet the needs of the town and the selected developer (see Figure 11.7). The commuter rail line is still on schedule to be up and running by 2008, and the first homes in the transit-oriented

development were scheduled to break ground in the summer of 2003.

Cornelius' proactive planning regime moved to consolidate this town center vision in the spring of 2003 when it commissioned the Lawrence Group to prepare a master plan for its remaining land area around the TOD and along the train line, about six square miles, in collaboration with its neighbors, the towns of Davidson and Huntersville. The Lawrence Group set up another public charrette, and the resultant master plan balanced the opportunities for development, particularly spurred by transit and the recent provision of sewer service, with the conservation of some of the last large areas of open farmland in the county (see Plate 53).

Within the study area for this last piece of the puzzle, and immediately to the east and south of the Transit-oriented Development, sits 656 acres

**Figure 11.7** Revised TOD Master Plan Layout, Cole Jenest and Stone, Landscape Architects, 2001. This plan retained many elements of the original DPZ plan, but revised parts of the street pattern to suit detailed topographical conditions. The commuter rail line makes a shallow arc on the left-hand edge of the drawing, and the train station will be located next to the pedestrian connection across the tracks to the adjacent town center. The mixed-use development discussed in this chapter is immediately off the drawing on the left-hand side. (Drawing courtesy of Cole Jenest and Stone)

(254 hectares) of working farmland that has been in the ownership of one family since it was granted during the reign of King George III. The land was conveyed by the British admiral and peer, Lord Anson from what was then Anson County, which extended all the way from the Charlotte area to the Mississippi River, about 600 miles to the west, illustrating the vast scale of colonial America. Listed on the National Register of Historic Places this land is destined by family decree to remain undeveloped for generations to come. While this is prime developable land (all good farmland is!) which would allow improved connectivity between Cornelius and Davidson, its presence as a huge 'central park' immediately next to centers of denser development, has great environmental and historic benefit for the community. Accordingly, in our final study, we concentrated future development well away from this land, and around the location of another future commuter train station at the southern edge of this master plan area, two-and-a-half miles south from the location of the Cornelius town center station. Here we created a new employment-led TOD merged with a park-and-ride facility, as the conditions were very similar to the Mooresville/Mount Mourne case study in Chapter 9: good road access to Interstate 77, and large tracts of developable land held by only a handful of property owners. This plan was just recently finished when this book was completed in the early summer of 2003. We await with interest to see if this companion development to the Cornelius town center and the Mount Mourne employment center reaches an equivalent level of fulfillment!

## CRITICAL EVALUATION OF CASE STUDY

We have many good things to say about this case study, having been involved in its initial phases and then observing the concepts coming to fruition by virtue of the skills and talents of others. We have one caveat, however. This bold, entrepreneurial vision of a new town center has been implemented in a series of conservative neo-classical buildings. These structures use the past as something to copy as a restrictive model, rather than something to interpret afresh, as a typology. This retreat into imagery from the past to concoct a style for new buildings is a common American problem, and well known in Britain too, where the fine line between a discerning respect for tradition and a cozy nostalgia for an invented past is often blurred. In this instance, as in many others

including Huntersville's Birkdale Village, historicist architecture has been the means of gaining popular and economic success. It is a perplexing commentary on our times that if the bold planning and urban design moves in the town center of Cornelius had been rendered in equally bold contemporary architecture (which can be perfectly compatible with New Urbanism) it is most unlikely that elected officials would have backed the project, nor the citizens embraced it. In 2003 in America, we live in a time of very conservative popular taste, and while as artists and architects we long for the opportunity to marry contemporary design with Smart Growth planning, as urban designers, we realize it may take another generation before our society's cultural quest for shallow nostalgia deepens into something more aesthetically profound.

On a much more positive note, it is clear that this case study has achieved the highest level of implementation of any in the book. This is due largely to its lengthy time period, early plans in the form of student projects having been discussed as far back as 1993. It has taken 10 years to reach its current status, still unfinished but moving forward piece by piece. The successful implementation of good design ideas has been driven by the proactive leadership of the town, both elected officials and staff, and their aggressive seeking of public–private partnerships that could combine the energy and efficiencies of the private sector with the long-term vision of the public authority, and using modest public investments to leverage major private money.

Of particular note are the connections made by the town outward from its new central core. Town officials recognized that to be an active center, the old mill site had to become the focus of something larger than itself. Accordingly, through several changes of elected officials, most of whom shared a common vision, town staff made sure the new town center was connected to high-density transit opportunities – and compensatory open space preservation – along the rail line they shared with their neighboring towns. This perspective is an exemplar for us all, and reinforces our fundamental belief in the connectedness of scales in Smart Growth and New Urbanism. Even when we work at the scale of the block, we are always thinking beyond the site boundaries and grappling with the larger context. One block relates to the blocks around it, then to the whole neighborhood, and then to the whole town, and in this instance to a collaborative regional vision with adjacent municipalities. The block is the crucible of the region as much as the region is the incubator of the block.

# Afterword

This book has attempted to weave together several strands of urban thought into one coherent narrative around a central premise: the best way to plan communities is to design them in detail. We chose to illustrate this theme with an insider's view of the design and planning process, believing that laying bare the successes and disappointments of our own work could accomplish five things. First, for those who find urban design a fuzzy concept, using case studies of typical projects could demystify the concepts and techniques of the discipline, rendering it more accessible to non-designers. Second, the detailed description of real-life examples could reveal the potential that Smart Growth and New Urbanist strategies have for communities large and small in their struggle for more sustainable ways of living and building.

Third, we hope that our case studies will illuminate the similarities in technique and the differences in political context between British and American practice. Fourth, by displaying our concepts, theories, and results on site, the work can function as an open book for students in both countries, demonstrating how professionals work in practice, and how ideas taught in studios and lecture halls by architecture professors can be directly relevant to critical practice. And fifth, it could support others like ourselves who work hard to save America from itself. We are not alone.

One of the first things architects learn as professionals is something they are rarely taught at in school, except perhaps as a lecture in Professional Practice: their work as architects and urban designers is founded on collaboration and compromise. Furthermore, compromise need not be the dirty word that besmirches architectural genius. Clients, contractors, surveyors, engineers and planners all play valid and important roles in creating buildings, and what is true for architecture is magnified in the wider worlds of urban design and town planning. The charrette is justly touted as a great method of getting community input and buy-in to complex planning issues, but that forum is equally useful in contextualizing the designer's skill, casting him or her in a role that goes beyond that of an independent professional. The urban designer is part of a creative team that includes representatives of many other disciplines as partners, along with non-professionals and citizens.

When minds are open, charrettes can be great learning vehicles for designers as well as the general public. Throughout the book we've emphasized the use of traditional urban forms and typology as a means of bridging past, present and future, and of using history and theory to enrich our designs amidst the development realities in American towns and cities. Being alert to the power of traditional sources does not imply that architectural design can't or shouldn't evolve. Within the urban frame of people-centered public space, architecture can experiment, evolve and adapt. Similarly, using typologies doesn't imply our designs are fixed; we do not necessarily know the solution before we begin.

Typologies are starting points for designers, generic foundation stones of structures that take particular shape according to local circumstances. This local understanding comes only by listening and involving local people as partners in the enterprise of shaping their community. One reason why the Mooresville and Greenville charrettes were successful was because local participation was excellent. The design team learned a great deal from people in the area, and the master plans were greatly improved by the process.

Through our case studies, we have deliberately illustrated a real-life mixture of success and disappointment. We don't say 'failure' because none of the projects 'failed'. Even the Raleigh example, where our contract did not include any provisions for implementation, leaving the master plan alone and vulnerable to the vagaries of future decisions, did not 'fail', although it did certainly not succeed as much as we would have liked. We take some heart that in knowing that planners in Raleigh, as in many cities across the USA, are working hard to improve the planning system, and our plan might have made the task of our Carolina colleagues a little easier. Our plan also helped support the efforts of the Triangle Transit Authority to bring commuter train service to the region, and, especially we think, helped the community to appreciate the economic and social advantages that transit-oriented villages provide, as opposed to building bare-bones park-and-ride lots at the station sites.

Apart from the Cornelius town center with its longer time span, all these projects were planned during the years 2000 and 2002. In America's recession-prone economy, burdened by threats of global terrorism and a general loss of confidence, the impact of the plans on the ground has been modest – with the further exception of the Mooresville master plan – which helped attract a major corporate head-quarters to the site. This limited implementation within a one- to three-year period after completion of the plans should also not be judged a failure, because town building is a long-term process. It is not uncommon for a complex architectural project to take five years from inception to completion, and for urban design and town planning projects; this time frame can easily be doubled or tripled. We were very serious in the Greenville case study when we mapped out a potential implementation schedule that lasted 20 years!

For the professional, urban design is necessarily about deferred gratification. As experienced profession-als now in middle age, we know we may be retired before the plans we draw today take shape in the world. The trade-off for this long time scale is the scope of action and influence: we get to do a lot more than design buildings, honorable as that labor is. We get to design towns and cities! The public dynamism of urban design, and the constant interaction with communities trying to shape their future, are very satisfying architec-tural and planning endeavors. To continue analogies we've drawn from Gordon Cullen and Camillo Sitte, we urban designers are a bit like composers, whose music needs musicians to be heard. We create an urban score, but nothing happens unless other professionals and citizens play their parts by transforming our lines on paper and words on the page into political action and bricks and mortar. Delayed gratification it may be, but oh, the joys of composition!

We deliberately chose our case studies to illus-trate a hierarchy of urban scales: creating a regional framework for collaborative development among many municipalities; restructuring a faded subur-ban area in a large city around urban village centers; creating a new urban village on a greenfield site to make patterns of suburban growth more sustainable; revitalizing a poor inner-city neighbor-hood; and regenerating a decayed town center. Our work on these large and small projects has convinced us of one of New Urbanism's central

propositions – continuity and connections in design thinking exist between all scales of urbanism, from the region to the block.

Some professional opinion still maintains that Smart Growth operates at a large scale of 'planning,' while New Urbanism concerns itself with the smaller, 'design' scale of individual projects (Wickersham, 2003). In our view this is fundamentally mistaken: it perpetuates the divorce of planning from design. To take the design content out of Smart Growth, so it becomes just another set of planning policies, is to give it the kiss of death. Smart Growth, above all else, is about the *redesign* of our communities to help solve environmental and social problems, and to create new patterns of sustainable living in places that nourish the soul while providing for everyday necessities. Smart Growth and New Urbanism are indivisible; together they form a comprehensive approach to development, redevelopment and con-servation at all scales.

Our work is living proof that New Urbanism isn't just about making cute suburbs for the well-heeled middle class. It can, and should be an agency of social change and improvement. But one of the most severe testing grounds, for Smart Growth and New Urbanism alike, is in this arena of social equity. New Urbanism has garnered a reputation, somewhat unfairly, as merely a means of creating environments for the pleasure of the wealthier classes in American society. The economically distorted legacy of Seaside, and our enjoyment of Birkdale Village, in Huntersville, North Carolina, exemplify this problem. But this cat-egorization *is* unfair because it ignores, among other things, the great contributions to affordable housing evident in HOPE VI projects that are based squarely on New Urbanist principles. But the belief still lingers, and as we noted in Chapter 6, opponents of Smart Growth have developed a potentially powerful new tactic of branding Smart Growth as 'snob growth', the preserve of a wealthy upper-middle class that excludes lower income families and individuals. To overcome this slur is vital, but aspects of American society make it a very difficult challenge.

For an allegedly 'classless' culture, America in the twenty-first century is handicapped by a stratification based on money and race, all too self-evident in the form of the nation's cities. Low- and moderate-income households are often concentrated in parts of cities many miles from centers of employment, with limited means of getting to and from workplaces, schools, and health services. Wealthy citizens keep poorer members of the community away from their suburban enclaves by means of large-lot exclusionary zoning that means smaller, more affordable homes can't be built in those locations. More rampant social and spatial segregation by means of gated communities is increasingly commonplace. On occasion, we've been interviewed by towns seeking consultants for a new comprehensive plan, only to find that our stated ideals about the importance of social equity and affordable housing in all communities immediately disqualified us from further consideration. Such municipalities seek compliant consultants who will institutionalize discrimination, and they find them. However, we believe that to be complicit with this agenda is a reprehensible breach of professional ethics.

The equitable distribution of affordable housing throughout the community is both a founding principle of New Urbanism, and one of the hardest objectives to meet. America's sprawling settlement pattern means that on average, American households spend more money on transportation than on food, and only a fraction less than it takes to provide a roof over their head. Shelter consumes an average of 19 cents of every dollar, transportation 18 cents, and food, only 13 cents. For poorer households who desperately need money for decent housing, the distances between home and work mean that transportation costs alone take a whopping 36 cents out of every dollar, leaving too little for reasonable accommodation (Katz, 2003: p. 47).

While federal programs in America do provide support for affordable housing initiatives, it would be overly optimistic to hope for the implementation of a more proactive national policy mandating the equitable distribution of such accommodation in communities. It will be left to individual towns and cities to solve this problem as best they can. In this context, charrettes, master plans and new design-based zoning ordinances like the ones described in these case studies can help achieve social equity by designing it on the ground, neighborhood by neighborhood.

The authors don't want British readers to get too smug about the problems besetting America's towns and cities. The growing racial and class conflicts in Britain's inner cities, particularly in older failing urban areas in the north of the country bode ill for the future. Even in once prosperous industrial cities like Newcastle-upon-Tyne, which underwent decades of decline before fighting its way back to some semblance of urban health, the much-heralded and praiseworthy revitalization of the city center and quayside is contrasted with bitter urban decay in working class neighborhoods only a couple of miles away. This is not an isolated problem.

All is not sweetness and light in Albion's sceptered isle, and Americans who build their image of Britain from the BBC and Masterpiece Theater would be startled to comprehend the pressures and problems in British urban society. But, as we've said earlier in the book, there are national policies and support for planning and urban design that provide a framework for more comprehensive solutions than in America, and we're somewhat more optimistic about British cities than their American equivalents. In America, we simply have to work harder and put design to better use. As we hope we've shown in this book, design isn't simply an issue of aesthetics; it is a means of solving problems, and urban design provides the techniques for solving problems in cities through three-dimensional thinking. Contrary to Mies van der Rohe's assertion, in this case, less is *not* more. The extra third dimension provides designers and planners with more sophisticated tools to tackle urban problems than two-dimensional planning concepts that deal only with location and function. Urban design makes real places to live, to work, to shop, to worship, and to fall in love; urban planning makes only abstract models of cities.

The renaissance of American urban design is related in many ways to the British tradition of town planning – where the disposition of a community is organized according to physical criteria as well as social, economic and cultural considerations. It is the premise of the case studies that this kind of design-based planning can meet communities' needs in a way that conventional two-dimensional techniques cannot. Our work, and the work of many other professionals across the USA, reaffirms the tradition of physical master planning. We create a buildable vision and the means to implement it – as opposed to statistical planning methods that emphasize only analysis and policy formulation. The closer we get to the real world of places and people, the better we can solve the problems of cities, towns and neighborhoods. We, and others like us, are trying to reshape America for a sustainable future, one place at a time.

# The charter of the congress of the new urbanism

The Congress for the New Urbanism views disinvestment in central cities, the spread of placeless sprawl, increasing separation by race and income, environmental deterioration, loss of agricultural lands and wilderness, and the erosion of society's built heritage as one interrelated community-building challenge.

We stand for the restoration of existing urban centers and towns within coherent metropolitan regions, the reconfiguration of sprawling suburbs into communities of real neighborhoods and diverse districts, the conservation of natural environments, and the preservation of our built legacy.

We recognize that physical solutions by themselves will not solve social and economic problems, but neither can economic vitality, community stability, and environmental health be sustained without a coherent and supportive physical framework.

We advocate the restructuring of public policy and development practices to support the following principles: neighborhoods should be diverse in use and population; communities should be designed for the pedestrian and transit as well as the car; cities and towns should be shaped by physically defined and universally accessible public spaces and community institutions; urban places should be framed by architecture and landscape design that celebrate local history, climate, ecology, and building practice.

We represent a broad-based citizenry, composed of public and private sector leaders, community activists, and multidisciplinary professionals. We are committed to reestablishing the relationship between the art of building and the making of community, through citizen-based participatory planning and design.

We dedicate ourselves to reclaiming our homes, blocks, streets, parks, neighborhoods, districts, towns, cities, regions, and environment.

We assert the following principles to guide public policy, development practice, urban planning, and design:

## THE REGION: METROPOLIS, CITY, AND TOWN

1. Metropolitan regions are finite places with geographic boundaries derived from topography, watersheds, coastlines, farmlands, regional parks, and river basins. The metropolis is made of multiple centers that are cities, towns, and villages, each with its own identifiable center and edges.
2. The metropolitan region is a fundamental economic unit of the contemporary world. Governmental cooperation, public policy, physical planning, and economic strategies must reflect this new reality.
3. The metropolis has a necessary and fragile relationship to its agrarian hinterland and natural landscapes. The relationship is environmental, economic, and cultural. Farmland and nature are as important to the metropolis as the garden is to the house.
4. Development patterns should not blur or eradicate the edges of the metropolis. Infill development within existing urban areas conserves environmental resources, economic investment, and social fabric, while reclaiming marginal and abandoned

areas. Metropolitan regions should develop strategies to encourage such infill development over peripheral expansion.

5. Where appropriate, new development contiguous to urban boundaries should be organized as neighborhoods and districts, and be integrated with the existing urban pattern. Noncontiguous development should be organized as towns and villages with their own urban edges, and planned for a jobs/housing balance, not as bedroom suburbs.

6. The development and redevelopment of towns and cities should respect historical patterns, precedents, and boundaries.

7. Cities and towns should bring into proximity a broad spectrum of public and private uses to support a regional economy that benefits people of all incomes. Affordable housing should be distributed throughout the region to match job opportunities and to avoid concentrations of poverty.

8. The physical organization of the region should be supported by a framework of transportation alternatives. Transit, pedestrian, and bicycle systems should maximize access and mobility throughout the region while reducing dependence upon the automobile.

9. Revenues and resources can be shared more cooperatively among the municipalities and centers within regions to avoid destructive competition for tax base and to promote rational coordination of transportation, recreation, public services, housing, and community institutions.

## THE NEIGHBORHOOD, THE DISTRICT, AND THE CORRIDOR

1. The neighborhood, the district, and the corridor are the essential elements of development and redevelopment in the metropolis. They form identifiable areas that encourage citizens to take responsibility for their maintenance and evolution.

2. Neighborhoods should be compact, pedestrian-friendly, and mixed-use. Districts generally emphasize a special single use, and should follow the principles of neighborhood design when possible. Corridors are regional connectors of neighborhoods and districts; they range from boulevards and rail lines to rivers and parkways.

3. Many activities of daily living should occur within walking distance, allowing independence to those

who do not drive, especially the elderly and the young. Interconnected networks of streets should be designed to encourage walking, reduce the number and length of automobile trips, and conserve energy.

4. Within neighborhoods, a broad range of housing types and price levels can bring people of diverse ages, races, and incomes into daily interaction, strengthening the personal and civic bonds essential to an authentic community.

5. Transit corridors, when properly planned and coordinated, can help organize metropolitan structure and revitalize urban centers. In contrast, highway corridors should not displace investment from existing centers.

6. Appropriate building densities and land uses should be within walking distance of transit stops, permitting public transit to become a viable alternative to the automobile.

7. Concentrations of civic, institutional, and commercial activity should be embedded in neighborhoods and districts, not isolated in remote, single-use complexes. Schools should be sized and located to enable children to walk or bicycle to them.

8. The economic health and harmonious evolution of neighborhoods, districts, and corridors can be improved through graphic urban design codes that serve as predictable guides for change.

9. A range of parks, from tot-lots and village greens to ballfields and community gardens, should be distributed within neighborhoods. Conservation areas and open lands should be used to define and connect different neighborhoods and districts.

## THE BLOCK, THE STREET, AND THE BUILDING

1. A primary task of all urban architecture and landscape design is the physical definition of streets and public spaces as places of shared use.

2. Individual architectural projects should be seamlessly linked to their surroundings. This issue transcends style.

3. The revitalization of urban places depends on safety and security. The design of streets and buildings should reinforce safe environments, but not at the expense of accessibility and openness.

4. In the contemporary metropolis, development must adequately accommodate automobiles. It should do so in ways that respect the pedestrian and the form of public space.

5. Streets and squares should be safe, comfortable, and interesting to the pedestrian. Properly configured, they encourage walking and enable neighbors to know each other and protect their communities.

6. Architecture and landscape design should grow from local climate, topography, history, and building practice.

7. Civic buildings and public gathering places require important sites to reinforce community identity and the culture of democracy. They deserve distinctive form, because their role is different from that of other buildings and places that constitute the fabric of the city.

8. All buildings should provide their inhabitants with a clear sense of location, weather and time. Natural methods of heating and cooling can be more resource-efficient than mechanical systems.

9. Preservation and renewal of historic buildings, districts, and landscapes affirm the continuity and evolution of urban society.

# APPENDIX

# Smart growth principles

Appendix II sets out our set of Smart Growth principles dealing with the planning and the urban design of communities, prefaced with a set of more general policies. This is an expanded list from the one in Chapter 2; we have added notes *in italics* where the more exacting requirements of *sustainable development* extends and deepens these concepts of Smart Growth.

## General policies

1. Plan collaboratively amongst municipalities within a region.
2. Target public investment to support development in key areas and to discourage development in others. Extend suburban areas only in locations where they can be supported by existing public facilities and services or by simple and economic extensions of these services.
3. Reinforce the centers of cities, towns and neighborhoods. Locate regional attractions in city centers wherever possible, and not in suburban locations.
4. *Create developments that expand the diversity, synergism, and use of renewable resources in local economies* (Porter, 2000: p. 2).
5. Make development decisions predictable, fair and cost effective. Involve community stakeholders and citizens in the decision-making process.
6. Provide incentives and remove some legislative barriers to persuade and enable developers to do the right thing. Make it easy to build smart developments and harder to build sprawl.

## Planning strategies

7. Integrate land-use and transportation planning to minimize the number of trips by car and the distances driven. Provide a range of transportation choices to mitigate congestion.
8. Create a range of affordable housing opportunities and choices.
9. Preserve open space around and within the community, as working farmland, areas of natural beauty or areas with fragile environments.
10. Maximize the capacity of existing infrastructure by reusing derelict urban sites and filling in gaps in the urban fabric. Preserve historic buildings and neighborhoods and convert older buildings to new uses wherever possible. Minimize demolition.
11. Foster a distinctive sense of place as a building block of community development.

## Urban design concepts

12. Create compact, walkable neighborhoods with connected streets, sidewalks and street trees to make walking to work, to school, to the bus stop, or train station, or just walking for pleasure and exercise, safe, convenient and attractive.
13. Integrate offices and shops, along with community facilities such as schools, churches, libraries, parks and playgrounds into neighborhoods to create places to walk to and reduce vehicle trips. Design for densities that can support active neighborhood life. (The Denver Regional Air Quality Council estimated that urban designs

**235**

that follow these guidelines can reduce the Vehicle Miles Travelled [VMT] by as much as 10 percent [Allen, 16].)

14. Make public spaces the focus of building orientation and neighborhood activity. Move large car parks away from streets and screen them with buildings.

15. Use compact building designs and layouts to minimize consumption of land and conserve natural

resources. *Maintain and restore environmental attributes of development sites* (Porter, 2000: p. 2).

16. *Design buildings to reduce the consumption of energy and non-renewable resources and the production of waste and pollution* (Porter, 2000: p. 2).

To all of which we would add:

17. Think three-dimensionally! Envision your community in urban design detail.

# Extracts from a typical design-based zoning ordinance

# Haynie-Sirrine Neighborhood Zoning Overlay Code

| | NEIGHBORHOOD EDGE (NE) | NEIGHBORHOOD GENERAL (NG) | NEIGHBORHOOD CENTER (NC) | UNIVERSITY RIDGE VILLAGE CENTER (URVC) |
|---|---|---|---|---|
| **MIXED USE PROVISIONS** | Residential / Residential / Residential/Home Office; Cottage/Studio/Office, Garage/Workshop | Residential/Office / Residential/Office / Residential/Home Office; Cottage/Studio/Office, Garage/Workshop | Residential/Office/Hotel / Residential/Office/Hotel / Residential/Office/Hotel / Residential/Office/Hotel/Retail; Cottage/Studio/Office, Garage/Workshop | Residential/Office / Residential/Office / Residential/Office / Residential/Office / Residential/Office / Residential/Retail/Office; Cottage/Studio/Office, Cottage/Studio/Office |
| **SPECIFIC BUILDING TYPES PERMITTED** | Detached House – Street Lot Detached House – Alley Lot Civic Building | Detached House – Street Lot Detached House – Alley Lot Townhouse Apartment Building Civic Building | Detached House – Alley Lot Townhouse Apartment Building Shopfront Building Civic Building | Detached House – Alley Lot Townhouse Apartment Building Shopfront Building Workplace Civic Building |
| **PERMITTED OPEN SPACE TYPES** | Greenway Meadow Park Sportsfield | Greenway Park Sportsfield Green Square Plaza Community Garden Close Playground | Greenway Square Plaza Community Garden Close Playground | Greenway Square Plaza Community Garden Close Playground |
| **MAXIMUM HEIGHT** | 2½ Storys | 3 Storys | 4 Storys (exception-6 stories for Hotels) | 6 Storys |
| **SIGNAGE** | Arm Sign Only (Monument Signs for Civic Buildings only) | Arm Sign Only (Monument Signs for Civic Buildings only) | All Permitted Signage | |

| USE PROVISIONS | NEIGHBORHOOD EDGE (NE) | NEIGHBORHOOD GENERAL (NG) | NEIGHBORHOOD CENTER (NC) | UNIVERSITY RIDGE VILLAGE CENTER (URVC) |
|---|---|---|---|---|
| **Residential:** Premises available for long-term human habitation by means of ownership and rental, but excluding short-term letting of less than a month's duration | **Restricted residential:** The number of dwellings is restricted to one within a principal building and one within an ancillary building, and by the requirement of one assigned parking space for each. Both dwellings shall be under single ownership. *Permitted uses:* Single Family homes and Duplexes | **Limited residential:** The number of dwellings is limited by the requirement of 1.5 assigned parking spaces for each dwelling, a ratio that may be reduced according to the shared parking standard. *Permitted uses:* Single Family homes, Duplexes, and Multi-Family dwellings | **Open residential:** The number of dwellings is limited by the requirement of 1.5 assigned parking spaces for each dwelling, a ratio that may be reduced according to the shared parking standard. *Permitted uses:* Single Family homes, Duplexes, and Multi-Family dwellings | **Open residential:** The number of dwellings is limited by the requirement of 1.5 assigned parking spaces for each dwelling, a ratio that may be reduced according to the shared parking standard. *Permitted uses:* Single Family homes, Duplexes, and Multi-Family dwellings |
| **Lodgings:** Premises available for short-term human habitation, including daily and weekly letting | **Restricted lodging:** The number of bedrooms available for lodging is restricted to one within an ancillary building, and by the requirement of one assigned parking space for each leasable bedroom in addition to the requirement of two spaces for a dwelling. *Permitted uses:* Rental Cottages (in outbuildings) | **Limited lodging:** The number of bedrooms available for lodging is limited by the requirement of one assigned parking space for each bedroom, in addition to the parking requirement for each dwelling. Food service may only be provided in the morning. *Permitted uses:* Rental Cottages and Bed and Breakfast Inns | **Open lodging:** The number of bedrooms available for lodging is limited by the requirement of one assigned parking space for each bedroom, in addition to the parking requirement for each dwelling. Food service may be provided at all times. *Permitted uses:* Hotels and Inns, Rental Cottages | **Open lodging:** The number of bedrooms available for lodging is limited by the requirement of one assigned parking space for each bedroom, in addition to the parking requirement for each dwelling. Food service may be provided at all times. *Permitted uses:* Hotels and Inns, Rental Cottages |
| **Office:** Premises available for the transaction of a general business, but excluding retail sales and manufacturing | **Restricted office:** Customary home occupation uses are permitted only provided the office use is restricted to the first floor or ancillary building and by the requirement of one assigned parking space for each 250 square feet, in addition to the parking requirement for each dwelling. *Permitted uses:* Home Occupations | **Restricted office:** Customary home occupation uses are permitted only provided the office use is restricted to the first floor or ancillary building and by the requirement of one assigned parking space for each 250 square feet, in addition to the parking requirement for each dwelling. *Permitted uses:* Home Occupations | **Open office:** The area available for office use is limited by the requirement of one assigned parking space for each 250 square feet, a ratio that may be reduced according to the shared parking standards. *Permitted uses:* Office Uses, Live-Work Units | **Open offices:** The area available for office use is limited by the requirement of one assigned parking space for each 250 square feet, a ratio that may be reduced according to the shared parking standards. *Permitted uses:* Office Uses, Live-Work Units |
| **Retail:** Premises available for the commercial sale of merchandise and prepared foods, but excluding manufacturing | **Restricted retail:** Retail use is forbidden within residential buildings; with the exception that one neighborhood storefront (in the first story of a corner location) shall be permitted for each 300 dwelling units in a neighborhood. *Permitted uses:* Day Care Centers | **Restricted retail:** Retail uses is forbidden within residential buildings; with the exception that one neighborhood storefront (in the first storey of a corner location) shall be permitted for each 300 dwelling units in a neighborhood. *Permitted uses:* Neighborhood Store (on corner lots only) and Day Care Centers | **Open retail:** The area available for retail use is limited by the requirement of one assigned parking space for each 250 square feet of gross retail space, a ratio that may be reduced according to the shared parking standards. *Permitted uses:* Retail Uses, Restaurants, Entertainment Uses, Day Care Centers, Convenience Stores *Excluded uses:* Automotive, Road and Heavy Equipment Sales and Service, Adult Establishments and Adult Video Stores, Drive-Through Uses | **Open retail:** The area available for retail use is limited by the requirement of one assigned parking space for each 250 square feet of gross retail space, a ratio that may be reduced according to the share parking standards. *Permitted uses:* Retail Uses, Restaurants, Entertainment Uses, Day Care Centers, Convenience Stores and Drive-Through Facilities (subject to the issuance of a Conditional Use Permit) *Excluded uses:* Automotive, Boat, Heavy Equipment Sales and Service, Adult Establishments and Adult Video Stores |
| **Manufacturing:** Premises available for the creation, assemblage, and repair of items including their retail sale except when such activity creates adverse impacts | **Restricted manufacturing:** Manufacturing uses are forbidden. | **Restricted manufacturing:** Manufacturing uses are forbidden. | **Restricted manufacturing:** Manufacturing uses are forbidden. | **Limited manufacturing:** The area available for manufacturing use is limited to the building. The parking requirement shall be negotiated according to the specific manufacturing activity. *Permitted uses:* Light Manufacturing Uses (no outdoor storage permitted) |
| **Civic:** Premises available for not-for-profit organizations dedicated to religion, arts and culture, education, government, social service, transit, and other similar functions | **Open civic:** Civic uses shall be permitted, except those uses that exceed 25 000 square feet shall be subject to the issuance of a Conditional Use Permit. | **Open civic:** Civic uses shall be permitted, except those uses that exceed 25 000 square feet shall be subject to the issuance of a Conditional Use Permit. | **Open civic:** Civic uses shall be permitted, except those uses that exceed 25 000 square feet shall be subject to the issuance of a Conditional Use Permit. | **Open civic:** Civic uses shall be permitted, except those uses that exceed 25 000 square feet shall be subject to the issuance of a Conditional Use Permit. |

# Haynie-Sirrine Neighborhood Zoning Overlay Code

## APARTMENT BUILDING

*Description: A multiple unit building with apartments vertically arranged and with parking located below or behind the building. Units may be for rental or for sale on condominium ownership or may be designed as continuing care facilities. The ground floor may be available for commercial uses.*

## Lot Requirements

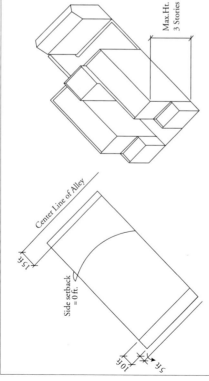

Center Line of Alley

Side setback = 0 ft.

Max. Ht. 3 Stories

15 R
10 R
5 R
5 R

**Setbacks:**

*Front* (Maximum): 10 feet

*Sides:* 0 feet (Corner–4 feet)

*Rear:* 15 feet from centreline of alley

*Parking and Vehicular Access:* Primary vehicular access is provided using a rear lane or alley only. Off-street parking should be located in the rear yard only. No curb cuts or driveways are permitted along the frontage.

*Building Lot Coverage (Maximum):* 50 percent

*Maximum Height:* 3 Stories (4 Stories in NC)

*Accessory Structures:*
*Side/Rear Setback:* 0 feet
*Maximum Footprint:* 650 square feet

*Encroachments:* Balconies, stoops, stairs, chimneys, open porches, bay windows, and raised doorways are permitted to encroach into the rear yard only. Upper story balconies may encroach into the right-of-way up to five feet with permission from the City.

## Architectural Requirements

### General Requirements

1. Usable porches and stoops should form a predominate motif of the building design and be located on the front and/or side of the building. Usable front porches are at least six feet deep and extend more than 50 percent of the façade. Garage doors are not permitted on the front elevation of any apartment building.

2. Garage doors are not permitted on the front elevation of any apartment building.

3. Fences or walls shall be no greater than eight feet in height behind the front building line. Fences shall be no greater than four feet in height and walls no greater than three feet in height in the front yard setback.

4. All building elevations visible from the street shall provide doors, porches, balconies, and/or windows. A minimum of 60 percent of front elevations, and a minimum of 30 percent of side and rear building elevations, as applicable, shall meet this standard. "Percent of elevation" is measured as the horizontal plane (lineal feet) containing doors, porches, balconies, terraces and/or windows. This standard applies to each full and partial building store.

5. All front entrances shall be raised from the finished grade (at the building line) a minimum of 1½ feet.

6. All multifamily and infill buildings shall provide detailed design along all elevations. Detailed design shall be provided by using at least three (3) of the following architectural features on all elevations as appropriate for the proposed building type and style (may vary features on rear/side/front elevations):

   a) Dormers
   b) Gables
   c) Recessed or covered porch entries
   d) Cupolas or towers
   e) Pillars of posts
   f) Eaves (minimum six-inch projection)
   g) Off-sets in building face or roof (minimum 16 inches)
   h) Bay windows (minimum four-inches wide)
   i) Balconies
   j) Decorative patterns on exterior finish (e.g. scales/shingles, wainscoting, ornamentation and similar features)
   k) Decorative cornices and roof lines (for flat roofs)

### Materials

4. Residential building walls shall be wood clapboard, wood shingle, wood drop siding, primed board, wood board and batten, brick, stone, stucco, approved vinyl, or similar material. Accessory buildings with a floor area greater than 150 square feet shall be clad in materials similar in appearance to the principal structure.

5. Garden walls may be of brick, stone or stucco matching the principal building. Front yard fences shall be wood picket or wrought iron only. Side and rear yard fences may be chain link, wood, wrought iron, or similar material. All side and rear yard fences over four feet in height shall be wood or similar material.

6. Residential roofs shall be clad in wood or asphalt shingles, clay tile, or standing seam metal (copper, zinc, or terne) or material similar in appearance and durability.

### Configurations

1. Main roofs on residential buildings shall be symmetrical gables or hips with a pitch between 4 : 12 and 12 : 12. Monopitch (shed) roofs are allowed only if they are attached to the wall of the main building. No monopitch roof shall be less than 4 : 12.

2. Two wall materials may be combined horizontally on one façade. The heavier material should be below.

3. Exterior chimneys shall be finished in brick or other material approved by the Planning Department.

4. The crawlspace of buildings shall be enclosed.

### Techniques

4. Overhanging eaves may expose rafters.

5. Flush eaves shall be finished by profiled molding or gutters.

6. All rooftop equipment shall be enclosed in building material that matches the structure or is visually compatible with the structure.

*Multifamily Building*

*Multifamily Building*

*Eightplex*

*Multifamily Building*

# SHOPFRONT BUILDING

*Description: A small-scale structure which can accommodate a variety of uses. A group of shopfront buildings can be combined to form a mixed-use neighborhood center. Individual shopfront buildings can be used to provide some commercial service, such as a neighborhood store, in close proximity to homes. Office buildings, hotels and inns can be placed in shopfront buildings.*

## Lot Requirements

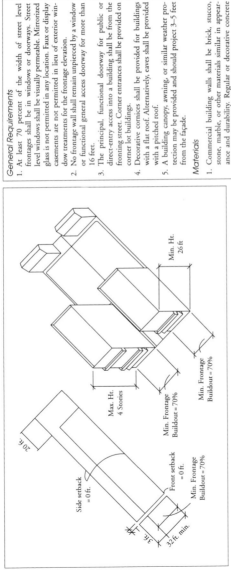

Side setback = 0 ft.

20 ft.

Front setback = 0 ft.

Min. Frontage
Buildout = 70%

3 ft.

32 ft. min.

Max. Ht.
4 Stories

Min. Frontage
Buildout = 70%

Min. Ht.
26 ft

Min. Frontage
Buildout = 70%

**Minimum Height:** 26 feet

**Maximum Height:** four stories

**Setbacks:**
 *Front (Maximum):* 0 feet
 *Sides:* 0 feet
 *Rear:* 20 feet

**Frontage Buildout (Min.):** 70 percent

**Parking and Vehicular Access:** Primary vehicular access is provided using a rear lane or alley only. Off-street parking shall be located in the rear yard only. No curb cuts or driveways are permitted along the frontage.

**Encroachments:** Upper story balconies may encroach into the right-of-day up to three feet with permission from the city.

**Accessory Structures:**
 Side/Rear Setback: 0 feet

## Architectural Requirements

### General Requirements

1. At least 70 percent of the width of street level frontages shall be in windows or doorways. Street level windows shall be visually permeable. Mirrored glass is not permitted in any location. Faux or display casements are not permitted in lieu of exterior window treatments for the frontage elevation.
2. No frontage wall shall remain unpierced by a window or functional general access doorway for more than 16 feet.
3. The principal, functional doorway for public or direct-entry access into a building shall be from the fronting street. Corner entrances shall be provided on corner lot buildings.
4. Decorative cornices shall be provided for buildings with a flat roof. Alternatively, eaves shall be provided with a pitched roof.
5. A building canopy, awning, or similar weather protection may be provided and should project 3–5 feet from the façade.

### Materials

1. Commercial building walls shall be brick, stucco, stone, marble, or other materials similar in appearance and durability. Regular or decorative concrete block may be used on building walls not visible from a public street or as an accent material only. All accessory buildings shall be clad in materials similar in appearance to the principal structure.
2. Pitched roofs shall be clad in wood or asphalt shingles, clay tile, or standing seam metal (copper, zinc, or terne) or materials similar in appearance and durability.
3. Signs on the inside of glazed openings may be neon.

### Configurations

1. All visibly exposed façades shall have a recognizable base course, which shall align with the sill level of the first storey consisting of, but not limited to: thicker walls, ledges, or sills; integrally textured materials such as stone or other masonry; integrally colored and patterned materials such as smooth finished stone or tile; lighter or darker colored materials, mullions, or panels; and/or planters.
2. All visibly exposed façades shall have a recognizable top consisting of, but not limited to: cornice treatments, other than just colored stripes or bands, with integrally textured materials such as stone or other masonry or differently colored materials; sloping roof with overhangs and brackets; stepped parapets; and/or a cornice which shall terminate or cap the top of a building wall.
3. Two wall materials may be combined horizontally on one façade. The heavier material shall be below.
4. Sky-lights shall be flat (non-bubble).

### Techniques

7. Stucco shall be float finish.
8. Windows shall be set to the inside of the building face wall.
9. All rooftop equipment shall be enclosed in building material that matches the structure or is visually compatible with the structure.

*Mixed Use*

*Mixed Use*

*Mixed Use*

*Mixed Use*

*Mixed Use*

*Genary Store*

STREET TYPES AND STANDARDS

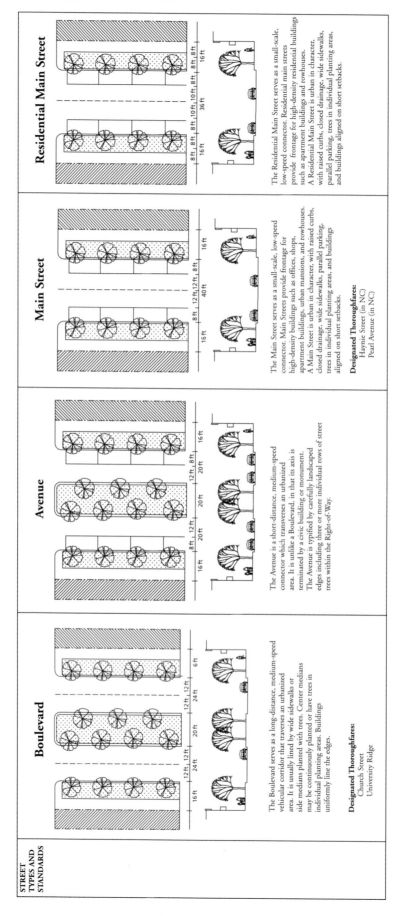

## Boulevard

The Boulevard serves as a long-distance, medium-speed vehicular corridor that traverses an urbanized area. It is usually lined by wide sidewalks or side medians planted with trees. Center medians may be continuously planted or have trees in individual planting areas. Buildings uniformly line the edges.

**Designated Thoroughfares:**
Church Street
University Ridge

## Avenue

The Avenue is a short-distance, medium-speed connector which transverses an urbanized area. It is unlike a Boulevard, in that its axis is terminated by a civic building or monument. The Avenue is typified by carefully landscaped edges including three or more individual rows of street trees within the Right-of-Way.

## Main Street

The Main Street serves as a small-scale, low-speed connector. Main Streets provide frontage for high-density buildings such as offices, shops, apartment buildings, urban mansions, and rowhouses. A Main Street is urban in character, with raised curbs, closed drainage, wide sidewalks, parallel parking, trees in individual planting areas, and buildings aligned on short setbacks.

**Designated Thoroughfares:**
Haynie Street (in NC)
Pearl Avenue (in NC)

## Residential Main Street

The Residential Main Street serves as a small-scale, low-speed connector. Residential main streets provide frontage for high-density residential buildings such as apartment buildings and rowhouses.
A Residential Main Street is urban in character, with raised curbs, closed drainage, wide sidewalks, parallel parking, trees in individual planting areas, and buildings aligned on short setbacks.

# PARKING STANDARDS

## GENERAL PRINCIPLES

1. Parking lots should not dominate the frontage of pedestrian-oriented streets, interrupt pedestrian routes, or negatively impact surrounding neighborhoods. Lots should be located behind buildings or in the interior of a block whenever possible.

2. Parking areas shall not abut pedestrian-oriented street intersections or civic buildings, be adjacent to squares or parks, or occupy lots which terminate a vista.

3. No off-street parking area shall be located within any front yard except for single-family residential uses. All off-street parking spaces for multifamily buildings shall be in the rear yard only.

4. Parking lots shall not occupy more than 1/3 of the frontage of the adjacent building or no more than 75 feet, whichever is less.

5. All parking areas visible from the right-of-way shall be screened from view. Parking structures shall be wrapped by buildings along the primary façade.

6. Off-street parking areas shall be designed to facilitate adequate movement and access by sanitation, emergency, and other public service vehicles without posing a danger to pedestrians or impeding the function of the parking area.

7. Off-street parking areas shall be designed so that parked vehicles do not encroach upon or extend onto public rights-of-way, sidewalks, or strike against or damage any wall, vegetation, utility, or other structure.

8. Large surface parking lots should be visually and functionally segmented into several smaller lots. Alternative parking area designs incorporating planting island and trees shall create separate and distinct outdoor rooms for no more than 36 cars per room. The size of any single surface parking lot shall be limited to three acres, unless divided by a street or building.

9. All parking areas shall be curved using a standard curb with a minimum width of one feet six inches. Landscape islands shall be similarly curved.

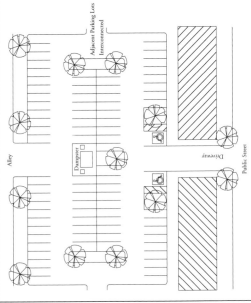

*Alley*

*Adjacent Parking Lots Interconnected*

*Dumpster*

*Driveway*

*Public Street*

## AISLE AND DRIVEWAY WIDTHS

1. Parking area aisle widths shall conform to the following table, which varies the width requirement according to the angle of parking.

| Aisle Width | Angle of Parking | | | | |
|---|---|---|---|---|---|
| | 0 | 30 | 45 | 60 | 90 |
| One Way Traffic | 13 | 13 | 13 | 18 | 20 |
| Two Way Traffic | 19 | 19 | 20 | 22 | 24 |

2. Driveways shall be a maximum of 12 feet in width for one-way traffic and 24 feet in width for two-way traffic. In no case shall a driveway width exceed 24 feet, except as required by the City of Greenville.

## PARKING SPACE DIMENSIONS

1. Parking space dimensions (other than those designed for the disabled) shall be a minimum of (twenty) feet long and (nine) feet wide. Parking spaces shall be dimensioned in relation to curbs or aisles, so long as their configuration, area, and dimensions satisfy the requirements of this Section.

2. Parallel parking space dimensions or disabled parking shall be a minimum of twenty feet by (eight) feet.

## MINIMUM PARKING RATIOS

All square footage is in leasable square feet. Uses less than 2500 leasable square feet are exempt from parking requirements. Parking requirements may be satisfied using on-street parking in front of buildings or public lots with 300 feet of primary building entrances.

| Single family Home | 2 spaces |
|---|---|
| Multi-family Home | 1 per bedroom (up to 2 required) |
| Commercial Uses | 1 per 250 sq ft |
| Restaurants | 1 per 4 seats |
| Light Industrial | 0.25 per 1000 sq ft or non-office space |
| Bed and Breakfast Inns and Hotels | 1 per bedroom |
| Civic Uses | No minimum |

## SHARED PARKING STANDARDS

1. The joint use of shared off-street parking between two uses may be made by contract between two or more adjacent property owners. Adjacent lots shall be interconnected where practical.

2. Developments that operate at different times may jointly use or share the same parking spaces with a maximum of one-half of the parking spaces credited to both uses, if one use is a church, theater, assembly hall or other use whose peak hours of attendance will be at night or on Sundays, and the other use or uses are ones that will be closed at night or on Sundays or upon the normal hours of operation.

# Extracts from general development guidelines

## 2.4.4 RURAL NEIGHBORHOOD CENTERS

*The CORE Planning and Design Workshop Report identified a site for a Rural Neighborhood Center in the historic Carpenter Community.*

*A Rural Neighborhood Center is equivalent in size to the Convenience Center noted earlier, but scattered in buildings generally not exceeding 6000 square feet in footprint area around a central public space such as a prominent intersection or open space.*

*The following recommendations are specific to the existing Carpenter Historic District, but provide a general template for dealing with other small scale rural centers that may be developed in the future.*

*Historic Carpenter in Cary, NC*

## Guidelines

1. New buildings should be consistent with the existing historic character and built fabric.

2. New commercial or mixed-use development should be in detached buildings at a scale compatible with existing development and historic precedents, generally not exceeding the 6000 square feet limit previously noted. They should be residential in scale and character, for example, by using pitched roofs and front porches. New buildings generally should not exceed two storeys.

3. A significant public open space, like, for example, a village green, should be constructed within the area created by existing and new buildings. The space should be large enough to accommodate civic festivities and events such as a farmers' market. For these purposes, the green should not exceed one acre in size, and have an informal aesthetic in plan and planting design.

4. To reinforce the importance of such a special rural place, a new public building, like a library, museum or community center should be sited on or immediately adjacent to the green, and in harmony with the existing historic buildings and other new construction. A transit stop for future local bus transit should also be located adjacent to the new green.

5. To ensure the continued relevance and public use of this historic rural crossroads, the green should be connected into the proposed greenway system for the area. New medium-density housing, between 2–6 units per acre, should be constructed between the historic center and the adjacent Carpenter Village development. The streets in this new housing development should be connected into Carpenter Village and to the historic rural crossroads area. The rural character of the crossroads should be preserved by shielding this new housing from the viewshed along Morrisville-Carpenter Road. This can be done by means of careful site planning to locate new housing behind existing tree lines and ridge lines.

## 5.1 SUSTAINABLE DEVELOPMENT PRACTICES

*Preservation and renewal of historic buildings, districts, and landscapes affirm the continuity and evolution of civic life. All buildings should provide their inhabitants with a clear sense of location, weather, and time. Natural methods of heating and cooling can be more resource efficient than mechanical systems.*

*The adaptive reuse of historic structures conserves resources and maintains the character of the community*

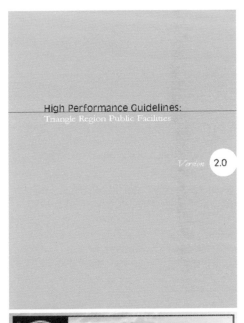

*Use of TJCOG's High Performance Standards can result in efficient, cost-effective, durable, and environmentally sound buildings and landscapes*

### Guidelines

1. Building designers should provide the anticipated rating of proposed buildings according to either the current US Green Building Council's LEED standard or the current Triangle J Council of Governments' High Performance Guidelines standard.

   These standards cover resource efficiency and environmental impacts, including many of the site-related items addressed in this document. The anticipated rating should include a description of the specific anticipated points achievable. The TJCOG High Performance Guidelines can be viewed at:

   http://www. tjcog.dst.nc. us/hpgtrpf.htm.

   The LEED standard is available at: http://www. usgbc.org.

2. The adaptive reuse of the valuable historic building stock is an effective sustainable practice and is encouraged.

3. Existing vegetation and large specimen trees should be preserved and incorporated into the site design in order to create a natural landscape and that give the impression of a mature landscape.

4. Consider utilizing drought tolerant plants and other xeriscape techniques. These include: amending the soil, mulching, grouping plants by water need, and utilizing water-efficient irrigation equipment and schedules.

## 5.2   BUILDING PLACEMENT

*A primary task of all urban architecture and landscape design is the physical definition of streets and public spaces as places of shared use. Streets lined by buildings rather than parking lots are more interesting to move along, especially for pedestrians, and provide a safer environment.*

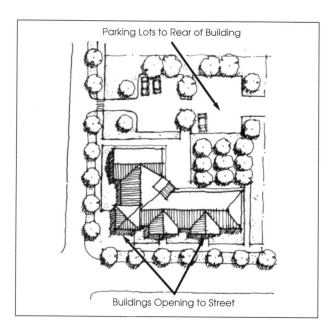

Parking Lots to Rear of Building

Buildings Opening to Street

*Locate buildings on the corner to create pedestrian interest and reduce the visual impact of parking*

*Locate residential buildings close to the sidewalk to create pedestrian interest along the frontage and maximize the functional use of the rear yard*

### Guidelines

1. Locate buildings close to the pedestrian street (within 25 feet of the curb), with off-street parking behind and/or beside buildings.

2. Outside of Mixed-use Activity Centers, buildings on infill lots should generally be setback a distance equal to an average of all buildings within 300 feet on the same side of the street.

3. If the building is located at a street intersection, place the main building, or part of the building, at the corner. Parking, loading or service areas should not be located at an intersection.

4. To maximize the street frontage of buildings and minimize the street frontage of parking lots, buildings should be articulated so that the long side fronts the street.

5. Pedestrian circulation should be an integral part of the initial site layout. Organize the site so that the buildings frame and reinforce pedestrian circulation, and so that the pedestrians walk along building fronts rather than along or across parking lots and driveways. Also arrange buildings to create view corridors between pedestrian destinations within and adjacent to the site including building entrances, transit stops, urban open space, and nearby public amenities including parks and greenways.

## 5.3 STREET LEVEL ACTIVITY

*The sidewalks remain the principal place of pedestrian movement and casual social interaction. Designs and uses should be complementary to that function.*

*Sidewalks should encourage casual social interaction*

*Porches and stoops create a semi-public outdoor space that encourages pedestrian activity*

*Small sidewalk displays help bring the indoors outside and add pedestrian interest*

## Guidelines

1. The ground floors of buildings in Mixed-use Activity Centers should be encouraged to contain public or semipublic uses such as retail or entertainment uses with direct entry from the street. In residential areas, the predominate architectural feature of the home should be porches and stoops. These features encourage pedestrian activity by providing an attractive destination and an interesting journey.

2. Retail activities within buildings should be oriented toward the street and have direct access from sidewalks through storefront entries.

3. Buildings should have at least one primary entrance facing a pedestrian-oriented street. Alternatively, a primary entrance may be directly accessed by a sidewalk or plaza within 20 feet of the entrance (except single family detached homes).

4. Street level windows should be transparent to permit views to the interior and to provide exterior security through "eyes on the street."

5. Open-air pedestrian passageways (with or without overhead cover) are generally more visible and more inviting than interior hallways. This can be an attractive, successful location for store entries, window displays, and/or restaurant/café seating.

6. Take the "indoors" outdoors by spilling interior space (e.g. dining areas, small merchandise displays) onto walkways and plazas and bring the "outdoors" into the building by opening interior spaces (e.g. atriums) to views and sunshine.

**249**

# Extracts from urban design guidelines

## 2.0 INTRODUCTION AND OVERVIEW OF MIXED-USE CENTERS

The Mixed-use Center encourages the development of compact, urban buildings that compliment the surrounding neighborhoods and are supported by existing and planned transportation networks constructed to support the traffic demands of both the auto and the pedestrian. Mixed-use Centers should be designed around a square, plaza, or other urban open space that can serve as a focal point for community activities.

Mixed-use Centers are historically formed near the convergence of large, coherent neighborhoods and near the intersection of major City streets.

This runs counter to the current Comprehensive Plan where most Focus Areas are designated at the intersection of thoroughfares. Unless a substantial investment is made to redesign these roads to permit the pedestrian traffic that Mixed-use Centers generate, the location of the Core should be moved to the mid-block away from the intersection. This slight shift in the Focus Areas will permit the Mixed-use Centers to function as true pedestrian-friendly environments as well as maintain the efficiency of the intersections.

The Mixed-use Center is typically defined by three organizing elements: the Core, a Transition, and the Edge.

The Core of a Mixed-use Center is finite in size, typically radiating 1/8 to 1/4 mile (or a five-minute walk for the average adult) from the "Main-Main" intersection or a primary focal point such as a significant urban open space (e.g. Moore Square Park). The Core consists of the most intense urban buildings in both massing and use and is the center of pedestrian activity. Buildings in the Core are often vertically mixed-use, providing opportunities for housing and office uses above ground-level retail. Like most successful Main Streets across the United States, the retail and restaurant uses should be physically concentrated in the Core to provide a critical mass of shopping and pedestrian activities that identifies it as a destination. Corridors of predominately mixed-use buildings typically form the entryways into the formalized Core.

The Transition area, due to its physical proximity to the Core, is the ideal location for medium- to

*Images of pedestrian-scaled Neighborhood Centers*

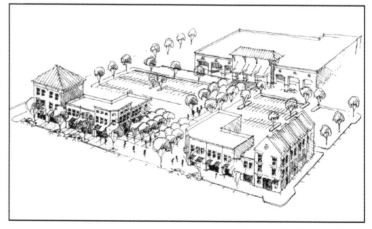

*A Typical Neighborhood Center*

high-density (where appropriate) housing. The housing is therefore supported by the Core and vice-versa along a fine network of well-connected, pedestrian-scaled streets. In addition, where transit stops are located within the Core, there is a significant user population within walking distance. The Transition area, by its name, serves as a transition from the intensity of the Core to its surrounding, supporting neighborhood areas. The size of Transition area is largely a function of its walking distance to the Core. For Neighborhood and Village Centers, this distance is typically 1/8 mile and 1/4 mile respectively, though this distance may be increased to 1/2 mile around a rail transit station.

*Rendering courtesy of Shook*

The Edge is typically not a part of the Mixed-use Center as it is typically comprised of predominately single-family housing. While these areas should be seamlessly connected to the Core by pedestrian-oriented streets, transitions from the "neighborhood" to the "center" should be accomplished through the proper design of the public realm of the street (including the use of traffic calming features on existing streets) as well through appropriate massing, scale, and architectural design of the buildings.

For the purposes of these Guidelines two Mixed-use Centers have been identified: the Neighborhood Center and the Village Center. While both share basic urban design principles, the size (acreage) of the Core area and the permitted height of buildings is differentiated.

*Images of a new Village Center (Birkdale Village in Huntersville, NC)*

In general, Neighborhood Centers have a maximum distance from the center of the Core area to the Edge of 1/4 mile or a five-minute walk for the average adult. The Five Points and Glenwood South areas are an example of a historic Neighborhood Center. Neighborhood Centers are most often comprised of uses similar to a typical Grocery Store-anchored shopping center, though they front on a pedestrian-friendly grid of streets rather than a large parking lot.

Village Centers typically radiate 1/2 mile (10-minute walk) from the center of the Core to the Edge. Examples of Village Centers include Hillsborough Street and Cameron Village. An excellent model of a new Village Center is Birkdale Village, located in Huntersville, NC.

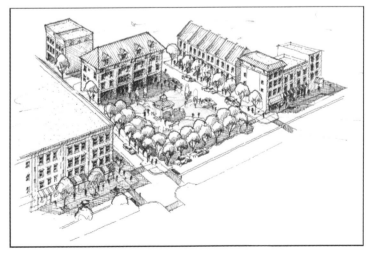

*A Typical Village Center with urban open space as focal element*

## 4.1 GENERAL STREET DESIGN PRINCIPLES

*It is the intent of these guidelines to build streets that are integral components of community design. Streets should be designed as the main public spaces of the City and should be scaled to the pedestrian.*

*The Guidelines encourage the development of a network of interconnecting streets that disperse traffic while connecting and integrating neighborhoods with the existing urban fabric of the City. Equally as important, the Guidelines encourage the development of a network of sidewalks and bicycle lanes within the rights- of-way that provide an attractive and safe mode of travel for cyclists and pedestrians.*

*Pedestrian-oriented Streets have an activated public realm with formal landscaping where the building frontages open out to the sidewalk.*

*These Guidelines are applicable to all streets up to and including major thoroughfares, particularly those that enter a Mixed-use Center. Streets that are within a Mixed-use Center should be designed and posted as low-speed (20– 35 mph) connectors. The Recommended Street Design Standards for these streets are contained in Appendix III.*

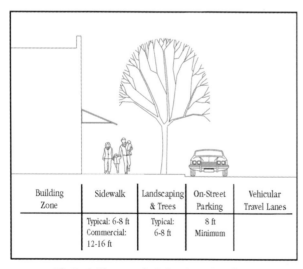

**The Basic Elements of a Pedestrian-oriented Street**

| Building Zone | Sidewalk | Landscaping & Trees | On-Street Parking | Vehicular Travel Lanes |
|---|---|---|---|---|
| | Typical: 6-8 ft Commercial: 12-16 ft | Typical: 6-8 ft | 8 ft Minimum | |

## Guidelines

1. Sidewalks should be 5–8 feet wide and located on both sides of the street. Sidewalks in commercial areas should be a minimum of 12–16 feet wide to accommodate sidewalk uses such as vendors, merchandizing, and outdoor seating.

2. Streets should be designed with street trees planted in a manner appropriate to their function. Commercial streets should have trees which compliment the face of the buildings and which shade the sidewalk. Residential streets should provide for an appropriate canopy, which shades both the street and sidewalk, and serves as a visual buffer between the street and the home. The typical width of the street tree landscape strip is 6–8 feet. This width ensures healthy street trees, precludes tree roots from heaving the sidewalk, and provides adequate pedestrian buffering. Street trees should be at least $6^{1}/_{4}$ inches caliper and should be consistent with the City landscaping, lighting and street sight distance requirements.

3. In Core areas, trees may be planted in tree wells with grates over the top to protect the roots. Irrigation should be provided. Unit pavers are preferred over concrete.

4. Planted medians are encouraged on multi-lane roads to provide additional tree canopy and reduce the visual height-to-width ratio of the overall streetscape. They also provide for safe, convenient pedestrian refuges at crossings.

5. Wherever possible, street locations should account for difficult topographical conditions, by avoiding excessive cuts and fills and the destruction of significant trees and vegetation outside of street rights-of way on adjacent lands.

*A Pedestrian-oriented Street is detailed with interesting storefronts, landscaping, furniture wide sidewalks and on-street parking*

*Pedestrian wayfinding signs and other kiosks give pedestrians advantages over the automobile*

## Guidelines

6. Closed or gated streets are strongly discouraged.

7. On-street parking provided should be parallel. Curb or angle parking is permitted only on low-volume, low-speed streets.

8. Where on-street parking is provided, the landscape strip should be planted in grass at-grade. This will enable people to walk directly from their car to the sidewalk. Shrubs, ground covers, trees and raised planters should be located so as not to conflict with opening car doors or pedestrians' access to and from on-street parking.

9. Streets should be designed so pedestrians have convenient and safe means to cross streets. Allowable treatments may include but not be limited to roundabouts, raised pedestrian crosswalks, multi-way stops, "bulb-outs," alternative pavement treatments, and signals at crosswalks when warranted.

10. Streetscape designs should include a system of pedestrian wayfinding signs, kiosks and other environmental graphics to supply directions to the pedestrian. This should be done in a unified comprehensive manner for Mixed-use Centers.

11. Landscaping and pedestrian features such as bump outs and tree planters need only be placed at the end of the block and at mid-block-crossings. Mid-block crossings are necessary where the block face is more than 200 feet.

12. Angle parking is encouraged in commercial areas as a way to provide additional, convenient parking spaces for merchants and restaurants.

*Diagonal parking is more convenient and plentiful per linear foot than parallel parking and is encouraged in heavy commercial areas*

**255**

# Bibliography

## INTRODUCTION

Blake, P., 1974. *Form Follows Fiasco: Why Modernism Hasn't Worked*, Boston: Little, Brown.

Booker, C., 1980. *The Seventies*, London: Allen Lane.

Campbell, B. 'The Queenies that Betrayed the Gorbals', *The Independent*, (London): 15 September, 1993.

Coleman, A., 1985. *Utopia on Trial*, London: Hillary Shipman.

Congress for the New Urbanism, Leccese, Michael, and Kathleen McCormick, editors, 1999. *Charter of the New Urbanism*, New York: McGraw-Hill.

Dutton, J.A., 2000. *New American Urbanism: Reforming the Suburban Metropolis*, Milan: Skira.

G.B. Deputy Prime Minister and Secretary of State for the Environment, Transport and the Regions, 2000: *Our Towns and Cities: The Future: Delivering an Urban Renaissance* (Cm 4911). London: Stationery Office.

Gold, J.R., 1997. *The Experience of Modernism: Modern architects and the future city*, London: E & FN Spon.

Hall, P., 2002. *Cities of Tomorrow: an Intellectual History of Urban Planning and Design in the Twentieth Century*, 3rd Edition, Oxford: Basil Blackwell.

Hughes, R., 1980. *The Shock of the New*, London: BBC Publications.

Katz, P., 1994. *The New Urbanism: Toward an Architecture of Community*, New York: McGraw-Hill.

Kunstler, J.H., 1993. *The Geography of Nowhere: the Rise and Decline of America's Man-Made Landscape*, New York: Simon & Schuster

Lubbock, J., 1995. *The Tyranny of Taste: the Politics of Architecture and Design in Britain, 1550–1960*, New Haven, CN: Yale University Press.

Pocock, D., and Hudson, R., 1978. *Images of the Urban Environment*, London, MacMillan.

Ravetz, A., 1980. *Remaking Cities*, London: Croom Helm.

Rogers, R. G., 1999. *Towards and Urban Renaissance*, London: E & FN Spon.

## CHAPTER 1

Alexander, C., and others, 1977. *Pattern Language: Towns, Buildings, Construction*, New York: Oxford University Press.

Alexander, C., and others, 1987. *A New Theory of Urban Design*, New York: Oxford University Press.

Banham, R., 1963. 'CIAM,' in Hatjie, G., editor, 1963. *Encyclopedia of Modern Architecture*, London: Thames and Hudson.

Benfield, F.K., Raimi, M.D., and Chen, D.D.T., 1999. *Once There Were Greenfields: How Urban Sprawl is Undermining America's Environment, Economy and Social Fabric*. Washington, D.C.: National Resources Defense Council.

Broadbent, G., 1990. *Emerging Concepts of Urban Space Design*, Van Nostrand Reinhold.

Brooke, S., 1995. *Seaside*, Gretna, Louisiana: Pelican Publishing Company, Inc.

Castells, M., 1989. *The Informational City: Information technology, Economic Restructuring and the Urban-Regional Process*. Oxford: Blackwell.

Castells, M., 1997. *The Information Age: Economy, Society, and Culture, 1: The Rise of the Network Society*. Oxford: Blackwell.

Castells, M., 1977. *The Power of Identity: The Information Age: Economy, Society and Culture, Volume I*. Oxford: Blackwell.

Chase, J., Crawford, M., and Kaliski, J., 1999. *Everyday Urbanism*, New York: The Monacelli Press.

Coleman, A., 1985. *Utopia on Trial: Vision and Reality in Planned Housing*, London: Hilary Shipman.

Cullen, G., 1961. *Townscape*, London: The Architectural Press.

Dear, M., 1995. 'Prologomena to a post modern urbanism,' in Healey, P. et al., (eds) *Managing Cities: The New Urban Context*, London: Wiley, 27–44.

Dennis, M., 1981. 'Architecture and the Postmodern City,' in the *Cornell Journal of Architecture*, I, p.48–67.

Duffy, F., 1997. *The New Office*, London: Conran Octopus Ltd.

Florida, R., 2002. *The Rise of the Creative Class: And How It's Transforming Work, Leisure, Community and Everyday Life*. New York: Basic Books.

Garreau, J., 1991. *Edge City: Life on the New Frontier*, New York: Doubleday.

Garreau, J., 2001. 'Face to Face in the Information Age,' Unpublished conference paper, *City Edge 2: Centre vs. Periphery*, Melbourne, Australia.

Gastil, R., 2000. Preface to *New American Urbanism: Re-forming the Suburban Metropolis*, by John A. Dutton. Skira Architectural Library.

Giedion, S., 1941. *Space, Time and Architecture: the Growth of a New Tradition*, Cambridge, MA: Harvard University Press, 5th edition, 1967.

Gilder, G., 2000. *Telecosm: How Infinite Bandwidth Will Revolutionize Our World*. New York: Free Press.

Gold, J.R., 1997. *The Experience of Modernism: Modern architects and the future city*, London: E & FN Spon.

Graham S., and Marvin, S., 1996. *Telecommunications and the city: electronic spaces, urban places*, London: Routledge.

Hall, P., 1998. *Cities in Civilisation*, New York: Pantheon Books.

Hall, P., 2002. *Cities of Tomorrow: An Intellectual History of Urban Planning and Design in the Twentieth Century* (3rd Edition), Oxford: Blackwell Publishing.

Hanchett, T.W., 1998. *Sorting Out the New South City: Race, Class and Urban Development in Charlotte, 1875–1975*, Chapel Hill: University of North Carolina Press.

Harvey, D., 1989. *The Condition of Postmodernity: An Enquiry into the Origins of Cultural Change*. Oxford: Basil Blackwell.

Hitchcock, H.R., and Johnson, P., 1932. *The International Style*, New York: Museum of Modern Art.

Holyoak, J., 1993. 'The Suburbanisation and Re-urbanisation of the Residential Inner City,' in Hayward, R., and McGlynn, S., editors, *Making Better Places: Urban Design Now*, Oxford: Butterworth Architecture.

Howell, P., 1993. 'Public Space and the Public Sphere: Political Theory and the Historical Geography of Modernity,' in *Environment and Planning D: Society and Space*, 11: 303–22.

Jacobs, Jane, 1962. *The Death and Life of Great American Cities*, London: Jonathan Cape. Previously published 1961, New York: Vintage Books.

Jameson, F., 1991. *Postmodernism, or, The Cultural Logic of Late Capitalism*. Durham, NC: Duke University Press.

Jencks, C., 1977. *The Language of Postmodern Architecture*, London: Academy Editions.

Kaliski, J., 1999. 'The Present City and the practice of City Design,' in Chase, J., Crawford, M., and Kaliski, J., 1999. *Everyday Urbanism*, New York: The Monacelli Press.

Kelly, K., 1998. *New Rules for the New Economy: 10 Radical Strategies for a Connected World*. New York: Viking.

Kotkin, J., 2001. 'The New Geography of Wealth.' Reis.com, Techscapes, December; available on-line at www.reis.com/learning/insights_tech-scapesart.cfm?art=1.

Le Corbusier, 1929. *The City of Tomorrow and its Planning*, London: John Rodker. Translated from the 8th French Edition of *Urbanisme* with an introduction by Frederick Etchells (reprinted 1947 by The Architectural Press). In: *Essential Le Corbusier: L'Esprit Nouveau Articles*, 1998. Oxford: The Architectural Press.

Le Corbusier, 1925. 'La Rue' (The Street), reprinted in Le Corbusier and Jeanneret, P., 1964. *Le Corbusier and Pierre Jeanneret: The Complete Architectural Works*, Vol.1, 1919–1929, Zurich: Editions d'Architecture, London: Thames and Hudson.

Le Corbusier, 1942. *Charte Athènes*, Paris. Reprinted 1973, trans. by Anthony Eardley, New York: Grossman Publishers.

Lloyd, R., and Clark, T.N., 2001. 'The City as Entertainment Machine,' in Kevin Fox Gotham, (ed), *Critical Perspectives on Urban Redevelopment. Research in Urban Sociology*, Vol. 6 Oxford: JAI Press/Elsevier, 375–378.

Kreiger, A., and Lennertz, W., editors, 1991. *Towns and Town-Making Principles*, New York: Rizzoli.

Malpass, P., 1979. 'A re-appraisal of Byker, Parts 1 & 2: Magic, myth and the architect,' *The Architects' Journal*, 19/1979 and 20/1979.

MacCormac, R., 1973. 'Housing form and land use: new research.' *RIBA Journal*, Nov. 549–51.

McDougall, I., 1999. 'The New Urban Space,' *City Edge Transcripts*, the Proceedings of the City Edge Conference: Private Development vs Public Realm, City of Melbourne, Australia, 29–35.

Mitchell, W.J., 1995. *City of Bits: Space, Place, and the Infobahn*. Cambridge, Mass.: MIT Press.

Mitchell, W.J., 1999. *e-topia:'Urban Life, Jim – but not as we know it.'* Cambridge, Mass.: MIT press.

Mohney, D., and Easterling, K., 1991. *Seaside: Making a Town in America*, New York: Princeton Architectural Press.

Mumford, L., 1962. 'The Sky Line: Mother Jacobs' Home Remedies,' *New Yorker*, 1st December, 1962. Republished in Mumford, 1968. *The Urban Prospect*, New York: Harcourt, Brace and World, 194.

Nairn, I., 1955. *Outrage*, London: The Architectural Press

Nairn, I., 1957. *Counter-attack against Subtopia*, London: The Architectural Press

Oldenburg, R., *The Great Good Place: Cafés, Coffee Shops, Community Centers, Beauty parlors, General Stores, Bars, Hangouts, and how they get you through the day*, New York: Marlowe and Co.

Pawley, M., 1971. *Architecture versus Housing*, London: Studio Vista Ltd.

Pevsner, N., 1936. *Pioneers of the Modern Movement: from William Morris to Walter Gropius*, London: Faber and Faber.

Power, N.S., 1965. *The Forgotten People*, Evesham: Arthur James Limited.

Richards, J.M., 1940. *An Introduction to Modern Architecture*, Harmondsworth: Penguin.

Rogers, J.R., and Rogers, A.T., 1996. *Charlotte: Its Historic Neighborhoods*, Dover, New Hampshire: Arcadia Publishing.

Rowe, C., and Koetter, F., 1978. *Collage City*, Cambridge, Mass.: MIT Press.

Santayana, G., 1905. *Life of Reason, Reason in Common Sense*, New York: Scribner's.

Sennett, R., 1971. *The Uses of Disorder: Personal Identity and Community Life*. London: Allen Lane.

Sennett, R., 1974. The Fall of Public Man, New York: Alfred A. Knopf.

Sexton, R., 1995. *Parallel Utopias: Sea Ranch and Seaside: the Quest for Community*, San Fransisco: Chronicle Books.

Sitte, Camillo., 1889. *City Planning according to Artistic Principles*, Vienna: Verlag von Carl Graeser. Text reissued with detailed commentary by Collins, George R., and Christiane Crasemann Collins, 1965. *Camillo Sitte and the Birth of Modern City Planning*, New York: Random House: revised edition, 1986. New York: Rizzoli.

Soja, E., 1989. *Postmodern Geographies*, London: Verso.

Van Eyck, A., 1962. *Team10 Primer*, in Jencks, C., and Kropf, K., editors. 1977. *Theories and Manifestoes of Contemporary Architecture*, Chichester, Sussex: Academy Editions.

Watson, S., and Gibson, K., editors, 1995. *Postmodern Cities and Spaces*, Oxford: Blackwell.

Webber, M.M., 1964a. 'The Urban Place and the Nonplace Urban Realm, in: Webber, M.M., Dyckman, J.W., Foley, D.L., Gutenberg, A.Z., Wheaton, W.L.C. and Wurster, C.B., *Explorations in Urban Structure*, 79–153. Philadelphia: University of Pennsylvania Press.

Webber, M.M., 1964b. 'Order in Diversity: Community without Propinquity,' in Wingo, L., Jr., editor, *Cities and Space: the Future Use of Urban Land*, 23–153. Philadelphia: University of Pennsylvania Press.

Wofle, Ivor de, (ed.), 1971. *Civilia: the End of Sub Urban Man*, London: The Architectural Press.

Young, M., and Wilmott, P., 1992. *Family And Kinship In East London*, Berkeley: University of California Press. (First published by Routledge & Kegan Paul, 1957).

## CHAPTER 2

Adler, J., 1995. 'Bye-Bye, Suburban Dream,' *Newsweek*, May 15th, pp. 41–53.

Alofsin, A., 1989. 'Broadacre City: The Reception of a Modernist Vision, 1932–1988,' in Alofsin, A., and Speck, L., editors, 1989. 'Modernist Visions and the Contemporary American City.' *Center: A Journal for Architecture in America*, Volume 5. Austin, TX.: The Center for the Study of American Architecture, University of Texas at Austin.

Archer, J., 1983. 'City and Country in the American Romantic Suburb,' *Journal of the Society of Architectural Historians*. XLII: 2, May.

Baldassare, M., 1986. *Trouble in Paradise:The Suburban Transformation of America*, New York: Columbia University Press.

Barnett, J., 1986. *The Elusive City: Five Centuries of Design, Ambition and Miscalculation*, New York: Harper and Row.

Benfield, F.K., Raimi, M.D., and Chen, D., 1999. *Once There Were Greenfields: How Urban Sprawl Is Undermining America's Environment, Economy and Social Fabric*, New York: National Resources Defense Council/Surface Transportation Policy Project.

Benfield, F.K., Terris, J., and Vorsanger, N., 2001. *Solving Sprawl: Models of smart growth in communities across America*, New York: National Resources Defense Council.

Bohl, C.C., 2002. *Place Making: Developing Town Centers, Main Streets, and Urban Villages*, Washington, D.C.: Urban Land Institute.

Booth, G., Leonard, B., and Pawlukiewicz, M., 2002. *Ten Principles for Reinventing America's Suburban Business Districts*, Washington, D.C.: Urban Land Institute.

Brookings Institution Center on Urban and Metropolitan Policy, Bruce Katz, Director. 2002. *Adding It Up: Growth Trends and Policies in North Carolina*. 17. Washington, D.C.: The Brookings Institution.

Buchanan, C., 1963. *Traffic in Towns: a study of the long term problems of traffic in urban areas*, London: Ministry of Transport.

Burchell, R., et al., 1997. *Costs of Sprawl Revisited: The Evidence of Sprawl's Negative and Positive Impacts,'* Transportation Research Board and National research Council. Washingtron DC: National Academy Press.

Burchell, R.W., and Listokin, D., 1995. *Land, Infrastructure Housing Costs and Fiscal Impacts Associated with Growth: The Literature on the Impacts of Sprawl versus Managed Growth*, Cambridge, Mass.:Lincoln Institute of Land Policy Study Working Paper.

Calthorpe, P., and Fulton, W., 2001. *The Regional City*, Washington DC: Island Press.

Cervero, R., 1986. *Suburban Gridlock*, New Brunswick, New Jersey: Center for Urban Policy Research.

Cervero, R., 1989. *America's Suburban Centers – The Land Use-Transportation Link*. Boston, MA.: Unwin Hayman.

Clawson, M., 1971. *Suburban Land Conversion in the United States: An Economic and Governmental Process*, Baltimore: John Hopkins University Press.

Clawson, M., and Hall, P., 1973. *Planning and Urban Growth: An Anglo-American Comparison*, Baltimore: John Hopkins University Press.

Duany, A., Plater-Zyberk, E., and Speck, J., 2000. *Suburban Nation: The Rise of Sprawl and the Decline of the American Dream*. New York: North Point Press.

Ewing, R., Pendall, R., and Chen, D., 2002. *Measuring Sprawl and its Impact: the Character & Consequences of Metropolitan Expansion*, (Smart Growth America, accessed 17th November 2002); available from http://www.smartgrowthamerica.org; Internet.

Fishman, R., 1987. Bourgeoise Utopia: The Rise and Fall of Suburbia, New York: Basic Books, Inc.

Gans, H.J., 1976. *The Levittowners; ways of life and politics in a new suburban community*, New York: Pantheon Books.

Gruen, V., 1973. *Centers for the Urban Environment: Survival of the Cities*, New York: Van Nostrand Reinhold.

Hall, P., 1998. *Cities in Civilisation*, New York: Pantheon Books.

Hall, P., 2002. *Cities of Tomorrow: An Intellectual History of Urban Planning and Design in the Twentieth Century* (3rd Edition), Oxford: Blackwell Publishing.

Hegemann, W., and Peets, E., 1922. *The American Vitruvius: An Architect's Handbook of Civic Art*, New York: The Architectural Book Publishing Company. Reprinted 1990 with an Introduction by Alan J. Plattus, preface by Leon Krier and an Introductory Essay by Christiane Crasemann Collins. New York: Princeton Architectural Press.

Howard, E., 1898. *Tomorrow: A Peaceful Path to Real Reform*. London: Swan Sonnenschein.

Institute of Transportation Engineers. 1994. *Traffic Engineering for Neo-Traditional Neighborhood Design*. Washinton, D.C.: ITE.

Jackson, K.T., 1985. *Crabgrass Frontier: the Suburbanization of the United States*, New York: Oxford University Press.

Kay, J.H., 1997. *Asphalt nation: how the automobile took over America and how we can take it back*. New York: Crown Publishers Inc.

Kelbaugh, D. editor, 1989. *The Pedestrian Pocket Book*. New York: Princeton Architectural Press.

Killingworth, R., Earp, J., and Moore, R., 2003. 'Health Promoting Community Design.' Special issue of the *American Journal of Health Promotion*, Sept/Oct. 2003.

Krier, L., 1984. *Houses, Palaces, Cities*. London: AD Editions.

Kunstler, J.H., 1993. *The Geography of Nowhere: The Rise and Decline of America's Manmade Landscape*, New York: Simon and Schuster.

Kunstler, J.H., 1996a. 'Home from Nowhere,' *Atlantic Monthly*, Volume 278, No. 3, September, pp. 43–66.

Kunstler, J.H., 1996b. *Home from Nowhere: Remaking Our Everyday World for the Twenty-first Century*, New York: Simon and Schuster.

Lancaster, O., 1959. *Here, of All Places: The Pocket Lamp of Architecture*, London: John Murray.

Langdon, P., 1994. *A Better Place to Live: Reshaping the American Suburb*, Amherst, Mass.: University of Massachusetts Press.

McHarg, I., 1969. *Design with Nature*, Garden City, New York: Doubleday, Natural History Press.

O'Neill, D.J., 2002. *The Smart Growth Tool Kit: Community Profiles and Case Studies to Advance Smart Growth Practices*, Washington, D.C.: Urban Land Institute.

Putnam, R., 2000. *Bowling Alone: The Collapse and Revival of American Community*, New York: Simon and Schuster.

Riesman, D., 1950. *The Lonely Crowd: A Study of the Changing American Character*, New Haven: Yale University Press.

Rowe, P.G., 1991. *Making a Middle Landscape*, Cambridge, Mass.: MIT Press.

Solomon, D., 1989. 'Fixing Suburbia,' in Kelbaugh, D., editor. *The Pedestrian Pocket Book: a New Suburban Design Strategy*, New York: Princeton Architectural Press in association with the University of Washington.

Southworth, M., and Ben-Joseph, E., 1997. *Streets and the Shaping of Towns and Cities*, New York: McGraw-Hill.

Spirn, A.W., 1984. *The Granite Garden: Urban Nature and Human Design*, New York: Basic Books.

Srikameswaram, A., 2003. 'Studies find walkable communities are healthier,' in the Pittsburgh Post-Gazette, Aug. 29th, 2003.

Stern, R., 1981. 'La Ville Bourgeoise,' in Stern, R. and Massengale, J., 'The Anglo-American Suburb,' *Architectural Design*, 51.

Stilgoe, J.R., 1988. *Borderland: Origins of the American Suburb, 1820–1939*, New Haven, Conn.: Yale University Press.

Unwin, R., 1909. *Town Planning in Practice: an Introduction to the art of designing Cities and Suburbs*, London: T. Fisher Unwin. Reprinted 1994, with a new preface by Andres Duany and a new introduction by Walter L. Creese. New York: Princeton Architectural Press.

U.S. Department of Health and Human Services, 2001. *Healthy People in Healthy Communities*, Washington, D.C.: U.S. Government Printing Office.

Venturi, R., Scott-Brown, D., Izenour, S., 1972. *Learning from Las Vegas*, Cambridge, Mass.: MIT Press.

Ward, S., editor, 1992. *The Garden City: Past, Present and Future*, London: E & FN Spon.

Whyte, W.H., 1956. *The Organization Man*, New York: Simon and Schuster.

Whyte, W.H., 1988. *City*, New York: Doubleday.

## CHAPTER 3

Allen, E., 1999. 'Measuring the environmental footprint of the New Urbanism,' *New Urban News*, Volume 4, Number 3, May/June 1999, pp.16–18.

Arendt, R.G., 1994. *Rural by Design: Maintaining Small Town Character*. Chicago: APA Planners Press.

Arendt, R.G., 1996. *Conservation Design for Subdivisions: A Practical Guide to Creating Open Space Networks*, Washington, D.C.: Island Press.

Baker, B., 2003. 'Manufacturing Success,' in ULI – the Urban Land Institute, 2003. *Urban Land: Europe*, Winter 2003, Vol. 5., No. 1. Washington, D.C.: the Urban Land Institiute.

Bohl, Charles C., 2002. *Place Making: Developing Town Centers, Main Streets, and Urban Villages*, Washington, D.C.: Urban Land Institute.

Bohl, C., 2003. 'The Return of the Town Center,' in Lineman, P., and Rybczynski, W., 2003, *Wharton Real Estate Review*, Spring 2003.

Booth, Geoffrey, Leonard, Bruce, and Pawlukiewicz, Michael, 2002. *Ten Principles for Reinventing America's Suburban Business Districts*, Washington, D.C.: Urban Land Institute.

Broadbent, G., 1990. *Emerging Concepts in Urban Space Design*, London: Van Nostrand Reinhold.

Brookings Institute Center on Urban and Metropolitan Policy and the Fannie Mae Foundation. 1998. *A Rise in Downtown Living*. Washington D.C.: The Brookings Institute and the Fannie Mae Foundation.

Calthorpe Associates, 1992. *Transit-Oriented Development Design Guidelines*, San Diego, CA: City of San Diego.

Calthorpe, P., 1993. *The Next American Metropolis: Ecology, Community and the American Dream*, New York: Princeton Architectural Press.

City of Toronto, Various authors, 1995. *Making Choices: Alternative Development Standards*, Toronto: Ontario Ministry of Housing and Ministry of Municipal Affairs.

Congress for the New Urbanism, 1998. *Charter of the New Urbanism*, available at: http://www.cnu.org/charter.html.

Congress for the New Urbanism, 2000. *Charter of the New Urbanism*. New York: McGraw-Hill.

Congress for the New Urbanism, 2002. *Greyfields into Goldfields: Dead Malls Become Living Neighborhoods*, San Francisco: Congress of the New Urbanism.

County Council of Essex, 1973. *A Design Guide for Residential Areas*. Essex: County Council of Essex.

Cullen, G., 1961. *Townscape*, London: The Architectural Press.

Davidson, Town of, 2000. *Zoning Regulations*, Davidson, NC: Town of Davidson.

Department of the Environment, Transport and the Regions, 2000. *Planning Policy Guidance Note 3: Housing*. London: DETR.

Duany, A., and Plater-Zyberk, E. with Kreiger, Alex, and William Lennertz, editors, 1991. *Towns and Town-making Principles*, New York: Rizzoli.

Duany, A., and Plater-Zyberk, E., 2002. *The Lexicon of New Urbanism, Version 3.2*, Miami, FL.: DPZ & Co..

Ellis, C., 2002. 'The New Urbanism: Critiques and Rebuttals,' *Journal of Urban Design*, Volume 7, Number 3, 261–291.

*Emerging Trends in Real Estate,* 1999. New York: Pricewaterhouse-Coopers and Lend Lease Real Estate Investments.

Eppli, Mark J., and Tu, Charles C., 1999. *Valuing The New Urbanism: The Impact of the new Urbansim on prices of Single-Family Homes*,Washington, D.C.: Urban Land Institute.

Forty, A., and Moss, H., 1980. 'A Housing Style for Troubled Consumers: the success of the Pseudo-Vernacular,' *Architectural Review*, February, pp. 72–8.

Hall, P., 2002. *Cities of Tomorrow: An Intellectual History of Urban Planning and Design in the Twentieth Century* (3$^{rd}$ Edition), Oxford: Blackwell Publishing.

Hammond, A., and Walters, D., 1996. *Town of Huntersville Zoning Ordinance*, Huntersville, NC: Town of Huntersville.

Hegemann, W., and Peets, E., 1922. *The American Virtuvius: an Architect's Handbook of Civic Art*. Reprinted 1990. New York: Princeton Architectural Press.

Jacobs, J., 1962. *The Death and Life of Great American Cities*, London: Jonathan Cape, 1962

Huxtable, A.L., 1997. *The Unreal America: Architecture and Illusion*, New York: New Press.

Ingersoll, R., 1989. 'Postmodrn urbanism: forward into the past,' *Design Book Review*, 17, pp. 21–25.

Jacobs, Jane, 1962. *The Death and Life of Great American Cities*, London: Jonathan Cape. Previously published 1961, New York: Vintage Books.

Kaliski, J., 1999. 'The Present City and the Practice of City Design,' in Chase, J., Crawford, M., and Kaliski, J., 1999. *Everyday Urbanism*, New York: The Monacelli Press.

Keane, T., and Walters, D., 1995. *The Davidson Land Plan*, Davidson, NC: Town of Davidson.

Kelbaugh, D., editor, 1989. *The Pedestrian Pocket Book: A New Suburban Design Strategy*, New York: Princeton Architectural Press.

Koolhas, R., and Mau, B., 1995. *S,M,L,XL*. New York: The Monacelli Press Inc.

Krier, R., 2003. *Town Spaces: contemporary interpretations of traditional urbanism*, Basel: Birkhauser.

Landecker, H., 'Is new urbanism good for America?' *Architecture*, 84(4), pp. 68–70.

Langdon, P., 2003a. 'Zoning reform advances against sprawl and inertia,' *New Urban News*, Volume 8, Number 1, Jan/Feb. 2003, pp.1–3.

Langdon, P., 2003b. 'The right attacks smart growth and New Urbanism,' *New Urban News*, Volume 8, Number 3, April/May 2003, pp. 1, 7–8.

Lynch, K., 1960. *The Image of the City*, Cambridge, MA.: MIT Press.

O'Neill, D.J., 1999. *Smart Growth: Myth and Fact*, Washington, D.C.: Urban Land Institute.

O'Neill, D.J., 2002. *The Smart Growth Tool Kit: Community Profiles and Case Studies to Advance Smart Growth Practices*, Washington, D.C.: Urban Land Institute.

Perry, C.A., 1929. *The Neighborhood Unit: A Scheme for Arrangement for Family Life Community*. (Regional Study of New York and its Environs, VII, Neighborhood and Community Planning, Monograph One, 2–140). New York: Regional Plan of New York and its Environs.

Porter, Douglas R., et al., 2000. *The Practice of Sustainable Development*, Washington, D.C.: Urban Land Institute.

Rybczynski, W., 1995. 'This old house: the rise of family values in architecture,' *New Republic*, May, pp. 14–16.

Rybczynski, W., 2003. 'The Changing Design of Shopping Places,' in Lineman, P., and Rybczynski, W., 2003, *Wharton Real Estate Review*, Spring 2003.

Safdie, M., 1997. *The City After the Automobile*, New York: Basic Books.

Schmitz, A., et al., 2003. *The New Shape of Suburbia: Trends in Residential Development*, Washington, D.C.: Urban Land Institute.

Steuteville, R., editor, 2001. 'Consistent market found for NU,' *New Urban News*, Volume 6, Number 1, Jan./Feb. 2001.

Sitte, C., 1889. *City Planning according to Artistic Principles*, Vienna: Verlag von Carl Graeser. Text reissued with detailed commentary by Collins, G.R., and Collins, Christiane C.C. 1965. *Camillo Sitte and the Birth of Modern City Planning*, New York: Random House. Revised edition, 1986. New York: Rizzoli.

Sudjic, D., 1992. *The 100 Mile City*, San Diego: Harcourt Brace & Company.

Taylor, N., 1973. *The Village in the City: Towards a New Society*, London: Temple Smith.

Unwin, R., 1909. *Town Planning in Practice*. Reprinted 1994, New York: Princeton Architectural Press.

ULI-the Urban Land Institute, 1998. *ULI on the Future of Smart Growth*. Washington, D.C.: ULI.

Venturi, R., Scott-Brown, D., and Izenour, S., 1972. *Learning from Las Vegas: The Forgotten Symbolism of Architectural Form*. Cambridge, Mass.: MIT Press.

Venturi, R., and Scott-Brown, D., 1968. 'A Significance for A&P Parking Lots, or Learning from Las Vegas,' Architectural Forum, March 1968, pp. 37–43.

Warrick, B., and Alexander, T., 1998. *Changing Consumer Preferences*, Washington, D.C.: Urban Land Institute.

## CHAPTER 4

Alexander, C., Ishikawa, S., and Silverstein, M., 1977. *A Pattern Language: Towns, Buildings, Construction*, Oxford: Oxford University Press.

Alexander, C., Neis, H., Anninou, A., and King, I., 1987. *A New Theory of Urban Design*, Oxford: Oxford University Press.

Argan, G.C., 1963. 'On the typology of architecture,' trans. Joseph Rykwert, in Nesbit, K. editor, 1996. *Theorizing a New Agenda for Architecture: An Anthology of Architectural Theory 1965–1995*. New York: Princeton Architectural Press. First published in *Architectural Design* no. 33, December.

Bohl, C.C., 2002. *Place Making: Developing Town Centers, Main Streets, and Urban Villages*, Washington, D.C.: Urban Land Institute.

Broadbent, G., 1990. *Emerging Concepts in Urban Space Design*, London: Van Nostrand Reinhold.

Calthorpe, P., 1993. *The Next American Metropolis: : Ecology, Community and the American Dream*, New York: Princeton Architectural Press.

Colquhoun, A., 1967. 'Typology and Design Method,' in Nesbit, K. editor, 1996. *Theorizing a New Agenda for Architecture: An Anthology of Architectural Theory 1965–1995*. New York: Princeton Architectural Press. First published in *Arena 83*, June 1967.

Craycroft, R., 1989. *The Neshoba County Fair: Place and Paradox in Mississippi*. Starkville: Center for Small Town Research and Design, Mississippi State University.

Cullen, G., 1961. *Townscape*. London: The Architectural Press.

De Quincy, Quatremere, 1832. *Dictionnaire Historique de l'Architecture*. Paris.

Dovey, K., 1999. 'Democracy and Public Space?' *City Edge Transcripts*, the Proceedings of the City Edge Conference: Private Development vs Public Realm, City of Melbourne, Australia, 45–51.

Durand, J.N.L., 1805. *Precis des Leçons d'Architecture*, XIII. Paris.

Gosling, D., 1996. *Gordon Cullen: Visions of Urban Design*, London, Academy Editions.

Hudnutt, W.H. III., 2002. 'Thoughts on Civic Leadership and the Future of Cities,' in ULI – the Urban Land Institute. *ULI on the Future: Cities Post-9/11*. Washington, D.C., the Urban Land Institute.

Krier, R., 1979. 'Typological and Morphological Elements of the Concept of Urban Space,' *Architectural Design*, 49 (1).

Krier, R., 1979. *Urban Space*. London: Academy Editions.

Locke, J., 1687. *An Essay Concerning Human Understanding* (ed. A.D. Woozley), 1964, London: Collins Fontana Library.

Marshall, A., 2000. *How Cities Work: Suburbs, Sprawl and the Roads Not Taken*. Austin, Texas: Austin University Press.

McDougall, I., 1999. 'The New Urban Space,' *City Edge Transcripts*, the Proceedings of the City Edge Conference: Private Development vs Public Realm, City of Melbourne, Australia, 29–35.

Moneo, R., 1978. 'On Typology,' *Oppositions 13*, Cambridge, Mass: MIT Press.

Pocock, D., and Hudson, R., 1978. *Images of the Urban Environment*, London: MacMillan.

Rossi, A., 1966. *L'Architettura della citta*, ed. Marsilio, Padua; trans. Ghirado, D. and Ockman, J. 1982 as *The Architecture of the City*, Cambridge, Mass: MIT Press.

Rybczynski, W., 1995. 'This old house: the rise of family values architecture,' New Republic, May, 14–16.

Rybczynski, W., 1995. *City Life: Urban Expectations in a New World*. New York: Scribner.

Safdie, M., 1997. *The City After the Automobile*. New York: Basic Books,

Sorkin, M., 2001. *Some Assembly Required*, Minneapolis: University of Minnesota Press.

Sandercock, L., 1999. 'Café Society or Active Society?' *City Edge Transcripts*, the Proceedings of the City Edge Conference: Private Development vs Public Realm, City of Melbourne, Australia, viii–xi.

Sudjic, D., 1992. *The 100 Mile City*. New York: Harcourt Brace.

Tibbalds, F., 1992. *Making People Friendly Towns: Improving the public environment in towns and cities*. Harlow: Longmans.

Trancik, R., 1986. *Finding Lost Space: Theories of Urban Design*. New York: Van Nostrand Reinhold.

Vidler, A., 1978. 'The Third Typology,' in Nesbit, K., editor., 1996. *Theorizing an New Agenda for Architecture: An Anthology of Architectural Theory 1965–1995*. New York: Princeton Architectural Press.

## CHAPTER 5

Atlanta Regional Commission (ARC) 2000. *Smart Growth Toolkit*, Atlanta: ARC. Available at www.atlantaregional.com/qualitygrowth/planning/toolkits.html

Barnett, J., 1974. *Urban Design as Public Policy: Practical methods for Improving Cities*, New York: McGraw-Hill.

Beatley, T., 2000. *Green Urbanism: Learning from European Cities*, Washington D.C.: Island Press.

Beatley, T., and Manning, K., 1997. The Ecology of Place: *Planning for Environment, Economy and Community*, Washington, D.C.: Island Press.

Broadbent, G., 1990. *Emerging Concepts in Urban Space Design*, London: Van Nostrand Reinhold.

Brown, T.D., and Lewis, C.S., 1996. *The Town of Cornelius Land Development Code*, Cornelius, NC: Town of Cornelius.

Burke, M., 1997. 'Environmental Taxes gaining Ground in Europe.' *Environmental Science and Technology News*. Vol. 31, No. 2, pp. 84–88.

Calthorpe Associates, 1992. *Transit-Oriented Development Design Guidelines*, San Diego, CA: City of San Diego.

County Council of Essex planning staff, 1973. *A Design Guide for Residential Areas*, Essex: County Council of Essex.

Cullen, G., 1967. 'Notation 1–4,' *The Architects Journal (Supplements)*, May 31, 1967, July 12 1967, August 23 1967, September 27 1967.

Department of the Environment, Transport and the Regions, 1994. *Sustainable Development: The UK Strategy*. London: DETR.

Department of the Environment, Transport and the Regions, 1995. *Planning Policy Guidance Note 1' General Policy and Principles*. London: DETR.

Department of the Environment, Transport and the Regions, 2000. *Planning Policy Guidance Note 3: Housing*. London: DETR.

Department of the Environment, Transport and the Regions/Commission for Architecture & the Built Environment, 2000. *By Design: Urban Design in the Planning System: Towards Better Practice*. London: DETR.

Department of the Environment, Transport and the Regions/Commission for Architecture & the Built Environment, 2001. *By Design: Better Places to Live: A Design Companion to PPG 3*. London: DETR.

Duany, A., and Plater-Zyberk, E., 1991. 'Urban Code: The Town of Seaside,' in Mohney, D and Easterling, K. editors, 1991. *Seaside*, New York: Princeton Architectural Press.

Duany, A., and Plater-Zyberk, E., 1991. 'Codes,' in *Towns and Town-Making Principles*, Kreiger, A., and Lennertz, W., editors, 1991, New York: Rizzoli.

Dutton, J.A., 2000. *New American Urbanism: Reforming the Suburban Metropolis*, Milan: Skira.

Ellin, N., 1999. *Postmodern Urbanism*, rev. ed., New York: Princeton Architectural Press.

Ferris, H., 1922. 'The New Architecture,' *New York Times Book Review and Magazine*, March 19, 1922.

Hall, P., 1998. *Cities in Civilisation*, New York: Pantheon Books.

Hall, P., 2002. *Cities of Tomorrow: An Intellectual History of Urban Planning and Design in the Twentieth Century* (3rd Edition), Oxford: Blackwell Publishing.

Hall, R., 2003. 'Why the sprawl lobby has clout'. *The Charlotte Observer*, 19 May, 2003.

Hammond, A., and Walters, D., 1996. *Town of Huntersville Zoning Ordinance*, Huntersville, NC: Town of Huntersville.

HUD (U.S. Department of Housing and Urban Development) (2000) *HOPE VI: Building Communities, Transforming Lives*, Washington, D.C.: HUD.

HUD (U.S. Department of Housing and Urban Development) (2000) *Strategies for Providing Accessibility & Visitability for HOPE VI and Mixed Finance Homeownership*, by Urban Design Associates, Washington, D.C.: HUD.

Hudnutt, W.H. III., 2002. 'Thoughts on Civic Leadership and the Future of Cities,' in ULI – the Urban Land Institute. *ULI on the Future: Cities*

*Post-9/11*. Washington, D.C., the Urban Land Institute.

Katz, B., 2003. 'The Permanent Campaign,' *Urban Land*, 62, 5. May, 45–52.

Keane, T., and Walters, D., 1995. *The Davidson Land Plan*, Davidson, NC: Town of Davidson.

Leach, J.F., 1980. *Architectural Visions: The Drawings of Hugh Ferris*, New York: Whitney Library of Design.

McDougall, I., 1999. 'The New Urban Space,' *City Edge Transcripts*, the Proceedings of the City Edge Conference: Private Development vs Public Realm, City of Melbourne, Australia, 29–35.

National Association of Homebuilders (NAHB), no date. *The Truth About Property Rights*, Washington, D.C.: NAHB.

Sandercock, L., 1999. 'Café Society or Active Society?' *City Edge Transcripts*, the Proceedings of the City Edge Conference: Private Development vs Public Realm, City of Melbourne, Australia, viii–xi.

Sitte, C., 1889. *City Planning according to Artistic Principles*, Vienna: Verlag von Carl Graeser. Text reissued with detailed commentary by Collins, G.R., and Collins, Christiane C.C. 1965. *Camillo Sitte and the Birth of Modern City Planning*, New York: Random House. Revised edition, 1986. New York: Rizzoli.

Tiesdell, S., 2002. 'The New Urbanism and English Residential Design Guidance: A Review,' in *Journal of Urban Design*, Volume 7, No. 3, October 2002.

Various authors, 1995. *Celebration Pattern Book*, Orlando, Florida: The Walt Disney Company.

World Commission on Environment and Development, 1987. *Our Common Future*, Oxford: Oxford University Press.

## CHAPTER 6

Aldous, T., 1992. *Urban Villages: A concept for creating mixed-use urban developments on a sustainable scale*, London: Urban Villages Group.

Aldous, T., editor, 1995. *Economics of Urban Villages: A report by the Economics Working Party of the Urban Villages Forum*, London: Urban Villages Forum.

Baker, B., 2003. 'Manufacturing Success,' in ULI – the Urban Land Institute, 2003. *Urban Land: Europe*, Winter 2003, Vol. 5., No. 1. Washington, D.C.: the Urban Land Institiute.

Booth, Geoffrey, Leonard, Bruce, and Pawlukiewicz, Michael, 2002. *Ten Principles for Reinventing America's Suburban Business Districts*, Washington, D.C.: Urban Land Institute.

Calthorpe, P., and Fulton, W., 2001. *The Regional City*, Washington DC: Island Press.

Congress for the New Urbanism, 2002. *Greyfields into Goldfields: Dead Malls Become Living Neighborhoods*, San Francisco: Congress of the New Urbanism.

Darley G., Hall, P., and Lock, D., 1991. *Tomorrow's New Communities*, York: Joseph Rowntree Foundation.

Ewing, R., 1996. *Best Development Practices*, Chicago: American Planning Association.

Hirschhorn, J., 2003. 'Behind Enemy Lines at the Anti-Smart Growth Conference.' Viewed at http://www.planetizen.com/oped/item.php?id= 82, March 2003.

Lang, J., 2000. 'Learning from Twentieth Century Urban Design Paradigms:Lessons for the Early Twenty-first Century,' in Freestone, R., editor, 2000. *Urban Planning in a Changing World: The Twentieth Century Experience*. London: E & FN Spon.

Lucy, W.H., and Phillips, D.L., 2001. *Suburbs and the Census: Patterns of Growth and Decline*, Washington, D.C.: Brookings Institution Center on Urban & Metropolitan Policy, available at www.brook.edu/dybdocroot/es/urban/census/lucy.pdf

McIlwain, J.K., 2002. 'A New Century – a New Urban Form: Location and Affordability of Housing in a Postmodern World,' in the Urban Land Institute, 2002. ULI on the Future: Cities Post 9/11. Washington, D.C.: the Urban Land Institute.

O'Connell,T., and Johnson, H.L., 2003. 'Financing Affordable Housing,' *Urban Land*, 62, 5. 32.

Schmitz, A., 2003. *The New Shape of Suburbia: Trends in Residential Development*, Washington, D.C.: Urban Land Institute.

Sucher, D., 1995. *City Comforts: How to Build an Urban Village*, Seattle: City Comforts Press.

*The Charlotte Observer*, 2003. 'Boomtown Burdens,' Charlotte, N.C.: March 24–27, 2003.

Wates, N., 2000. *The Community Planning Handbook: How people can shape their cities, towns and villages in any part of the world*, London: Earthscan Publications Ltd.

Whyte, W.H., 1980. *The Social Life of Small Urban Spaces*, Washington, D.C.: The Conservation Foundation.

## CHAPTER 7

ITE Technical Council Committee 5P-8, chaired by Spielberg, F.L., 1994. *Traffic Engineering for Neo-traditional Neighborhood Design*, Washington, D.C.: Institute of Transportation Engineers.

North Carolina Department of Transportation, Division of Highways, 2000. *Traditional Neighborhood Development (TND) Guidelines*, Raleigh, N.C.: NCDOT

The Lawrence Group Architects of North Carolina Inc., 2003. *Centre of the Region Enterprise: General Development Guidelines*, Davidson, N.C.: The Lawrence Group.

Triangle J Council of Governments and The Lawrence Group Architects of North Carolina Inc., 2003. *Centre of the Region Enterprise: Planning and Design Workshop Report*, Davidson, N.C.: The Lawrence Group.

## CHAPTER 8

The Lawrence Group Architects of North Carolina Inc., 2002. *City of Raleigh, NC, Urban Design Guidelines*, Davidson, N.C.: The Lawrence Group.

## CHAPTER 9

Santos, R., 2003. 'Open Space as an Amenity,' in Schmitz, A (2003). *The New Shape of Suburbia: Trends in Residential Development*, Washington, D.C.: Urban Land Institute.

## CHAPTER 10

The Lawrence Group Architects of North Carolina Inc., 2003. *Haynie-Sirrine Neighborhood Master Plan, Greenville, SC*, Davidson, N.C.: The Lawrence Group.

Duany Plater-Zyberk & Company, 2002. *The Lexicon of the New Urbanism, Version 3.2*, Miami, FL.: DPZ & Co.

## CHAPTER 11

Brown, T.D., and Lewis, C.S. eds., 1996. The Town of Cornelius Land Development Code, Cornelius, NC: Town of Cornelius.

Brown, T.D., 2002. *Planning for a Transit-Oriented Future: The Town of Cornelius Land Development Code and Planning Initiatives*, unpublished Masters Thesis, University of North Carolina at Charlotte.

Hylton, T., 2000. *Save Our Land: Save Our Towns*, Harrisburg, PA: Rb Books and Preservation Pennsylvania.

Newsom, M., 1996. 'A Mecklenburg Miracle: How regional citizens are having a say on growth,' *The Charlotte Observer*, June 1, p.14.

## AFTERWORD

Katz, B., 2003. 'The Permanent Campaign,' *Urban Land*, 62, 5. May, 45–52.

Wickersham, J., 2003. 'EIR and Smart Growth,' *Urban Land*, 62, 5. May, 24–7.

## APPENDICES

Appendix I

Congress for the New Urbanism, Leccese, Michael, and Kathleen McCormick, editors, 1999. *Charter of the New Urbanism*, New York: McGraw-Hill.

## APPENDIX II

Porter, Douglas R. et al., 2000. *The Practice of Sustainable Development*, Washington, D.C.: Urban Land Institute.

## Appendix III

The Lawrence Group Architects of North Carolina Inc., 2003. *Haynie-Sirrine Neighborhood Master Plan, Greenville, SC*, Davidson, NC.: The Lawrence Group.

## Appendix IV

The Lawrence Group Architects of North Carolina Inc., 2003. *Centre of the Region Enterprise: General Development Guidelines*, Davidson, NC.: The Lawrence Group.

## Appendix V

The Lawrence Group Architects of North Carolina Inc., 2002. *City of Raleigh, NC, Urban Design Guidelines*, Davidson, NC.: The Lawrence Group.

# Index

References to illustrations are shown in italics.